# Teach Yourself®
# HTML 4

# Teach Yourself<sup>®</sup> HTML 4

**Stephanie Cottrell Bryant**

**IDG Books Worldwide, Inc.**
An International Data Group Company

Foster City, CA • Chicago, IL • Indianapolis, IN • New York, NY

**Teach Yourself® HTML 4**

Published by

**IDG Books Worldwide, Inc.**

An International Data Group Company

919 E. Hillsdale Blvd., Suite 400

Foster City, CA 94404

www.idgbooks.com (IDG Books Worldwide Web site)

ISBN: 0-7645-7512-0

Printed in the United States of America

10 9 8 7 6 5 4 3 2 1

1P/QT/QZ/ZZ/IN

Distributed in the United States by IDG Books Worldwide, Inc.

Distributed by CDG Books Canada Inc. for Canada; by Transworld Publishers Limited in the United Kingdom; by IDG Norge Books for Norway; by IDG Sweden Books for Sweden; by IDG Books Australia Publishing Corporation Pty. Ltd. for Australia and New Zealand; by TransQuest Publishers Pte Ltd. for Singapore, Malaysia, Thailand, Indonesia, and Hong Kong; by Gotop Information Inc. for Taiwan; by ICG Muse, Inc. for Japan; by Intersoft for South Africa; by Le Monde en Tique for France; by International Thomson Publishing for Germany, Austria and Switzerland; by Distribuidora Cuspide for Argentina; by LR International for Brazil; by Galileo Libros for Chile; by Ediciones ZETA S.C.R. Ltda. for Peru; by WS Computer Publishing Corporation, Inc., for the Philippines; by Contemporanea de Ediciones for Venezuela; by Express Computer Distributors for the Caribbean and West Indies; by Micronesia Media Distributor, Inc. for Micronesia; by Chips Computadoras S.A. de C.V. for Mexico; by Editorial Norma de Panama S.A. for Panama; by American Bookshops for Finland. Authorized Sales Agent: Anthony Rudkin Associates for the Middle East and North Africa.

For general information on IDG Books Worldwide's books in the U.S., please call our Consumer Customer Service department at 800-762-2974. For reseller information, including discounts and premium sales, please call our Reseller Customer Service department at 800-434-3422.

For information on where to purchase IDG Books Worldwide's books outside the U.S., please contact our International Sales department at 317-596-5530 or fax 317-596-5692.

For consumer information on foreign language translations, please contact our Customer Service department at 800-434-3422, fax 317-596-5692, or e-mail rights@idgbooks.com.

For information on licensing foreign or domestic rights, please phone +1-650-655-3109.

For sales inquiries and special prices for bulk quantities, please contact our Sales department at 650-655-3200 or write to the address above.

For information on using IDG Books Worldwide's books in the classroom or for ordering examination copies, please contact our Educational Sales department at 800-434-2086 or fax 317-596-5499.

For press review copies, author interviews, or other publicity information, please contact our Public Relations department at 650-655-3000 or fax 650-655-3299.

For authorization to photocopy items for corporate, personal, or educational use, please contact Copyright Clearance Center, 222 Rosewood Drive, Danvers, MA 01923, or fax 978-750-4470.

Library of Congress Cataloging-in-Publication Data

Bryant, Stephanie Cottrell.

   Teach Yourself HTML 4 / Stephanie Cottrell Bryant.

     p.  cm.

   Includes bibliographical references.

   ISBN 0-7645-7512-0 (alk. paper)

   1. HTML (Document markup language)   I. Title.

QA76.76.H94B793 1999

005.7'2--dc21                      99–22673

                                       CIP

# ABOUT IDG BOOKS WORLDWIDE

Welcome to the world of IDG Books Worldwide.

IDG Books Worldwide, Inc., is a subsidiary of International Data Group, the world's largest publisher of computer-related information and the leading global provider of information services on information technology. IDG was founded more than 30 years ago by Patrick J. McGovern and now employs more than 9,000 people worldwide. IDG publishes more than 290 computer publications in over 75 countries. More than 90 million people read one or more IDG publications each month.

Launched in 1990, IDG Books Worldwide is today the #1 publisher of best-selling computer books in the United States. We are proud to have received eight awards from the Computer Press Association in recognition of editorial excellence and three from Computer Currents' First Annual Readers' Choice Awards. Our best-selling *...For Dummies*® series has more than 50 million copies in print with translations in 31 languages. IDG Books Worldwide, through a joint venture with IDG's Hi-Tech Beijing, became the first U.S. publisher to publish a computer book in the People's Republic of China. In record time, IDG Books Worldwide has become the first choice for millions of readers around the world who want to learn how to better manage their businesses.

Our mission is simple: Every one of our books is designed to bring extra value and skill-building instructions to the reader. Our books are written by experts who understand and care about our readers. The knowledge base of our editorial staff comes from years of experience in publishing, education, and journalism — experience we use to produce books to carry us into the new millennium. In short, we care about books, so we attract the best people. We devote special attention to details such as audience, interior design, use of icons, and illustrations. And because we use an efficient process of authoring, editing, and desktop publishing our books electronically, we can spend more time ensuring superior content and less time on the technicalities of making books.

You can count on our commitment to deliver high-quality books at competitive prices on topics you want to read about. At IDG Books Worldwide, we continue in the IDG tradition of delivering quality for more than 30 years. You'll find no better book on a subject than one from IDG Books Worldwide.

John Kilcullen
Chairman and CEO
IDG Books Worldwide, Inc.

Steven Berkowitz
President and Publisher
IDG Books Worldwide, Inc.

*Eighth Annual Computer Press Awards ≥1992*

*Ninth Annual Computer Press Awards ≥1993*

*Tenth Annual Computer Press Awards ≥ 1994*

*Eleventh Annual Computer Press Awards ≥1995*

# Credits

*Acquisitions Editor*
Debra Williams Cauley

*Development Editor*
Laura E. Brown

*Technical Editor*
Chris Stone

*Copy Editors*
Dennis Weaver, Corey Cohen,
Tim Borek

*Book Designers*
Daniel Ziegler Design, Cátálin Dulfu,
Kurt Krames

*Production*
IDG Books Worldwide Production

*Proofreading and Indexing*
York Production Services

# About the Author

**Stephanie Cottrell Bryant** has designed Web pages professionally since 1995. She lives in Scotts Valley, California, with her husband John, her cat Allegro, and two retired racing greyhounds named Harry and Hammer. She is an active member of the National Writer's Union Santa Cruz/Monterey Local and served as a delegate in 1998.

Mrs. Bryant holds a Bachelor's Degree in Pre- and Early Modern Literature from the University of California, Santa Cruz. She encourages readers with questions or comments to email her at `steph@scottrell.com`.

*To my loving husband, John, in commemoration*
*of our paper anniversary.*
*And I shall love, because of you.*

# Welcome to
# Teach Yourself

Welcome to *Teach Yourself*, a series read and trusted by millions for nearly a decade. Although you may have seen the *Teach Yourself* name on other books, ours is the original. In addition, no *Teach Yourself* series has ever delivered more on the promise of its name than this series. That's because IDG Books Worldwide recently transformed T*each Yourself* into a new cutting-edge format that gives you all the information you need to learn quickly and easily.

Readers told us that they want to learn by doing and that they want to learn as much as they can in as short a time as possible. We listened to you and believe that our new task-by-task format and suite of learning tools deliver the book you need to successfully teach yourself any language or technology topic. Features such as our Personal Workbook, which lets you practice and reinforce the skills you've just learned, help ensure that you get full value out of the time you invest in your learning. Handy cross-references to related topics and online sites broaden your knowledge and give you control over the kind of information you want, when you want it.

## More Answers . . .

In designing the latest incarnation of this series, we started with the premise that people like you, who are beginning to intermediate computer users, want to take control of their own learning. To do this, you need the proper tools to find answers to questions so you can solve problems now.

In designing a series of books that provide such tools, we created a unique and concise visual format. The added bonus: *Teach Yourself* books actually pack more information into their pages than other books written on the same subjects. Skill for skill, you typically get much more information in a *Teach Yourself* book. In fact, *Teach Yourself* books, on average, cover twice the skills covered by other computer books — as many as 175 skills per book — so they're more likely to address your specific needs.

# WELCOME TO TEACH YOURSELF

## ... In Less Time

We know you don't want to spend twice the time to get all this great information, so we provide lots of timesaving features:

▶ A modular task-by-task organization of information: any task you want to perform is easy to find and includes simple-to-follow steps.

▶ A larger size than standard makes the book easy to read and convenient to use at a computer workstation. The large format also enables us to include many more code listings and illustrations.

▶ A Personal Workbook at the end of each chapter reinforces learning with extra practice, real-world applications for your learning, and questions and answers to test your knowledge.

▶ Cross-references appearing at the bottom of each task page refer you to related information, providing a path through the book for learning particular aspects of the software thoroughly.

▶ A Find It Online feature offers valuable ideas on where to go on the Internet to get more information or to download useful files.

▶ Take Note sidebars provide added-value information from our expert authors for more in-depth learning.

▶ An attractive, consistent organization of information helps you quickly find and learn the skills you need.

These *Teach Yourself* features are designed to help you learn the essential skills about a language or technology in the least amount of time, with the most benefit. We've placed these features consistently throughout the book, so you quickly learn where to go to find just the information you need — whether you work through the book from cover to cover or use it later to solve a new problem.

You will find a *Teach Yourself* book on almost any technology subject — from Windows to XML to C++. Take control of your learning today, with IDG Books Worldwide's *Teach Yourself* series.

# Teach Yourself
## More Answers in Less Time

Go to this area if you want special tips, cautions, and notes that provide added insight into the current task.

Search through the task headings to find the topic you want right away. To learn a new skill, search the contents, chapter opener, or the extensive index to find what you need. Then find — at a glance — the clear task heading that matches it.

## Creating an HTML Document

An HTML document is essentially a text file with special tags to help your Web browser display its content. In some ways, an HTML file is like a word processor document; the text and graphics are the focus of the document, but formatting information, such as boldface type and font sizes, is included to help the program display and print the document correctly. When you try to open the document in a program that cannot "read" the formatting information, the formatting is lost, or the document itself is garbled.

So, too, with HTML documents. If you try to open an HTML document with a program that does not read HTML, the formatting will be lost or the document itself will look like gibberish. Similarly, if you try to open a non-HTML document in a Web browser, it will not look the same as an HTML document, and may even look like gibberish as well.

HTML has gone through many revisions during its history, and there is now an element you can use to tell the Web browser which version of HTML you're using. It's called the <!DOCTYPE> element, and many HTML authoring tools automatically put this element at the top of a new Web document. Later, I'll show you how to use <!DOCTYPE>s when your Web page uses style sheets, frames, or XML. For now, use the following <!DOC-TYPE> element as the first line in your HTML 4.0 Web page:

```
<!DOCTYPE HTML PUBLIC "-//W3C//DTD HTML
4.0//EN"
"http://www.w3.org/TR/REC-html40/strict.dtd">
```

This <!DOCTYPE> statement says that the document uses the HTML 4.0 Document Type Definition, as defined by the World Wide Web Consortium (W3C), and found at **http://www.w3.org/TR/REC-html40/strict.dtd**.

After you've included the <!DOCTYPE> element, insert the <HEAD> element. Since the <HEAD> element of the Web page is not actually displayed in the browser, it's a good place to hide code that doesn't belong elsewhere. For example, you can put comments, JavaScript code, and copyright notices in the <HEAD> element. In addition, there's a special element, called a <META> tag, that belongs in the <HEAD> section. <META> elements will be covered later, since they're used primarily to index your Web page and provide specific information to search engines.

### TAKE NOTE

#### SAVING AS HTML

Depending on the authoring tool you use, saving your document as HTML may be fairly simple or it might be downright complicated. For example, a Web authoring tool that is designed to write Web pages will probably use HTML as the default file type. However, if you're using a text editor (such as Notepad or SimpleText) or a word processor (such as Microsoft Word or Corel WordPerfect), then you may have to change the file type when you save. If you ever have trouble opening a Web page that was created using a text editor or word processor, check the filename extension, and the file type to be sure that it really did save as an HTML file.

Learn the concepts behind the task at hand and why the task is relevant in the real world. Timesaving suggestions and advice show you how to make the most of each skill.

After you learn the task at hand, you may have more questions, or you may want to read about other tasks related to the topic. Use the cross-references to find different tasks to make your learning more efficient.

**CROSS-REFERENCE**

For more information on Web authoring tools, see Appendix C. To review HTML tag syntax, see Chapter 1.

**FIND IT ONLINE**

A document structure HTML reference guide can also be found at **http://www.tue.nl/bwk/cheops/via/maker/html4/html.htm#struct.**

Use the Find It Online element to locate Internet resources that provide more background, take you on interesting side trips, and offer additional tools for mastering and using the skills you need. (Occasionally you'll find a handy shortcut here.)

18

# WELCOME TO TEACH YOURSELF

> The current chapter name and number always appear in the top right-hand corner of every task spread, so you always know exactly where you are in the book.

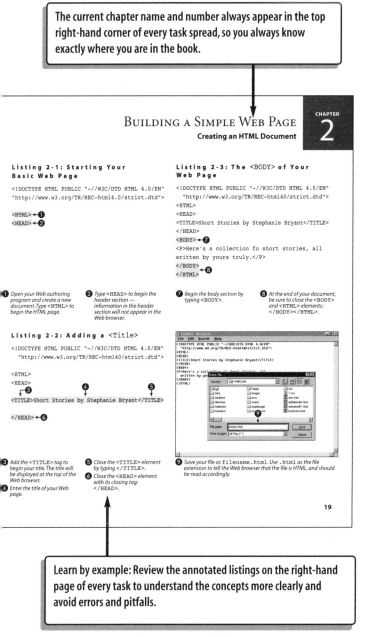

## Who This Book Is For

This book is written for you, an intermediate computer user who isn't afraid to take charge of his or her own learning experience. You don't want a lot of technical jargon; you *do* want to learn as much about a language as you can in a limited amount of time. You need a book that is straightforward, easy to follow, and logically organized, so you can find answers to your questions easily. And you appreciate simple-to-use tools such as handy cross-references and visual step-by-step procedures that help you make the most of your learning. We have created the unique *Teach Yourself* format specifically to meet your needs.

> Learn by example: Review the annotated listings on the right-hand page of every task to understand the concepts more clearly and avoid errors and pitfalls.

# Personal Workbook

It's a well-known fact that much of what we learn is lost soon after we learn it if we don't reinforce our newly acquired skills with practice and repetition. That's why each *Teach Yourself* chapter ends with your own Personal Workbook. Here's where you can get extra practice, test your knowledge, and discover ideas for using what you've learned in the real world. There's even a Visual Quiz to help you remember your way around the topic's software environment.

## Feedback

Please let us know what you think about this book, and whether you have any suggestions for improvements. You can send questions and comments to the *Teach Yourself* editors on the IDG Books Worldwide Web site at **www.idgbooks.com**.

## Personal Workbook

**Q&A**

**1** How do you include a title in the HEAD section?

**2** What is the link anchor element?

**3** How do you include a background graphic?

**4** How many heading levels are there?

**5** In the <IMG> element, height and width are measured in what units?

**6** What does the <HR> element do?

**7** Name two accessibility issues discussed in this chapter.

**8** What element do you put at the top of your HTML document?

ANSWERS: PAGE 434

34

After working through the tasks in each chapter, you can test your progress and reinforce your learning by answering the questions in the Q&A section. Then check your answers in the Personal Workbook Answers appendix at the back of the book.

# WELCOME TO TEACH YOURSELF

Another practical way to reinforce your skills is to do additional exercises on the same skills you just learned without the benefit of the chapter's visual steps. If you struggle with any of these exercises, it's a good idea to refer to the chapter's tasks to be sure you've mastered them.

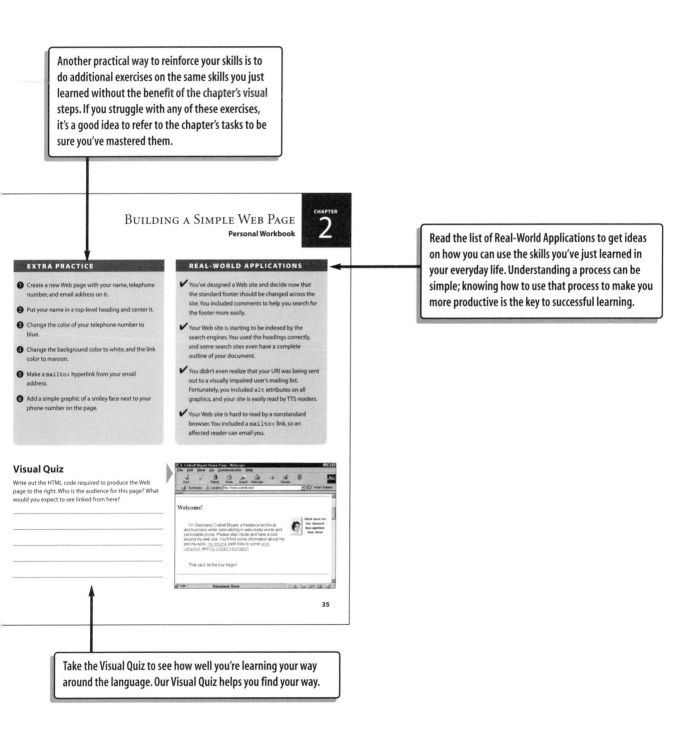

## BUILDING A SIMPLE WEB PAGE
**Personal Workbook**

**CHAPTER 2**

Read the list of Real-World Applications to get ideas on how you can use the skills you've just learned in your everyday life. Understanding a process can be simple; knowing how to use that process to make you more productive is the key to successful learning.

### EXTRA PRACTICE

1. Create a new Web page with your name, telephone number, and email address on it.

2. Put your name in a top-level heading and center it.

3. Change the color of your telephone number to blue.

4. Change the background color to white, and the link color to maroon.

5. Make a `mailto:` hyperlink from your email address.

6. Add a simple graphic of a smiley face next to your phone number on the page.

### REAL-WORLD APPLICATIONS

✔ You've designed a Web site and decide now that the standard footer should be changed across the site. You included comments to help you search for the footer more easily.

✔ Your Web site is starting to be indexed by the search engines. You used the headings correctly, and some search sites even have a complete outline of your document.

✔ You didn't even realize that your URI was being sent out to a visually impaired user's mailing list. Fortunately, you included `alt` attributes on all graphics, and your site is easily read by TTS readers.

✔ Your Web site is hard to read by a nonstandard browser. You included a `mailto:` link, so an affected reader can email you.

### Visual Quiz

Write out the HTML code required to produce the Web page to the right. Who is the audience for this page? What would you expect to see linked from here?

Take the Visual Quiz to see how well you're learning your way around the language. Our Visual Quiz helps you find your way.

# Acknowledgments

Any project worth doing is worth doing with others. This book is no exception, and I'd like to thank all the people who pitched in and helped pull this book together, and to acknowledge their contributions to this project.

My thanks to the good people at IDG Books Worldwide, especially Debra Williams Cauley and Laura Brown, who edited the book and kept me on track, and to the technical editor, Chris Stone. My thanks also to copy editors Dennis Weaver, Tim Borek, and Corey Cohen, and to E. Shawn Aylsworth and other production personnel who helped make this book a reality.

Jonathan Kamin, WandaJane Phillips, Anne Martinez, and Lois Patterson contributed by writing chapters on subjects that completely baffle me. John Bryant provided uncomplaining technical support and consultation on an on-call basis; without him, this book would never have been possible. My thanks also to my assistant, Rudolph Malmgren III, who did paperwork and screenshots for me until the wee hours of the morning.

My thanks to my agent, Margot Maley and Waterside Productions, for helping pull things together, and giving me a few well-placed pushes in the right direction. Also, many thanks to the ever-patient National Writer's Union Santa Cruz Monterey Local 7 Steering Committee, particularly Steve Turner.

I have been blessed in having a family who have encouraged me in pursuing my writing, and who have allowed me the freedom to explore writing as a career. My thanks to my mother, Bonnie M. Beck, my sister, Jennifer Stamper, and my husband, John, for their love and support in that area.

# Contents

# CONTENTS

# CONTENTS

# CONTENTS

# CONTENTS

# CONTENTS

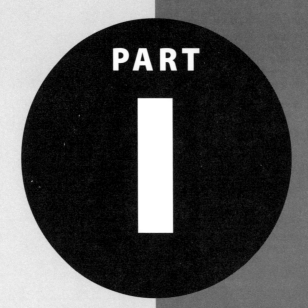

# PART

# I

# Getting Started

In this part, you learn the absolute basics of HTML (HyperText Markup Language) and Web design. This part covers the basic syntax of HTML, document structure, a basic Web page, tables, and accessibility.

HTML 4.0 addresses the issue of accessibility, as well as designing Web sites for all users. Too many Web sites take advantage of and misuse elements to produce cool effects. Unfortunately, these cool effects often are unreadable in many browsers, including (and especially) those used by people with visual or mobility disabilities. When you finish this part, you can build a basic Web site that will run in versions 4 and up of the popular Netscape Navigator and Microsoft Internet Explorer Web browsers. You'll be prepared to continue building your site with frames, forms, and style sheets, which are covered in Part II.

# CHAPTER

**MASTER THESE SKILLS**

▶ Learning HTML Syntax

▶ Developing Web Page Structure

▶ Adding Style and Substance

# The Basics

In this chapter, you'll learn a lot of the ground rules for HTML, including how to build a tag, and HTML's terminology and syntax. You'll also learn about using document structure, and visual versus significant HTML.

As in all computer languages, syntax, or how you structure the computer's instructions, is very important in HTML. Computers are notoriously unforgiving of syntax errors. A command without syntax is like a language without letters — it lacks the essential building blocks that make it understandable.

To bridge the gap between computers and humans, Web designers use several tools that serve as the common ground between man and machine. One such tool is document structure. Humans have a need for a well-structured document, in that we do not easily understand chaotic or disorganized writing. Computers need to know a document's structure in order to display it to humans in an organized and orderly fashion.

Humans and computers need different things from HTML. Humans need a visually pleasing and well-organized document, while computers just need to know how to display it this way. Because of this, HTML is used in two distinct ways.

First, HTML visually displays information in a Web browser. Layout, colors, and stylistic issues are important, and Web designers use a lot of proprietary tags to format the text.

Second, HTML displays information in a contextual, significant way, meaning the developer was less interested in how the pages looked than in providing information to the computer in an understandable manner. This leaves the visual formatting up to the computer, which is great, because it's *your* computer, not the Web designer's. While an individual Web browser or program may not have a method for displaying bold text, for example, it will have some method of rendering or emphasizing text using the `<STRONG>` element. The difference between bold, which is a visual typesetting element, and `<STRONG>`, which is a contextual element meaning strongly emphasized, is that the visual element will not be read by nonvisual or nongraphical browsers (such as text-only browsers and text-to-speech readers).

This chapter discusses the stylistic choices between visual and contextual Web sites, and how to strike a balance between the two.

# Learning HTML Syntax

HTML formats text, graphics, and structure in individual Web pages. HTML syntax refers to how those tags are structured. Web pages must use correct syntax in order for Web browsers to understand and display them correctly.

HTML consists of *elements*, which are made up of *tags*, which contain *attributes*, which often have *values*. An element is the general name for the set of tags and attributes defining some form of markup in HTML. For example, all headings are elements, and the top-level heading consists of two tags (one to open the heading, and one to close it), and a few optional attributes. For example, `<BODY background="images/background.gif">` is the tag for the `<BODY>` element, using the optional **background** attribute.

Each tag starts with a less-than sign, <, followed by the name of the element, such as `H1` for the top-level heading. Next come the attributes. One attribute for `H1` is **align**. You can align your heading to the left, right, or center. Left, Right, and Center are the available values to the **align** attribute. End the tag with the greater-than sign: >.

Most elements must also be closed. Closing tags look like opening tags, but without the attributes, and there is a / before the name of the element: `</H1>`, for example. The closing tag tells the Web browser to cease displaying that element's markup.

Some elements, of course, do not use any attributes, or should not. While it is possible to add styles to a line break (`<BR>`), for example, what would be the point?

Some elements do not have a closing tag. These elements are called "empty elements." Empty elements do something and then stop, and are no longer needed in the code. A line break is an empty element; once the line has broken, there are no further properties to deal with. An image is also an empty element, because its tags do not enclose anything.

There are two types of elements: *block* and *inline*. A block element creates a new block of text and graphics. Block elements usually create a line break or paragraph break when they are opened or closed. The most common block element is the text paragraph, but others are heading tags, horizontal rules, structural elements such as `<DIV>`, and others.

An inline element is simply an element that does not cause a line or paragraph break. Like the inline italics in a word processing document, it does not affect the entire block of text. Images are now considered inline elements in current browsers (older ones cannot handle inline JPEGs). Very few elements can be both an inline element and a block element.

Table 1-1 provides a quick reference for the parts of a tag, along with examples. All HTML tags must be enclosed in <> brackets. In the examples, bold sections correspond to the current tag property.

---

**CROSS-REFERENCE**

In Chapter 2, you'll actually write your first Web page, starting with the `<HTML>`, `<HEAD>`, and `<BODY>` elements

**FIND IT ONLINE**

The W3C's HTML 4.0 specification discusses the origins of elements and attributes at **http://www.w3.org/TR/REC-html40/intro/sgmltut.html#h-3.2**.

### SCRIPTING SYNTAX

JavaScript, Jscript, VBScript, and cascading style sheets all have a different syntax for the elements you put in your Web page. Although any Web browser that can understand those elements should be able to understand their syntax, don't get confused by a different way of writing code. Scripting elements and style sheets were originally developed and implemented as ways to extend HTML, not as additions to HTML itself, and they were developed by companies such as Netscape and Microsoft to grant their Web browsers an "edge" over each other. Some of these elements have since been adopted by the World Wide Web Consortium (W3C) as part of HTML 4.0, but their syntax remains the same as when they were originally implemented.

### HTML IS NOT CASE-SENSITIVE

HTML elements and attributes are not case-sensitive, so you don't have to worry about using uppercase or lowercase in your tags, except when referring to filenames. Any value that is enclosed in quotation marks should be considered case-sensitive.

According to the W3C, attributes and values should be in lowercase. However, I have found that it is easier to locate and read tags in an HTML editor if the entire tag (except filenames and quoted values) is in uppercase. In keeping with the W3C standard, and to help you when you view other print references, I have used uppercase for elements, and lowercase for attributes throughout this book.

### Table 1-1: THE BIOLOGY OF A TAG

| Tag Property | Description | Example |
|---|---|---|
| ELEMENT | Defines what the tag does for the Web browser. | `<P>` |
| attribute | Extends the element with options, or source information. Some attributes are required for some tags. | `<INPUT type= "checkbox" checked>` |
| Value | The value of an attribute, such as the location of a source file, alignment option, sizing information, etc. An attribute's value follows the equals sign. | `<IMG src= "images/ icon.gif" border=0 align=Left ismap>` |

# Developing Web Page Structure

A Web document's structure consists of several elements. The first element tells the browser which version of HTML is used. Second, the <HEAD> element stores information about the document. Finally, the <BODY> element contains the document itself—images, text, hyperlink, and so forth. These elements are shown in Listing 1-1.

The <HEAD> doesn't appear directly in the Web browser, so you may put comments, search engine information, copyright notices, and scripting code in this element. In addition, style sheet information should be stored in the <HEAD> element. This element is the first part of the HTML file to load and be "read" by the Web browser.

An example of a simple <HEAD> element can be found in the code to the upper left on the next page. The <HEAD> tags should enclose any scripting and style sheet information, as well as the <META> elements, which help define the subject of the Web page for search engines and indexing sites. The author has also provided an HTML comment to give credit for the graphics used on the site. Anyone viewing the source of this Web page will see this information, but none of it is displayed in the document text itself.

The <BODY> element contains the document itself. Whatever you put in the <BODY> element will appear in the Web browser: text, graphics, hyperlinks, and so on. The only way to hide text or information in this element is to enclose it in a comment tag.

A <META> element is one way to provide information about your Web site to search engines, other Web authors, and Web servers. You can include any kind of information in a <META> tag. There is no closing tag to the <META> element.

<META> elements have two attributes: name and content. Name defines what the content's value will describe. For example, "Datetime" could be the value for the name. Then, a Web program would know that the numbers and letters under content represent the date and time, probably of the last modification. This is less important for search engines than it is for Web development teams. <META> elements are discussed in detail in Chapter 18.

*Continued*

## TAKE NOTE

### VIEW SOURCE

Any time you have a Web page loaded into the browser, you can view its HTML source code by using the View Source command. In both Internet Explorer and Netscape Navigator, this option (View ⇨ Source) is under the View menu on the menu bar.

### TEAMWORK IN HTML

Few Web designers work entirely alone, and if you ever have to work with another Web developer on the same Web pages, you'll need some way to keep track of your changes. Use the <META> element to note the author and editor of a Web page. Comment tags can include the most recent change, locations of content, and design notes.

## CROSS-REFERENCE
Comments are also discussed in Chapter 2.

## FIND IT ONLINE
The Web Developer's Virtual Library has an excellent tutorial on Web document structure at **http://www.stars.com/Tutorial/HTML/Structure/**.

## Listing 1-1: A Basic \<HEAD\> Section

```
<HEAD>
<LINK rel="STYLESHEET" TYPE="text/css"
href="campdown.css">


<!-- Clipart graphics probided by Corel
Corporation: http:/www.corel.com  -->


<META name="Keywords" content="Kansas City,
Camping, Family Entertainment, RV, Tent,
Fishing">
<TITLE>Welcome to Down Under Camp Resort in
Turney Missouri!</TITLE>
```
ⓐ ⓑ

ⓐ *The contents of the* `TITLE` *element appeats in the Web browser window, but not in the document itself.*

ⓑ *The colors and font are the result of the style sheet linked by the* `LINK` *element in the* `HEAD`.

■ *Part of Washtech's* \<HEAD\> *element:*`<META name="Keywords" content="Washington Alliance of Technology Workers, washtech, WashTech, Washtech, software, Washington state, high-tech industry, Seattle, Puget Sound, workers, union, organize, alliance, Microsoft, Boeing, Labor and Industries, overtime">`

## Listing 1-2: \<HEAD\> Elements

```
<HTML>

  <HEAD>
    <TITLE></TITLE>
    <LINK>
    <META>
    <STYLE></STYLE>
    <SCRIPT></SCRIPT>
    <BASE>
  </HEAD>
  <BODY>
    Web Page Content
  </BODY>

</HTML>
```

▲ *The elements available inside the* \<HEAD\> *of a Web document.*

# Developing Web Page Structure
*Continued*

Within the <BODY> element of your Web page, you should also have structure and form. Any good document needs to have structure. In the traditional world, you build structure with headings, sidebars, and whitespace — the margins around your text.

On the Web, you can use all these elements to visually structure your document. However, only headings will actually provide machine-readable document structure. Because of this, the <DIV> element was created.

<DIV> is a block element that enables Web authors to set aside or section-off an area of text and graphics. The <DIV> element can also help you structure Web pages by allowing you to name individual segments of your document, including headings, without using the heading elements, or having this structural information appear within the Web browser. Web browsers usually insert a line break after the <DIV> element closing tag. An example of using <DIV> elements is in Listing 1-2.

Similar to the <DIV> element, the inline <SPAN> element creates an artificial structure notation, although it is usually reserved for adding style sheet markup to a small phrase of text.

In addition to the <DIV> and <SPAN> elements, you can also structure your page visually with sidebars and whitespace. Although sidebars are discussed in Chapter 4, you can easily change the margins and whitespace of your document.

To change the margins within a block-level element (such as <DIV>, <P>, or <PRE>), use the `style`

attribute inside the opening tag for the block-level element: `<P style="margin-left: 10pt">` will add 10 points (a little less than half an inch on my 17" monitor) of whitespace to the left margin. An example is provided in the upper half of the next page. Note that the `style` attribute syntax is the same as for any other attribute in HTML: `attribute="Value"`. Style sheet syntax is different from the `style` attribute.

## TAKE NOTE

### ▶ TABLES AND STRUCTURE

Technically, tables don't affect Web page structure. However, when you use a table to visually lay out a Web page, the user should be left with the impression of a well-ordered page. For example, you can use a table to create a navigational or commentary sidebar to the left or the right, which will help "frame" the textual content, and give your users a visual break. Although a nonvisual program will not understand the layout structuring, you'll be providing the visual cues needed for your visual audience. Because tables "read" from left to right down the page, nonvisual programs will still be able to read the content of your Web page, but they will not render the visual layout as you created it.

**CROSS-REFERENCE**
Chapter 10 has more information on using style sheets to format and structure your text.

**FIND IT ONLINE**
The Index DOT HTML resource has a good inline style resource at **http://www.blooberry.com/html/style/syntax.htm#inline**.

## Listing 1-3: Structure Pages

```
<DIV name="Example" STYLE="color: #800000;
background: #F3DBAD; margin-left: 20pt;
margin-right: 20pt">
<H3>EXAMPLE:</H3>
<P>In Dragon NaturallySpeaking:<BR>
In NaturallySpeaking, you can switch back
and forth without touching the keyboard,
but you cannot select, copy, and paste text
from the Netscape window into the
NaturallySpeaking window. You <EM>can</EM>
do the reverse; copy and paste the
information from the NaturallySpeaking
window into another program, such as email
or word processing software.</P>
</DIV>
```

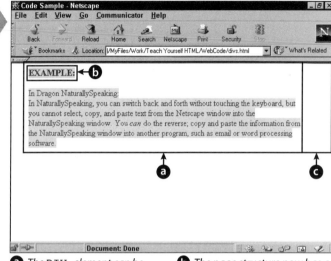

**ⓐ** The DIV element can be used to highlight and example with font and background colors and margins.

**ⓑ** The page structure now has a text section named "Example".

**ⓒ** Use the margin-left and margin-right values in the style attribute to increase the whitespace around a block of text.

## Listing 1-4: Using <SPAN> for Structure

```
<P><SPAN style="font-family: sans-serif;
font-weight: bold">In Dragon
NaturallySpeaking:</SPAN><BR>
In NaturallySpeaking, you can switch back
and forth without touching the keyboard,
but you cannot select, copy, and paste text
from the Netscape window into the
NaturallySpeaking window.</P>

<P><SPAN style="font-family: sans-serif;
font-weight: bold"> Now the above scenario
with IBM ViaVoice Gold:</SPAN><BR>
As you dictate, you switch between
navigator and ViaVoice. Only this time, you
can select the page, copy it to the
clipboard, switch back to ViaVoice
screen.</P>
```

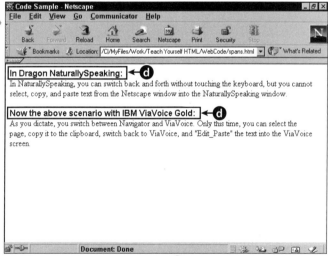

**■** The SPAN element is used here to format a subtitle without using a Heading element.

**ⓓ** The values in the style attribute instruct the web browser to use a sans-serif font in bold.

# Adding Style and Substance

Web browsers are not the only computer programs that read Web pages. Search engines, Web crawlers, and user agents (programs that search Web sites and send interesting URIs to users) all search the Web, each using a unique method.

Many new Web designers think that if you can't see it in the Web page, it doesn't matter. These designers use visual elements only, ignoring any structural elements that do not have a direct impact on the graphical design of their pages. Often, the Web site will be "browser-dependent," meaning that the Web user must have a certain Web browser — such as Netscape Navigator — installed in order for the site to work properly. Unfortunately, proprietary tags and extensions, plug-ins, and a constant preoccupation with visual elements results in an ineffective site, and may even cause a browser or system crash.

On the other end of the spectrum are Web sites that seem to be designed with the text browser in mind. A text-only browser, such as Lynx, will not show graphics or any special visual formatting in Web pages. The bottom-right figure on the facing page shows a Web page in a text-only browser.

Style versus substance. Visual elements against significant ones. How do you design for nongraphical programs and graphical Web browsers?

Although there's no easy answer to this problem, you can strike a balance between visual style and contextual substance. First, identify your audience. Are you on an intranet, where the entire company is using Internet Explorer? If so, you can use any visual formatting elements supported by that version of Internet Explorer. Does your site's content appeal to disabled users? Minimize your visual formatting, and create a speech-reader-friendly site. Assume that most of your users will have either the most recent version of their Web browser installed, or the one immediately preceding it. Use visual formatting only when other formatting elements are unavailable.

## Cross-Browser Compatibility

On the World Wide Web, about 40 percent use some variation of Netscape Navigator, 40 percent use Internet Explorer, and the other 20 percent are using other Web browsers. When you consider all the versions of Navigator and Internet Explorer that exist, you have some serious backward-compatibility issues. I'm not going to nitpick over each Web browser in this book. Instead, I note places where there have been compatibility problems in the past.

This book is about HTML 4.0, which includes the Cascading Style Sheets specification. Style sheets are supported by Internet Explorer 3.x and above, and Netscape Navigator 4.0 and above, as well as any browser that is HTML 4.0-compliant. Since Microsoft invented cascading style sheets, test your style sheet pages on Netscape, and vice versa, with frames. It stands to reason that the inventor of an element or technology will best support it, so test it on the "other guy" first.

**CROSS-REFERENCE**

Learn more about tailoring your site to your audience in Chapter 5.

**FIND IT ONLINE**

The Backward Compatibility Web page (http://www.delorie.com/web/wpbcv.html) shows you how well your Web site "degrades" in older browsers.

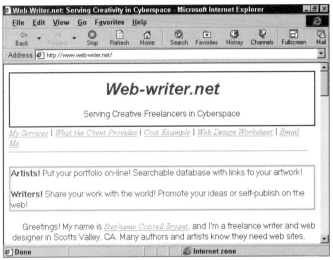

This Web site is designed for Internet Explorer 4 and Netscape Communicator 4 and above. The audience for this Web site mainly uses these browsers.

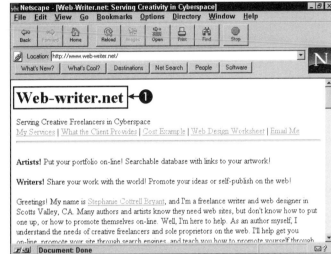

❶ This same site appears differently in Netscape Navigator 3.0. For example, the fancy banner at the top of the page is now just a text heading.

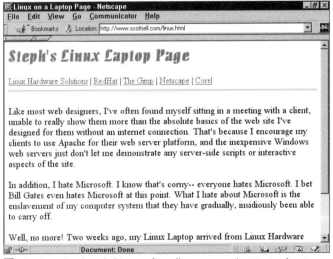

On the other hand, this text-friendly page uses just text colors to enhance the site, which looks fine in text-only browsers (which usually have few graphic or color options).

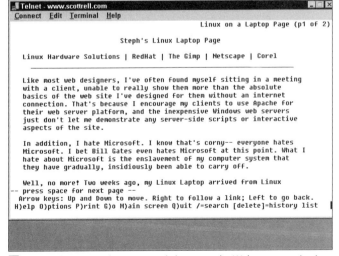

Even when viewed in a text-only browser, the Web page retains its meaning, and content is still readable. It still lacks the "flash" of more graphical and stylistic Web sites.

# Personal Workbook

## Q&A

**1** What's the difference between an element and an attribute?

_____

_____

_____

**2** Do you always need a closing tag for all elements?

_____

_____

_____

**3** Does any information from the <HEAD> element appear on the Web page?

_____

_____

_____

**4** How often should you repeat provocative words and phrases, such as "XXX, nudity, videogames" in your <META> elements?

_____

_____

_____

**5** Is it acceptable to include keywords in a <META> element that do not appear on the current page but do appear on other pages within the site?

_____

_____

_____

**6** Which one is an inline element, <DIV> or <SPAN>?

_____

_____

_____

**7** Do across-site headers and footers add anything valuable to a document's structure?

_____

_____

_____

**8** True or False: You should never use elements that provide only visual markup to the page.

_____

_____

_____

ANSWERS: PAGE 433

## EXTRA PRACTICE

① Open a Web page from the Internet in your Web browser. Find the title of the page in the browser.

② View the source code and find the <HEAD> element. (Hint: it's near the top!)

③ Identify the <META> elements (if any) and see if they describe the content of the Web page.

④ Look through the source code for comment tags, and read what they say.

⑤ Try to find the name of the Web designer, the HTML editor used, the last modified date, and information on the content of the site.

⑥ How much information about the site is in the <HEAD> element, and how much is in the body of the document?

## REAL-WORLD APPLICATIONS

✔ You search for a Web site containing information on the Lynx text-only Web browser. The word *lynx* has many different meanings, but the Web designers for the Lynx Web site have used many keywords in their <META> elements. You find the site quickly and easily.

✔ You like the graphics on a Web page and want to know if you can use them. In the source code, you find a comment with copyright information and an email address to write to for permission.

✔ You disagree with the opinions stated on a Web site. The author makes it clear that his opinions are his own, but forgot to identify himself on his page. You find the Web author's name in a <META> element, and contact him directly.

## Visual Quiz

This Web page is not the home page for the site. What kind of <META> elements would you expect to see in the <HEAD>, if any? Is this site designed for style or substance? Would you expect to be able to read this site with a text-only browser?

_____

_____

_____

_____

CHAPTER

**MASTER THESE SKILLS**

▶ **Creating an HTML Document**
▶ **Making Headings**
▶ **Adding Textual Paragraphs**
▶ **Creating a Hyperlink**
▶ **Using Graphics and Icons**
▶ **Customizing with Color**

# Building a Simple Web Page

A Web page is really little more than a text file with a series of markup tags to display it in a Web browser. In this chapter, you learn how to build a very basic Web page, complete with graphics, hyperlinks, and colorful backgrounds and text choices.

However, you'll leave the fancy frills, animation, and sound effects out of this first page. The basic Web page has an advantage over more complex Web pages: it will look good on nearly every Web browser available.

That's because you won't be confusing the Web browser. Any Web browser that can read HTML can display a simple Web page, no matter how obscure. The infamous "browser wars" have changed the way Web designers write HTML. And because HTML has been around for so long, and has changed so much over the past five years, it is nearly impossible to write pages that will look good in every Web browser.

The trick to writing effective Web sites lies in identifying your audience. You learned something about that in Chapter 1, and throughout this book I'll be pointing out ways to make your Web site

accessible to the largest audience possible. Later, when you move into more advanced and complex subjects, you'll always need the basics. As you write more complex Web sites, a simple, gizmo-free alternative may become an attractive option, even if it's just to tell users to upgrade their Web browsers!

HTML is an immensely flexible and varied language. As you've already seen in Chapter 1, the World Wide Web is rapidly becoming a limitless media, with literally thousands of ways to present data to the information-hungry public. How you choose to present that information is a matter of taste, style, and technological expertise. If you're reading this chapter, it's because you feel you need the expertise. When you're done with this chapter, you'll have enough expertise to publish a simple document with graphics; the kind of Web page that started the whole Web revolution.

And you may find that, with the instructions included in the "Customizing with Color" section of this chapter, the simple Web site presents your message in an effective, easy-to-read manner that is appreciated by everyone.

# Creating an HTML Document

An HTML document is essentially a text file with special tags to help your Web browser display its content. In some ways, an HTML file is like a word processor document; the text and graphics are the focus of the document, but formatting information, such as boldface type and font sizes, is included to help the program display and print the document correctly. When you try to open the document in a program that cannot "read" the formatting information, the formatting is lost, or the document itself is garbled.

So, too, with HTML documents. If you try to open an HTML document with a program that does not read HTML, the formatting will be lost or the document itself will look like gibberish. Similarly, if you try to open a non-HTML document in a Web browser, it will not look the same as an HTML document, and may even look like gibberish as well.

HTML has gone through many revisions during its history, and there is now an element you can use to tell the Web browser which version of HTML you're using. It's called the <!DOCTYPE> element, and many HTML authoring tools automatically put this element at the top of a new Web document. Later, I'll show you how to use <!DOCTYPE>s when your Web page uses style sheets, frames, or XML. For now, use the following <!DOC-TYPE> element as the first line in your HTML 4.0 Web page:

```
<!DOCTYPE HTML PUBLIC "-//W3C//DTD HTML
4.0//EN"
"http://www.w3.org/TR/REC-html40/strict.dtd">
```

This <!DOCTYPE> statement says that the document uses the HTML 4.0 Document Type Definition, as defined by the World Wide Web Consortium (W3C), and found at **http://www.w3.org/TR/REC-html40/strict.dtd**.

After you've included the <!DOCTYPE> element, insert the <HEAD> element. Since the <HEAD> element of the Web page is not actually displayed in the browser, it's a good place to hide code that doesn't belong elsewhere. For example, you can put comments, JavaScript code, and copyright notices in the <HEAD> element. In addition, there's a special element, called a <META> tag, that belongs in the <HEAD> section. <META> elements will be covered later, since they're used primarily to index your Web page and provide specific information to search engines.

## TAKE NOTE

### SAVING AS HTML

Depending on the authoring tool you use, saving your document as HTML may be fairly simple or it might be downright complicated. For example, a Web authoring tool that is designed to write Web pages will probably use HTML as the default file type. However, if you're using a text editor (such as Notepad or SimpleText) or a word processor (such as Microsoft Word or Corel WordPerfect), then you may have to change the file type when you save. If you ever have trouble opening a Web page that was created using a text editor or word processor, check the filename extension, and the file type to be sure that it really did save as an HTML file.

## CROSS-REFERENCE

For more information on Web authoring tools, see Appendix C. To review HTML tag syntax, see Chapter 1.

## FIND IT ONLINE

A document structure HTML reference guide can also be found at **http://www.tue.nl/bwk/cheops/via/maker/html4/html.htm#struct**.

## Listing 2-1: Starting Your Basic Web Page

```
<!DOCTYPE HTML PUBLIC "-//W3C/DTD HTML 4.0/EN"
"http://www.w3.org/TR/REC-html4.0/strict.dtd">


<HTML>    ← ❶
<HEAD>    ← ❷
```

❶ Open your Web authoring program and create a new document. Type <HTML> to begin the HTML page.

❷ Type <HEAD> to begin the header section — information in the header section will not appear in the Web browser.

## Listing 2-2: Adding a <Title>

```
<!DOCTYPE HTML PUBLIC "-//W3C/DTD HTML 4.0/EN"
  "http://www.w3.org/TR/REC-html40/strict.dtd">


<HTML>

<HEAD>
        ❸              ❹                    ❺
<TITLE>Short Stories by Stephanie Bryant</TITLE>

</HEAD>  ← ❻
```

❸ Add the <TITLE> tag to begin your title. The title will be displayed at the top of the Web browser.

❹ Enter the title of your Web page.

❺ Close the <TITLE> element by typing </TITLE>.

❻ Close the <HEAD> element with its closing tag: </HEAD>.

## Listing 2-3: The <BODY> of Your Web Page

```
<!DOCTYPE HTML PUBLIC "-//W3C/DTD HTML 4.0/EN"
  "http://www.w3.org/TR/REC-html40/strict.dtd">
<HTML>
<HEAD>
<TITLE>Short Stories by Stephanie Bryant</TITLE>
</HEAD>
<BODY>  ← ❼
<P>Here's a collection fo short stories, all
written by yours truly.</P>
</BODY>  ← ❽
</HTML>
```

❼ Begin the body section by typing <BODY>.

❽ At the end of your document, be sure to close the <BODY> and <HTML> elements: </BODY></HTML>.

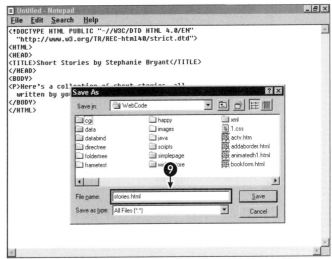

❾ Save your file as `filename.html`. Use `.html` as the file extension to tell the Web browser that the file is HTML, and should be read accordingly.

# Making Headings

As discussed in Chapter 1, headings provide the structure of your Web page. You learned why headings are needed. Now, you'll create and center them on your screen.

A heading can go anywhere inside the <BODY> element, in the document body.

Headings are most often used to define the structure of a document. However, many Web authors use them as a text formatting shortcut. Instead of altering the font itself, they may include it in a Heading element that is a close approximation of the "look" they wish to create.

Technically, that's using heading elements incorrectly, because not all Web browsers display headings the same way, although they will usually display the upper-level elements (1–3) in larger font, and lower-level elements (5–6) in smaller, often boldface font style.

If your audience will be using text-only browsers, such as Lynx, or when designing a Web site for the disabled, reserve headings for structural use only. It will save your readers a lot of headache when their "nonstandard" Web browsers display (or sometimes read aloud) your text in an inconsistent manner.

*Continued*

## TAKE NOTE

### HEADINGS AND TEXT READERS

Many disabled users, including visually impaired users, have text-to-speech (TTS) readers — computer programs that read aloud from a computerized document. These readers sometimes have special inflections or signals for hyperlinks and headings, so don't use a heading incorrectly if you think your audience may include disabled users. Unless your Web site is disconnected from the Internet, you will probably have a significant number of disabled people browsing and using your site.

### THE <HR> ELEMENT

Add a Horizontal Rule or <HR> element after major headings and section breaks. The Horizontal Rule gives your readers a visual clue that the subject is about the change. The <HR> element has no closing tag, and it includes a paragraph break at the end of the line.

**CROSS-REFERENCE**

Chapter 1 covers document structure and style.

**FIND IT ONLINE**

The W3C validator at **http://validator.w3.org/** can generate an outline of the document.

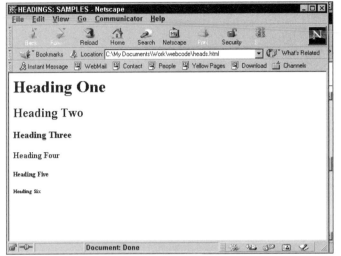

■ *Headings may display in a variety of ways in different Web browsers. Here's how they look in Netscape Communicator 4.0.*

## Listing 2-4: Headings

```
<!DOCTYPE HTML PUBLIC "-//W3C/DTD HTML 4.0/EN"
   "http://www.w3.org/TR/REC-html40/strict.dtd">
<HTML>
<HEAD>
<TITLE>Short Stories by Stephanie Bryant</TITLE>
</HEAD>
<BODY>
<H1>My Short Stories</H1>
<BODY>
<HTML>
```

❶ *To begin a "structurally sound" page, start with Heading 1. Type <H1>.*

❷ *Now type in the title of your page.*

❸ *Close the heading element with </H1>. You now have a top-level heading on your Web site.*

## Listing 2-5: Align Headings

```
<!DOCTYPE HTML PUBLIC "-//W3C/DTD HTML 4.0/EN"
   "http://www.w3.org/TR/REC-html40/strict.dtd">
<HTML>
<HEAD>
<TITLE>Short Stories by Stephanie Bryant</TITLE>
</HEAD>
<BODY>
<H1 align="center">My Short Stories</H1>
<HR>
<BODY>
<HTML>
```

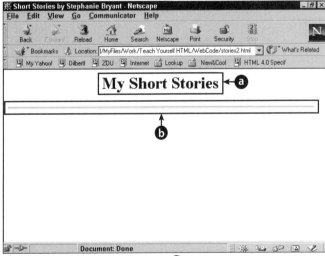

❶ *To center the heading, use the align attribute:* ALIGN=CENTER.

■ *You can also align headings to the* right *or* left.

❷ *Add <HR> after the heading element for a horizontal rule; it does not have a closing tag, and it creates an automatic paragraph break.*

# Making Headings

*Continued*

Heading tag syntax is fairly simple: `<H#>`, where # is the heading number desired. The element must be closed with `</H#>`. At the end of any heading line (when the element is closed), the Web browser puts in an automatic paragraph break; you do not need to add a paragraph break after a heading element. All headings can use the attributes discussed previously.

When you use additional headings, try to use them as a document structuring tool. `H1` should be the top-level heading, usually the title of the document itself. If you think of your document as a standard outline, `H2` should be the A heads, `H3` the B heads, and so forth.

There are six heading levels; Heading 6 is almost indistinguishable from normal text.

In Table 2-1, `H5` and `H6` are mentioned as being used for fine print and legal notices. Not only is this usage structurally unsound, it is also made obsolete with style sheets in HTML 4. I recommend using a paragraph style (using style sheets) called `"fineprint"` (using a smaller text size) in any document with legalese, copyright, or antispam notices.

## TAKE NOTE

### ▶ SEARCH ENGINES AND DOCUMENT HEADERS

Search engines, like Yahoo!, Excite!, AltaVista, and others, often use the document structure (as determined by the Headers) to categorize a document. The search engines used to use the Title, or META information, but they quickly found that unscrupulous Web designers would "load" these elements with irrelevant keywords, in hopes of attracting more traffic to their site.

When a search engine parses the headers, it will create a concept of the document based on what's in those headers, and it can then categorize the document more effectively. So if your document has the main topics enclosed in heading elements, it will be more likely to end up in the appropriate categories, where your potential audience is looking.

### ▶ DOCUMENT HEADERS AND VERIFICATION TOOLS

HTML verification tools also use heading elements to re-create document structure. This is usually done for the benefit of the Web author — you can see whether or not your document structure is actually present in the headings, or if it needs to be reorganized a bit.

## CROSS-REFERENCE

See Appendix A for a complete list of HTML elements, including headings.

## FIND IT ONLINE

BrowserCaps (**http://www.browsercaps.com/ config/Cv/Generated/test-headings.html**) shows how headings look in *your* browser.

## Table 2-1: HEADING ELEMENTS

| Heading | Tag | Use |
| --- | --- | --- |
| Heading 1 | <H1> | For top-level naming; usually for a page or chapter title. |
| Heading 2 | <H2> | Second-level naming; sections or parts in a document. |
| Heading 3 | <H3> | Subsections in a document — this is usually as far as your structure should require headings. |
| Heading 4 | <H4> | Rarely used for structure. |
| Heading 5 | <H5> | Rarely used for structure, but often used for "fine print" notices, such as disclaimers and copyright notices. |
| Heading 6 | <H6> | Often used incorrectly to format fine print text, such as disclaimers or copyright notices. |

### Listing 2-6: Subheadings

```
<BODY>
<H1 align="center">My Short Stories</H1>

<P>Here's a collection of short stories, all
written by yours truly.</P>

<H2>Science Fiction</H2>
<P>These science fiction stories are set in
the world of Aldervian.</P>
<BODY>
```

❶ ❷

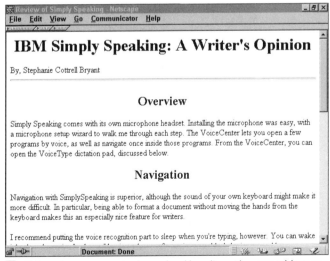

**IBM Simply Speaking: A Writer's Opinion**

By, Stephanie Cottrell Bryant

**Overview**

Simply Speaking comes with its own microphone headset. Installing the microphone was easy, with a microphone setup wizard to walk me through each step. The VoiceCenter lets you open a few programs by voice, as well as navigate once inside those programs. From the VoiceCenter, you can open the VoiceType dictation pad, discussed below.

**Navigation**

Navigation with SimplySpeaking is superior, although the sound of your own keyboard might make it more difficult. In particular, being able to format a document without moving the hands from the keyboard makes this an especially nice feature for writers.

I recommend putting the voice recognition part to sleep when you're typing, however. You can wake

❶ For second-level headings (and below), use <H2> (or the appropriate tag).

❷ Always remember to close your second-level heading elements with the </H2> tag.

■ Although you can center lower-level headings, they are seldom as effective as a centered title.

# Adding Textual Paragraphs

The main substance of your Web page is its text, and you should never let fancy graphics, plugins, or animation distract you from that fact. People go to the Web to find information, not to download silly pictures of an animated spider lumbering across the screen.

The basic text element is called <P>, standing for "paragraph." It does not need to be closed, although the </P> tag is optional, and may be useful if you're creating a highly structured Web page with very specific validation requirements.

The <P> element has one optional attribute, called align, which allows you to specify roughly where the text should appear on the screen. In addition, there are a couple of additional attributes that may be used when applying Cascading Style Sheets (CSS), which is discussed in Chapter 13.

A simple carriage-return in your text file has little or no meaning to HTML — the Web browser won't see or display it at all. It won't even put a space in there. When you begin a new paragraph, be sure to use the <P> element.

You can, however, create a line break without causing a paragraph break. The line-break element, <BR>, forces a line break wherever it appears — text will continue on the next line of the screen. <BR> has no closing tag.

## TAKE NOTE

### ▶ ALIGNMENT VERSUS JUSTIFICATION

Text alignment is not the same as text justification, although they are similar concepts. In a typical book or newspaper article, text is justified to both the left and right margins — the text fills to the margin and doesn't go over, creating smooth lines of text on either side. It takes some computer or typesetting wizardry to make the font stretch or shrink to those spaces as needed, and text justification is only available in HTML 4 through style sheets. Text alignment in HTML determines which side of the paragraph will be a smooth line — the left or the right, or neither (centered).

### ▶ CREATING HTML COMMENTS

In HTML, you can include comments that will not be read by the browser at all. These comments are used by Web design teams to make notes about the document, and to act as a guideline for further development.

For example, if you include a common header or footer across the Web site, you may wish to include a comment, such as <!— BEGIN FOOTER HERE —> to make searching and replacing the footer easier (replacing site-wide headers and footers is the most common complaint of Web designers).

Comment elements use the following syntax: <!— COMMENT —> where "COMMENT" is the text of your comment. Comments can span several lines without additional characters, and they do not have to use all capital letters, although it helps when you visually search for them.

## CROSS-REFERENCE

In Chapter 3, you'll learn how to change the font color and type within a paragraph.

## FIND IT ONLINE

See the W3C Style Guide at **http://www.w3.org/Provider/Style/Overview.html.**

### Table 2-2: PARAGRAPH ALIGN VALUES

| <P> Attribute | Text Alignment |
|---|---|
| <P align=left> | Left alignment, like normal text from a typewriter. |
| <P align=right> | Text is aligned to the right margin, but not justified on the left — it produces a ragged left column, but can be good for laying out pictures and text columns. |
| <P align=center> | Text is centered — similar to the <CENTER> element, but is part of the HTML 4.0 standard. |

### Listing 2-7: Adding Paragraphs

```
<H2>Science Fiction</H2>
<P>These science fiction stories are set in
the world of Aldervian.</P>
```

❶ Type <P>.

❷ Enter your text.

### Listing 2-8: Paragraphs and Linebreaks

```
<H2>Science Fiction</H2>
<P>These science fiction stories are set in
the world of Aldervian.</P>
<P>The main characters in this world are:
<BR>Elorids Marethina
<BR>Pelen Lethantor
<BR>Arronis Skyfire
</P>
```

❸ Each time you want a new paragraph break, add a <P>, not a carriage return.

❹ To cause a line break, use <BR>.

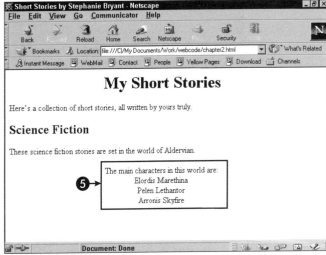

❺ To center a text paragraph, type <P align=center>.

# Creating a Hyperlink

Hyperlinks turn the World Wide Web *into* a web, by allowing authors to link to related sites, information, and resources. A hyperlink consists of the Anchor element with the `href` attribute, the location of the linked document, and the text being linked. The location is called the URI (Universal Resource Identifier), or URL (Universal Resource Location).

A URI generally takes the form of *http://www.domain. com/path/filename.html*. The topmost part of the URI is the domain name: `domain.com`, for example, followed by the hostname (which is the Web server). In this case, the hostname is `www`, and it's put before the domain name. Then, you have a forward slash and the path. The path is a directory structure within the Web server.

For example, in *http://www.netcom.com/members/ ~rtd/index.html*, the path consists of the `members` directory, followed by the `~rtd` subdirectory (`~rtd` is inside `members`, which is why it appears after it in the path name). This is an example of an *absolute URI*, used for sites outside your own domain.

There's another type of URI, the *relative URI*, which locates a document based on where it is in relation to the current document. If your current document is in one directory, and the linked document (say it's called `file.html`) is in the same directory, you'd just link directly to the filename: `<A HREF="file.html">`.

The symbol `../` means to go up one directory in a relative URI — you can use it more than once to go up more than one directory level `<A HREF="../file.html">`. If you wish to go down one directory, simply type the name of the directory, a forward-slash, and the filename: `directory/file.html`. Finally, you can use these all in combination with each other `<A HREF="../`

`directory/file.html">`. The lower right-hand figure shows a directory structure; the URI of each document relative to the file named `Simply.html` is in italics.

A forward slash at the start of the URI means that you're going to the top of the domain `<A HREF"/~rtd/ index.html">`. On a page hosted at netcom, this would take the user to **http://www.netcom.com/ members/~rtd/index.html.** The underlined URIs in the lower right-hand figure also represent absolute URIs using this method. Do not use `http://` with internal URIs (relative or absolute).

## CROSS-REFERENCE

Chapter 6 covers additional attributes to the hyperlink element, especially how to open a hyperlink from one frame into another.

## FIND IT ONLINE

Check out the "Hypertext theory as if the WWWeb matters" page at **http://www.mcs.net/~jorn/ html/hyper.html.**

## Listing 2-9: Making a Hyperlink

```
<H2>Science Fiction</H2>
<P>These science fiction stories are set in
   the world of Aldervian.</P>
<P>The main characters in this world are:
<BR><A HREF="elordis.html">Elordis Marethina</A>
<BR>Pelen Lethantor                    ❶            ❷
<BR>Arronis Skyfire
</P>
```

## Listing 2-11: Internal Hyperlinks

```
<H2><A NAME="science_fiction">Science
Fiction</A></H2>
<P>These science fiction stories are set in
   the world of Aldervian.</P>              ❺
<P>The main characters in this world are:
<BR><A HREF="#elordis">Elordis Marethina</A>
<BR><A HREF="#pelen">Pelen Lethantor</A>
<BR><A HREF="character.html#arronis">Arronis
Skyfire</A>
                    ❻
</P>
```

■ *Decide which word or phrase makes an effective link, and the URI of the link's destination.*

❶ *Insert the hyperlink element before the word or phrase: <A href="filename.html">.*

❷ *At the end of the word or phrase, close the element with </A>.*

❺ *To link to a bookmark within a page (also known as an "anchor") use <A href="filename .html#bookmark">.*

❻ *You can link to a bookmark in the current file by using <A href="#bookmark">.*

■ *The bookmark name has a # sign before it, and it does not have a file extension.*

## Listing 2-10: Anchor Names

```
<H2><A NAME="science_fiction">Science
Fiction</A></H2>
               ❸
<P>These science fiction stories are set in
   the world of Aldervian.</P>
               ❹
<P>The main characters in this world are:
<BR>Elordis Marethina
<BR>Pelen Lethantor
<BR>Arronis Skyfire
</P>
```

❸ *To create an internal bookmark, use the <A name="bookmark"> element, where "bookmark" is a meaningful name for the bookmark.*

❹ *Close the bookmark anchor element with </A>.*

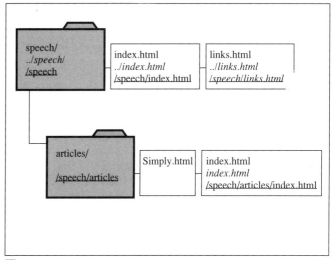

■ *In this figure, relative URIs (relative to* webaccess.html*) are shown in italics. Absolute URIs are underlined.*

# Using Graphics and Icons

Most Web pages use graphics and icons in some manner. Well-chosen graphics can contribute to an overall "look and feel" that is unique to your site. They give people visual clues about the site, and may serve well as navigation tools.

There are two formats of graphics on the World Wide Web: GIFs and JPEGs. JPEGs are usually used for photographs and full-color graphics, because they can store more graded color information through compression. GIFs are used for line art images and icons.

In HTML 4.0, all graphics are called "in-line" graphics, meaning they do not sit on a line by themselves. So, you can have a graphic in the middle of your text, or even have the text wrap around the graphic in a column.

Graphics are inserted into a Web page with the `<IMG>` element. The `<IMG>` element has a couple of required attributes and several optional ones. First and foremost is the `src` attribute. When you put an image into a Web page, the `src` attribute tells the Web browser where to find the image, much the same way the `href` tells the browser where to find a linked document.

You can align an image with the `align` attribute, much as you would align a paragraph. Simply include the `align=center` attribute (using whatever alignment you prefer: `center`, `left`, or `right`). If you place text after the graphic, the text will wrap around left- or right-aligned graphics, producing a magazine-style layout.

## TAKE NOTE

▶ **HEIGHT AND WIDTH**

The `height` and `width` attributes are especially important for the `<IMG>` element. Their values are measured in pixels.

When you include these attributes, your Web page will actually appear to load faster than it does, because the Web browser will be able to display text before the graphics finish loading.

Without these attributes to tell the browser how much space to leave, your audience will be stuck staring at a blank screen while the images download from the Web.

▶ **TRANSPARENT BACKGROUNDS IN IMAGES**

In GIF graphics, you can select one color (usually the background color) to appear transparent. That means the Web browser will not display anything in the graphic that is that color. Any background color or graphic you may have used will appear through the background of the graphic.

This feature can be useful when you want a graphic to appear to "float," but make sure your background color and your floating graphic contrast each other.

## CROSS REFERENCE

Chapter 6 has more information on creating and editing graphics, and using them as navigational maps for your Web site.

## FIND IT ONLINE

Bull's Backgrounds, Buttons, and Bars (**http://www. cbull.com/back.htm**) offers several free "accent" graphics.

## Table 2-3: IMG ATTRIBUTES

| Attribute Usage | Effect |
|---|---|
| align=center<br>align=left<br>align=right | Places the image to the right, left, or centered on the screen. May allow text to wrap around the graphic. |
| alt="More info this way!" | Provides a textual alternative to the graphic. |
| ismap | The ISMAP attribute has no value. It simply tells the browser that this graphic is an image map. |
| src="images/ icon.gif"> | Provides the location of the graphic — this is a mandatory attribute. |

## Listing 2-12: Including Images

```
<IMG SRC="images/icon.gif"> ← ❶
<H1 align="center">My Short Stories</H1>
<IMG SRC="images/icon.gif" height=25 width=100>
                                    ❷        ❸
```

❶ *Start with the basics:* <IMG src="images/icon. gif">. *Note that the URI of the graphic is in quotes.*

❷ *Add height and width attributes.*

❸ *Note that the* height *and* width *values are in pixels, and are not enclosed in quotes.*

■ *There is no closing tag to the* <IMG> *element.*

## Listing 2-13: Using Attributes in the <IMG> Tag

```
<H1>
<A href="index.html">
<IMG SRC="images/icon.gif" alt="Home Icon" ← ⓐ
  align="left"></A>
Home Page Central ⓑ
<A href="index.html"> ← ⓒ
<IMG SRC="images/icon.gif" border=0></A> ← ⓒ
</H1>
                              ⓓ
```

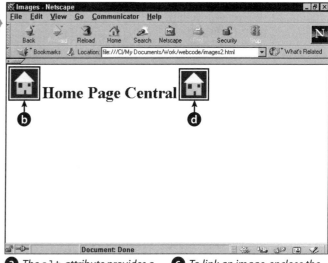

ⓐ *The* alt *attribute provides a text alternative while the image loads.*

ⓑ *Use the* align *attribute to place the image to the left, right, or centered.*

ⓒ *To link an image, enclose the* <IMG> *element in the hyperlink elements.*

ⓓ *To link without a blue hyperlink outline, add* border=0 *to the* <IMG> *element.*

**29**

# Customizing with Color

In my own Web sites and pages, I like to use color to create a certain "look and feel." When you surf the Web, try to take note of the pages that make an impression on you, and the ones that don't. Using specific colors across your site will help your audience remember you, and they take no longer to download than an ordinary Web page.

To tell the Web browser which colors to use, you need to determine the RGB color code. This code is in the form of a six-digit number, where the first two digits refer to the amount of red in the color, the second two refer to the amount of green in the color, and the third two refer to the amount of blue in the color.

The hardware and software setup of the user's machine will have an effect on how the colors show up. Video boards, display screens, and even Web browsers can all produce slight color variations. Usually, it's not a significant difference. But once in a while someone will view your site with an unusual configuration and find it difficult to read. For that reason, you should try to test your Web site on as many different computers as possible. The WebTV display models in most electronics stores will give you a "free peek" at how the colors of your site (and other design elements) appear in the WebTV browser. Libraries and universities often have older hardware and software, so you can see if your site "degrades" gracefully. And although it won't help with the hardware issue, you can download a shareware or freeware copy of most Web browsers available today.

*Continued*

## Colors Can Be "Turned Off" By the User

All browsers that have color options (and some that don't) allow users to set a particular color scheme and use it for every site that they encounter. That means they can override your color scheme with their own defaults. Make sure your graphics won't "disappear" or become meaningless if someone chooses a different color scheme. Common color schemes include the following:

▶ White background, black text, and blue hyperlinks
▶ Black background with white text and yellow hyperlinks
▶ Gray background, black text, and blue hyperlinks (this is the Netscape default color scheme)

Just because these are the most common, however, does not mean that they are the only ones. Some users may have the colors set to a very sharp contrast, while others may have increased the font size all over the screen to be able to read it better (I've done this on my own system — 17 years of eyeglasses and you'll try anything). Some people just pick their favorites, or colors that are especially soothing.

**SHORTCUT**

Windows 95 comes with a simple Paint program and calculator for an inexpensive color picker and converter.

**FIND IT ONLINE**

The Inquisitor Mediarama Color Page Builder (**http://www.inquisitor.com/hex.html**) lists color codes to include in your Web site.

## TABLE 2-4 COMMON RGB COLOR CODES

| RGB Color Code | Common Name |
| --- | --- |
| #000000 | Black |
| #800000 | Dark red |
| #008000 | Green |
| #000080 | Navy |
| #800080 | Purple |
| #008080 | Teal |
| #808080 | Gray |
| #FF0000 | Red |
| #FFFF00 | Yellow |
| #0000FF | Blue |
| #FFFFFF | White |

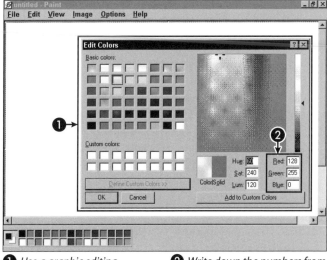

**1** Use a graphic editing program to choose the color you desire.

**2** Write down the numbers from the Red, Green, and Blue values. These will be numbers between 0 and 256.

**3** Open Calculator in Scientific mode.

**4** Enter the 256 code for Red.

**5** Click the Hex radio button and write down the two-digit number (it may include a letter) for Red.

■ Repeat these steps for Green and Blue.

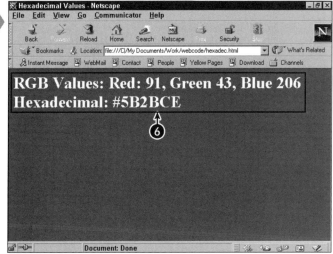

**6** Now put each of the two-digit codes together: RRGGBB. That's your RGB color code for that color.

# Customizing with Color

*Continued*

You should always choose colors that complement the graphics and icons in your Web page. When you've chosen your colors, you can apply them to your page background, text, and hyperlink colors, which can be any colors you want in HTML.

Changing a color scheme within a page is done in the <BODY> element, because it affects nearly every item in the body of the Web page. When you change page colors, be sure to view the page before uploading it to the World Wide Web. In fact, look at it on as many different computers as you possibly can so you can make sure it's not just your computer making it look good.

You can also include a background graphic instead of a color. To do this, include the attribute `background="image.gif"` (where image.gif is your background graphic) inside the <BODY> element.

The background graphic must be a GIF file, and it will "tile" across the screen. So, if the graphic is narrow, it will repeat itself horizontally multiple times. If it's short, it will repeat itself vertically.

Try to avoid using very large graphics, hoping for a "watermark" effect. It rarely works, and users with a very large screen will easily see a repetition in the watermark.

Background graphics override background colors in most Web browsers.

**CROSS-REFERENCE**

Colors are also discussed in Chapter 3 and Chapter 9.

**FIND IT ONLINE**

Netscape's Web site has information on background and foreground colors at **http://home.netscape.com/ assist/net_sites/bg/index.html**

## Listing 2-14: Changing Background Colors

```
<!DOCTYPE HTML PUBLIC "-//W3C/DTD HTML 4.0/EN"
   "http://www.w3.org/TR/REC-
html40/strict.dtd">
<HTML>
<HEAD>
<TITLE>Short Stories by Stephanie
Bryant</TITLE>
</HEAD>
<BODY BGCOLOR="#FFFFFF"> ◄─❶
<H1>Water Wheel</H1>
<HR>
```

❶ *To change the background color to white, insert the attribute* bgcolor="#FFFFFF" *into the <BODY> tag.*

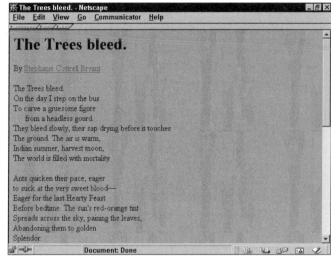

■ *To change the background color to a graphic, use* background="images/image.gif". *In this example, I used a low-contrast graphic as the background.*

## Listing 2-15: Changing Text Colors

```
<!DOCTYPE HTML PUBLIC "-//W3C/DTD HTML 4.0/EN"
   "http://www.w3.org/TR/REC-
html40/strict.dtd">
<HTML>
<HEAD>
<TITLE>Short Stories by Stephanie
Bryant</TITLE>
</HEAD>
<BODY BACKGROUND="ltwood.gif" TEXT=#FFFF00"
   LINK="#75D854" ALINK="00FFFF">
<H1 align="center">My Short Stories</H1>
```

❷ *To change the text color, use* text="#RRGGBB".

❸ *A standard, unvisited hyperlink is called link.*

❹ *The visited hyperlink attribute is vlink, and an active hyperlink, currently being clicked, is called* alink.

■ *Test your hyperlink colors by looking at them in a Web browser before you publish.*

■ *When you're done, you'll have an attractive, quick-loading page that helps others find and use your site.*

# Personal Workbook

## Q&A

**1** How do you include a title in the HEAD section?

_____

_____

_____

**2** What is the link anchor element?

_____

_____

_____

**3** How do you include a background graphic?

_____

_____

_____

**4** How many heading levels are there?

_____

_____

_____

**5** In the <IMG> element, height and width are measured in what units?

_____

_____

_____

**6** What does the <HR> element do?

_____

_____

_____

**7** Name two accessibility issues discussed in this chapter.

_____

_____

_____

**8** What element do you put at the top of your HTML document?

_____

_____

_____

ANSWERS: PAGE 434

## EXTRA PRACTICE

**1** Create a new Web page with your name, telephone number, and email address on it.

**2** Put your name in a top-level heading and center it.

**3** Change the color of your telephone number to blue.

**4** Change the background color to white, and the link color to maroon.

**5** Make a `mailto:` hyperlink from your email address.

**6** Add a simple graphic of a smiley face next to your phone number on the page.

## REAL-WORLD APPLICATIONS

✔ You've designed a Web site and decide now that the standard footer should be changed across the site. You included comments to help you search for the footer more easily.

✔ Your Web site is starting to be indexed by the search engines. You used the headings correctly, and some search sites even have a complete outline of your document.

✔ You didn't even realize that your URI was being sent out to a visually impaired user's mailing list. Fortunately, you included `alt` attributes on all graphics, and your site is easily read by TTS readers.

✔ Your Web site is hard to read by a nonstandard browser. You included a `mailto:` link, so an affected reader can email you.

## Visual Quiz

Write out the HTML code required to produce the Web page to the right. Who is the audience for this page? What would you expect to see linked from here?

_____

_____

_____

_____

_____

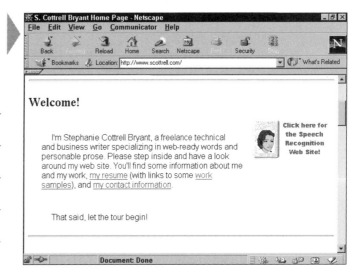

# CHAPTER 3

**MASTER THESE SKILLS**

▶ Formatting Text

▶ Adding Quotations

▶ Using Subscript and Superscript

▶ Creating a List

▶ Rendering Code

# Text in HTML

In this chapter, you learn how to format text for the Web. You'll be able to make different types of paragraphs, and you'll learn how to make individual paragraphs stand out from the rest.

I've already discussed how text is crucial to Web design. All the information and data you put on your Web site must go through one final filter before it is read by a human being. It must be displayed as text on a screen.

Reading onscreen text is difficult. When you read a book, light hits the paper and is reflected back, forming letters and words. When you watch a movie in a theater, light is projected through the film and onto the screen. Studies show that it is easier to process visual information when it is projected or reflected. Computer screens provide information through a backlit display, which means the light is actually shining up *through* your text. Add to this the problem of resolution — computer screens will never quite be as "real" as printed text — and you can understand why people are reluctant to read long spans of text online.

Good Web design means understanding the limitations of the electronic world. Although text is important, don't put too much of it on your Web page. Break it up with sidebars, tables, and graphics. Use whitespace to provide visual relief. And finally, put the most important information at the top. Users should be able to decide if the document is important in the first screen of text (100–200 words). In fact, no Web document designed for the general public should be longer than 500 words. That doesn't mean you shouldn't put longer articles on the Web — just make sure any links to them identify the depth, and therefore the audience, of the piece (for example, "Technical Information on our Products" or "Media Release on the Latest Version of our Product").

This chapter helps you display your text so it can be easily read and understood online, but it is up to you to make sure the content is worthwhile and interesting to your audience.

# Formatting Text

Adding boldface, italics, and underlining to text adds emphasis to words and phrases, and can be critical in delivering your message to your audience.

In HTML, there are two ways to apply these kinds of formatting changes to text. The easiest way is to use the `<B>` (bold), `<I>` (italic), and `<U>` (underline) elements to tell the Web browser how to change the text.

You can also use the `<EM>` and `<STRONG>` elements to make those changes. `<EM>` stands for "Emphasis," and is usually displayed as italicized text. `<STRONG>` stands for, well, "Strong text," which is usually set in boldface.

Why would you use `<EM>` and `<STRONG>` instead of the others? Well, it all comes back to Web browsers and meaning. Emphasis and Strong mean something. When a nonstandard Web browser encounters them, it will usually have some means of displaying or reading the text to convey its meaning. Bold, italics, and underline are meaningless. A Web browser can't tell if an item is italicized to show emphasis or to denote the title of a book.

Bold, Italics, Underline, Emphasis, and Strong have only the optional attributes available to all HTML 4.0 elements.

There's a special type of block element called an `<ADDRESS>`. Web browsers usually display this element on its own line, italicized, and it is supposed to be used for email addresses only.

The `<PRE>` element will "preformat" the text. For example, this code sample:

```
<P>The quick brown fox jumped over the lazy
dog.</P>
<PRE>But then the dog ran away.</PRE>
```

would look like this in your Web browser:

The quick brown fox jumped over the lazy red dog.
`But then the dog ran away.`

The `<PRE>` element creates a new line, and must be closed with `</PRE>`. In addition, any blank spaces and new lines you put within a `<PRE>` element will be formatted in HTML. The last figure has an example of preformatted text, below regular, default-style text.

*Continued*

*Continued*

## TAKE NOTE

### FORMATTING TEXT WITH STYLE SHEETS

There are still other ways you can format text. Using style sheets, you can change the color, size, weight, and style of the text. You can even include a strikethrough style and paragraph justification. It's a lot more flexible than the elements available through HTML.

### SGML: THE REASON BEHIND EM AND STRONG

SGML, the *Standard Generalized Markup Language*, is the precursor to HTML. The concepts behind SGML are fairly simple: provide a markup language that can be read in many different ways by different machines without losing any meaning.

**CROSS-REFERENCE**
SGML is discussed in Chapter 10.

**FIND IT ONLINE**
More information on SGML and using meaningful elements can be found at **http://www. pineapplesoft.com/reports/sgml/**.

## Listing 3-1: Simple Text Formatting

```
<P>
In HTML, there are two ways to apply these
kinds of formatting changes to text. The
easiest way is to use the <B>bold</B>
<I>italic</I>, and <U>underline</U> elements
to tell the Web browser how to change the
text. The upper-left and upper-right figures
show you how to do that.
</P>
```

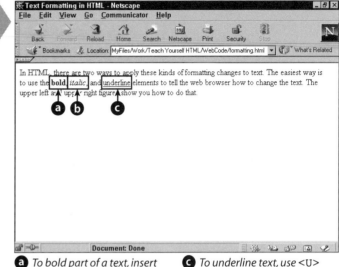

**a** To bold part of a text, insert `<B>` before the text section and `</B>` after it.

**b** To italicize text: `<I>`*italicized text goes here*`</I>`.

**c** To underline text, use `<U>` and `</U>`. Be sure to close all your text formatting elements!

## Listing 3-2: Text Formatting in HTML

```
<P>Why would you use <EM>EM</EM> and
<STRONG>STRONG</STRONG> instead of the others?
Well, it all comes back to Web browsers and
meaning. Emphasis and Strong mean something.
When a nonstandard Web browser encounters
them, it will usually have some means of
displaying or
reading the text to convey its meaning. Bold,
italics, and underlining are without context.
Web browsers can't determine if a phrase is
italicized to provide emphasis, or to denote
the title of a book.</P>
```

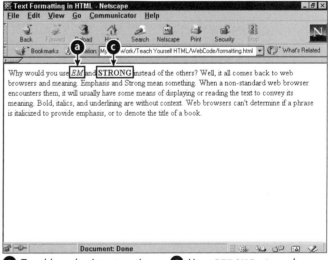

**a** To add emphasis to a section, use `<EM>`.

**b** `<EM>` must also be closed: `</EM>`.

**c** Use `<STRONG>` to make a strong point, such as in a passage or a sentence summing up a paragraph.

**d** `<STRONG>` must be closed with `</STRONG>`.

# Formatting Text
*Continued*

It's great to know how to change a document's text and hyperlink colors, but what if you want to change the font itself, or the color of just one section?

You can change the text style of individual words, phrases, or sentences. There are some good reasons to do this, but there are also many reasons not to.

One reason you'd want to change the font style is to emphasize or create a heading without actually using a heading element. If you don't want that heading to be noted by search engines, then you could use the <FONT> element to change the appearance of your font without attaching a meaning to the change.

A good reason *not* to change your font styles is to prevent confusion, and to accommodate that portion of your audience that has steadfastly clung to an older browser out of loyalty, ignorance, or want of RAM. The <FONT> element overrides the colors you set in the document <BODY> element, but it is not overridden by the user's Web browser. As a result, you may get some strange results if you fiddle around with the font colors in your document.

One solution to the many problems with the <FONT> element is to use Cascading Style Sheets (CSS). When used correctly, Style Sheets enable Web authors to suggest a display format for particular sections of text, and the user's Web browser can overlook them. In fact, older Web browsers (which do not use CSS) automatically overlook Style Sheets, presenting the information in the default text style.

## TAKE NOTE

### ▶ HTML 4.0 INCLUDES <FONT> ELEMENT

The W3C has drafted a working proposal for HTML 4.0. Although HTML 4.0 is moving quickly into a new standard called XML (Extensible Markup Language), this specification includes the <FONT> element. Netscape 3.0 and above, and Internet Explorer 3.0 and above, support the <FONT> element.

However, you should always write basic HTML pages as though someone with an older browser is going to see it. If you decide to use the <FONT> element to change size or colors on a basic Web page, use relative sizing (size=+1 instead of size=4), and choose colors that will show up on white, black, and gray backgrounds if set in the browser preferences.

### ▶ THE <BASEFONT> ELEMENT

The <BASEFONT> element can be included at the top of an HTML document. Similar to the text attribute in the <BODY> element, the <BASEFONT> element changes the font all throughout the document. However, it's far more flexible, because you can change every attribute available in the <FONT> element with the <BASEFONT> element.

**CROSS-REFERENCE**

Information on Cascading Style Sheets can be found in Chapter 10.

**FIND IT ONLINE**

http://www.mcsr.olemiss.edu/~mudws/font.html gives reasons why and when you should *not* use the <FONT> element.

## Table 3-1: FONT ATTRIBUTES

| Attribute | Example | Effect |
|---|---|---|
| color | `<FONT color= "#800000">` | Changes the color of the font to the RGB hexadecimal value: in this case, maroon. |
| face | `<FONT face= "Arial">` | Changes the Font typesetting to Arial. Can be used with any font name, but the user browsing your site must have the font installed for it to work. |
| size | `<FONT size="5">` | Increases the font size from 3 (the default) to 5. Font sizes range from 1 to 7. |
| | `<FONT size=-1>` | Increases the font size by adding 1 from the current size (usually 3). Since some people automatically have the font sizes set larger or smaller than normal, this allows relative sizing to take place. |

### Listing 3-3: Formatting the `<Font>` Element

```
<P>How do you change your text font?
<FONT COLOR="#008000">Or the color of just one
section?</FONT></P>
<P>
<FONT face="Arial" size=+2>You can change the
text style of individual words, phrases, or
sentences.</FONT>
<FONT SIZE="6"> There are good reasons to do
this, but many reasons not to.</FONT>
```

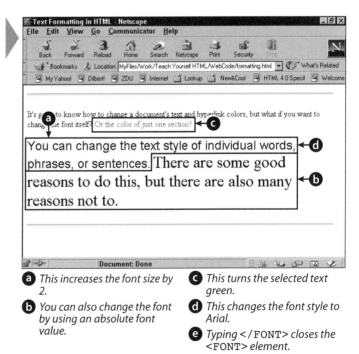

**ⓐ** This increases the font size by 2.

**ⓑ** You can also change the font by using an absolute font value.

**ⓒ** This turns the selected text green.

**ⓓ** This changes the font style to Arial.

**ⓔ** Typing `</FONT>` closes the `<FONT>` element.

# Adding Quotations

Providing quotations on a Web site is an often-overlooked but important aspect of the Web. It has to do with your voice. You don't want your voice to be the only one heard on your Web site. Your opinion may count for something, but it gains respect when backed by someone else's opinion, too.

For product pages, an appropriate reviewer's quote may make or break a sale. Academic Web authors may need to put academic quotations up, such as source information, lecture notes, or similar attributed material. You might simply wish to put your favorite Shakespearean line somewhere on your Web site.

Whatever your reason for using quotations, you want to make them stylistically correct, so they'll appear in everyone's Web browser. The `<BLOCKQUOTE>` element has been a part of HTML ever since users wanted a way to indent a paragraph of text. Use the `<BLOCKQUOTE>` element any time you have a multiline quotation that you wish to set off. The top two elements on the facing page show you how to use the `<BLOCKQUOTE>` element.

The other type of quotation is called an inline quote. Typically, this is one line of text or less, and you include it in a paragraph of regular text. To insert a quotation into a line of text, simply enclose it in the `<Q>` element.

Both elements have an optional attribute called `cite`, which allows you to include the URI of the source document (provided it is on the World Wide Web). Oddly enough, you can (and should) use the `<CITE>` element itself to provide a reference source for your quotation. This element will appear on a line by itself, usually in italics.

## TAKE NOTE

### ▶ NESTING QUOTATIONS

Quotations can be nested: that is, you may use the `<Q>` element inside a `<BLOCKQUOTE>` element. You can also use the `<Q>` element within the `<Q>` element. In American English, when you quote a quotation: "He said to her 'But I'm not an American!'" you use double quotes to start the quotation, and single quotes for within the quotation. In other languages, that's not the case, so using the `<Q>` element to insert your quote marks means they'll show up correctly in other languages. That's especially true if you add the `lang` attribute with nested quotations. For American English, use `lang="en-us"`.

### ▶ USING QUOTE-MARK CHARACTERS

Although double-quote marks are automatically inserted when using the `<Q>` element, if you decide not to use the `<Q>` element for an inline quotation, you'll need to insert them yourself. Because HTML uses quote marks as a special character, you should use the character entities instead of the traditional quote marks found on your computer keyboard. Those entities are `&#171;` for an open-quote mark, and `&#187;` for a close quote.

**CROSS-REFERENCE**

More special characters can be found in Chapter 9.

**FIND IT ONLINE**

Bartlett's Familiar Quotations is available online at **http://www.mirrors.org.sg/bartlett/**.

## Listing 3-4: Quotations

```
<BLOCKQUOTE ◄─ⓐ
CITE="http://www.mirrors.org.sg/bartlett/ ◄─ⓒ
138.38.html">
Let me not to the marriage of true minds<BR>
Admit impediments: love is not love<BR> ◄─ⓑ
Which alters when it alteration finds<BR>◄─┘
</BLOCKQUOTE>
<CITE>Shakespeare, Sonnet cxvi</CITE> ◄─ⓓ
```

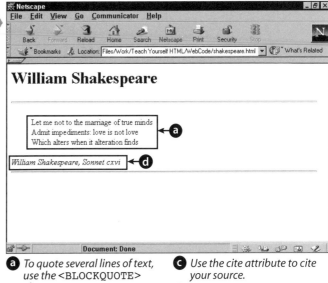

ⓐ To quote several lines of text, use the <BLOCKQUOTE> element.

ⓑ Use line and paragraph breaks between lines and stanzas.

ⓒ Use the cite attribute to cite your source.

ⓓ Always give author credit when providing a quote.

## Listing 3-5: Special Quote Characters

```
<P>◄─❶
Bill Gates said: &#171;It's my belief that
every computer will have speech and
linguistics built into it, because that's the
world of discourse that we live in. I'm not
saying the keyboard will go away, but a
substantial part of the operating system will
be this ability.&#187;◄─❹
```
(❸ and ❷ labels point to the `&#171;` and `&#187;` character references)

## Listing 3-6: Using the <Q> tag

```
<P>◄─❺
<Q LANG="en us">Ah, yes, I wrote the
<Q LANG="en us">Purple Cow</Q>-<BR>
I'm sorry, now, I wrote it!</Q>
<P>
<CITE>Gelett Burgess</CITE>
```
(❼ points to LANG, ❻ points to <Q> tags, ❽ points to "I wrote the")

❶ To make an inline quotation using quote mark characters, start with a normal <P> element.

❷ Type the sentence to enclose in quotes.

❸ Before the quotation, put &#171; and after it, put &#187;.

❹ The semicolons are very important to special character syntax.

❺ To make an inline quotation, start with the sentence in a normal <P> element.

❻ Enclose the quote in <Q> tags.

❼ Remember to use a lang attribute: <Q lang="en-us">.

❽ This line contains a nested quote.

# Using Subscript and Superscript

Subscript and superscript elements place text slightly raised or slightly lowered with respect to the rest of the line. They are inline elements — there is no line-break after they're closed.

The subscript element, `<SUB>`, places text below the line of normal text. This is especially useful in footnotes and glossary notes, which you can then link to a bookmarked reference at the end of the document. For example, `The VC2000 is a highly-compliant source for manufacturing widgets<SUB><A HREF="#note1">1</A></SUB>` would provide a hyperlink to the source of the quotation, or perhaps a definition of the jargon word "widget."

As you might have guessed by now, superscript does the opposite; it places text *above* the line of normal text. While you can also use the superscript element for referencing footnotes, its more common use is in chemical and mathematical notation: `a<SUP>2</SUP> + b<SUP>2</SUP> = c<SUP>2</SUP>` is the same as $a^2 + b^2 = c^2$. Note that there are no spaces between the variable being squared, and the superscript 2. Rarely will you place spaces between a letter and a superscript or subscript character. The purpose of this element is to provide a reference or notation, neither of which generally takes a space between it and the item noted.

Finally, you may write a page in a language that requires superscript text. An example of this is in the French abbreviation for Mademoiselle. When writing "Mlle.", it is proper to put the "lle" above the line, and it is therefore appropriate to use the superscript element to achieve this effect.

The superscript and subscript elements only have the standard attributes available to all elements; `id`, `class`, `lang`, `dir`, `title`, `style`, and scripting attributes such as `onclick` and `onmouseover`.

Footnotes. Endnotes. Chemical or mathematical notation. Foreign languages. There are literally hundreds of reasons you might use subscript and superscript *correctly*. Simply put, E doesn't equal mc squared on the Web without them.

## TAKE NOTE

### ▶ INCLUDING TRADEMARK SYMBOLS

Web designers often misuse the `<SUP>` element to produce the little TM on business documents: `<SUP><FONT size=1>TM</FONT></SUP>`.

Although they're covered in Chapter 9, I'm going to share with you the special character code for the trademark symbol: `&#153;`. Whenever you're tempted to use the `<SUP>` element for a trademark symbol, use `&#153;` instead.

### ▶ USING ENDNOTES IN HTML

In HTML, a footnote is linked in the body of a section, and explained either at the bottom of the section or at the bottom of the Web page itself. Endnotes, however, are at the end of the entire paper (some papers span several pages), or on a page by themselves. Unless your notes are very long, use footnotes in HTML so that users don't have to bounce back and forth between two different pages, or put them into a frame for easy reference.

### CROSS-REFERENCE
Chapter 9 has more information about special characters for mathematical notation and formulae.

### FIND IT ONLINE
http://ccwf.cc.utexas.edu/~egumtow/calculus/index.html uses the `<SUP>` tag extensively to illustrate calculus.

### Listing 3-7: Subscript in Matematical Notation

```
<P>
Confidence interval for the pop. variance
<B>
<FONT FACE="Symbol">s</FONT><SUP>2</SUP>:
(<I>n</I> -√1)<I>s</I><SUP>2</SUP>/
<FONT FACE="Symbol">C</FONT><SUP>2</SUP>
<SUB><FONT FACE="Symbol">a</FONT>/2</SUB>
</B>   to   
<B>
(<I>n</I> - 1)<I>s</I><SUP>2</SUP>/
<FONT FACE="Symbol">C</FONT><SUP>2</SUP>
<SUB>1-<FONT FACE="Symbol">
a</FONT>/2</SUB></B>
```

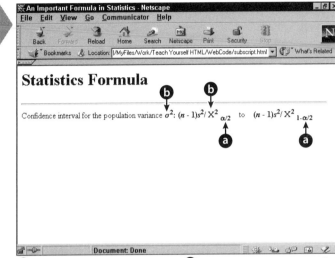

**a** To subscript scientific notation, use the <SUB> element. You can subscript as many characters as you wish within a line.

**b** This example uses a special font to display Greek letters and symbols.

### Listing 3-8: Subscript in Academic Notation

```
<P>
Timothy Rockwood was born July 5, 1727 in
Medway, Massachusetts. He died, February 21,
1806, in Holliston, Massachusetts.
<SUP><A HREF="#1" NAME="up1">1</A></SUP>
</P>
<HR>
<P>
<A NAME="1">1.</A> <CITE>A Historical and
Genealogical Record of the Descendants of
Timothy Rockwood. By E.L. Rockwood, 1856,
page 11</CITE> <A HREF="#up1">Return to
text</A></P>
```

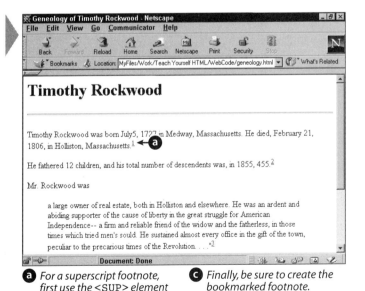

**a** For a superscript footnote, first use the <SUP> element to raise the text.

**b** Next, link the footnote number to a bookmark.

**c** Finally, be sure to create the bookmarked footnote.

# Creating a List

In HTML, you can create a numbered or bulleted list, nest lists into one another (like an outline), change the style of bullets or numbers, and define terms in list form. A numbered (ordered) list automatically increments each item by one. A bulleted (or unordered) list uses the same symbol — usually a round bullet mark — beside each item.

Lists are one of the most beautiful elements in HTML, because they are easy to use and extremely flexible. Instead of renumbering each time you insert an item into the list, you can take advantage of the ordered list to number it for you. Want to change a bulleted list to numbered? You only have to change two tags — one at the start of the list and one at the end.

Creating a list is also easy. You start by opening the list element: <OL> for ordered lists, and <UL> for unordered lists. Before each item in the list, use the list item element, <LI>. The list item closing tag </LI> is optional, but closing the list element itself is not.

To create a definition list, start with <DL>, which stands for "Definition List." A definition list is more like a two-column table; the first item in a pair is a term that must be defined, and the second is the definition. Definition list code is shown in the lower left of the next page, with results displayed in the lower right-hand figure.

*Continued*

## Using Bullet Icons in Unordered Lists

Ever see a really cool list, with colored bullets beside each item? Want to make one yourself?

Using bullet icons is easy, but it diverges from the HTML standard. When you use a bulleted icon, you "break" the list; it's no longer a list, in fact. Instead, use the line break element (<BR>) after each list item. At the beginning of the new line, insert your bullet icon graphic <IMG src="images/bullet.gif" height=5 width=5 alt="*">. It's not a good way to make a list, because programs and text readers won't be able to understand that it is a list. But it's visually indistinguishable from a list in Netscape Navigator and Microsoft Internet Explorer.

**CROSS-REFERENCE**

In Chapter 6, you learn how to create special bullets for your unordered lists.

**FIND IT ONLINE**

AndyArt's HTML Tips on Lists (**http://www. andyart.com/ht_lists.htm**) offers a quick look at building basic HTML lists.

## Listing 3-9: Building an Ordered List

```
<H2>How to find a Web site</H2>
<OL> ◄─ⓐ
 ┌─►<LI>Go to <A HREF="http://www.yahoo.com">
 ⓑ Yahoo!</A> Web Site.
 │  <LI>Type in a keyword to search for.
 └─ <LI>Scroll down the list of sites and find
one that matches.
</OL> ◄─ⓒ
```

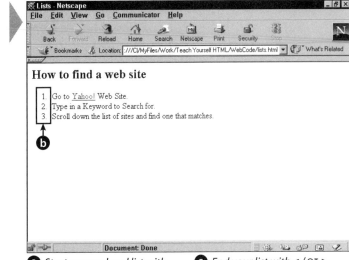

ⓐ Start your ordered list with <OL>.

ⓑ Each item must be preceded with the <LI> tag.

ⓒ End your list with </OL>.

## Listing 3-10: Creating a Definition List

```
<DL> ◄─ⓐ
    <DT>Definition List</DT> ◄─ⓑ       ⓒ
   <DD>A 2-column list used to define terms and
to provide information about individual
items.</DD>
    <DT>Ordered List</DT> ◄─ⓑ         ⓒ
    <DD>A numbered list, often used to indicate
steps in a procedure, or to prioritize
items.</DD>
<DT>Unordered List</DT> ◄─ⓑ
<DD>A bulleted list, used to highlight product
features or to list items without a
priority.</DD>
</DL> ◄─ⓓ
```

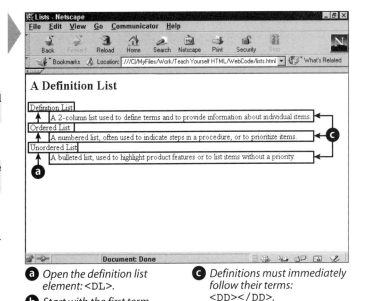

ⓐ Open the definition list element: <DL>.

ⓑ Start with the first term element: <DT>. Close it with </DT>.

ⓒ Definitions must immediately follow their terms: <DD></DD>.

ⓓ The definition list element must be closed with </DL>.

# Creating a List
*Continued*

In addition to the simple list elements, there are a number of things you can do to liven up your list to make it more exciting. As I've already mentioned, you can use graphics instead of bullets. Although imperfect HTML, it will do the job if you need it to.

Another way to change the style of any list is with the type, start, and value attributes. The type attribute lets you change the appearance of the list item markers (bullets or numbers, depending on which type of list).

In an ordered list, type can be set to any of the following values: 1, a, A, i, I. The default value is 1, indicating normal, Arabic numerals. However, if you change it to I, for example, you'll have Roman numerals for your numbering scheme. You can change the type of any individual list item by putting the type attribute inside the <LI> element tag. By putting the type inside the <OL> tag, you change it for the entire list.

In an unordered list, type can have the values disc, square, or circle. The disc is the default; it's a round, filled-in bullet. The square is a filled-in box, and the circle is an unfilled circle.

Now, suppose you're using an ordered list, but you don't want to start at number 1. Perhaps it's an excerpt from an outline, or you're using a different numbering scheme. Put a start attribute in the <OL> element tag to change the starting number. For example, <OL start="2"> will make the first list item number 2. If you use both a start attribute and a type attribute, the first list item will be the start value, in whatever type you specified (so <OL type="A" start="4"> will result in the first list item being named "D".

Finally, you can change the value of any list item with the value attribute. Again, this attribute is only useful for ordered lists. You can set the value to whatever numeric value you like. The ordered list will begin numbering from that value on up. So, if you set <LI value="3">, the list item after that one will automatically have a value of 4.

## Nesting Lists

Just as you can nest quotes, you can also nest lists, even different types of lists. It's simple: instead of putting a list item element, start a new list. The new list will appear to be a subordinate list to the list item directly above it. The figure at the lower left shows a nested list. The code for that list is found in the lower-left code sample.

By using the type attribute, you can bring a certain amount of order to a nested list. The code sample and figure show how.

**CROSS-REFERENCE**

Appendix B contains an HTML attribute reference.

**FIND IT ONLINE**

View **http://www.w3.org.TR/REC-html40/index/ elements.html** for the complete list of HTML elements.

## Table 3-2: LIST ATTRIBUTES

| Attribute | Values | Effect |
|---|---|---|
| type circle | disc, square, | In an unordered list, changes the bullet style to a solid-colored square or an open (unfilled) circle. The default is disc, a solid-colored circle. Has been replaced by style sheets. |
| | 1, a, A, i, I | Changes the numeral style in an ordered list; Arabic numbers (default), lowercase letters, uppercase letters, lowercase Roman numerals, and uppercase Roman numerals. Has been replaced by style sheets. |
| start | *any integer* | In an ordered list, changes the first item number to the integer specified. Has been replaced by style sheets. |
| value | *any integer* | In a list item, this changes the number of the item; useful in altering ordered lists. Has been replaced by style sheets. |
| style | - | Replaces the above attributes without making them obsolete. |

## Listing 3-11: A Nested List

```
<H2>Membership Committee Notes</H2>
<OL type="I"> ← a
<LI>Membership Goals
<OL type="A"> ← b
<LI>Gain new members</LI>
<LI>Retain current members</LI>
   <UL type ="square" name="actions"> ← b
   <LI>call lapsed members</LI>
   <LI>send prelapse postcards</LI>
   <LI>annual, personal contact</LI>
   </UL> ← c
<LI>Increase member participation</LI>
</OL> ← c
<LI>Committee Duties
<!-- LIST CONTINUED -->
</OL>
```

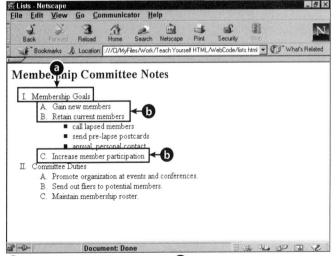

**a** To make a nested list, start with a standard list.

**b** Under the item that serves as a heading for the nested list, put <UL> for a nested unordered list.

**c** Be sure to close all nested list elements with </UL> or </OL>.

# Rendering Code

By its very nature, the Internet tends to draw the technologically minded. Originally the domain of military and academic applications, it has a strong history in science and technology, not merely because of its purely technological nature.

"Code" describes the syntax and elements that make up a machine-readable program or file. When you write HTML, you are writing code, although it is a far cry from a C program. Still, code must be written in very specific syntax or the computer cannot understand it, and the program, Web page, script, or applet won't work.

The <CODE> element is one way for all these "techies" to put their samples into HTML. Computer code is usually rendered in text with a fixed-width font, as it has been all throughout this book. That's an accepted method of showing that what you're writing is supposed to be read by a machine. When read by a Web browser, text within the <CODE> element should also be displayed in a fixed-width font. Because some Web browsers will be set up to display the <CODE> element in a unique or individual way, you should reserve this element only for code samples you put on the World Wide Web.

The <CODE> element can be used inline to describe code snippets or elements that you do not need to set off by themselves. You can also use it with a paragraph element, such as <P> or <PRE> to display a block of code.

## TAKE NOTE

### ► USING SPECIAL CHARACTERS

HTML uses several characters as part of its syntax. As you already know, element tags must be enclosed in <> symbols. As you might guess, you can't use those symbols in HTML without the Web browser trying to read the tags inside.

If you're trying to render code onto the Web, especially HTML code, use the special characters, as discussed in Chapter 9, for any special symbols you might need to use.

### ► PRE AND TT ELEMENTS

The <CODE> element will render code into a monotype font for you, but it is definitely designed to be a significant element; everything within the <CODE> tags should be code, nothing more.

However, you may be wondering how to display monospace text when it's not code. Do you use the <CODE> element because it achieves the desired effect? Of course not. Use the <PRE> tag for blocks of monospace text, and the <TT> element for inline monospace text.

**CROSS-REFERENCE**

Chapter 11 has more information about customizing tags to reflect their content.

**FIND IT ONLINE**

The CODE element is used extensively at **http://www.eskimo.com/~scs/C-faq/faq.html**.

## Table: 3-3 WAYS TO DISPLAY CODE

| Element | Usage |
|---------|-------|
| <CODE> | Inline element to denote a code fragment. |
| <PRE> | Block element to use monospace font and preformatted whitespace. |
| <TT> | Inline element that uses monospace font but has no meaning attached. |

Happy Face Source Code — Netscape

**Happy Face Source Code**

The following is the JavaScript code to put in your <HEAD> element.

```
<SCRIPT Language="JavaScript">
function happyFaces() {
        if (document.MoodGetter.mood[0].checked) {
                document.images[0].src = "face1.gif";
                document.styleSheets[2].disabled = true;
                document.styleSheets[1].disabled = true;
                document.styleSheets[0].disabled = false;
        }
        if (document.MoodGetter.mood[1].checked) {
                document.images[0].src = "face2.gif";
                document.styleSheets[0].disabled = true;
                document.styleSheets[2].disabled = true;
                document.styleSheets[1].disabled = false;
        }
        if (document.MoodGetter.mood[2].checked) {
                document.images[0].src = "face3.gif";
```

Document: Done

■ *A sample of JavaScript, as shown using the <CODE> and <PRE> elements.*

### Listing 3-12: Displaying Code in HTML

```
<P>This is the Hello World Program in C.  Note
that the <CODE>#include</CODE> command
requires a <CODE>#</CODE> symbol before it.
Leave it out, and you'll have a syntactical
error!</P>
<PRE><CODE>/* Hello World Program */
#include &lt;stdio.h&gt;

main()
{
  (void)printf("Hello, World!\n");
  return(0);
}
</CODE></PRE>
```

Hello World in C — Netscape

**Hello, World!**

This is the Hello World Program in C. Note that the #include command requires a # symbol before it. Leave it out, and you'll have a syntactical error!

```
/* Hello World Program */
#include <stdio.h>

main()
{
        (void)printf("Hello, World!\n");
        return(0);
}
```

Document: Done

**ⓐ** Use the <CODE> element for inline code.

**ⓑ** For blocks of code, use the <PRE> element. Using <CODE> in a block element adds significance.

**51**

# Personal Workbook

## Q&A

**1** How would you put text into a foreign language font that you knew your users would have installed?

_____

_____

_____

**2** How do you include a trademark symbol on a Web page?

_____

_____

_____

**3** What are the three types available in unordered lists?

_____

_____

_____

**4** Can you nest different types of lists?

_____

_____

_____

**5** How do you change the starting value of an ordered list?

_____

_____

_____

**6** Name the two ways to cite sources in HTML 4.0 quotations.

_____

_____

_____

**7** How would you display a fragment of code within a paragraph?

_____

_____

_____

**8** What's the difference between Emphasis (<EM>) and Italic (<I>) text?

_____

_____

_____

**ANSWERS: PAGE 435**

## EXTRA PRACTICE

❶ Write a page describing your favorite hobbies. Put each of your hobbies in dark red text (Hint: The RGB code for dark red is #800000).

❷ Create an unordered list of your hobbies, and place special emphasis on the one you like most.

❸ Put your favorite (or any) quote about your favorite hobby at the bottom of the Web page. Use appropriate citation and source information.

❹ Make the quotation a footnote of your favorite (emphasized) hobby.

❺ In the same HTML page, show the code for your list as it appears in your HTML page.

❻ Change the unordered list type to empty circles instead of discs as bullets.

## REAL-WORLD APPLICATIONS

✔ You're writing a Web page and want to include some of your ASCII artwork. You use the <PRE> elements to keep parts of your artwork aligned.

✔ You're putting product information online, including blurbs from reviews. You use the cite attribute to keep track of who said what about your product.

✔ In the internal Web site, you're in charge of action lists for all personnel. You use unordered lists to highlight company goals, and ordered lists to prioritize actions that will achieve those goals.

✔ You're writing a Web page about Year 2000 solutions. The <CODE> element lets you share your solutions online.

## Visual Quiz

What elements are evident on this page? How else could you display this information? Is this the most effective way to show these samples?

_____

_____

_____

_____

_____

```
Lists - Netscape
File  Edit  View  Go  Window  Help

How to find a web site

   1.  Go to Yahoo! Web Site.
   2.  Type in a Keyword to Search for.
   3.  Scroll down the list of sites and find one that matches.

A Definition List

Definition List
        A 2-column list used to define terms and to provide information about individual items.
Ordered List
        A numbered list, often used to indicate steps in a procedure, or to prioritize items.
Unordered List
        A bulleted list, used to highlight product features or to list items without a priority.

<H2>A Definition List</H2>
<DL>
<DT>Definition List</DT>
<DD>A 2-column list used to define terms and to provide information about ind
<DT>Ordered List</DT>
<DD>A numbered list, often used to indicate steps in a procedure, or to prior
<DT>Unordered List</DT>

                     Document: Done
```

# CHAPTER

# Tables

Tables are currently the method of choice for displaying data and for laying out Web pages. Originally intended for data display, they quickly gained popularity as layout tools, allowing Web authors to force information to look like a traditional printed page, with columns, sidebars, and whitespace.

In this chapter, you'll learn how to create a table, change its cells, format individual rows and columns, and how to use tables for laying out a Web page.

The basics of table creation and formatting are fairly simple to learn, which is why they're covered early in this book. However, tables require a lot of abstract thinking in HTML. You cannot simply see the table and make it look the way you want to, unless you use a WYSIWYG (What You See Is What You Get) Web editor. Let me strongly caution against using a WYSIWYG editor, however; they invariably change your code to reflect the editor's particular idea of style, which can be a real pain if you're really trying to learn HTML.

The biggest problem encountered is that, in HTML, tables are written in rows from the left to the right, top to bottom, just as English is read. However, if you're designing a table to include columnar data (such as a price estimate) or to feature a comparison chart, you might already think of your data in columns. So instead of wanting to input each row of information, you try to input each column. Although a typical spreadsheet program works that way, and a WYSIWYG editor can handle that kind of data entry, you will find it very hard to wrap your mind around rows in HTML tables. Think of your table data as rows instead of columns, and they'll be a snap to create.

Tables have been used for laying out Web pages since these pages were first invented. Because most Web browsers now support tables, there are few problems with this method. However, older browsers and nonvisual browsers may not support layout tables the way you expect. Keep your layout tables simple and you'll have fewer problems with other kinds of browsers.

# Creating a Basic Table

Your first table will be fairly simple. It will have two columns, two rows, and one heading row. It will also have a caption. Start by creating the `<TABLE>` element: `<TABLE></TABLE>`. The `<TABLE>` element has several optional attributes. First, you can add or remove a `border`. Border values are pixels, so `<TABLE border=1>` will create a table with a one-pixel-wide border around each cell. In some Web browsers, this border is actually a little wider than one pixel because of the beveled edges, which give the border a slightly raised appearance.

Another attribute to the `<TABLE>` element is the `bgcolor` attribute. Similar to the `bgcolor` in the `<BODY>` element, `bgcolor` changes the background color for the table. It can also be used in individual cells and rows. If you change the background color of a table, be sure that the background is light enough that it does not interfere with the text color, or use the `<FONT>` element or style sheets to change the text color within the table itself. Like most color effects, the `bgcolor` attribute is being phased out in favor of style sheets. For now, however, you can use it to change the background color of your table. Table backgrounds are not supported by older browsers, although they are part of the HTML 4.0 specification.

Tables can be nested within one another. So, you can have one table inside the data cell of another table. This can get *very* confusing in HTML code; use indentation and comments to keep track of which table you're in!

## TAKE NOTE

### ▶ PROVIDING ALTERNATE TEXT FOR TABLES

Tables have long been problematic for nongraphical browsers. Traditionally, they are read or displayed from left to right, going down, row by row. Some text-only browsers will display pipe marks (|) and hyphens to indicate borders, but most will not. The `summary` attribute of the `<TABLE>` element allows you to include a text description of the table, not unlike the `alt` attribute of the `<IMG>` element.

### ▶ CENTERING IN TABLES

As you know by now, there are three ways to center information in HTML. The first is to use the `<CENTER>` element, which will center your text but is generally considered poor design. The other way is to use the `align=center` attribute, which is available for nearly every block element.

Tables are a block element. If you use the `align=center` attribute in the `<TABLE>` element, your entire table will be centered. If you use `align=center` in an individual row, the contents of the cells for that row will be centered. Finally, `align=center` in any of the individual cells will center the data within the cells only. Naturally, you can use any alignment value — `center`, `left`, or `right`.

## CROSS-REFERENCE
One of the easiest ways to edit a table is with an HTML editing program. Several are described in Appendix C.

## FIND IT ONLINE
Jonny's Crashcourse in Tables () provides a table-building tutorial.

## Listing 4-1:A Simple Table

```
<TABLE border=1>
<TR>
  <TH>Item</TH>
  <TH>Cost</TH>
  <TH>Quantity</TH>
  <TH>Total Cost</TH>
</TR>
<TR>
  <TD>InterNIC domain name
  registration fee</TD>
  <TD>$35</TD>
  <TD>2 years</TD>
  <TD>$70</TD>
</TR>
</TABLE>
```

**ⓐ** To create a basic table, start with the `<TABLE>` element and use the border attribute to include a border.

**ⓑ** Create the first row in your table: `<TR>`.

**ⓒ** Add table header cells: `<TH></TH>`.

**ⓓ** Add a table data cell with the `<TD>` element in a new row: `<TR><TD></TD></TR>`.

## Listing 4-2:Captions and Colors

```
<TABLE border=1 align=center bgcolor="#C0C0C0"
dir=ltr>
<CAPTION>Price Estimate for Web Design<CAPTION>
<TR>
  <TH>Item</TH>
  <TH>Cost</TH>
  <TH>Quantity</TH>
  <TH>Total Cost</TH>
</TR>
```

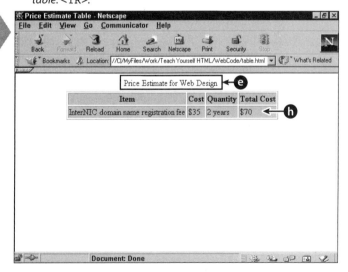

**ⓔ** The optional `<CAPTION>` element adds a table caption.

**ⓕ** To center the table, add `align=center` to the `<TABLE>` element.

**ⓖ** Table columns are read left to right by TTS readers and Web browsers. To change that direction, use the dir attribute (`dir=rtl`) in the `<TABLE>` element.

**ⓗ** Add a background color with the bgcolor attribute: `#C0C0C0` is a shade of gray.

# Changing Cell Size and Structure

ells are the smallest group of data in a table. Individual cells should contain only one item of data. In the previous task, you made your first table. That table had two columns and three rows (including the heading), for a total of six individual cells.

Cells can be specially formatted in HTML using particular attributes. Some of those attributes can be inherited from the <TABLE> element or the individual row. Some can even be inherited from a column using the <COLGROUP> element.

To begin with, you can change the spacing and padding of each cell in a table by changing the cellspacing or cellpadding attributes in the <TABLE> element. The cellspacing attribute determines the width in pixels of the white portion of the table border. See the top-right figure for an example of a very wide cellspacing. Cellpadding is similar to cellspacing, except that it defines the width in pixels of whitespace between the cell contents and the border of the table. If the table has an invisible border (border=0), the cell contents will seem to float, separated from all other information. You can see why this is beneficial in a language that hasn't provided very well for whitespace.

Next, you can also change the alignment — vertical or horizontal — of the contents of a cell. Use the align attribute in the <TD> or <TH> elements to align the text. Align the contents vertically with the valign attribute: <TD align=center valign=top> will center the cell contents and place them at the top of the cell (default is in the middle). Valign can take the values top, bottom, middle, and baseline, which will align the content of all cells in the row by the first line of text, but won't necessarily align them to the top of the cell nor align the last line of text in any way.

Finally, you can span cells from one cell to another. Use the rowspan attribute to increase a cell's size vertically, and the colspan attribute to increase it horizontally. The value for rowspan and colspan is equal to the number of rows or columns you'd like to increase the cell by. Do not create overlapping cells — it's illegal HTML and will produce poor results, if any.

## TAKE NOTE

### ▶ CHANGING TABLE CELL COLORS

To change the background color of a table cell, insert the bgcolor attribute into the <TD> element, just as you would for the <BODY> element or the <TABLE> element. Then, change the font colors using the <FONT> element, or scrap the whole bgcolor attribute entirely and use a style sheet instead, which will degrade better in older browsers.

### ▶ EMPTY CELLS

To create an empty cell that still has border spacing, insert a line break (<BR>) into the cell. The line break won't increase the whitespace, but it will create an empty cell.

## CROSS-REFERENCE

Chapter 3 has more details on the align attribute.

## FIND IT ONLINE

For a great example of various tables, see The Table Sampler at *http://www.netscape.com/assist/ net_sites/table_sample.html*.

## Listing 4-3: Cell Alignment

```
<TR>
  <TD valign="top">InterNIC domain name
  registration fee.</TD>
  <TD valign="top">$35</TD>
  <TD valign="top">2 years</TD>
  <TD valign="top" align="right">$70</TD>
</TR>
<TR>
  <TD valign="top">Web site design</TD>
  <TD valign="top">$50</TD>
  <TD valign="top">9 hours</TD>
  <TD  valign="top" align="right">$450</TD>
</TR>
```

❶ *Change the vertical alignment with the* valign *attribute; I find* valign=top *makes very clean rows.*

❷ *Use the* align *attribute for horizontal alignment;* align=right *works well for columns of numbers.*

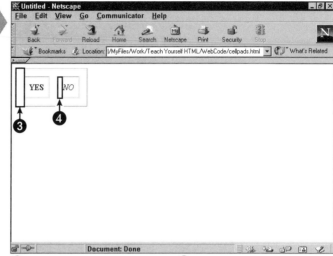

❸ *Change the space between the cell and the table border with the* cellpadding *attribute in the* <TABLE> *element:* cellpadding=10.

❹ *Change the space within the border with* cellspacing=15.

■ Cellspacing *and* cellpadding *are only defined in the* <TABLE> *tag.*

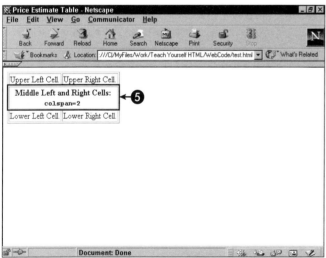

❺ *To span a column, use the* colspan *attribute:* colspan=2.

■ *Make sure the rows with spanned columns and the number of unspanned cells in other rows equal each other.*

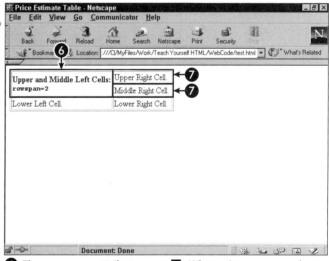

❻ *The* rowspan *attribute spans rows.*

❼ Rowspan *always increases a row's size downward — make sure there's another row beneath it!*

■ *When using* rowspan, *be sure to use the* valign *attribute for a balanced look.*

# Editing Rows

HTML groups data cells into rows using the <TR> element, as shown in the upper left and right table examples. The HTML comments name each row in the table. Each <TR> element indicates a new row in the table, and rows are displayed in sequence (the first row is the top row, and so on). There is no corresponding <TC> element for table columns.

That means it's sometimes hard to put columnar data into tables. For example, the table shown to the lower right has columnar data, in the form of a price estimate. As you can see, I had to make certain that each row had enough cells, and that all columns contained the same type of data.

You can put table head, footers, and body rows into structural elements known as <THEAD>, <TFOOT>, and <TBODY> elements. Presumably, <THEAD> and <TFOOT> data will be printed at the top and bottom of pages when the Web page is sent to the printer. You can have more than one <TBODY> element; in fact, that's how you group rows within the table body. Each of these elements surrounds and groups <TR> elements, and they take all the standard optional attributes as well as alignment attributes (which are applied to all cells within the group's rows).

If you use these elements, the <TFOOT> element must come before the <TBODY> element in your HTML, so Web browsers can display footer information before the many rows of data load. Unfortunately, these elements don't degrade very well; Netscape 4.0 and IE 3.0 will display the table foot before the table body.

To include table head and body structural information without displaying the <TFOOT> first, simply omit the <TFOOT> element. Sure, you won't have a footer on the printed page of your table in IE 4.0. But you will be cross-browser compatible, combining the best of IE 4.0 with the universal appeal of other Web browsers.

## TAKE NOTE

### ▶ USING ROWSPAN AND COLSPAN IN ROWS

When you design a table, take out a piece of scratch paper and jot down the number of cells you need in each row. Each time you create a cell in a row, jot down one tick mark. When you use the colspan attribute, mark off one tick for each column spanned. That way, you'll never have too many or too few cells in your table row.

Similarly, each time you create a rowspan, the cell spanning the row counts as one (or more, if it also spans columns) cell for that row. The other cells will "fit in" around it. For that reason, it's very important to have the same number of cells in each row.

## CROSS-REFERENCE
Need help picking a background color? Chapter 2 shows you how!

## FIND IT ONLINE
An excellent example of tables is at **http://www.blue-gauntlet.com/catalog/weapons/foil/electric/blades.html**.

## Listing 4-4: A Simple Table

```
<TABLE>
<TR> <!-- Table Row # 1 -->
    <TD>Upper Left Cell.</TD>
    <TD>Upper Right Cell.</TD>
</TR>
<TR> <!-- Table Row # 2 -->
    <TD>Lower Left Cell.</TD>
    <TD>Lower Right Cell.</TD>
</TABLE>
```

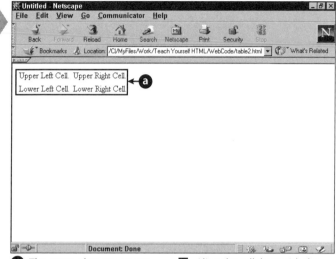

**ⓐ** *The* `<TR>` *elements create table rows.*

**■** *Align the cell data with the* `align` *attribute:* `align=center`.

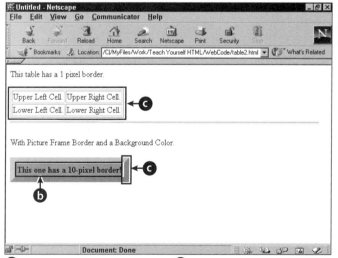

**ⓑ** *Change the background color of your table cells with* `bgcolor`.

**ⓒ** `Border=1` *creates a table border; use 1 or 2 pixels for a table border, 10–12 for a picture frame.*

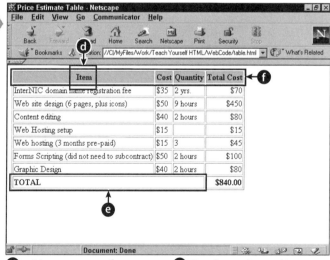

**ⓓ** `Align=center` *forms headings in the table.*

**ⓔ** `Colspan` *spans text or whitespace into unused columns, removing border lines from empty cells.*

**ⓕ** *Bgcolor can be used in a* `<TR>` *element as well as the* `<TABLE>` *element and cell elements.*

61

# Formatting Columns

Even though HTML 4.0 doesn't group table data into columns, it does allow you to format entire columns with the <COL> and <COLGROUP> elements. Unfortunately, these elements are only supported in Internet Explorer 3.x and above, although they are part of the HTML 4.0 specification.

Within each <COLGROUP>, you can have many <COL> elements. A <COL> element defines an individual column within the <COLGROUP>. However, the <COLGROUP> element may also contain formatting information for all the columns inside the group.

The span element is the only required attribute to the <COLGROUP> and <COL> elements. It defines how many columns to format. For example, if you have four cells in each row, then you have four columns. If any of those cells span columns, count the number of columns spanned and add it to the rest of the cells.

Use the align attribute to align the text within each cell of the column to the right, left, or center. The align attribute can also take a value called justify, but this does not work in any browser I tested it on.

Similarly, you can align column data vertically with the valign attribute. This attribute takes the values top, bottom, middle, or baseline; these values work the same as in table rows.

Finally, you can edit the width of the columns. Use width="value" to specify how wide (in pixels) to make each column in the <COLGROUP> or the individual column.

The other way to format columns is to change each cell within the column, as described earlier in this chapter. It's tedious, and leads to some very long code. However, it's compatible with Netscape as well as many of the nonstandard browsers.

## TAKE NOTE

### SPANNING CELLS IN DIFFERENT COLGROUPS

You might have already figured out that the <COLGROUP> element doesn't prevent you from spanning <COL> elements with individual cells. However, just because you can doesn't mean you should. The individual cell may take the property of the first <COL> element or the second <COL> element, or it may cause the table to not display properly at all.

### STYLE SHEETS AND COLUMNS

Since both the <COLGROUP> elements and style sheets were invented by Microsoft, you'd think you could use style sheets in columns with confidence — any browser supporting the <COL> element should also support style sheets, right? Wrong. Internet Explorer 4.0 (which comes with Win98) supports styles in columns and column groups, but IE 3.0 (which recognizes both style sheets and column groups) doesn't put them together.

**CROSS-REFERENCE**

Chapter 13 has more information on scripting attributes that you can use in column groups.

**FIND IT ONLINE**

Microsoft has information on attributes for <COLGROUP> at **http://www.microsoft.com/ workshop/author/dhtml/reference/data/ colgroup_members.htm**

## Listing 4-5: Column Groups

```
<COLGROUP span=3 align="right">
<COL span=1 align="center" bgcolor="#CCCCCC">
<COL span=1 align="left">
<COL span=1 valign="bottom" width=50%>
</COLGROUP>
```

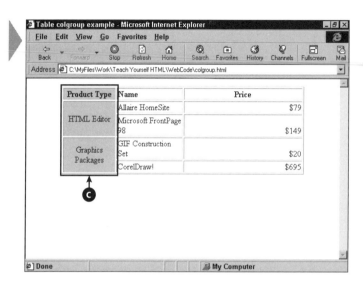

**a** *To create a column for formatting, insert* `<COLGROUP span=3></COLGROUP>` *after your* `<TABLE>` *or* `<CAPTION>` *elements.*

**b** *Adding* `align=right` *in the opening* `<COLGROUP>` *tag aligns the text to the right.*

**c** *To format individual columns, include* `<COL>` *elements before the closing* `</COLGROUP>` *tag.*

## Listing 4-6: Classes in Column Groups

```
<STYLE TYPE="text/css">
.financial {text-align: right;}
.types {background: #CCFF33;}</STYLE>
<BODY BGCOLOR="#FFFFFF">
<TABLE align=center cellspacing="2"
  border="1" width=80%>
<COLGROUP span=3> <COL span=1
  align="center" bgcolor="#CCCCCC"
  class="types"> <COL span=1 align="left">
<COL span=1 valign="bottom" align=right
  width=50% class="financial"></COLGROUP>
```

**1** *The style* `class` *"types" formats the product type by giving it a yellow background.*

**2** *The financial* `class` *aligns all the text to the right, giving a clean column for dollar figures.*

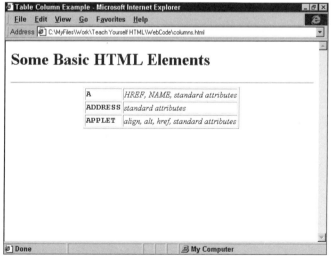

■ *Another example of using column groups to format cell data.*

63

# Using Tables for Layout

When tables first became part of HTML, Web authors were overjoyed. Finally, a way to display raw data without using the `<PRE>` element!

And then we got greedy. We wanted to use tables to create columns, like in a magazine. Tables started to be used for text columns, sidebars, and right- or left-hand navigation columns. In response, Netscape and Microsoft made a few extensions to tables in their Web browsers (extensions are elements and attributes that aren't supported by any other browser). These new attributes could define the width of the table or individual cells, allowed cell spanning, background colors, and many of the cool attributes you've already learned about.

Web authors used these new attributes to lay out their pages. Web design became a simple formula: make a table with no border, one row, and just two cells. Put your navigation information in the left cell, and make it very, very thin. Put your content in the right cell. Voilà! You've forced the Web browser to display exactly what you want it to display, in magazine format.

Well, not exactly. You see, even though tables are usable as layout tools, and even though nearly every site I visit uses them that way, they aren't very cross-browser compatible. In fact, you and I could be using the exact same version of the same browser, and I may have to scroll to the right to see all the text in the table, while you'd see the whole table, with lots of whitespace around it. As soon as a Web designer defines the width attribute (in pixels) in a table, he or she stops designing for all users, and is only designing for those who share the same screen resolution and window width.

If you absolutely *must* use tables for layout, and you've found that cascading style sheets don't solve your problem, then follow this list of Table Dos and Don'ts.

**CROSS-REFERENCE**

Using tables for layout is becoming obsolete in HTML 4.0. See Chapter 10 for information on laying out a document with style sheets.

**FIND IT ONLINE**

The W3C has a design rationale for using tables at **http://www.w3.org/TR/REC-html40/ appendix/notes.html#notes-tables.**

## Table Tips

▶ Specify `width` in percentages: the percent of the window each column or cell should fill.

▶ Use narrow graphics within your table.

▶ Use the `bgcolor` attribute or style sheets to highlight a sidebar.

▶ Design for a screen resolution of no more than 640 480 pixels.

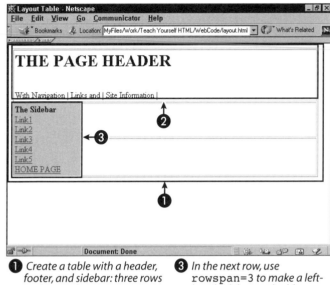

❶ Create a table with a header, footer, and sidebar: three rows and two columns.

❷ In the first table cell, use `colspan=2` to make the header.

❸ In the next row, use `rowspan=3` to make a left-hand sidebar, and add a background color with `bgcolor`.

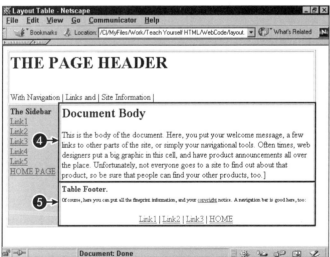

❹ Put your body text and information into the second cell of the second row (next to the sidebar cell).

❺ Put the site-wide footer or navigation bar in the only cell in the third row.

❻ Use the `<MULTICOL>` element by inserting the opening tag before the columnar section.

❼ The `<COLS>` element is required: `cols=2`.

■ Close the `<MULTICOL>` element at the end of the columnar section. Elements within the `<MULTICOL>` section will still be read and displayed correctly.

# Personal Workbook

## Q&A

**1** How do you create a table without a border?

_____

_____

_____

**2** How many columns are in a table?

_____

_____

_____

**3** What is _cell spanning_?

_____

_____

_____

**4** How do you create a table heading?

_____

_____

_____

**5** Why would you not use the `<COLGROUP>` element?

_____

_____

_____

**6** How do you change the width of a table or its columns?

_____

_____

_____

**7** Why should you use a `summary` attribute, and where?

_____

_____

_____

**8** What's the difference between `align` and `valign`, and what are their respective values?

_____

_____

_____

ANSWERS: PAGE 435

## EXTRA PRACTICE

❶ Create a simple table with three columns and three rows.

❷ Put some sample data (like Name, Favorite Movie, Age) in the second and third rows of data cells.

❸ Make the top row a heading row, and put appropriate column titles in the cells.

❹ Change the background color of the second row of cells.

❺ Align all the data in the third column (Age) to the right (there's more than one way to do this!).

❻ Now add a row with one cell that spans all three columns. Write **Table's Done! Tables are Fun!** in the cell data area. Test it on your browser.

## REAL-WORLD APPLICATIONS

✔ Your Web site has a listing of all your favorite songs, the CDs they're on, and links to the artists' Web sites. You put this information into a three-column table for easier reading.

✔ You want to publish a price comparison chart online, but each product division has several versions of the product. You use rowspan to help group products by division, while keeping individual version information separate.

✔ You want a special look and feel for your Web site and think tables are the way to go. You create a borderless table with a colored sidebar for easy navigation of your site.

✔ You want to highlight the picture of your dog that you put on your Web site. You use a very thick border to create a picture frame effect.

## Visual Quiz

What are some design issues with this page? How did the author create it? Identify each table, and any special formatting you see in the table. (Hint: there are nested tables on this page.) When you're done, go to **http://www.campdownunder.com/facilities97.html** and view the source code.

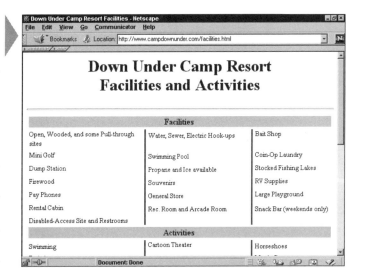

_____

_____

_____

_____

# CHAPTER 5

# Audience and Accessibility

I've talked a lot about accessibility in this book, and this chapter really gets into the nitty-gritty of Web site accessibility. In this chapter, you'll learn how to identify your audience and their needs, how to make your site accessible to the largest portion of that audience, how to test your Web site, and how to make a multilingual site. Finally, no amount of planning and accessibility will be enough, so you'll also learn how to encourage Web users to talk back to you, and how to get more information about your online visitors.

The most important thing about your Web site is the information you're trying to share. And perhaps the most important thing about that information is whom you're trying to share it with. Don't overlook the power of your targeted message. The Internet is too wide and varied an experience to assume that you'll be able to reach everybody.

Computers have long been a crucial tool for many disabled users. Not only do computers provide a communication and learning resource independent of physical abilities, the Internet has turned them into the ultimate virtual office. From research to email, computers are helping people with disabilities interact more smoothly with coworkers, friends, and family on a level never before available.

As the "baby boomer" generation gets older, a new wave of computer users is discovering that the monitor is just a little harder to read, and the mouse isn't what it used to be to an arthritic or carpal-tunnel-afflicted wrist. As a Web designer, you can't afford to alienate any part of your audience, especially not those who are more likely to use the Web on a regular basis.

This chapter will give you lots of advice and ideas, but it's ultimately up to you to find out what works and what doesn't. I can tell you to use bright colors and animations on a child's site, but if your Web site is for children with a particular disability, then you might sacrifice the blinking lights for something more effective. A site for teenagers should have tons of graphics and "cool stuff," but not if it's for the Teen Lynx User Group. Start with something that you like, then ask people from your audience what they like or dislike about the site. In the end, you'll find something you both can agree on.

# Identifying the Audience

One of the first things you should ask yourself before designing your Web site is who will be using the site? Is it a company Web site, to sell your product or service? If so, then you should already have a good idea of who your audience is — it's the same audience as your product's market, or that percentage of it that is surfing the Internet.

Many beginning Web authors start out with no idea who their audience is. They're just throwing a few things together, stuff they like, to learn how to code HTML. Without realizing it, they're writing Web pages for an audience, too. Their audience consists of people who share their interests (or the ones they put on the Web page), and who have the same software and hardware setup as they do.

The easiest audience to design for is a company intranet. You already know which Web browsers the audience uses, because the company has had them installed on all the computers. However, an intranet is almost always informative. Rather than flash and sparkle, employees are seeking very specific pieces of information, which they need to do their jobs.

When you know your audience, you can ask them specific questions about using your Web site, so you can improve it. You'll know when you've achieved a good Web site because you'll be able to ask your audience what they like and dislike about the site, and when the dislikes are few and correctable, you will have finally reached your audience.

## TAKE NOTE

### CHILDREN AND PICTURES

When you're developing a site for children, use meaningful pictures and icons, and less text. Children relate well to bright, colorful images, and they can often figure out what an icon means without needing to read the text.

Colorful images make an impact on families as well. Reds and bright blues are more likely to catch a person's attention, as are animated graphics.

### DISABLED AUDIENCES

Most of this chapter will focus on making your Web site usable to a disabled audience. Disabilities that can affect a person's ability to surf the net include repetitive-stress syndrome (RSI), carpal tunnel, paralysis, arthritis, visual impairment (not limited to blindness), deafness, learning disabilities, color-blindness, underdeveloped motor skills, autism, epilepsy, brain damage, and even back pain.

If your site addresses the elderly (which is a growing population on the net), be sure it's enabled for visually impaired users, as well as those whose hands may not always be able to work a mouse or a keyboard. Avoid obnoxious flashing animations (and the <BLINK> element) if you think that even one light-induced epileptic may surf your site. A number of Web users are now surfing without a mouse, using the keyboard or speech commands to control their Web browsers.

**CROSS-REFERENCE**

Chapter 6 will help you design low-bandwidth images for your site.

**FIND IT ONLINE**

pwWebSpeak, the text-to-speech browser shown in the above example, is available as a demo version at **http://www.prodworks.com.**

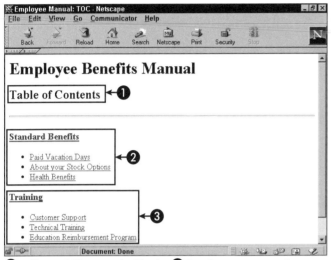

**①** Offer a quickly scanned table of contents for employees to use.

**②** Use a flat Web structure, with links to all sections of the site from one centralized area.

**③** Put the most commonly accessed information at the top of each page.

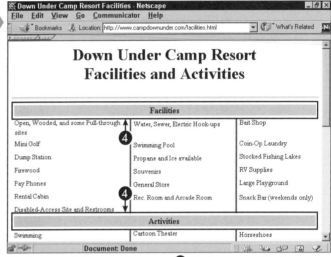

■ A commercial Internet site must be professional, yet easy to read. Use background and table colors to create visual impact without slow-loading graphics.

**④** Limit your use of flashy graphics, but don't ignore the power of visual stimuli.

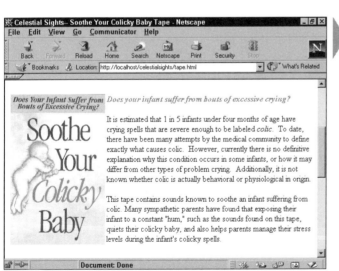

■ This site targets stressed out parents with colicky babies. Note the use of simple graphics and easily read text.

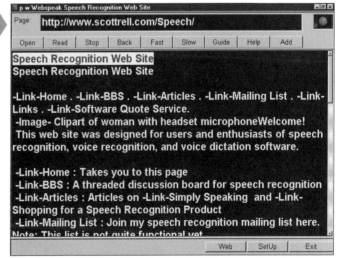

■ This Web site is designed for visually impaired users, as seen in a popular text-to-speech browser, pwWebSpeak. The browser's default text and color scheme, large yellow text on black background, is designed for those with poor vision.

# Making a Site Accessible

Now that you know who'll be accessing your site, design your site to be usable by those people. This means taking into account the users' Web browsers, hardware configuration, etc. Is your site going to be used by older people, families, general consumers? Assume they're all using a 15-inch monitor at 640   480 screen resolution. Is it a site for IT professionals? Make sure it's text friendly, as many UNIX users have text-only Web browsers. Does your site discuss typography and page layout for print professionals and graphic designers? Then you can assume they'll have a display setup that rivals or exceeds yours.

When you plan your Web site, consider these common barriers to accessibility:

▶ Frames are very hard to navigate without a mouse. They're also annoying on small screens and low resolutions. Finally, they are not supported by text-only browsers.

▶ Tables are supported poorly in text-only browsers, but are good for displaying raw data. When you force their sizes and widths, users without high-end display systems must scroll to the right to read the entire table. Tables can often be circumvented by using other design elements, such as site-wide headers and footers. Use the new `summary` attribute to provide a text alternative to your table.

▶ Graphics are not usually a problem, but many users do not use or view graphics. Users may turn off the graphics with their Web browsers to save on download time, or to assist a speech reader Web browser. `Alt` attributes in the `<IMG>` element will help describe the graphic to users who do not choose to display it.

▶ Animated graphics, although attention-getting, are irritating when used on pages that are pure content, not navigational pages. Very intrusive animation can cause some light-sensitive users to have difficulty concentrating on your message. Finally, users can stop animations (after they load) in many Web browsers.

▶ Forms are one of the more recent changes towards accessibility. To navigate a form with the keyboard, users use the Tab key to move from one form field to another, going down the form in the order they were written into the HTML page. This can cause some problems, especially if there are additional hyperlinks (such as advertisements) in the middle of your form. Use the `<FIELDSET, LEGEND>` elements, and the `tabindex` (all described in Chapter 8) attribute to help users navigate your form without using the mouse.

## TAKE NOTE

### ▶ WEB BROWSER ACCESS

You may have noticed that the same barriers to accessibility are also barriers to cross-browser compatibility. What's important is that you decide what audience you'll design for, and which browsers those users use the most. Then, design your Web site for the majority of the browsers using your site. However, use all the tricks and tools in this chapter and throughout this book to make your site as universally accessible as possible without losing the message to the rest of your audience.

## CROSS-REFERENCE
More information on forms can be found in Chapter 8.

## FIND IT ONLINE
The HTML Writer's Guild (http://www.hwg.org/) offers several mailing lists for Web design and audience issues.

## Listing 5-1: Targeting Frames

```
<FRAMESET ROWS="20%,*"
    <FRAME NAME="upper" SRC="upper.html"
        MARGINWIDTH="10" MARGINHEIGHT="10"
        SCROLLING="auto" FRAMEBORDER="yes"
    <FRAME NAME="bottom" SRC="bottom.html"
        MARGINWIDTH="10" MARGINHEIGHT="10"
        SCROLLING="auto" FRAMEBORDER="yes"
</FRAMESET>
```

**ⓐ** *Use frame borders to help distinguish between frames.*

**ⓑ** *When setting frame widths and heights, use percentages to degrade better.*

**ⓒ** *Name your frames with the name attribute of the <FRAME> element.*

**▇** *In the A element, use frame names and* target *attributes to open the page in the targeted frame.*

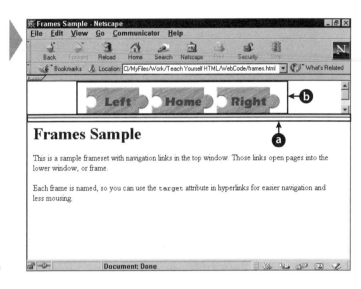

## Listing 5-2: Acessible Forms

```
<FORM ACTION="" METHOD="POST">
<B><U><FONT COLOR=" #CC0033">
    Name:</FONT></U></B>
<INPUT TYPE="Text" NAME="Name"
    VALUE="Name" ALIGN="LEFT" SIZE="20"
    MAXLENGTH="20" TABINDEX="1">
<B>ADDRESS: </B><INPUT TYPE="Text"
    NAME="address1" VALUE="Street"
    ALIGN="LEFT" SIZE="20" MAXLENGTH="20"
    TABINDEX="2"><BR>
<B>LINE 2:</B><INPUT TYPE="Text"
    NAME="address2" VALUE="Address Line 2"
    ALIGN="LEFT" SIZE="20"
    MAXLENGTH="20" NOTAB><BR>
<B>CITY: </B><INPUT TYPE="Text" NAME="city"
    VALUE="city" ALIGN="LEFT" SIZE="20"
    MAXLENGTH="20" TABINDEX="3">
```

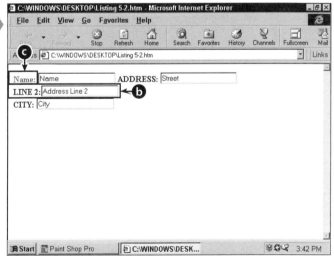

**ⓐ** *Use the* tabindex *attribute in form fields to decide in what order the fields will be selected using the Tab key.*

**ⓑ** *The* notab *attribute keeps an unnecessary field from being selected in the tab order.*

**ⓒ** *Use different colors and underlining to highlight required form fields.*

# Testing Your Site

I've mentioned before that you should always test your Web site on as many browsers as possible. Most Web browsers are available either for free, or as an evaluation download from the software company. For a general audience, you should try to have available Internet Explorer 3.0 and 4.0, and Netscape Navigator 3.0 and 4.0 for site testing.

For visually impaired audiences, a text-to-speech reader is best. However, text-to-speech readers are expensive. If you're stuck for an alternative, use a text-only browser, such as Lynx, to view your site. Be sure to look at your site in the graphical browsers with the graphics turned off (directions are on the next page for Internet Explorer and Netscape Navigator 4.0).

Of course, if you're designing for a company intranet, test with whatever Web browser is installed on the company sites, along with whatever plug-ins and helper applications are standard.

Take note of the accessibility barriers I mentioned earlier. Do they look less than perfect on other browsers? If you designed for just one Web browser, and you don't have control over what browser people will be using, then don't think that it will look "perfect" to everyone. Look at it with the other browsers and ask yourself: does this page lose its meaning when I look at it in this browser? If it does, then try to redesign it so it will send the same message to your audience, regardless of their hardware and software setup.

## TAKE NOTE

### ▶ INTERNET EXPLORER CONFLICT

If you install Microsoft Internet Explorer 4.0 on your Windows 95 or Windows NT computer, you will not be able to test Internet Explorer 3.0 on your system, because the files will have been overwritten by IE 4.0. You also won't be able to reinstall Internet Explorer 3.0 ever again, unless you do a complete uninstall and reinstall of the entire operating system, preferably with a version that predates IE 4.0. Believe it or not, that's actually deliberate, but it sure is a pain for Web designers!

In contrast, Netscape makes its previous versions available for downloading at their site, and you can download and install them in as many ways as you like.

### ▶ SHARING RESOURCES

Naturally, not everyone can have all the Web browsers installed on his or her machine all the time. A common solution is to exchange testing resources with other Web designers. You can ask on certain newsgroups and mailing lists if people will take a look at your Web site and tell you how it looks. Some designers will also send you a screen capture of the site, and if you ask people to focus on a specific accessibility barrier, you'll receive answers that are more useful to the design issues you're really testing for. Be sure to reciprocate later, though, and offer others the benefit of your Web browser wisdom.

### CROSS-REFERENCE
Chapters 10 and 11 offer information and tips on installing and using different Web browsers.

### FIND IT ONLINE
The BrowserWatch site (**http://browserwatch. internet.com/**) has information on current and not-so-current Web browsers.

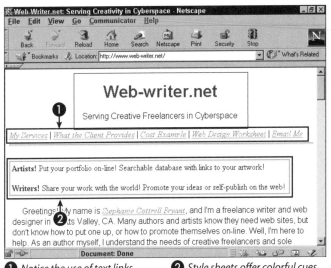

❶ Notice the use of text links instead of graphics for a clean-looking page.

❷ Style sheets offer colorful cues without slow-loading graphics.

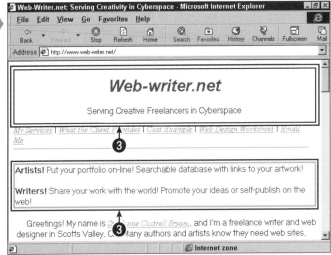

❸ A well-designed site looks good across browsers, although not everything is identical.

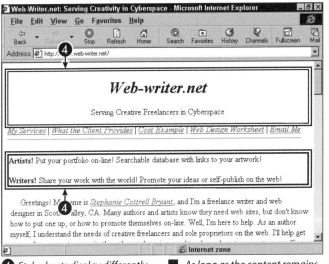

❹ Style sheets display differently across browsers, and even different versions of the same browser.

■ As long as the content remains legible, don't change a page just because one element looks slightly different than another.

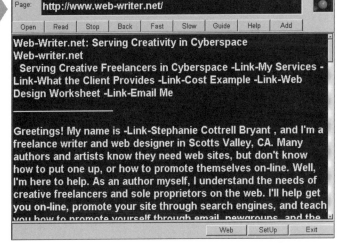

■ Notice how the text-only page eliminates all style sheet information and colors. Any graphics on this page would display their text-only alt attributes, as well.

# Using Multiple Languages

The World Wide Web is definitely an international enterprise, and a multilingual resource for all. As a result, the people who surf over to your site may not read your native language.

In Chapter 3, I discuss how to use an alternative font face to provide a different character set for your site. In reality, that's just a "hack" — a workaround that Web designers have developed to be able to do what they want to without tripping over HTML standards.

To begin with, you must be able to write in the (human) language of your document. It sounds like a no-brainer, but there are some people who believe the multiple language support means the Web is some universal translator that will magically turn their English pages into Japanese. No, **you** have to be able to translate into Japanese, or use one of the many translation programs available on the Web.

You also have to tell the Web browser what language the Web page is in, using the `lang` attribute. There is no standard default; a Web browser that is distributed in China will not have U.S. English as its default language, although the user can install and support multiple languages. Specifying the content language is illustrated in the second figure.

Finally, you should be sure to test your foreign language page in a browser that supports that foreign language. If it doesn't look right, go back and put `lang` attributes into every element that relates to the page content. Sometimes, you'll still have to use a <BASEFONT> element in the <HEAD> to force an unusual font to be used.

## TAKE NOTE

### ▶ USING THE DIR ATTRIBUTE

Many languages, such as Hebrew, are not read from left to right across the page. For these languages, use the `dir` attribute. Dir can have values of LTR or RTL, meaning left to right, and right to left, respectively. To use `dir` to change the direction of an entire HTML document, put it in the HTML element at the top of the page. If your directional text is just a block element, such as a quote or sample, then include it in the block element used (such as <BLOCKQUOTE>). Finally, you can use `dir` in an inline element, including <SPAN>, which does not cause any formatting in and of itself.

### ▶ CHARACTER ENCODING AND HTML

Some alphabets, such as the Cyrillic alphabet, have characters that are not easily rendered in the Latin-1 (Western European) alphabet. To use these alphabets, you can change the *charset* (character set) of your document. The most common charset you'll encounter is ISO-8859-1, also known as Latin-1, the Western European alphabet. ISO-8859-5 includes Cyrillic characters. SHIFT_JIS and EUC-JP are for Japanese character sets. You can specify the character set in a <META> element: `<META http-equiv="Content-Type" content="text/html; charset=ISO-8859-5">` for a Cyrillic document, for example.

**CROSS-REFERENCE**

Chapter 9 discusses character sets and encoding in depth.

**FIND IT ONLINE**

The UNICODE Charset Informational Page is at **http://www.terena.nl/projects/multiling/unicode/index.html**.

## Table 5-1: LANGUAGE VALUES

| Lang value | Language |
|------------|----------|
| en | English |
| fr | French |
| it | Italian |
| nl | Dutch |
| el | Greek |
| es | Spanish |
| pt | Portuguese |
| ar | Arabic |
| he | Hebrew |
| ru | Russian |
| zh | Chinese |
| ja | Japanese |
| hi | Hindi |
| ur | Urdu |
| sa | Sanskrit |

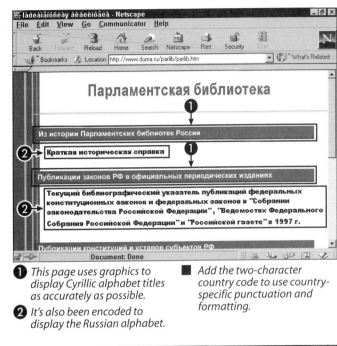

❶ This page uses graphics to display Cyrillic alphabet titles as accurately as possible.

❷ It's also been encoded to display the Russian alphabet.

■ Add the two-character country code to use country-specific punctuation and formatting.

### Listing 5-3: Charset Definitions

```
<HTML>
<HEAD>
<META HTTP-EQUIV="CONTENT-TYPE"
CONTENT="TEXT/HTML; CHARSET=X-CP1251">
</HEAD>
```

▲ The <META> element uses the charset attribute to set the character set to the Russian alphabet, "X-CP1251." Other alphabets are available, such as for Asian and Arabic languages.

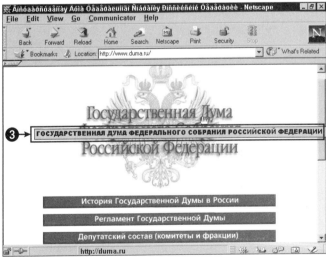

❸ Done correctly, alt text appears in the correct character set.

# Encouraging Feedback

Perhaps one of the hardest parts of designing a Web site is knowing how effectively your message is getting across to your audience. Once you've designed the site, you have a responsibility to the users of that site to provide them a means of responding to you. After all, even a computer book author includes her email address!

One way to encourage user feedback is to provide a hyperlink to your email address on each page. Another is to have an online form for users to complete; it should ask specific questions about the site, as well as about the user filling in the form. The user profile questions are to make sure the person commenting is part of your target audience. The site-related questions are to provide focus to their critique.

But how do you get people to go to the feedback form? Well, some people just go there automatically. Most of your audience, however, will probably have to be invited. Some ways to invite user comments:

► Put the following message on your Web page: "Comments are always welcome. Please use the **feedback form** for your remarks."
► Give them an incentive: Offer a drawing for a free item, or make it part of the registration form for a downloadable program.

You can also offer a mailing list or an online threaded forum. A mailing list sends email out to everyone on the list, and the members of the list can often reply to the list as well. This can increase your Web site's visibility, and your audience will be more likely to tell you what interests them.

An online forum, or bulletin board, is a Web-based, threaded discussion group in which users can post and read messages by subject. A forum is similar to a mailing list, but forums don't attract the same volume — probably because users must actively visit them, while lists are sent to their email addresses automatically.

Whatever you do to encourage feedback on your site, respond quickly to the feedback. If someone emails you asking for a URL, reply that day with the URL, or tell them you don't know where to find it. Don't be afraid to say you don't know something, but be willing to look it up.

**CROSS-REFERENCE**

Running bulletin board, guestbook, and form scripts will be discussed in Chapter 14.

**FIND IT ONLINE**

Guestpage.com (**http://www.guestpage.com/**) offers free guestbook services to any Web site.

■ *This chat system has a Halloween theme. Colors and graphics fit into the theme, but they're easily overridden by the Web browser preferences.*

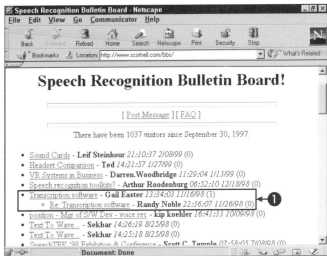

❶ *A threaded bulletin board system allows users to post help requests and receive information from others. Users can also post useful information, such as conference dates and workarounds.*

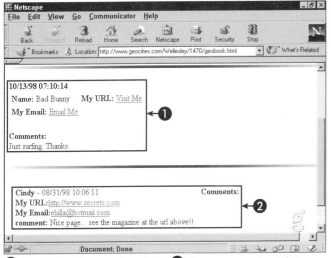

❶ *A guestbook is a nonthreaded place for people to sign their names and make a few comments.*

❷ *Here, someone has left the URL to their magazine's home page.*

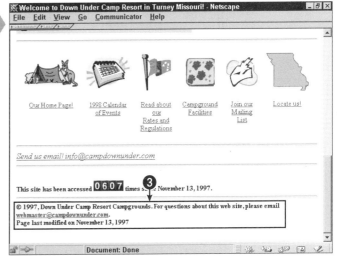

❸ *Include a* `mailto:webmaster` *hyperlink on each page of your site: users who have trouble with an individual page will click there first.*

# Personal Workbook

## Q&A

**1** Name two common barriers to accessibility for older users.

_____

_____

_____

**2** What are the benefits of designing for an intranet?

_____

_____

_____

**3** What are the drawbacks of an intranet?

_____

_____

_____

**4** How many Web browsers should you test your Web page on?

_____

_____

_____

**5** What's a low-bandwidth alternative to graphics?

_____

_____

_____

**6** Name one problem with animated graphics.

_____

_____

_____

**7** How can you encourage users to respond to your site?

_____

_____

_____

**8** What's one of the first steps in designing your Web site?

_____

_____

_____

ANSWERS: PAGE 436

## EXTRA PRACTICE

1. Ask a friend of a different generation what they like and don't like about the Web and the Internet. This person is your test audience.

2. Using his or her input, design a site about your favorite book or movie.

3. Ask your test audience to look at your site and tell you if they would read that book or watch that movie, based on the information in the site.

4. Change your site so your test audience will be swayed by your review.

5. Now, add some method for users to submit their ideas and discussion online.

6. Double-check your site in at least five different Web browsers (different versions count, too!).

## REAL-WORLD APPLICATIONS

✔ Your company is opening an office in Tokyo. You work with a translator to put the company manual into Japanese, and use the Japanese character encoding to put it online.

✔ You're designing a Web page for the elementary school science fair. You use lots of colorful graphics and online activities, and place pictures of the kids' projects online.

✔ Two weeks before a product launch, the leading Web browsers go through yet another change. You can test Web browsers for compatibility, and are confident your site will survive the "upgrade."

✔ Although you didn't realize it, your personal recipe page has become a big hit with the over-50 crowd. They keep coming back to share their recipes with you on your guestbook or bulletin board system.

## Visual Quiz

Who's the audience for this Web page? What will filling in the form do? What would you change on this site to encourage people to use this service? Would paid advertising work on a site like this?

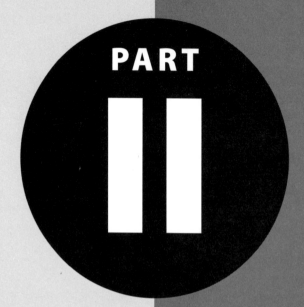

# PART

# II

# Beyond the Basics

In this part, you learn how to create Web-ready graphics, frames, and online forms. You also learn how to use more advanced HTML elements and tags in your Web pages. This part is designed as a "next step" to learning HTML. Image design is a major part of the Internet. If you're not a graphic designer, it can be tricky to know how to use available tools. Because of this, I've included on the CD-ROM the shareware version of the popular graphics program PaintShop Pro. Chapter 6 teaches you how to use it. Similarly, Chapter 7, "Building Frames," and Chapter 8, "Forms," teach you how to design effective, professional pages using those design features of HTML.

Finally, Chapter 9, "Advanced Tags," introduces some rarely used HTML elements that are extremely powerful. Special characters and symbols, more advanced applications of META elements, and mathematical notation may not be what you think you need now, but a professional designer knows they exist and isn't afraid to use them.

When you finish reading this part, you'll know how to use HTML to create a framed site or an online form. You'll know when and how to use special characters for symbols, and create an image.

CHAPTER **6**

# Images and Image Maps

This chapter shows you how to use commonly available software to create images that will liven up the visual appearance of your pages. There are two image formats commonly in use on the Web: GIF and JPEG, with a third, PNG, just coming into use. GIFs are generally used to create line drawings and simple images for icons, while JPEGs are used for complex images, such as photographs, with many colors. There is enough overlap, however, that your choice of file format may hinge on which version of your images makes a smaller file.

The more graphics you place on a page, the longer it takes to load. A large number of moving images can make the eye tire pretty quickly, and may also serve to confuse rather than to enlighten. And research has shown that a page that takes more than 15 seconds to load drives away potential visitors.

One simple rule to help you decide when to employ graphics is *never send a graphic to do the job of text*. Simple text links can get your visitors to other parts of your site just as easily as a graphic button without increasing load time.

Nonetheless, a bit of graphics can certainly do a lot to make your page distinctive. You can add your company logo to your page headers, and may want to use other images as illustrative points.

You *may* also want to use text icons when a particular typeface is strongly identified with your company's image. One of the limitations of Web technology is that no matter what fonts you place on your page, they are not displayed on your visitors' browsers if the fonts are not installed on the visitors' systems.

Another use for graphics is *image maps*. HTML allows you to make areas of a graphic into "hot spots," to which you can attach a link. The graphic image may consist solely of text or of an actual picture.

All the examples in this chapter use the complete version of Paint Shop Pro, a trial version available on the accompanying CD. If you have another image editing program that you prefer, feel free to use it.

# Creating a GIF Image

With minimal drawing skills, you can create a simple, yet effective GIF image. I'm going to take you through all the steps of using Paint Shop Pro to create an image of a wheel. If a text caption is added, this can work as an icon on your page. In the next task, you build on this icon to create an animated GIF.

Paint Shop Pro has several toolbars, which are called *palettes*. Most of these can be either floating or anchored in the program window. You need to use the Color Palette, the Tool Palette, and the Control Palette. All of these palettes appear in the upper-right figure on the facing page.

The Control Palette changes to match the tool you are using, and you often need to use the Tool and Control Palettes together. For example, if you use the Line tool, first choose the color for the line, then use the Control Palette to set the width of the line to draw.

You also need to become familiar with the Color Palette, and the ways to manipulate color. Paint Shop Pro comes with a "safety palette," which contains only the 216 colors that can safely be displayed in any browser. By default, this is the only palette included with Paint Shop Pro, but you can create and save as many palettes as you need.

To work effectively with Paint Shop Pro, you need to become familiar with the tools on the Tool Palette. Many of them are advanced tools for subtle image manipulations, and are beyond the scope of this book.

*Continued*

## TAKE NOTE

### ▶ PAINT SHOP PRO: BASIC TOOLS TO USE

▶ The Pointer tool, which looks like an arrow, is used mainly for dragging windows and selected parts of images.

▶ The Zoom tool (a magnifying glass) has the same effects as the View ⇨ Zoom In and View ⇨ Zoom Out commands.

▶ The Shape tool, represented by a solid square, can be used to draw squares, rectangles, circles, and ellipses.

▶ The Line tool, represented by a diagonal line, is used for drawing straight lines.

▶ The Paintbrush tool is used for freehand drawing (it can also draw straight lines).

▶ The Text tool is used to place text in your image; you have access to all the fonts and styles installed on your system and can select the justification of the text to suit your purpose.

▶ The dropper can be used to "pick up" a color from an image for use elsewhere.

▶ The Flood Fill tool, a paint can, can be used to create gradient, as well as solid fills, when used with the Control Palette.

## SHORTCUT

Press Ctrl+Alt+G to toggle the grid on and off. Click the Magnifying Glass tool to choose zoom values from the Control Palette.

## FIND IT ONLINE

To check for the latest upgrade to Paint Shop Pro, go to http://www.jasc.com/pspdl.html.

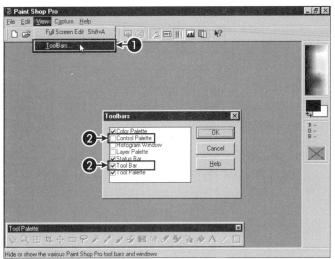

① *Choose View ⇨ Toolbars to display the Toolbars dialog box.*

② *Click the Control and Tool Palette options. The other three options are defaults.*

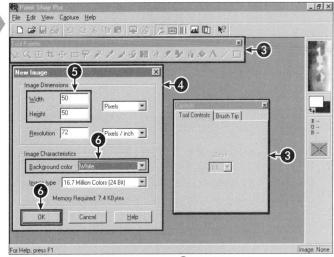

③ *Arrange the Tool and Control Palettes.*

④ *Choose File ⇨ New to display the New Image dialog box.*

⑤ *Set the width and height to 50 pixels.*

⑥ *Set the background color to White. The default color depth is 16.7 million colors. Click OK.*

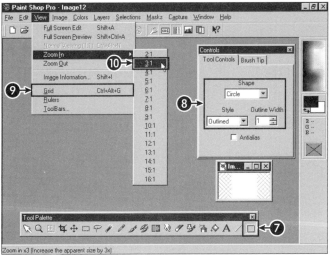

⑦ *Select the Shape tool.*

⑧ *In the Control Palette, set the shape to Circle, the style to Outlined, and the Outline Width to 1.*

⑨ *Choose View ⇨ Grid to display a grid on the image work area.*

⑩ *Choose View ⇨ Zoom In to set the display to three times actual size.*

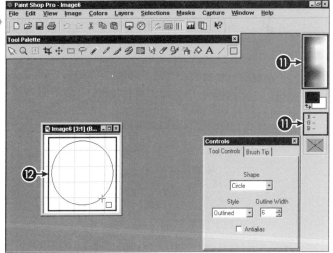

⑪ *Click your pointer on the left edge of the Color Palette to choose black for the foreground color. The RGB values should all be 0.*

⑫ *Position your pointer in the center of the grid and drag it diagonally to a vertex to center your circle.*

# Creating a GIF Image
*Continued*

You've drawn the rim of a wheel. Next you'll draw spokes and a hub using the Line and Shape tools. You may also need to use the Paintbrush to touch up the edges. You'll make the image transparent so that only the wheel itself shows up on your page.

To use Paint Shop Pro effectively, you need to acquaint yourself with its handling of color. On the right edge of the screen is the Color Palette, showing gradations from red through violet (top to bottom) and from black to white (left to right). When you move your pointer over this area, it becomes a Dropper. The color over which you are hovering shows in the lower square below the palette, marked with an X. The RGB values (degree of intensity of red, green, and blue, respectively) appear just above it, expressed in values from 0 to 255. To choose a color as the background click it with your right mouse button. To choose a color as the foreground color, click with the left mouse button. They appear in the square immediately below the Color Palette. (The foreground color is in front.) To reverse foreground and background, click on the two-headed arrow in the lower-left corner of that square.

You may need more precise control over your colors. You may have a hard time finding a true red by hovering, for example, and you absolutely cannot get a gray from the palette. To control values directly, click on either the foreground or background square, depending on where you want to use the color. This displays the Colors dialog box, which appears in the upper-left figure. Here you have many ways of choosing a color:

▶ From the Basic Colors grid, you can choose any of the displayed colors. These will show up as unmixed colors at all color depths.

▶ From the ring to the right, you can choose a precise RGB value by clicking on the shade you want. The color you choose appears in the leftmost of the two squares below the ring.

▶ From the square inside the ring, you can set the hue, saturation, and luminance by clicking on the part of the square that represents the shade you want.

▶ You can enter RGB and hue, saturation, and luminance values directly.

▶ You can enter the HTML code for a color in the field provided.

## TAKE NOTE

### ▶ CHOOSING "BROWSER-SAFE" COLORS
Not all colors are properly rendered in all browsers. A file called *Browser Safe Colors.gif* appears on the CD. It shows all 216 browser-safe colors, with their RGB values and HTML codes. Sometimes the easiest way to get the color you want is to look it up in the file and enter the value in the HTML code field.

## CROSS-REFERENCE
To review the way colors are handled in HTML, see Chapter 2.

## FIND IT ONLINE
http://www.users.interport.net/~giant/COLOR/1ColorSpecifier.html has a chart of RGB and HTML values.

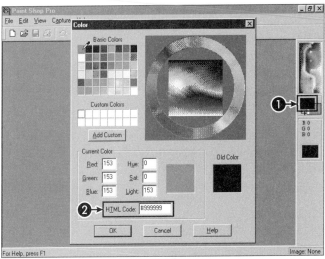

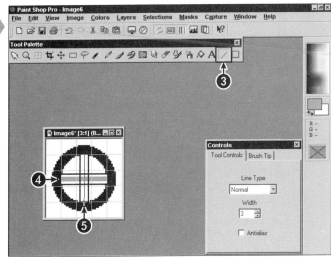

**①** Click on the foreground color square to bring up the Colors dialog box.

**②** Enter the HTML code #999999 to choose a browser-safe shade of gray.

**③** Choose the Line tool. Set the line width to 3.

**④** Click the left inner edge of the circle. Draw a horizontal line to the right inner edge.

**⑤** Click the top inner edge of the circle. Draw straight down to the bottom inner edge.

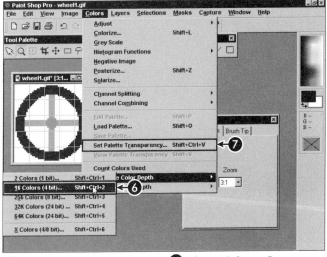

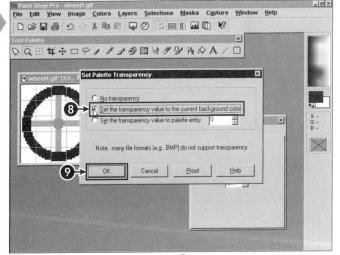

**■** Open the Colors dialog box and choose Red from the basic colors, choose the Shape tool, set the width to 4, and center the hub.

**⑥** Choose Colors ➪ Decrease Color Depth ➪ 16 Colors.

**⑦** Choose Colors ➪ Set Palette Transparency.

**⑧** Set the transparency value to the screen background color.

**⑨** Click OK and save the image as wheel1.gif.

# Animating a GIF

To add some razzle-dazzle to your page, you may want to use *animated GIF* files. These are most often used for banner ads, which you may exchange with other sites to draw traffic to your page. They may also be used to draw attention to specific points on your page. In this section, you create an animated GIF based on the wheel image you created in the previous task. You create four related images and use a special piece of software to create an animation.

First, to create the images, make three copies of the original wheel. (You will have to set the transparency to match your original—it isn't copied.) You then command to rotate each image a different degree: 22.5 degrees, 45 degrees, and 62.5 degrees.

There are several ways you can go here. The best image will result from selecting just the center of the wheel, excluding the rim.

- ▶ If you're really good with freehand, you can use the Lasso to select just this area.
- ▶ You can also use the Selection tool, with the shape set to Circle in the Control Palette. If this works, you get the best result, but it's difficult to center the circle perfectly, and you may miss part of a spoke or include a bit of rim. If you're going to try this method, first zoom out as much as you can. And don't be afraid to try again if the circle isn't where you want. Just click outside the selected area to undo the selection. Besides, you can always touch up the images later.
- ▶ Finally, you can rotate the entire image, which is the most accurate in including everything but may make a bit of a mess of the rim.

When you have saved the new images as `wheel2.gif`, `wheel3.gif`, and `wheel4.gif`, respectively, you're ready to animate the image.

Paint Shop Pro includes a simple Animation Studio as an installation option. Once it's installed, you can run it from Paint Shop Pro's File menu. Choose File ➪ Animation Wizard. Just accept the defaults on the first four screens.

The Open dialog box lets you choose multiple files using the Ctrl or Shift key, so you can choose all your files at once. On the fifth screen, click Add Image and select all four wheel images. Use the buttons to place them in the correct order, click Next, and then click Finish. To see the result of an animation, click View ➪ Animation. When you save the file, a complex dialog box appears. Click Customize, and change the palette to eight colors. Otherwise, the image will appear in two colors.

## TAKE NOTE

### ▶ TOUCHING UP

If you need to touch up the edge between two colors, use the Dropper to select the colors on either side of the edge, one with the left button and the other with the right. You can then alternate buttons to alternate between the two colors.

## CROSS-REFERENCE

Other Web and graphics tools are discussed in Chapter 12.

## FIND IT ONLINE

You can download a free version of yet another animator, Ulead's GIF Animator, at **http://www.ulead.com**.

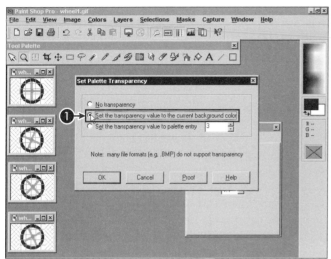

■ *Press Ctrl+C to copy the original image and Ctrl+V three times to create three identical copies.*

① *Press Shift+Ctrl+V to open the Set Palette Transparency dialog box and choose "Set the transparency value to the current background color."*

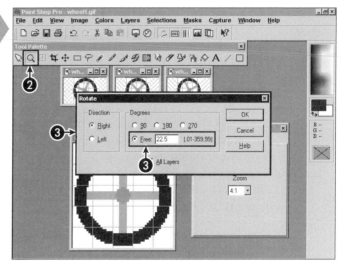

② *Enlarge the second image with the Zoom tool.*

■ *Set the Selection tool to Circle and select the area inside the rim.*

③ *Press Ctrl+R to open the Rotate dialog. Choose Free rotation. Enter 22.5.*

■ *Rotate the centers of the remaining images to 45 and 62.5 degrees.*

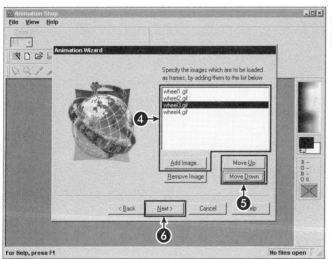

■ *In the Animation Shop, choose File ⇨ Animation Wizard. Click Next through the first four pages.*

④ *Click Add Image, and select the four wheelx.gif files.*

⑤ *Use the Move Up and Move Down buttons to place the files in the proper order.*

⑥ *Click Next.*

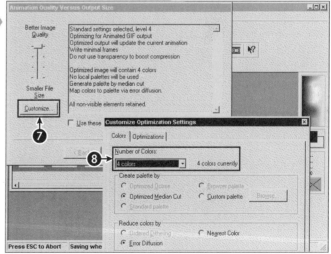

■ *Choose View ⇨ Animation to see the result. Choose File ⇨ Save and name the graphic wheel.gif.*

⑦ *In the Animation Quality Versus Output Size dialog box, click Customize.*

⑧ *Change the number of colors from 4 to 8. Click OK. Click Next twice, then click Finish.*

# Working with JPEG Images

JPEG images are generally used when you require photographic quality. You may use JPEGs, for example, to place portraits of your top executives on your About Us page, or show images of your products for an online catalog.

JPEGs use a compression formula to squeeze unnecessary information out of the file. Although JPEGs theoretically have 16.7 million colors, your actual image may require many fewer colors. Various graphics tools let you control the degree of compression. Often, you can compress a JPEG a great deal without losing quality.

To acquire a JPEG image, you can

▶ Scan an image with your scanner.

▶ Purchase one on a CD of royalty-free images.

▶ Have your photos returned to you on disk rather than on paper.

▶ Use a digital camera.

▶ Download it from the Web; if you do, be sure to inquire whether it's copyrighted, and whether you can use it if it is.

Sometimes a photographic image may reach you in a file format other than JPEG. If so, you can load it into Paint Shop Pro and use the Save as Type command in the Save dialog box to convert it to JPEG.

The upper-left figure shows how to acquire an image from either a scanner or a digital camera. Paint Shop Pro has built-in support for TWAIN-32-compliant scanners.

Your scanner documentation will tell you if it qualifies. When you choose the Acquire command, your scanner window pops up and automatically previews the image. You may want to change the scanning area to focus on only part of the image. As you can see in the lower-left image, the Image menu contains many effects you can use to sharpen or alter your image. You can even change the size of the entire image if it's too big. Paint Shop Pro retains an Undo History if you don't like the changes you made.

Perhaps your image needs touching up. You can select areas with the Lasso tool, and blur (or sharpen) them, say, to make the background less prominent. You can blur particular spots using the Blur tool (a pointing finger). Or you can remove blemishes by using the Clone Brush tool (two parallel paintbrushes) to copy a background area over the blemish. Using the Crop tool and its Control Palette, you can select an area of the image and crop to just the selected area.

## TAKE NOTE

### ▶ ZOOMING WITH THE MOUSE

If you have a mouse with a wheel, and the image is not so big that the window has scroll bars, then turning the wheel zooms the image in and out.

## CROSS-REFERENCE

See Chapter 2 for instructions on writing the code to insert an image into your Web page.

## FIND IT ONLINE

Seattle Filmworks (**http://www.filmworks.com**) will deliver your 35mm pictures on diskette.

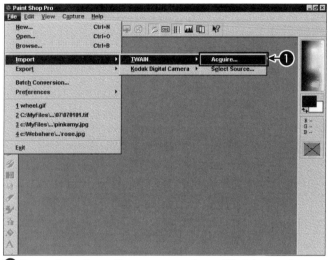

**①** *To acquire an image from a scanner, choose File ▷ Import ▷ TWAIN ▷ Acquire.*

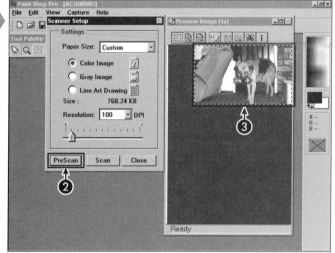

**②** *The scanner window appears. Preview or prescan the image.*

**③** *If you wish, and if your scanner supports it, crop the image so only the desired portion is scanned.*

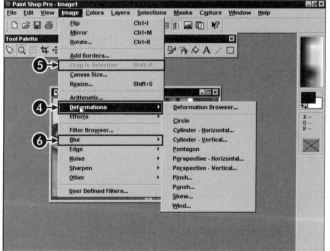

**④** *Use commands on the Image menu, such as Deformations, to add special effects to your image.*

**⑤** *Use the Crop tool to resize the image by clicking Crop to Selection.*

**⑥** *Use the Blur tool to hide blemishes.*

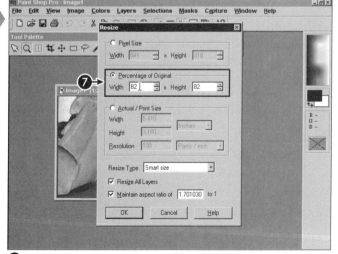

**⑦** *Use the Image ▷ Resize command to reduce the image. Enter the percentage of the original to which it should be reduced.*

■ *If you leave other settings alone, you get a proportional resize.*

■ *Save the image as type JPEG.*

# Creating a Design Element

This section illustrates how to create a design element, in this case a button that changes its appearance when the mouse moves over it. This means you need to create two versions of the button. One of the characteristics of a button image is the visually raised border, light on the top and left and dark on the bottom and right. You can pick colors that relate to your image and draw the borders by hand using the Line tool. But it's much easier to use the Image ⇨ Effects ⇨ Buttonize command, which does the whole thing for you.

If you have a library of textures, and it includes a texture that goes with your design theme, you may want to create a textured button. If not, you can create a button with a solid or a gradient background.

In the upper-left image on the next page, I used a portion of a textured background image, which I copied and pasted as a new image. If you want a solid background, you can also create a new image of about 75    25. If the result doesn't appear to be the right size, close it and start again with different dimensions.

The next step is to buttonize it. This creates the appearance of a beveled edge. You can control several aspects of the way the button is formed:

▶ You can set the height and width in pixels; I generally favor a height and width of 2 or 3 for small text buttons.

▶ You can set the opacity from 0 to 100 percent. The default is 100. Less than 50 tends to make the border disappear. A number in the 60s results in a border of the same colors as the background, but quite visible. Complete opacity yields a border in black and gray.

▶ You can choose a solid or a transparent edge. The default is solid. If you use transparent, with an opacity setting of 80 percent or more, the border appears to be rounded rather than beveled.

When you've adjusted the border to your liking, save the image. You won't be adding the text just yet, because you'll use this image as a blank to make a variety of buttons. If you want a button that appears to be depressed when the mouse passes over it, you need to make a second copy that's been inverted.

*Continued*

## TAKE NOTE

### MAKING YOUR BUTTONS TRANSPARENT

If your page uses a background image, and you want the buttons to match your background, you don't have to paste bits of the background texture into the buttons. Instead, make the background color transparent. Be sure to use a background color that more or less matches your background image, so that you'll be able to see text when you add it.

**CROSS-REFERENCE**

See Chapter 2 for instructions on adding a graphic into your page.

**SHORTCUT**

Use Ctrl+I for Image ⇨ Flip. Use Ctrl+V for Edit ⇨ Paste ⇨ As New Image.

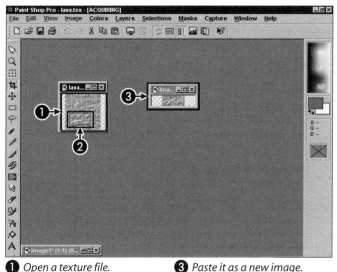

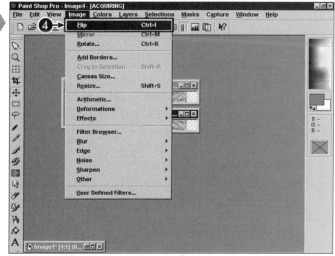

❶ Open a texture file.

❸ Paste it as a new image.

❷ Select a rectangular portion
suitable for a button. Copy it.

■ Paste a second copy of the
image.

❹ Choose Image ➪ Flip to turn
the image upside down. This
allows the button to look the
same after it's flipped a
second time.

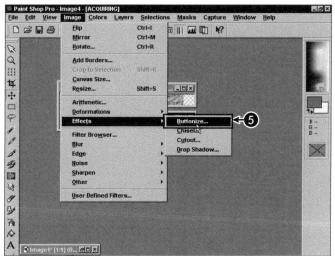

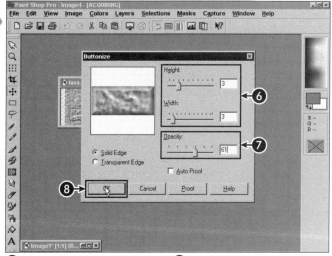

❺ Choose Image ➪ Effects ➪ Buttonize from the menu.

❻ Set the border Height and
Width to 3.

❼ Set the opacity to 61.

❽ Choose OK.

■ Repeat the procedure for the
flipped button.

# Creating a Design Element
*Continued*

You now have a regular button and an inverted button, but the inversion isn't complete. You have to flip the second button a second time. This will restore the background to its original appearance, but reverse the bevel so that it appears to slant inward rather than outward.

Now you're ready to add text. To add text, you use the Text tool. Before you do, make sure you've saved both images. Call them `buttonu` and `buttond,` and save them as GIFs. These will be blanks for all the buttons on your page. You don't want to reduce the colors yet, because then there won't be any color left over for you to use as text.

When you use the Text tool, you must first choose the foreground color to use for the text; otherwise, the text appears in the background color, which is pretty useless. I'll use white on this texture, but if you've chosen a light-colored texture, you should choose a color that will contrast.

As usual, you'll find it easier to see what you're doing if you zoom the image out. To start, click with the pointer. Eventually, the Add Text dialog box appears. Here, you can choose any font on your system, in any size and style. But you have to be sensible. There's a tradeoff. On the one hand, the font you choose will appear properly in any graphical browser, because it's displayed as a graphic. On the other, you're working with a very small image, and a fancy font will most likely be illegible. You're probably best off with plain old Arial, Times Roman, or MS Serif or Sans Serif, unless you've got another font that's equally legible at small sizes. If you want to display fancier text, you'll need to work with a larger image.

When you've finished this task, you'll have a pair of "Next" buttons, as well as the blanks you've created. You can use the blanks to make any other buttons you require. Most likely you'll want at least "Home" and "Back" buttons; depending on the structure of your site, you may also want "Up" or other navigational features. You can apply the principles you learn in this task to make a wide variety of buttons. If you don't like the beveled look, you might try some of the other effects. The cutout effect also makes an interesting button.

## TAKE NOTE

### ► USING GRADIENT FILLS

To create a gradient, choose the Flood Fill tool (the paint can), and in the Control Palette choose the type of gradient you want. Then, choose the foreground and background colors to blend. The Options button on the Control Palette lets you vary many aspects of the gradient. You'll just have to experiment with them to find out what they all do. Unfortunately, you won't be able to use a gradient on a small image such as a button, but they are great for banners.

**CROSS-REFERENCE**

See Chapter 18 for use of the `onmouseover` command.

**SHORTCUT**

Use Ctrl+E for Edit ⇨ Paste ⇨ As New Selection. Use F12 for File ⇨ Save As.

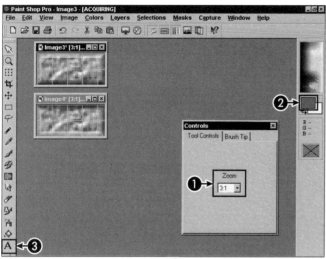

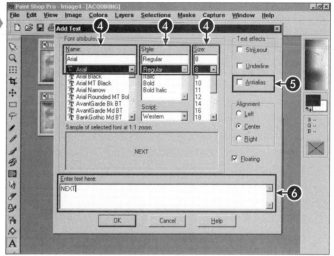

■ *Use the Image ▷ Flip command on the second image to invert it a second time.*

**①** *Zoom in on the image.*

**②** *Choose a contrasting foreground color.*

**③** *Click on the Text tool.*

■ *Click your mouse in the middle of one of the images.*

**④** *Choose Arial for your font, Regular style and 8 points.*

**⑤** *Uncheck Antialias.*

**⑥** *Enter NEXT in the text box and click OK.*

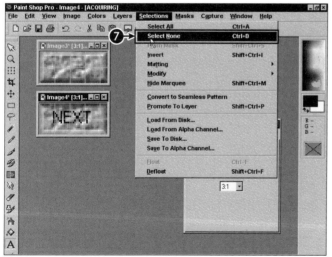

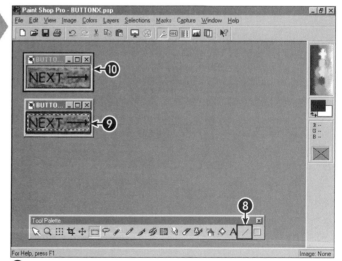

**⑦** *Drag and drop the text into the center of the button. Choose Selections ▷ Select None to anchor the text to the background.*

**⑧** *Choose the Line tool.*

**⑨** *Draw an arrow pointing to the right. Copy the text and the arrow.*

**⑩** *Select the other button graphic, and paste the copy.*

■ *Position it and click outside the selection to anchor it. Save the images as* nextbtnu.gif *and* nextbtnd.gif.

# Reducing Download Time

A s you know, the more graphics you use, the slower your pages download. Therefore, you must use your graphics judiciously.

Fortunately, there are several things you can do to improve the download time for your pages, even with graphics. First, you can make your images smaller. Second, if you want to display a group of photo-quality images, you can make a *thumbnail page* of small copies of the pictures, each linked to a single page containing the full-size image. This lets your visitors see what's available with a minimal hit against download time, and then view only the images they are interested in. You can create a crude thumbnail page in Paint Shop Pro, as described in the first figure.

Finally, you can reduce the file size of the images you use. One obvious way is to reduce the number of colors in a GIF file. If this doesn't shrink the file sufficiently, sometimes converting the image to a JPEG yields greater improvement. I tried this with the navigation buttons you created in the previous task and reduced the file size from 2K to 1K. (You may not experience an equivalent gain if your background image is less complex than the one I used.) Occasionally, you may find that you can reduce a file by converting from JPEG to GIF. It depends on the characteristics of the file.

Several programs can help you reduce the file size of your JPEG images with minimal loss of quality. Paint Shop Pro can help you reduce the file size somewhat, as shown in the upper right-hand figure.

An easier to use, but more limited, program is Ulead's SmartSaver 3.0. This tool does a spectacular job of adjusting compression, comparing the results using different settings and different file types. A pair of windows lets you compare the original (on the left) and the compressed version (on the right) for size and quality. You can see the effects of different settings immediately.

SmartSaver includes built-in tools for cropping and resizing images (as does LView Pro), so you have all the tools you need to improve an image's download time in one place.

## TAKE NOTE

### ▶ COMPRESSING A JPEG IMAGE

With Ulead's SmartSaver, you can reduce an image file with little technical knowledge. As the second illustration shows, I was able to compress the photo from about 136K to about 8K. That yields a tolerable increase in the load time for a page with few graphics. The default compression is 85 percent. I was able to compress down to 65 percent with little loss of quality by altering other settings. Since the second view pane provides immediate feedback, I could see the results without worrying about technical issues.

## CROSS-REFERENCE

For a practical application of some of these techniques, see Chapter 22.

## FIND IT ONLINE

To use Ulead SmartSaver online for free, or download the trial version, go to **http://www.ulead.com/webutilities/frwhere.htm**.

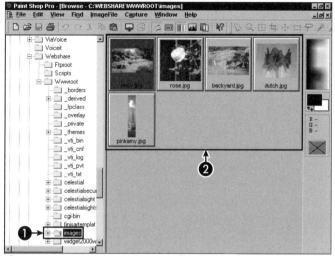

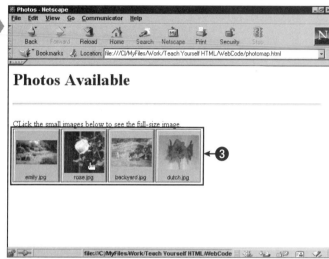

**1** Group the files to display in a single folder. Use the File ⇨ Browse command (or press Ctrl+B), and choose that folder.

**2** Paint Shop Pro creates a window containing just the files in that folder.

**3** Use a screen capture program to capture that window, and save the result as a JPEG file.

■ Turn it into a clickable image map that users can choose to view images from.

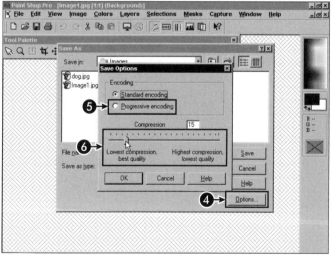

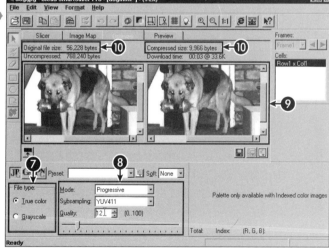

**4** When saving, choose Options for compressing and decompressing JPEG files.

**5** Choose Progressive encoding for more efficient encoding.

**6** The higher the compression, the lower the quality of the JPEG image.

**7** Choose the file color type in SmartSaver.

**8** Choose the degree and manner of compression.

**9** Compare the original to the compressed version for quality.

**10** Compare the file size of the original with that of the compressed version.

# Writing Client-Side Image Maps

Image maps are graphic images, portions of which are linked to other files. You might see an actual map, for example, on which you can click on various areas and get information about what's located there.

Image maps come in two varieties: *client-side* and *server-side*. Client-side maps are executed entirely on the user's browser. Because there are no calls to the server to execute a client-side map, they execute more quickly. Moreover, you can test them on your own computer.

Unfortunately, some browsers (such as Internet Explorer and Netscape Navigator versions 2.0 and below) don't support client-side maps. This is not true of a server-side map. Fortunately, it's possible to combine client-side and server-side maps.

To create a client-side map, you use areas in the form of rectangles, circles, and polygons. You then define the *hot spots* — those areas that can be linked — by their coordinates. See the table for details. To demonstrate this, I drew the image you see in the upper-left figure. I used the Shape tool to draw the outline of the rectangle and the circle, and the Line tool to draw the polygon freehand. Just for fun, I used the Fill tool to fill the areas and the background with different colors, using a radial gradient in the Control Palette.

To get the coordinates, point your mouse at the upper-left corner and note the two numbers in the left corner of the status bar. Those are the coordinates of the mouse pointer relative to the upper-left corner of the image. Just point to the relevant corners and note the values, which you use in your code. For the circle, the grid pattern comes in handy. Once you've got the center, follow the grid to an edge, then use the difference from the value you already recorded. Here are the values for the three illustrated objects:

| Shape | Coordinates |
| --- | --- |
| Rectangle | 21,23; 99,84 |
| Circle | 156,56; 35 |
| Polygon | 222,27; 252,27; 271,53; 249,89; 226,89; 206,52 |

You don't have to be absolutely precise with the coordinates. As long as you more or less define the hot spot, your visitors' mouse pointers will change to a hand when they hover over the area.

The code for a map based on these areas appears on the facing page. On the following page, you learn a more common use for image maps, with the full code for presenting one.

Of course, you must save the image to your site, as well as the code.

*Continued*

## TAKE NOTE

▶ **PITFALLS IN IMAGE MAP CODING**

Note that several of the commands for image maps *must* be in all caps. Notice also that the coordinates are listed sequentially, separated only by commas. It's up to the browser to sort out the relationships.

**CROSS-REFERENCE**

For details on placing an image on an HTML page, see Chapter 2.

**FIND IT ONLINE**

A complete tutorial on image maps appears at http://aace.virginia.edu/go/Web Tools/Imagemap/home.html.

## Using the Shape Tool and Flood Fill Effectively

The Shape tool lets you choose whether to create your shapes as outlines or as solid blocks of color. If you want to use a gradient fill, you should create outlines, and set the outline width to at least 2. Otherwise, the fill color will "bleed" into the background. Similarly, to draw polygons to be filled, set your line width to at least 2.

### Table 6-1: COORDINATES REQUIRED FOR IMAGE MAP SHAPES

| Shape | Coordinates |
|---|---|
| Rectangle | Upper left, lower right |
| Circle | Center, length of radius |
| Polygon | Every vertex |

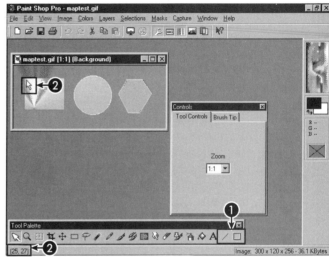

**❶** *Create shapes using the Shape tool and the Line tool.*

**❷** *Use the mouse pointer to find out the coordinates of the vertices of your shapes; for circles, determine the center and radius.*

### Listing 6-1: Code to Define an Image Map

```
<IMG SRC="shapes.gif" USEMAP="#maptest"
 ismap>
<MAP NAME="maptest">
  <AREA SHAPE="RECT" COORDS="21,23,99,84"
href="../squarepage.html">
  <AREA SHAPE="CIRCLE" COORDS="156,56,35"
href=../roundpage.html">
  <AREA SHAPE="POLYGON" COORDS="222,27,252,
   27,271,53,249,89,226,89,206,52"
href="../oddpage.html">
</MAP>
```

▲ *This image map defines three hot spots, each with a different shape.*

# Writing Client-Side Image Maps

*Continued*

Now that you have the basics of client-side mapping, I'm going to demonstrate a common application — a navigation bar to be used in the left frame of a two-frame page. You might ask, why not just use a table with a series of text links? Or a series of separate buttons?

First, a table with text is normally the preferred solution, but this site's look depends on the use of a particular font, which may not be installed on its visitors' computers. You can keep the text from reverting to a default by displaying it as graphics. Second, a series of buttons requires a separate call to the server for each one. Thus, an image map loads more quickly.

Since that's true, why not just insert the map into each page? Because when it's in a frame, it has to be downloaded only once, improving the overall performance of the site.

The upper-left figure shows the beginning of the map. The company name appears in the top of the image. In the text box, I've typed all the names of the pages, separated by line spaces. I'll insert the entire block at once, avoiding problems of uneven vertical spacing. I've also turned Antialias on, because this font, at a larger size than our previous example, is likely to have ragged edges without antialiasing.

Finally, I click OK and position the text. Once that's done, I decrease download time by reducing the colors to 16 and saving the image as a GIF file.

Now all that's left is the mapping. This image has plenty of space between the intended hot spots, so it's just a matter of defining more-or-less precise rectangles. The first, around the company name, is linked to the home page.

The others are linked to the various pages that appear in the right frame. Note that in the code example, in the `<IMG>` tag, everything from the `alt` attribute to the end is optional. Your map will work perfectly well without these elements.

## TAKE NOTE

### ▶ PROVIDING ALTERNATIVES TO IMAGE MAPS

If you examine the code, you'll notice that the `alt` attribute can't be used easily to substitute for all the information provided by the image. This can limit the usefulness of the page to visually impaired persons and people who have graphics turned off. For this reason, all the right-frame pages in this site have both a series of navigation buttons (with appropriate `alt` attributes ) and text links at the bottom of the page.

### ▶ DEFINING A DEFAULT URL

If you want the entire image to be "hot," you can define a default URL. To do so, add another line just before the closing `</MAP>` tag. This line should define the coordinates of your entire map. In the example shown here, the code would be:

```
<AREA SHAPE="RECT" COORDS="0, 0, 100, 460" HREF="../index.htm">
```

**CROSS-REFERENCE**

For information on creating frames, see Chapter 7.

**FIND IT ONLINE**

http://www.marketscape.com/support/docs/ Publisher/wcd00521.htm shows how to convert server-side image maps to client-side maps.

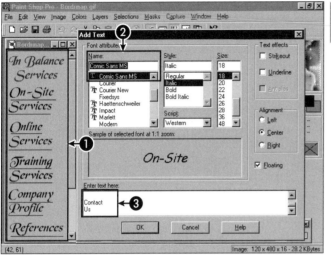

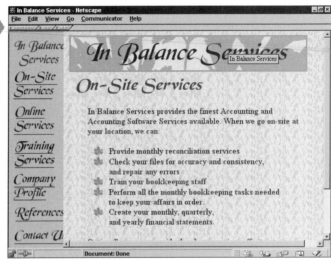

**1** Create a narrow, vertical image suitable for a left border.

**2** Choose the display font to use.

**3** Enter the names of the pages to be linked to, separated by carriage returns.

■ This image shows the navigation bar in use on a page.

### Listing 6-2: Image Map Code

```
<A HREF="left.htm/map"><!—tells the name of the file containing this information, and that it
is a map>
<IMG SRC="bordrmap.gif" ismap usemap="#LNavBar" ALT="Site Navigation" height="480" width="110"
border="0"></A>
<p>
<MAP NAME="LNavBar">
  <AREA SHAPE="RECT" COORDS="0, 1, 100, 65" HREF="../index.htm">
  <AREA SHAPE="RECT" COORDS="0, 72, 100, 142" HREF="../service1.htm">
  <AREA SHAPE="RECT" COORDS="0, 146, 100, 213" HREF="../service2.htm">
  <AREA SHAPE="RECT" COORDS="0, 219, 100, 283" HREF="../training.htm">
  <AREA SHAPE="RECT" COORDS="0, 288, 100, 351" HREF="../profile.htm">
  <AREA SHAPE="RECT" COORDS="0, 355, 100, 403" HREF="../referenc.htm">
  <AREA SHAPE="RECT" COORDS="0, 407, 100, 453" HREF="../contact.htm">
</MAP>
```

▲ This code defines the shapes and hyperlinks for a navigation bar.

# Writing Server-Side Image Maps

Creating server-side image maps is not much more difficult than creating client-side maps. But the technique is different. To create a server-side map, you must

1. Create the image.
2. Determine the coordinates of the hot spots.
3. Create an *external map file* — an ASCII text file defining the hot spots and the hyperlinks to which they point. This file must have the extension .map.
4. Create a hypertext reference in your document, pointing to the external map file.

To define the example in the previous task as a server-side map, you would create the navbar.map, as shown in the upper half of the next page.

An external map file and a client-side map have several important differences:

▶ You *must* have a default element, and it must appear first, rather than last.
▶ The names of the shapes — rect, circle, polygon — must be in lowercase.
▶ The order of the elements — shape, target page, coordinates — is different.
▶ You must have a web server that can handle server-side image maps.

Once you've created and saved this file (you can use Notepad or any other plaintext editor), you can supply the reference to it in the code for your page. The reference takes the following form:

```
<A HREF="location of the map file">
<IMG SRC="image name" ismap></A>
```

In this instance, it would read as follows:

```
<A HREF="http://www.inbalserv.com/
navbar.map">
<IMG SRC="bordrmap.gif ismap></A>
```

You can create an internal map like the one on the previous page, and an external map file like the one shown above. The only change you need to make to the internal map to include the external one is to change the line

```
<A HREF="left.htm/map">
```

to

```
<A HREF="http://www.inbalserv.com/
navbar.map">
```

## TAKE NOTE

### ▶ NCSA AND CERN IMAGE MAPS

Image maps were first developed by two organizations; NCSA and CERN. Although they've become fairly standardized, there are minor differences between them, and even among different implementations of them. Check which standard your Web server uses before creating a server-side image map.

**CROSS-REFERENCE**

More information on Web servers is in Chapter 17.

**FIND IT ONLINE**

Tucows Software Archive has a collection of image map utilities at **http://tucows.tierranet.com/imap95.html**.

### Listing 6-3: Code for the Map File in NCSA Format

```
default ../index.htm 0, 0, 100, 460
rect ../index.htm 0, 1, 100, 65
rect ../service1.htm 0, 72, 100, 142
rect ../service2.htm 0, 146, 100, 213
rect ../training.htm 0, 219, 100, 283
rect ../profile.htm 0, 288, 100, 351
rect ../referenc.htm 0, 355, 100, 403
rect ../contact.htm 0, 407, 100, 453
```

▲ *This code defines a server-side navigation bar in NCSA format.*

### Listing 6-4: Code for the Map File in CERN Format

```
rect (0,1) (100,65) ../index.htm
rect (0,72) (100,142) ../service1.htm
rect (0,146) (100,213) ../service2.htm
rect (0,219) (100,283) ../training.htm
rect (0,288) (100,351) ../profile.htm
rect (0,355) (100,403) ../referenc.htm
rect (0,407) (100,453) ../contact.htm
default ../index.htm
```

▲ *This code defines a server-side navigation bar in CERN format.*

■ *The server-side image map looks and works just like a client-side image map, with two major differences. It works on older browsers, but it's more of a drain on server resources.*

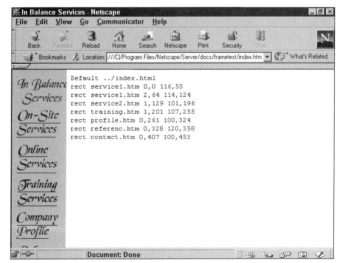

■ *The results of using a CERN image map on an NCSA-compliant Web server.*

# Personal Workbook

## Q&A

**1** What are the three graphic file formats that can be used on the Web?

_____

_____

_____

**2** When is a JPEG preferable to a GIF?

_____

_____

_____

**3** What Paint Shop Pro tools might you use to select part of an image?

_____

_____

_____

**4** How do you select foreground and background colors in Paint Shop Pro?

_____

_____

_____

**5** What are the six values that define a color?

_____

_____

_____

**6** Name three ways you can reduce the download time for an image.

_____

_____

_____

**7** What are the three shapes you can use to define a hot spot in an image map?

_____

_____

_____

**8** What are the advantages and disadvantages of client-side image maps vis-à-vis server-side image maps?

_____

_____

_____

_____

**ANSWERS: PAGE 437**

## EXTRA PRACTICE

**1** Create an image of a rectangle with a gradient fill. Make it rotate.

**2** Add text to your rectangle to make a banner.

**3** Scan an image, reduce it to 75 percent, and see how far you can reduce the color depth while keeping the image usable.

**4** Create a block image with text areas to use as a site map.

**5** Define coordinates for the text area, and use them in a client-side map.

**6** Use the same coordinates to write a server-side map.

## REAL-WORLD APPLICATIONS

✔ You've created an animated GIF and discover it stands in a rectangle of blue, which contrasts badly with your page background. You go back to the source images, change the background to transparent, and re-create the animation.

✔ You've put some photos on one of your pages, and discover that it now takes two minutes to download. You reduce the size of the photos, decrease the color depth, and compress the images, to yield a download time of 40 seconds.

✔ Your client, an art gallery owner, wants to show all her paintings for sale on the Web. You scan in the photos to a single folder, give the files meaningful names, and use Paint Shop Pro's Browse feature to create a thumbnail page.

## Visual Quiz

Identify at least 10 of the tools in the Paint Shop Pro Tool Palette.

_____

_____

_____

_____

_____

_____

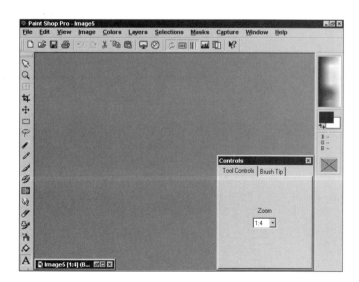

CHAPTER

**MASTER THESE SKILLS**
- ▶ Designing a Frameset
- ▶ Making Your First Frame
- ▶ Targeting Frames
- ▶ Scripting Frames
- ▶ Navigating with Frames
- ▶ Creating Ugly Frames That Work

# Building Frames

I've often felt that frames are one of the most abused features in HTML. How many times have you gone to a Web site and watched with dismay as your screen was suddenly filled with a bunch of irritating frames, all of which take forever to load? Worse, one of the frames is just a rotating advertisement banner — and it refreshes every 30 seconds, turning your computer (and your Internet connection) into someone else's advertising venue.

However, frames are the only way to display multiple HTML pages on the same screen at the same time. You could open several windows on your Web browser, but then you'd have to switch between them several times. With frames, you can design a site that allows users to access several windows of information simultaneously. Those windows of information should be related, however, or users will resent the loss of precious screen space for irrelevant material.

HTML frames have become almost ubiquitous in the world of the Web. Most of the time, they're used to control how a user navigates a site. Studies have shown that Web users don't use a navigation bar or menu unless it's in the top screen of a document. In fact, many Web users never even scroll down to the second screen, so navigation bars at the bottom of a Web page should be a redundant copy of one on the top. Or, use a frame to permanently set your navigation tools in one place on the screen.

In this chapter, I'm going to show you how to build a frameset (the file which sets up the frames), how to open a page in one frame using a hyperlink in another, and how to use scripting elements to make your frames do cool stuff. Most importantly, you'll learn how to make your frameset look good *and* be usable and effective. You'll also learn about frames that look "ugly" but enhance your site and help users navigate. Sometimes a frame needs to sacrifice perfect design for clarity and usability.

Because of their design issues, frames are an advanced HTML topic, and should be treated as such. Don't start your first Web site with a frame. Start it in basic HTML, and when it outgrows the basic site structure, redesign it as a framed site. That way, you'll already have enough Web-ready documents to justify the "real estate" loss.

# Designing a Frameset

A frameset is similar in syntax to an ordinary HTML document, but its code looks completely different from most Web pages. For starters, in HTML 4.0, frameset documents use a different <DOCTYPE> element at the head of the page. In addition, framesets don't have a <BODY> element.

Most importantly, however, framesets look different when rendered onscreen. Every framed page with a scrollbar reduces the available screen width and space, making your site look more and more cramped and uncomfortable. The fewer frames you have, the better off you'll be. And, every frame used correctly will make the site seem less cramped and more useful.

Start by deciding why you need to frame your HTML pages. Do you want to create space for an advertising banner? Put a site-wide navigation menu to one side of the screen? Compare two documents side by side?

On the next page, there are examples of several types of frame layout. Naturally, you can use or combine these styles however you like. But there are four questions you should ask yourself when you design a frameset:

1. Which frame will change the most?
2. How will users navigate this frameset?
3. What visual cues will show that it's a frame and how to use it?
4. How will this frameset help my audience use my Web site?

Remember the layout tables? Well, try to keep the same design issues in mind when you design frames. However, although frames are a part of HTML 4.0, they weren't part of HTML 3.2 (the previous specification). Thus, older browsers (and not too old, either) might not use any or all of the frame attributes described in this chapter. For example, targeting frames, frame widths, and border attributes may not work correctly in older browsers. Or, they may work, but not the way you expect them to. The most popular Web browsers, Microsoft Internet Explorer 3.0 and above and Netscape Navigator 3.0 and above, do support almost all of the frame attributes I cover in this chapter. But you should always feel free to test your pages in any older Web browser before launching your site.

## Frames and Screen Width

In typical HTML design, you only need to worry about screen width when you design large graphics and layout tables. However, frames fill the browser window, and you need to remember that when you design them.

Most users browse with their Web browser windows maximized, meaning they fill the available screen. This means typical screen resolutions are in effect. Typical screen resolutions on a PC-compatible computer are 640 480, 800 600, 1,024 768, and 1,260 1,024. These numbers represent a screen that is, for example, 640 pixels wide and 480 pixels high. Macintosh screens tend to be taller, rather than wide, although they have a much greater variety available.

**CROSS-REFERENCE**

These design issues are all similar to ones discussed in Chapter 5.

**FIND IT ONLINE**

For some fun with frames see "THE I HATE FRAMES PAGE" at **http://sac.uky.edu/~bymoor0/ hatethem/hframe.htm**.

```
<HTML>
<HEAD>
<TITLE>A 2-Column Frameset </TITLE>
<FRAMESET cols="50%,  *">

        <FRAME name="leftframe"          <FRAME name="rightframe"
              src="left.html">                 src="right.html">

   left.html                            right.html
      <HTML>                               <HTML>
      <HEAD>                               <HEAD>
      <TITLE> Left Frame</TITLE>           <TITLE> Right Frame</TITLE>
      </HEAD>                              </HEAD>
      <BODY>                               <BODY>
      <H1>The Left Frame</H1>              <H1>The Right Frame</H1>
      <HR>                                 <HR>
      </BODY></HTML>                       </BODY>
                                           </HTML>

   </FRAME>                              </FRAME>


</FRAMESET>
</HTML>
```

■ *A sample structure for a framed site.*

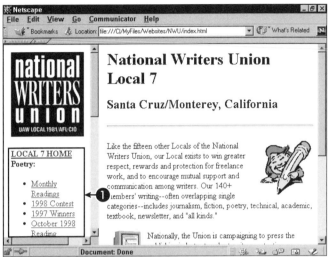

➊ *This site uses frames for navigation; the left navigation bar remains the same when you click its links.*

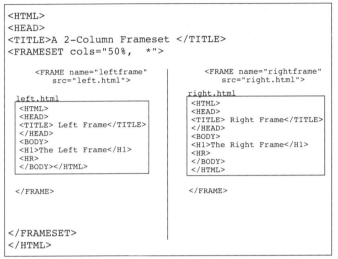

➋ *This chat room uses a frame on top to provide chat tools for users.*

➌ *The chat conversation refreshes every minute for a dynamic experience.*

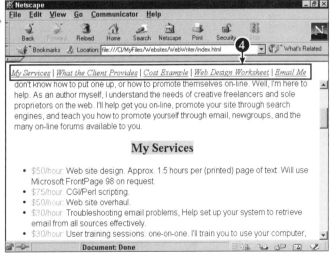

➍ *This site has a thin, unobtrusive navigation bar at the very top of the frameset.*

# Making Your First Frame

There are two main differences between a frameset and any other HTML document. The first difference is the `<DOCTYPE>`. As I've already mentioned, the `<DOCTYPE>` defines what kind of HTML document you're creating. For example, is it a simple HTML file, or does it use visual markup?

Frames have their own `<DOCTYPE>`, such as, `<!DOCTYPE HTML PUBLIC "-//W3C//DTD HTML 4.0 Frameset//EN" "http://www.w3.org/TR/REC-html40/frameset.dtd">`.. This document type declaration should be the first line of your HTML document, even before the `<HTML>` element.

Follow the `<DOCTYPE>` with your `<HTML>` element, and then the `<HEAD>` element. Include a title; this will appear at the top of the browser window when a user looks at your frameset. Don't include style sheet information; put that into the individual pages that appear in the frames.

The next major difference is the `<BODY>` element. Framesets don't have a `BODY` element, so remember not to put one in. Instead, start declaring the frameset by opening the `<FRAMESET>` element. Inside the `<FRAMESET>`, you can define the number of rows or columns inside that frame, as well as how large each row or column should be.

You can also nest `<FRAMESET>` elements, the same way you can nest tables. You can split a row into two columns, or a column into multiple rows. Nested framesets are kind of the "bread and butter" of advanced frame design.

Finally, you should always have a backup plan for Web browsers that don't support frames. The `<NOFRAME>` element goes around a normal HTML document inside the frameset document, to direct users to the correct page, or to instruct them on obtaining a newer Web browser. This is perhaps one of the most effective ways to split your Web site into two separate groups (those who have a modern browser, and those who are using an old or nonstandard browser).

## TAKE NOTE

### ▶ FRAME BORDERS

When you create a frameset, you have to decide if there will be a visible border or not, and whether or not that border may be resized by the user. Resizable borders are a good thing from the user's perspective; they can reduce the size of an unneeded navigation frame while reading an online document. On the other hand, they might take the opportunity to minimize ad banners or other important design elements on your site.

Note that shared borders must have the same border elements, or the defaults (resizable frames and a thin border) will be used.

### ▶ FLOATING FRAMES

In Internet Explorer 3.0 and above, you can "float" frames by giving them a specific height, width, and space around them. These frames will appear within the document itself, similar to a table or a graphic. The main difference is that you'll be able to change the content within the floating frame, like an embedded window or document.

## CROSS-REFERENCE

See Chapter 13 for more information on positioning HTML margins.

## FIND IT ONLINE

A basic frames tutorial is available at **http://www.geocities.com/BourbonStreet/Delta/9978/frames.htm**.

## Listing 7-1: A Simple Frameset

```
<HTML>
<HEAD><TITLE>Frames</TITLE></HEAD>    ◀—❶
<FRAMESET ROWS="20%,*">
</FRAMESET>
  ❸  ❹
</HTML>
  ❷
```

## Listing 7-3: Frame Margins and Borders

```
<HTML>
<HEAD><TITLE>Frames</TITLE></HEAD>
<FRAMESET ROWS="20%,*">
  <FRAME NAME="upper" SRC="upper.html"
❾→MARGINHEIGHT="10" SCROLLING="auto"
  FRAMEBORDER="yes">
  <FRAME NAME="bottom" SRC="bottom.html"
    MARGINHEIGHT="10" SCROLLING="auto"◀—⓫
    FRAMEBORDER="no">
</FRAMESET>
  ❿
```

❶ Begin the frameset with a standard HTML document, but without the <BODY> element.

❷ Add a <FRAMESET> element.

❸ The <FRAMESET> must include either a rows or a cols attribute.

❹ The value of these attributes should be the width or height, in pixels or percentage.

❾ Optional <FRAME> attributes include marginheight and marginwidth, which set the margins for the framed documents.

❿ Make frame borders visible or invisible with the frameborder attribute.

⓫ Set the scrolling attribute to allow an automatic scroll bar.

## Listing 7-2: Adding Frames

```
<HTML>
<HEAD><TITLE>Frames</TITLE></HEAD>
<FRAMESET ROWS="20%,*">
❺→<FRAME NAME="upper" SRC="upper.html">
  <FRAME NAME="bottom" SRC="bottom.html">
</FRAMESET>      ❻            ❼
<NOFRAMES>
Please go to the <A HREF="bottom.html">
Content Page</A> if your web browser does
not support frames.
</NOFRAMES>
</HTML>
            ❽
```

❺ Now, add a <FRAME> element.

❻ Include the src attribute, the URI of the file to display inside the frame.

❼ <FRAME> elements must have a name attribute, starting with an alphanumeric character.

❽ Use <NOFRAMES> for older Web browsers.

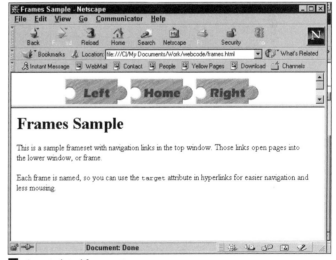

■ A completed frameset.

# Targeting Frames

Once you've created your frameset, you need some way of navigating through them. Most framesets consist of a main content frame bordered by other frames containing banners, navigation menus, and similar design elements.

But what happens when you click on a hyperlink inside a frame? Well, usually it opens the new page inside the same frame. That can make things hard to read when using a narrow navigation menu. When you click a hyperlink in a frameset, the page could open

- ▶ Inside the same frame
- ▶ Within another frame in the frameset
- ▶ In another frame within a child or parent frameset
- ▶ A new frameset over the current one (replacing whatever windows were there)
- ▶ In another frame, and forces another frame to reload or open a new page
- ▶ A new Web browser window
- ▶ In the current window, replacing the current frameset

As you can see, there are quite a few ways to manipulate your frame content through hyperlinks. By default, hyperlinks open within the same frame.

To open a hyperlink in another frame, you would use the `target` attribute: `<A HREF="sample.html" target="_top">`. However, if you want to open a frame inside a different frame in the frameset, you must first specify the `name` of each frame, and target that frame. For example, `<FRAME name="content">` would name a particular frame as "content". Clicking the hyperlink `<A HREF="info.html" target="content">` would open the Web document inside the "content" frame.

You can also target all the frames within a frameset, and all the links inside a frame, by putting the `target` attribute inside the `<FRAME>` elements. `<FRAME`

`name="navigation" target="content">` would produce a frame named "navigation", which opens all its links into the "content" frame. As you can see, there are many possibilities.

*Continued*

## TAKE NOTE

### ▶ PARENT AND CHILD FRAMES

Because framesets can be nested, some frames are "parent" frames of others. While this isn't terribly important most of the time, it becomes crucial when dealing with scripts and when you use the reserved name _parent as a target.

Suppose you had a frameset with the following code:

```
<FRAMESET cols="200,*">
  <FRAMESET rows="50%, *">
    <FRAME name="frame1"
src="frame1.html">
    <FRAME name="frame2"
src="frame2.html">
  </FRAMESET>
  <FRAME name="main" src="frame3.html">
</FRAMESET>
```

This nested frameset creates a three-frame set. The main frameset is split into two columns, and the left-hand column is split into two rows. Now, if you target the _parent from inside frame 2, it will open in the entire frame.

But if frame2.html is a frameset in itself, then targeting _parent will open the page into the parent frameset, as defined here.

## CROSS-REFERENCE
Hyperlinks are discussed in detail in Chapter 2.

## FIND IT ONLINE
http://www.newbie.net/sharky/frames/intro.htm has a five-lesson tutorial on frames.

# Frame-Naming Conflicts

At some point, you might end up with two frames with the same name. Usually, this is the result of opening one frameset into an existing frameset. HTML 4.0 has special rules on handling these kinds of conflicts. First, the browser will look inside the deepest frameset for the named frame. If no frame of that name exists, it will look in the parent frame, then the parent frameset. It will continue to work its way up until it finds a frame of that name.

If the browser doesn't find a frame of that name, it will open a new frame and give it that name.

For example, `<A HREF="content.html" target="content">` will open the content.html page into the "content" frame. But suppose there's no "content" frame? No problem. The Web browser will create a new browser window and open "content.html" into it.

## Listing 7-4: Nested Framesets

```
<HTML>
<HEAD><TITLE>Frame 2</TITLE></HEAD>
<FRAMESET ROWS="50%, *">
    <FRAME NAME="frame4" SRC="frame4.html"></FRAME>
    <FRAME NAME="frame5" SRC="frame5.html"></FRAME>
</FRAMESET>
</HTML>
```

❷ ❶

❶ Frame 2 adds frames 4 and 5 to the current frameset.

❷ Notice that each frame is still named, so hyperlinks and scripts can open in a particular frame.

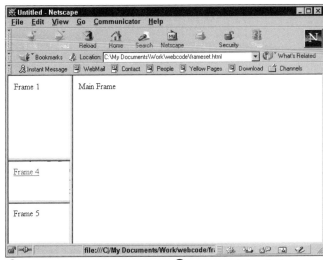

❶ frame2.html is itself a frameset, which means it adds its frames to the current frameset.

❷ The hyperlink called Frame 4 targets the _parent frame.

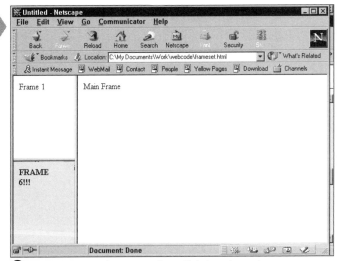

❸ When you open the Frame 4 hyperlink, it replaces the frame2.html frameset. The result is the original frameset, which is the parent of the frame2.html frameset.

# Targeting Frames

*Continued*

Frame names must begin with an alphanumeric character, not a symbol. However, a number of "reserved names" exist, which have special properties in HTML frames. The reserved names are `_blank`, `_self`, `_parent`, and `_top`. Each one of these reserved names has a special purpose in frames, and does something unique.

A hyperlink that targets `_blank` opens a page in a new, unnamed browser window. Use `_blank` frame targets when your hyperlink takes someone outside your site. For example, if you have a list of hyperlinks, the ones belonging to other people should open into new windows. Why? Well, yours isn't the only site using frames, and nothing's quite as irritating as a framed site inside the little content frame of another (framed) site. Also, you might not want to be associated as the owner of that site's content. Unfortunately, if the link opens inside your frameset, it will appear to be a part of your site — not such a great thing after all. In Netscape Navigator, `_new` is the same as `_blank`, but it's not part of the HTML standard.

The `_self` target opens the page inside the current frame. That's the default for most Web browsers; if there's no target specified, then the link opens inside the current frame. That's useful for hyperlinks inside of content frames, which you want to open more content into the frame.

When you target `_parent` frames, you're really targeting the frame in which your current frame resides.

Finally, `_top` opens the link in the current browser window, replacing the entire frameset. Think of a browser window as a box. Inside the box, you might have a frameset, and several named frames within that frameset. When you open a hyperlink into another frame, the content just gets shuffled around in the box. But when you open it into the `_top`, the entire box empties and is filled with whatever page that hyperlink led to.

## TAKE NOTE

### ▶ THE BASE TARGET

Set the default target for all the navigation hyperlinks by using a `target` attribute in the `<BASE>` element of the navigation frame document. For example, `<BASE target="content">` inside the `<HEAD>` element of a document will open all hyperlinks into the "content" frame. This is the only reliable way to set the default target for a document or a frame in HTML 4.0.

### ▶ TARGETS IN JAVASCRIPT

JavaScript and Dynamic HTML (DHTML) use frame targets and named windows when controlling Web content. JavaScript in particular can be a little tricky when you target from a frame with a base target. Depending on the Web browser, JavaScript will use the base target instead of the `target` attribute specified in the JavaScript program. You can work around this by removing the base target from your framed page.

## CROSS-REFERENCE
See Chapter 22 to develop your site's identity; frames maintain that look and feel across the site.

## FIND IT ONLINE
Another good frames tutorial can be found at **http://members.aol.com/harvillo/index.html**.

## Listing 7-5: Targeting Frames

```html
<B>A FEW FRAMES LINKS</B>
<UL>
<LI><A HREF="http://www.livesoftware.com/jrc"
  TARGET="_blank">The JavaScript Resource
  Center</A>
<LI><A HREF=
  "http://www.geocities.com/SiliconValley/
  7116/" TARGET="_blank">JavaScript Planet</A>
<LI><A HREF="javascript.html" target="_self">My
  Own JavaScript Page</A>
<LI><A HREF="frameset.html" target="_blank">A
  Sample Frameset</A>
</UL>
```

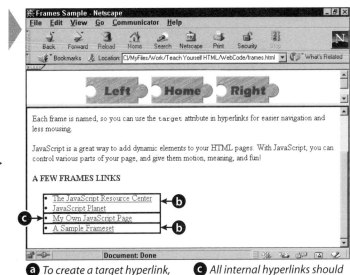

**ⓐ** To create a target hyperlink, start with a basic hyperlink.

**ⓑ** Add the target attribute: `target="_blank"` to open outside links in a new window.

**ⓒ** All internal hyperlinks should `target _self` or another frame in the frameset.

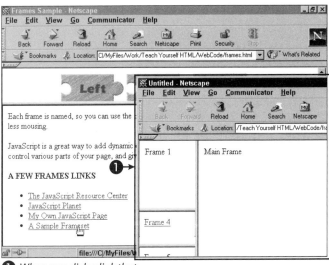

**❶** When you click a link that targets "_blank", it opens a new, unnamed browser window.

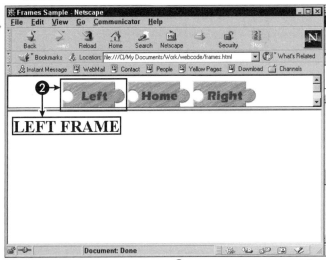

**■** The `<BASE target>` of the top frame is "bottom," the frame below it.

**❷** When a user clicks the "Left" icon, the bottom frame opens a file called "left.html."

# Scripting Frames

To script a frame, use JavaScript, VBScript, and whatever other scripting language the Web browser might recognize, all of which are discussed in detail in Chapter 18.

However, you can do some really awesome things with a scripted frame. For example (and this is the least of the many things you can do, by the way), when a user holds his or her mouse over a hyperlink or navigation button, the main content can change to reflect his or her choice, without needing to click on the hyperlink. That's useful for help menus, navigation tools, and games applications.

The first two figures on the next page show the form to create a four-frame array in JavaScript, available at FURL at **http://www.dscnet.com/furl/**. Although it doesn't look like much, the URLs were saved in a cookie, so when the user returns to the form, their URLs will automatically be inserted into the form, and their previous setup will be restored. You can use cookies to save user settings for your framesets as well.

The second example is a script I downloaded from the script author's Web site directly at **http://www.geocities.com/Paris/LeftBank/2178/**. The script creates a drop-down, folder-style directory structure for navigating lists of URLs and Web pages. It's by far one of the most useful little JavaScripts for site navigation I've seen in a long time.

If you decide to use scripts or Dynamic HTML to change your frames on the fly, you'll need to know a few things about frames. First, every frame in your page must be named. If it's not named, you won't be able to control anything inside the frame. DHTML uses the Document Object Model (DOM) as a way to use any item in a Web page in a script. Because frames are usually named anyway, they tend to be used quite a bit in DHTML. In one of the most cooperative efforts in the DHTML arena, both Netscape Navigator and Microsoft Internet Explorer call frames in the same way.

You can also control floating windows the same way you control frames. That's useful for creating scripts that use a floating remote control, pop-up advertisements, and site maps. With Dynamic HTML, you can launch stand-alone applications — such as calculators and design scripts — into a separate window, and have the results transferred directly into your Web site.

## TAKE NOTE

### ▶ ALTERNATE FRAMES INFORMATION

As in JavaScript, you should always count on the non-enabled browser hitting your site. The <NOFRAMES> element goes around any HTML markup you'd like to include as an alternative to those who go "frameless." In general, browsers that don't recognize frames will also ignore scripting languages, so as long as you include an alternate Web page in the <NOFRAMES> element, you can probably skip the <NOSCRIPT> element in your script.

**CROSS-REFERENCE**
JavaScript and other client-side scripting languages are discussed in Chapter 18.

**FIND IT ONLINE**
See the JavaScript Tip of the Week at **http://webreference.com/javascript/**.

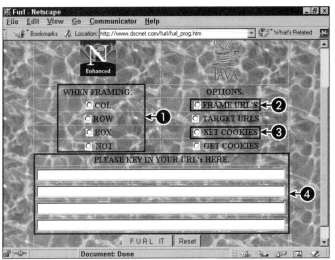

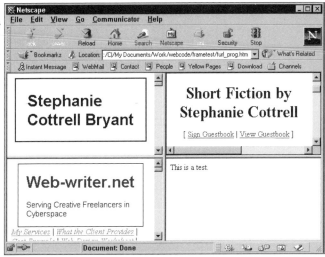

**❶** Decide how your URLs will appear.

**❷** The Frame URLs option puts all the URLs listed in the bottom boxes into the frameset.

**❸** Set Cookies to return to the same URLs later.

**❹** Put up to four absolute URLs in the bottom boxes.

■ The result of the FURL JavaScript.

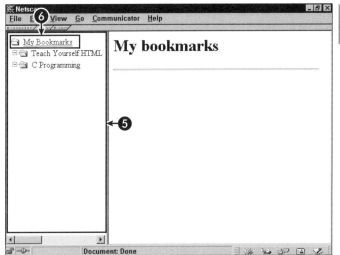

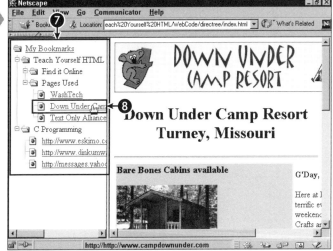

**❺** In this JavaScript-enabled site, the left-hand frame holds a Windows-like directory structure.

**❻** Click the top folder to see the directory's contents.

**❼** As you can see, the directories continue to expand.

**❽** Documents have a different icon to visually denote a Web page to open into the right-hand frame.

# Navigating with Frames

In this section, you learn how to create a frame that actually helps people navigate a Web site, from start to finish. You put together all the design elements you've learned so far, and see how to make a navigation tool that really works.

For the first example, I use an article that I wrote about one aspect of fiction writing. The article is quite long, about 10 pages when printed. So, I wanted to provide a certain amount of internal navigation. The basic structure of the document is fairly straightforward, and is shown in the Table of Contents, shown in the upper left-hand figure.

First, start by breaking the document down into smaller sections. Put bookmarks at the top of each section. Section headings are a good idea as well, to provide a visual cue for users.

In a separate Web page, make a simple list of each bookmark and its title. Some bookmarks are in subsections from the rest of the document. If you want to create graphical buttons for each section, go ahead.

Now, create the frameset. This is a pretty simple frame; I made two columns, one thinner than the other. The left-hand column will contain the navigation buttons, so I named it "navigation." The right-hand column contains the content, so it's named "content. Here's the code:

```
<FRAMESET COLS="191,*">
  <FRAME NAME="navigation"
SRC="FantasyTOC.html"
  MARGINWIDTH="0" MARGINHEIGHT="0"
SCROLLING="auto"
  FRAMEBORDER="yes">
```

```
<FRAME NAME="content"
SRC="FantasyWorld.html"
  MARGINWIDTH="10" MARGINHEIGHT="10"
  SCROLLING="auto" FRAMEBORDER="no">
</FRAMESET>
```

You could also create your navigation frame without a border. That saves about three pixels of screen width, and can be less intrusive visually. In each frame that shares the border, use `frameborder="no"`. However, for navigation bars, you should include a visual cue anyway, so a different background color might be in order, as shown in the third figure.

This technique also works for a site with multiple pages and departments. I'll show you that kind of example next.

*Continued*

## Margins and Buttons

In our example, the frame margins are set at 0, both in the frameset and in the page itself (using style sheets). However, if you set the `marginheight` or `margin-width` to something higher than 0, it will add to the margin of the elements inside the document itself.

In other words, if you find that your frame has a lot of extra whitespace (not necessarily a good thing in a navigation menu), check the margins of both the frame and the document inside it.

**CROSS-REFERENCE**

See Chapter 6 for more information on designing a graphical navigation bar.

**FIND IT ONLINE**

For suggestions on designing navigation plans, see

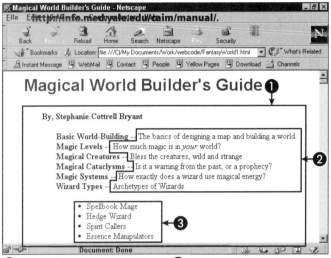

❶ The table of contents was originally a list of hyperlinks at the top of this document.

❷ Note that the list also provides a short description of each section.

❸ Because of the larger screen width, I could also include the "Wizard Types" subsections.

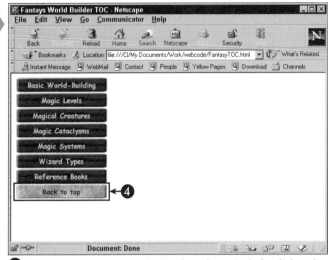

❹ When you create your navigation bar, always include a link to the home page or top of the Web document.

■ Because it's to be used in a frame, this navigation bar leaves out descriptions and subsections.

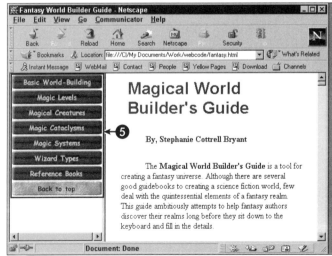

❺ The left-hand frame should be wide enough to read your links or graphics without scrolling.

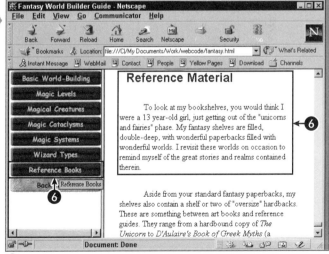

❻ When a user clicks the "Reference Books" link, the right-hand page jumps to the bibliography.

# Navigating with Frames

*Continued*

The previous example works as an introduction to frame navigation, but most sites are more complicated than that. Frames are usually needed only on sites with several topics and subtopics. Many departmentalized sites show only the top level of the site's hierarchy in their site-wide navigation schemes, and the navigation within a particular department may be less than standardized. As a result, users may find the department they're looking for but get lost in actually trying to find the information they need.

In this lesson, you'll see how to apply the same framed navigation concepts to a departmentalized site. Instead of one long document that's been broken into shorter parts, this site consists of several pages and departments, each with a specific purpose. When the users first go to the site, they see the default screen, shown in the first figure.

Now, when a user selects an item on the left-hand navigation bar, the item opens a page into the right-hand frame, the content frame. The title frame doesn't change; nothing links into it, and all it does is provide a site-wide title bar.

Suppose you go into one of these departments, such as "Chat Rooms," and there are some additional navigation buttons you'd like to use. Although adding another navigation bar on the left would look "clunky," you could do it. However, there's space to the right and at the bottom that you haven't taken advantage of.

Suppose the "Chat Rooms" link opens a page called "chat.html." That page would itself be a frameset, as shown in the third figure. When you put it inside the content frame of the original frameset, it shows up as the last figure, and you've added a separate navigation frame for an individual department of your site. Now, users in the chat area will always have a navigation tool for the subdepartment as well as the entire site. If you maintain a consistent navigation scheme across your site, your users will appreciate the ease with which they can find what they're looking for.

## Framesets within Framesets

Remember when I discussed possible conflicts in named frames? Well, here's a good example of when one might occur.

The chat frameset consists of two frames, one on top and the other on the bottom. The top frame contains the content for this part of the site, while the bottom frame holds the navigation.

If we name the content frame "content," then in theory, links from the chat navigation bar should first try to open in the frame directly above it, and then any frames named "content" in the frameset surrounding it (the parent).

In practice, however, the frame opens in the first frame to be named "content," replacing the chat frameset.

That's just another good reason to give each frame a unique and meaningful name.

**CROSS-REFERENCE**

Chapter 22 covers site-wide graphics in depth.

**FIND IT ONLINE**

For a look at a navigation system that uses frames and is very confusing, see **http://www.theglobe.com**.

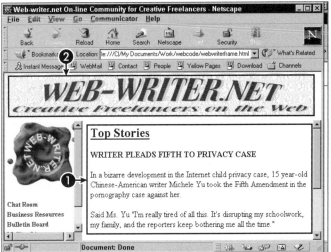

**1** In this online community frame, the main content window starts out with the day's headlines.

**2** The banner in the top frame provides an unchanging banner to help users know where they are on the Web.

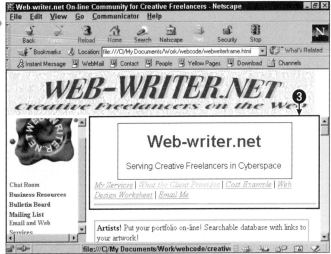

**3** When the user clicks a link in the left-hand navigation frame, it opens into the right-hand content frame.

**4** This chat room login screen uses frames to help users navigate within the chat room itself.

**5** With the chat room inside the site frame, you can see that the chat navigation links are for the chat room only.

■ The chat room navigation links "disappear" when you go to another department on the site.

# Creating Ugly Frames That Work

The next page shows a few "ugly" pages that work. That is, the pages do what they're supposed to do. Perhaps that's display advertisements, or help people navigate the site. They may not do their jobs in the most elegant manner, but they get the job done with a minimum of fuss.

The first example on the next page is a free chat room. The frames aren't overly elegant; the advertising banner at the top is especially intrusive, in my opinion. However, the frames do what they're supposed to do — help make using this chat site easy.

The second example is a page designed to put two different sides of a story side by side for comparison. The infamous Kenneth Starr report and the White House rebuttal, placed side by side so users can refer back and forth between them, and make their own decisions. This page, which I oh-so-creatively designed myself, is also a paragon of ugliness. There's no additional navigation, nor fancy buttons, bells, or special visual clues about where you are or where you're going. The left-hand column (with the Kenneth Starr report) is also too wide for the frame; notice the scroll bar at the bottom of that frame.

Finally, the "classic" example of an ugly frameset doing its job is the shopping cart. This example is a sample Web-based store. The example (a store that sells widgets) is fairly simple and straightforward. Text-based pages with simple forms and a simple navigation bar to the left allow users to add and remove items from a simple shopping cart. Online stores frequently use frames to help users navigate between product categories and the shopping cart utilities.

Creating a frameset that's "ugly but works" is different from creating one that's just plain ugly. *An ungainly frameset absolutely must serve a purpose.* For example, you might have a CGI application that really needs to have more than one screen of text available at the same time. Your FAQ page could have one frame with questions, hyperlinked to another with the answers. An online classroom might have the textbook loaded in one frame and the class discussion in another. The textbook would be harder to read in this kind of site, and a nonframed alternative site should certainly be provided in that case. But the value of being able to refer to an electronic text at the same time that you're discussing it is priceless.

## TAKE NOTE

### ADVERTISING FRAMESETS

Be wary of using frameset just for advertisements. Although ads are a valuable way to gain revenue for your Web site, they draw visitors *away* from your site. Make sure that the ads you put on your site won't turn people off with too many animations. And be extra careful about rotating banner ads in frames. They eat bandwidth and require the page to reload frequently, often interrupting the user's computer from downloading *your* pages.

**CROSS-REFERENCE**
Chapter 4 discusses common design flaws in tables; many apply to frames, too!

**FIND IT ONLINE**
Selena Sol's CGI archive is available at
**http://www.extropia.com/ products.html.**

# Ugly Frames That Don't Work

Sometimes, you run into a frameset that you think really should work, but it doesn't. Something about it makes the frame too confusing, or it takes too long to load. Usually, the same kinds of design flaws that ruin a good site also ruin a frame. These include

▶ Too many animated advertisements.

▶ Too many scroll bars: They eat screen space!

▶ Not enough visual cues: Make sure each frame is distinct.

▶ Inconsistent links: If the link goes to a chat site, call it "chat," not "chat," "discussion," and "talk."

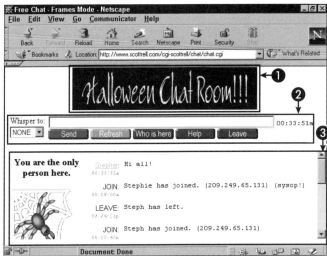

❶ The top frame contains the site header.

❷ This frame contains the chat room's toolbars and a form for submitting your chat conversation.

❸ The last frame contains the chat transcript, complete with a topic and user images.

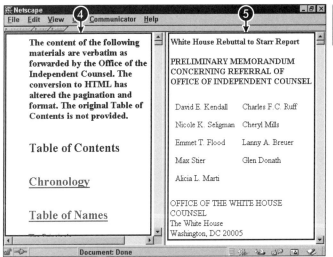

❹ The left-hand frame contains the Kenneth Starr report itself.

❺ On the right-hand frame, you can view the original White House rebuttal.

■ There's no additional navigation provided here, because each document stands alone.

■ This shopping cart Web store uses frames to navigate between products and the shopping cart utilities.

❻ The top-left frame provides a site-wide logo that does nothing but help users know where they are.

# Personal Workbook

## Q&A

**1** What's the first step in developing your frame?

_____

_____

_____

**2** What standard HTML element is not used in a frameset?

_____

_____

_____

**3** How do you create alternate text for a frameset?

_____

_____

_____

**4** What attributes are required in a <FRAME> element?

_____

_____

_____

**5** How can you adjust the frame's border and resizing ability?

_____

_____

_____

**6** What HTML element should you use to target hyperlinks in one frame to another frame?

_____

_____

_____

**7** What does the _top reserved name mean?

_____

_____

_____

**8** What happens when a hyperlink target cannot find the named frame?

_____

_____

_____

ANSWERS: PAGE 437

## EXTRA PRACTICE

① Create a standard frameset with two rows, one significantly smaller than the other.

② In the larger frameset area, put a nested, three-column frame.

③ Create four HTML documents: one horizontal (for the top), and three with a more vertical layout.

④ Create hyperlinks that target from the top frame into the first, second, and third frames.

⑤ Make the default target in your first and third frames be the second (center) frame.

⑥ Give all but the leftmost frame resizable borders and individual margins.

## REAL-WORLD APPLICATIONS

✔ Your CD inventory database has become too large for a simple Web page. You use frames and forms to make it easier to navigate.

✔ Your company home page consists of several independent departments. You use a frameset to keep the headers and footers consistent.

✔ As a law student, you need to compare a legal document with the notes you took in class. You put them side by side to quickly reference each page.

✔ Your Web site is getting a lot of traffic and attention, and you're being approached by advertisers. You put ads inside frames to keep them from cluttering your own pages.

## Visual Quiz

How was this frameset created? What design elements do you see in it? How would you design it differently?

_____

_____

_____

_____

_____

# CHAPTER 8

**MASTER THESE SKILLS**

- ▶ Identifying the Questions
- ▶ Designing the Form
- ▶ Collecting Special Information with Forms
- ▶ Using Scripts to Handle a Form
- ▶ Customizing Scripts

# Forms

Interactivity. It's the concept of being able to ask questions and receive answers, to change the way something works, to affect the world we live in.

On the World Wide Web, it's about being able to send and receive unique information through a Web browser. There are many forms of interactivity on the Internet: bulletin board systems, chat rooms, user preferences, VRML worlds, and feedback forms. In each system, you interact with other users, a graphical environment, or the Web site itself.

The most basic way to make your site interactive is through an online form. A basic form asks a question, logs the answer, and thanks the user for responding. More advanced forms may take the information provided and, in addition to logging it, send email to someone, provide user-specific content, or share the user's message with a chat room or online forum. Forms can also upload files to a Web server and help users create a unique experience for themselves.

Later, when you learn about JavaScript and Dynamic HTML, forms will be very important.

Most JavaScript and DHTML scripts use forms to create the dynamic aspects of the Web site. In some cases, JavaScript can validate the contents of a form before submitting it to a script, or even process the entire contents without ever using server resources. For the most part, those scripts convert or validate the user data, but they might also store user preferences in a set of cookies, which are stored on the user's computer and not on the Web server. With JavaScript and forms, you can create powerful applications that actually reduce the load on your Web server's resources.

This chapter teaches you how to design a basic Web form using the many types of form fields available. You'll also figure out what questions to ask, learn how to design a basic Web form, and learn about a few scripts to handle your form. I also show you how to adapt a script to your own purposes, and show you how to include hidden and password information in your forms.

# Identifying the Questions

Naturally, the first step in creating your form is figuring out what questions to ask, and what questions to require. In HTML, you can prevent a form from submitting if the required fields are not filled in. This is often used on the Web to require a name or email address on all forms.

Unfortunately, some Web sites require more information than they really need. Do you really need a user's telephone number when asking for comments on your Web site? Every piece of information you gather from someone is valuable, and Web users are becoming more and more wary of giving that data away for free. In addition, users may not know exactly who you are, or why you want this information; do you want the telephone number because you want to make a sales call, or sell the phone numbers to telemarketers, or so you can have a complete profile of all registered users?

Realistically, you should ask for and require only the information that you need for the purposes of that form. If it's not instantly obvious why you would need such information, then explain yourself. You might have fewer people filling out the form, but the ones who do will be happier about receiving that sales call. Explaining your motives also gives you a chance to explain your privacy policy; every Web site that asks for user data should have a public policy describing how and where they will use that data, and who they will authorize to use it as well.

Some common types of forms found in businesses are user feedback forms, requests for information, technical support queries, complaints, product registration, and online orders. In online communities, there are Web page authoring tools, email programs, customizable interface forms, and similar forms. In any Web site, you might also find an online contest form, which users fill out to win a prize.

## To Sell or Not to Sell?

If you collect enough customer data, you'll eventually be faced with the possibility of selling your mailing list. In some cases, you'll be approached by companies wanting to buy your list because they offer a similar or complementary product or service. In others, they just want to sell names and email addresses.

Using customer data gathered online is an ethical question that has yet to be resolved. Companies regularly sell their postal mailing lists, and the service you provide online may be worth the slight intrusion into the customer's privacy. You're not using any information that wasn't voluntarily given. But you're also not being entirely fair to the customer, who has trusted you with their personal information, and may not want to have it sold. You would be wise to offer the customer an "option out" from the mailing list when they first sign up, or you may face the possibility of alienating your customer and user base.

**CROSS-REFERENCE**

Chapter 5 has guidelines on designing for different audiences.

**FIND IT ONLINE**

Another good general style guide is at The Web Design Group: **http://www.htmlhelp.com/**.

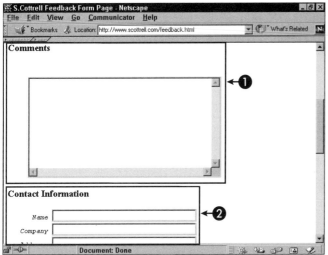

❶ A feedback form should ask for user comments.

❷ I also requested some contact information, in case I need to respond to the feedback.

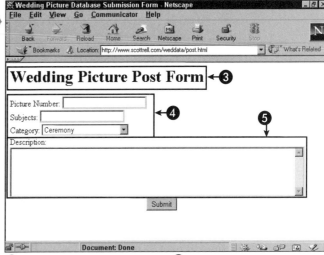

❸ This database form posts information to an online database.

❹ I request a picture ID number, the names of the subjects, and the category.

❺ Finally, a brief description will help users decide if they want to view the picture.

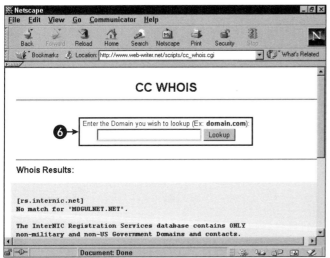

❻ This domain lookup form doesn't need any extra information; just the domain name.

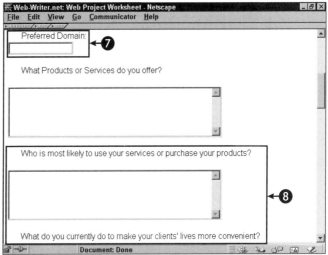

❼ This worksheet is for potential clients; by asking for a domain name, I can start registering their domain, if needed.

❽ The Web project worksheet asks about a company's commitment to their Web site, their audience, and their goals.

# Designing the Form

Once you've decided what questions to ask, and how to ask them, sit down and actually design out the form. The <FORM> element is the first element you'll need in your form. This requires three attributes: action, method, and enctype. The action refers to the URL of the CGI script that will handle the form's input, such as http://www.mydomain.com/cgi-bin/search.cgi.

The method can be "GET" or "POST." "GET" is usually used to request information, without making a permanent change to any files. "Post" is used when you want to save the form data to a file, or to somehow change a file based on information entered in the form. An example of "Get" would be a search engine; a search request doesn't add to a file or otherwise change the data on the server. "Post" could be used for registration pages, chat rooms, and online discussion forums.

Form fields must have two basic pieces of information: the name of the field, and the value. In text boxes, the value is entered by the user. In checkboxes, selection boxes, and radio buttons, the value is set in the form before the user ever fills in the fields.

Finally, the enctype is a media type used to encode the form data. The default is application/x-www-form-urlencoded, meaning the data will be submitted in a standard encoding scheme known as urlencoded. Unless you have specific instructions from the form's script, use the default encoding mechanism.

There are three basic form elements you can use for the form fields. The most complicated is called <INPUT>, and it's discussed later in this chapter. The other two are <TEXTAREA> and <SELECT>.

Use <TEXTAREA> to create a paragraph form field for your users to fill in and submit their comments, suggestions, or forum posts. <TEXTAREA> lets the user enter more than one line of text, which still must have a name (the value is whatever the user enters in the box). Required attributes include rows and cols; rows indicates the height of the box in fixed-width font rows, while cols are the number of characters wide a row will be. An option attribute is wrap, to determine the line wrapping in the field. wrap=off, the default, means the line will continue to scroll to the right. wrap=physical will wrap within the display, and enter all wrapping as displayed in the text box. Finally, wrap=virtual displays text wrapping but does not submit the text wrapping when the form data is submitted.

<SELECT> creates a drop-down box in which users may choose one or more options. An example of a drop-down box code is shown in the code at the top of the next page. In that example, the name of the selection choices is "browser," while the value is specified in the individual <OPTION> elements. <SELECT> requires a closing tag: </SELECT>.

*Continued*

## TAKE NOTE

### ▶ MULTIPLE SELECTIONS

Add the multiple attribute to a <SELECT> element for a multiselect box. Users will then be able to choose more than one item in the box, by holding down the Ctrl key while they click each choice.

**CROSS-REFERENCE**

All the form elements and attributes are given in Appendix B.

**FIND IT ONLINE**

Web Communications HTML Tutorial illustrates form design: **http://www.webcom.com/~webcom/html/tutor/forms/**.

## Listing 8-1: Drop-Down Selection Boxes

```
<P>Choose your Web Browser: <SELECT
   name="browser">
<OPTION value="nn3">Netscape Navigator 3.0
<OPTION selected value="nn4">Netscape
Navigator 4.0
<OPTION value="msie3">Microsoft Internet
Explorer 3.0
<OPTION value="msie4">Microsoft Internet
Explorer 4.0
<OPTION value="other">Text-Based or other
</SELECT>
```
ⓐ

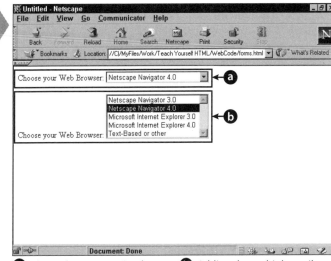

ⓐ *This code creates a simple drop-down box.*

ⓑ *Adding the multiple attribute to the <SELECT> element makes it a multiple-selection box.*

## Listing 8-2: Multiline Text Boxes

```
<FORM ACTION="/cgi-bin/script.cgi"
 METHOD="POST" ENCTYPE="application/
 x-www-form-urlencoded"><P>
Wrap is Off:<BR>
<TEXTAREA NAME="text area" COLS="50"
 ROWS="4" WRAP="OFF"></TEXTAREA><P>
Wrap is Physical:<BR>                         ⓐ
<TEXTAREA NAME="text area" COLS="50"
 ROWS="4" WRAP="PHYSICAL"></TEXTAREA><P>
Wrap is Virtual:<BR>            ⓑ
<TEXTAREA NAME="text area" COLS="50"
 ROWS="4" WRAP="Virtual"></TEXTAREA><P>
<INPUT TYPE="submit" value="Submit">
</FORM>                          ⓒ
```

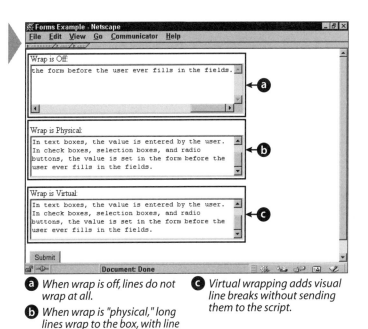

ⓐ *When wrap is off, lines do not wrap at all.*

ⓑ *When wrap is "physical," long lines wrap to the box, with line breaks being sent to the script.*

ⓒ *Virtual wrapping adds visual line breaks without sending them to the script.*

# Designing the Form
*Continued*

The <INPUT> form field element has a required attribute called `type`. Basically, `type` determines what kind of form field it is: a simple text field, radio buttons, checkboxes, or submit and reset buttons.

To create a simple text field, type `<INPUT type=text name="username" value="" size=10 maxlength=25>`. This would create a text field, 10 characters wide, which would accept up to 25 characters total. When submitted, the field's `name` would be "username" and the `value` would be whatever had been typed into the text field.

Radio buttons look like little dots which, when selected, exclude other radio buttons in the same group from being selected. Each set of radio buttons should be part of a group. For example

```
<P>Gender:<BR>
<INPUT type="Radio" name="gender" value="male"
checked> Male
<INPUT type="Radio" name="gender"
value="female"> Female
```

Although each radio button requires a separate element, they're all part of the same group because they share the same `name` — "gender" in this case. You can have more than one group of radio buttons; each group must have a unique `name`. Each button, however, has a different `value` — in this case, "male" and "female." Because male and female are mutually exclusive values, they're good choices for a radio button field. The `checked` attribute indicates that that particular radio button is selected by default.

Another "multiple-choice" <INPUT> field is called the "checkbox." The checkbox fields let users select more than one item in a group. Each checkbox field in the group has the same name, separate values, but they are not mutually exclusive. For example

```
<P>Bouquet Builder<BR>
<INPUT type="checkbox" name="flower"
value="rose"> Rose
```

```
<INPUT type="checkbox" name="flower"
value="daisy"> Daisy
<INPUT type="checkbox" name="flower"
value="iris">Iris
```

Checkboxes can also take the optional `checked` attribute. In this example, someone could build a bouquet online by checking off the flowers they want in the bouquet. These examples are all shown in the figures on the next page.

Finally, at the end of your form, there should be a way for customers to send the data to whatever `action` you specified. That's usually in the form of a button, called a Submit button, which is another `type` of <INPUT> called "Submit." The opposite `type` of button is called "Reset;" it just resets all the fields to their default values. The `value` of any button is what will be written on the button itself. Buttons do not need a `name` attribute.

```
<INPUT type="Submit" value="Send it in!">
<INPUT type="Reset" value="No, thanks.">
```

## TAKE NOTE

### ▶ TABINDEX AND NOTAB

Two more attributes available in any form element are the `tabindex` and `notab` attributes. In a form field element, `tabindex=1` will make that field the first item selected when a user presses the Tab key on their keyboard. By giving each form field a `tabindex` value, you'll help mobility impaired users navigate your form. The `notab` attribute, which does not take a value, removes that field from the tab order.

**CROSS-REFERENCE**

You can also apply scripting elements to Web forms. See Chapter 18 for more information.

**FIND IT ONLINE**

Another good forms tutorial is at **http://snowwhite.it. brighton.ac.uk/~mas/mas/courses/html/html2.html**.

## Listing 8-3
## Text Boxes and Radio Buttons

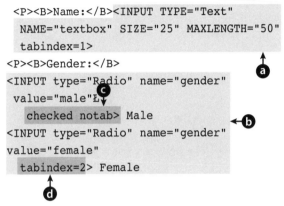

```html
<P><B>Name:</B><INPUT TYPE="Text"
 NAME="textbox" SIZE="25" MAXLENGTH="50"
 tabindex=1>
<P><B>Gender:</B>
<INPUT type="Radio" name="gender"
 value="male"
   checked notab> Male
<INPUT type="Radio" name="gender"
 value="female"
   tabindex=2> Female
```

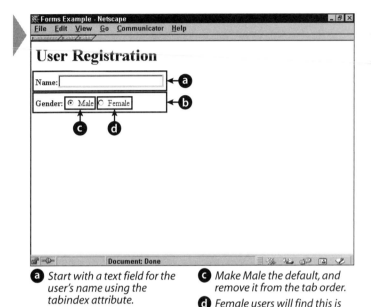

**a** Start with a text field for the user's name using the tabindex attribute.

**b** Add a form field for the user's gender; use radio buttons for mutually exclusive answers.

**c** Make Male the default, and remove it from the tab order.

**d** Female users will find this is the second item in the tab order.

## Listing 8-4: Checkboxes and Buttons

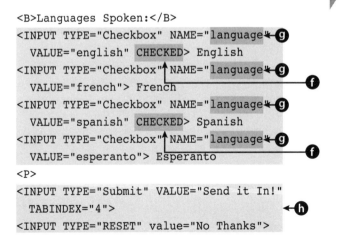

```html
<B>Languages Spoken:</B>
<INPUT TYPE="Checkbox" NAME="language"
  VALUE="english" CHECKED> English
<INPUT TYPE="Checkbox" NAME="language"
  VALUE="french"> French
<INPUT TYPE="Checkbox" NAME="language"
  VALUE="spanish" CHECKED> Spanish
<INPUT TYPE="Checkbox" NAME="language"
  VALUE="esperanto"> Esperanto
<P>
<INPUT TYPE="Submit" VALUE="Send it In!"
  TABINDEX="4">
<INPUT TYPE="RESET" value="No Thanks">
```

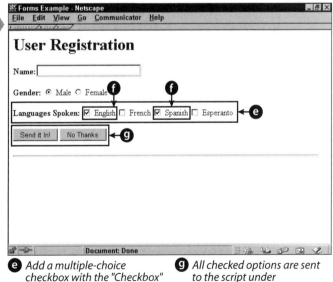

**e** Add a multiple-choice checkbox with the "Checkbox" type.

**f** Use the checked attribute to have multiple defaults.

**g** All checked options are sent to the script under "language."

**h** Create submit and reset buttons; use the value attribute to set a caption.

# Collecting Special Information with Forms

Forms have a few special fields to help you do special things. You may have been wondering how to create a password form that doesn't show the password onscreen, or how to make an image act as a submit button. In this section, I'll show you how to create a password field, hidden fields, a specialized submit button, and a file form.

First, a password form field is identical to a text field, with one major difference: the content entered is not shown onscreen and will sometimes even be scrambled before transmission. Code for a password field is

```
<B>Password:</B> <INPUT type="password"
name="password" size=10 maxlenght=15>
```

You might have seen some online forms that allow you to upload files to the Web server. Web-based email programs and certain Web server communities offer this as an alternative to FTP programs. The file form `type` only works on Netscape 2.0 and above, and Microsoft Internet Explorer 4.0 and above. The next page shows a screen shot of a page using passwords and a file upload ability:

```
<B>File to Upload:</B>
<INPUT type="file" name="upload" size=10>
```

You can also include hidden fields to the form. For example, to track which form the user filled out, or to submit the time, date, user data, or similar data with the rest of the form data:

```
<INPUT type="hidden" name="sourceform"
value="feedback.html">
```

Finally, you can change the way submit buttons work in your form. First, you can give a submit button a `name`. Ordinarily, when you create a submission button, you give it a `value`, which appears on the button itself. That

`value` is not sent with the rest of the form data; it has no `name`, and is therefore not significant.

However, if you specify a `name` for your submission button, the `name` and `value` of the submission button will be sent. While you might not care all that much about this feature, it can come in handy, especially when using JavaScript and other scripting languages to manipulate your form.

You can also change the submit form to use an image. This is often done to enhance the "look and feel" of a Web site. However, since reset buttons cannot use images this way, use this `<INPUT>` `type` on optional forms only, not on registration, online ordering, or user authentication forms — or have a text-based reset button as well.

```
<INPUT type="image"
src="images/sendbutton.gif"

alt="Send it in!">
```

## TAKE NOTE

### THE BUTTON ELEMENT

In HTML 4.0, there's a replacement element for the standard submit and reset buttons. It's the `<BUTTON>` element. It can have `name`, `value`, and `type` attributes, although only the `type` is actually required. The `<BUTTON>` element's `type` can be `reset`, `submit`, or `button`, which creates a scriptable push button. Any `<BUTTON>` element can use an image instead of a gray button, and they can contain content the same way any other block or inline element can contain content.

---

## CROSS-REFERENCE
Chapter 22 shows how to make image buttons.

## FIND IT ONLINE
Harvillo's Finest HTML Help (**http://members.aol.com/harvillo/index.html**) includes a neat Forms tutorial.

## Listing 8-5: Passwords and Upload Fields

```
<B>UserName:</B>
<INPUT TYPE="Text" NAME="username"
  SIZE="20" MAXLENGTH="20"><BR>
<B>Password:</B>
<INPUT TYPE="Password" NAME="pword"
  SIZE="20" MAXLENGTH="20"><BR>
<B>File to Upload:</B>
<INPUT TYPE="File" NAME="uploadfile"
  SIZE="20" MAXLENGTH="100"><BR>
```

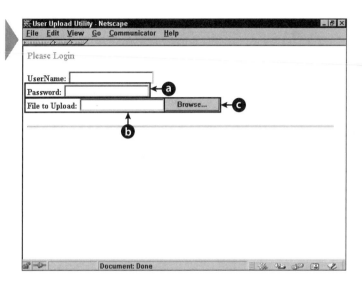

**ⓐ** The second field in this form is a password field; data entered here is not displayed onscreen.

**ⓑ** Create a file form field with `<INPUT type="file">`. This form field uploads files from the user's hard drive.

**ⓒ** A "Browse" button is automatically created by this type of field.

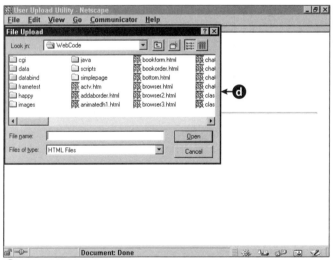

**ⓓ** Clicking the "Browse" button opens a Windows Explorer-style file browser.

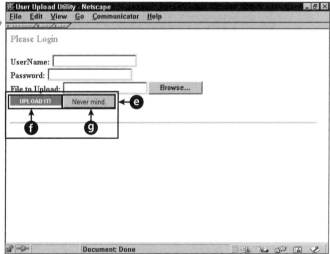

**ⓔ** Change the submit button to an image using the "Image" `type`.

**ⓕ** Use a `border` attribute to eliminate the blue hyperlink border in the Image button.

**ⓖ** The `value` for the reset button is also used as its caption.

# Using Scripts to Handle a Form

As you design your form, you need to specify an `action` in the `<FORM>` element. That `action` determines where the form data is sent, and what happens to it then.

There are basically two ways to handle form data. The easiest `action` to use is a mailto: form: `<FORM action="mailto:steph@scottrell.com" method="POST">`. That sends the form's data to my email address, although the data is nearly illegible because of the URL encoding type. An example of form data as sent to an email address is shown in the upper-left figure.

When you receive this gobbledygook of data, how do you make sense of it? This is what "urlencoding" means. It means additional characters are inserted into the data by the Web browser before it gets passed to the server (or sent by email). You need some way to unencode data like this. One way is to install a program on your home computer and "feed" the form data into it. If you know how to install software, then you know how to do that — you just install the program, and copy and paste the mailed form data into the program. An example of such a program, called FormKeeper, is shown in the upper-right figure.

The other way to handle form data is to use a CGI script. CGI scripts can do just about anything with form data, depending on how much work you want the server to do. You can decode and send the form results to an email address, add the data to a database or file, search for information, change a user profile (changes data in an existing file), create or upload a file, delete a file, or otherwise manipulate the data however you like.

Several free CGI scripts are available on the Internet, and these usually come with instructions for downloading and installing the programs. However, the usability of these scripts may vary; they're usually written by an individual, and given away as a promotion of their own scripting services, or as a gift to the Internet community. Some scripts are only free for nonprofit and educational institutions; all others must pay. In general, a good CGI script will cost around $100–300, depending on what it does and how well. Compared with the cost of a custom CGI programmer, that's relatively inexpensive for a commercially available script.

## .PL AND .CGI SCRIPTS

A file extension such as .pl or .cgi (or .html, for that matter) is simply a way to tell the operating system what type of file it is. Web servers often use those extensions when deciding how to handle files requested by a browser.

Although most servers will recognize .pl files (Perl files) as CGI programs, they might require a .cgi extension instead. You can change a .pl extension to .cgi, but it only works the other way around if the CGI is written in Perl. Just remember to change any references to the .pl file in the scripts or in your Web pages!

**CROSS-REFERENCE**

The CD-ROM includes FormPAL, a software program that creates forms.

**FIND IT ONLINE**

"CGI Made Really Easy" (**http://www.jmarshall. com/easy/cgi/**) is a good place to learn how to write a basic CGI script.

### Listing 8-6: URLencoded Data

```
required-to=scottrell%40scottrell.com
&success=http%3A%2F%2Fscottrell.com
%2Fconfirm.html
&subject=Feedback+From+Web+Site&Comments
=Good+Work%21
&Name=John+Bryant
&Company=User+Friendly+Computer+Products
&Address1=125+Main+St.&Address2
=Anytown&State=CA
&ZIP=95000&Telephone=%28408%29+XXX-XXXX
&FAX=%28408%29+XXX-
XXXX&E-mail=john%40domain.net
&MailingList=No&Contact=On
```

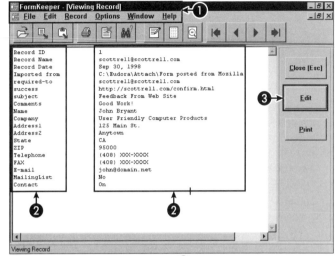

**1** FormKeeper is a program you install on your own computer, then import form results to it.

**2** Each form field is shown on the left; its value is to the right.

**3** You can even edit and change data, and save all the form results in a database.

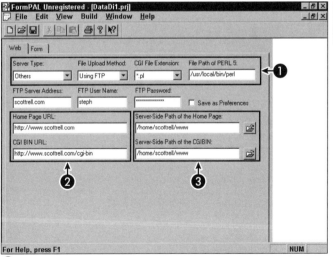

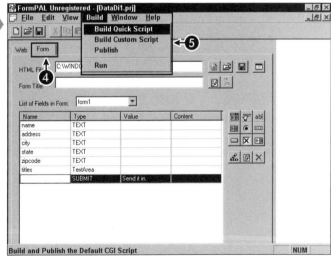

**1** Set up FormPAL by filling in your server type, upload method, and whether you use .pl or .cgi for scripts.

**2** Your home page and CGI BIN

URLs are what you'd type in the Web browser to get to those directories.

**3** The server-side paths are the actual locations on the Web server.

**4** FormPAL helps you design Web forms using a fill-in form and an external HTML editor.

**5** Click Build ➪ Build Quick Script to create and publish a quick form script for this form.

# Customizing Scripts

One of the hardest parts of using CGI scripts is that every Web server is different. Because CGI scripts are really little programs, they must be compatible with the operating system, Web server, and sometimes even hardware.

For this part of the chapter, I'm going to use a freely available form mailer script, called `formmail.cgi`. This script is available under the GNU license — basically, anyone can use it, modify it, and redistribute it, provided they also distribute the source code, and do it all for free. Other free scripts may have restrictions on how much you may change, or how you can use it (commercial vs. noncommercial use, for example).

To install the script on a UNIX computer, download `formmail.pl` (sometimes called `form-mail.pl` or `formmail.cgi`) and its documentation from the Internet into your Web server. At the UNIX prompt, type `which perl` to get the location of the Perl programming language. This will usually be something like `/usr/local/bin/perl`. Make sure the first line of the `formmail.pl` script matches the location. It should read: `#!/usr/local/bin/perl`

The following variables need to be modified in the Perl program before it will run. First, the mail program on your Web server. It's probably sendmail, so type `which sendmail` at the prompt. Put the results in the `mailprog` variable: `$mailprog = '/usr/lib/sendmail';`

Finally, change the recipient's address and referer's variable. The recipient address could be: `$recipient = 'youremail@domain.com';` You can also change this to a variable that will be read from the form when it's submitted. For example, you could have a hidden field in your form that would include the recipient's email address or even a text field if you want to be able to send the form results to anyone. To change the recipient to a results field, replace its value with `$FORM{'recipient'}`, and be sure to create a form field with a name and value for the recipient.

`$recipient = $FORM{'recipient'}`

In some versions of formmail, there's also a referer's variable, to prevent the form from being used outside your domain. Change this variable to your domain name (such as `scottrell.com`).

## Perl and Other CGI Languages

CGI runs programs, which are always written in individual programming languages. Most CGI scripts are written in Perl, C, or C++, although any programming language that's installed on the server can be used. C and C++ are popular choices because many programmers are familiar with those languages. Unfortunately, C programs must be compiled into something the computer can understand.

Perl is a very popular language for CGIs because it's small, fast, and easy to learn and use. Unlike C, Perl scripts do not need to be compiled to run. Finally, a large number of Perl libraries have been created to specifically deal with CGI applications.

**CROSS-REFERENCE**

Chapter 19 has more information on CGI scripting and developing your own scripts.

**FIND IT ONLINE**

See HTML forms and CGI scripts at
**http://www.speakeasy.org/~cgires/**.

## Listing 8-7: Formmail.pl

```
# $mailprog defines the location of your
# sendmail program on your UNIX
# system.
$mailprog = '/usr/sbin/sendmail'; ◄─ⓐ
# @referers allows forms to be located only #
on servers which are defined
# in this field. This fixes a security hole #
in the last version which allowed anyone # on
any server to use your FormMail
# script.
@referers = ('scottrell.com'); ◄─ⓐ
```

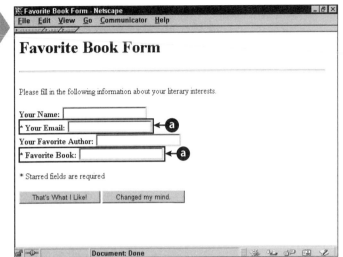

ⓐ *To customize* formmail.pl, *change the* $mailprog *and* @referers *variables. You can change other variables, too, or just use the form to send those variables through.*

## Listing 8-8: Putting the HTML and the CGI Together

```
                                                                          ─ⓑ
<FORM ACTION="cgi-bin/formmail.pl" METHOD="POST">
<INPUT TYPE="Hidden" NAME="recipient" VALUE="steph@scottrell.com">
<INPUT TYPE="Hidden" NAME="subject" VALUE="Favorite Book Form Results">  ◄─ⓒ
<INPUT TYPE="Hidden" NAME="required" VALUE="email,book">
<P><B>Your Name:</B> <INPUT TYPE="Text" NAME="realname" SIZE="20" MAXLENGTH="25">   ─ⓓ
<BR><B>* Your Email:</B> <INPUT TYPE="Text" NAME="email" SIZE="20" MAXLENGTH="25">
<BR><B>Your Favorite Author:</B> <INPUT TYPE="Text" NAME="author" SIZE="20" MAXLENGTH="30">
<BR><B>* Favorite Book:</B> <INPUT TYPE="Text" NAME="book" SIZE="20" MAXLENGTH="30">
<P>* Starred fields are required
<P>
<INPUT TYPE="Submit" VALUE="That's What I Like!">  <INPUT TYPE="RESET" value="Changed my
mind.">
</FORM>
```

ⓑ *In your HTML form, use the path to* formmail.pl *as the action.*

ⓒ *Include hidden fields for* recipient *(required by the* formmail.pl *script),* subject, *and* required.

ⓓ *The value for the hidden field named* required *should be other field names in the form.*

# Personal Workbook

## Q&A

**1** What kinds of information would you need in a user feedback form?

_____

_____

_____

**2** How do you protect your customers' data, and let them know you're protecting them?

_____

_____

_____

**3** What does the `action` attribute do? What's its value?

_____

_____

_____

**4** What's the difference between "`POST`" and "`GET`"?

_____

_____

_____

**5** How do you create a drop-down box?

_____

_____

_____

**6** How do you create a text box? What are the types of text wrapping available?

_____

_____

_____

**7** Name two ways to gather multiple-choice data.

_____

_____

_____

**8** How do you use a graphic instead of a submit button?

_____

_____

_____

**ANSWERS: PAGE 438**

## EXTRA PRACTICE

1. Write down three questions you'd ask someone applying for a job working for you (could be anything from a CEO position to yard work).

2. Create a Web form that asks for the applicant's name and phone number, and the answers to those three questions. Include a hidden field with the form's filename.

3. Create a submit button (image or otherwise) and a reset button for the form.

4. Upload the form and any scripts needed to your Web space.

5. Test the form by filling it in and submitting the data.

6. Use either a CGI script or form handling program to have the form results emailed to you.

## REAL-WORLD APPLICATIONS

✔ You've designed a Web site for musicians. By installing a CGI script and some forms, users at your site can contribute to an online calendar of gigs.

✔ Your company sells its products online. You design an order form to handle the order submissions, and use secure Web space to store the results for later retrieval.

✔ Your Aunt Martha never got the hang of email, but her local library has Web access. You put up an easy form for her to email you when she wants to chat.

✔ Better still, you install a program that lets Aunt Martha chat with you in real time, post messages to a discussion board with you, and check her own email from the Web!

## Visual Quiz

How would you have designed this form differently? What form elements are obvious? How did the designer create each visible field?

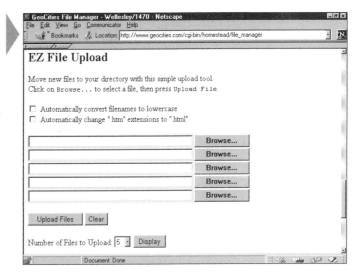

_____

_____

_____

_____

_____

**CHAPTER 9**

# Advanced Tags

If your Web site uses only the basic and intermediate HTML described up to this point, it can still be very serviceable and highly attractive to your visitors. Users will be able to enjoy your site and find information on it. With enough skill and time, you can have a very well designed site with attractive graphics, clear presentation, and general eye appeal. However, you may well want and need more from your Web site.

If you want to incorporate multimedia, mathematics, and special characters into your Web pages, or if you want to achieve certain special effects, you have to go beyond the basics that have been covered so far.

You can achieve certain special effects on your Web page by using browser-specific elements. In many cases, designing your page to match the capabilities of a specific browser is not a good idea as your audience will likely be limited, but in certain circumstances, doing so can be useful.

Making a Web site that stands out from the rest is no easy task. First, you need great content, and great design certainly helps as well. Next, you need to find a way to let the public know your page exists. Learn how to use HTML 4's indexing elements to give Web surfers a boost when they're looking for your site and don't even know it exists.

How about mathematical applications? Whether you're a teacher who wants to put a trigonometry module online, or a nuclear chemist sharing your findings with your colleagues, you will undoubtedly appreciate HTML 4's new mathematical capabilities.

Maybe studying and reading different languages happens to be your forte. If so, you will likely appreciate how HTML 4 has built-in capabilities to handle various character sets that match the characters used in other languages.

Attractive, catchy multimedia can dramatically increase the appeal of a site, particularly if you are attempting to attract a media-savvy audience. Many software vendors offer free plug-ins so that you can offer multimedia in a variety of formats. Learn how to incorporate various multimedia files, and use these plug-ins in your Web pages.

# Using Elements from Other Programs

HTML 4 is a sophisticated markup language that has been specifically designed so that it is not browser-dependent. However, you may wish to use elements that are not part of the HTML 4.0 specification, and which are browser-specific. With various versions of their respective browsers, Netscape and Microsoft introduced different elements that could each achieve intriguing special effects. You may prefer to stay away from these elements if you want all users to be able to enjoy your site equally, without needing specific versions of specific browsers. In many instances, users will not lose much or any content if their browsers can't support these elements — they will just miss out on the special effects.

The <MARQUEE> element was introduced in Microsoft Internet Explorer 2.0. It is still a quick, easy way to get animation on your Web page, but it is not ideal because only IE users will be able to see it. With the <MARQUEE> element, a scrolling message appears across the top of your Web page. You can control the text, the color, the spacing, and the speed of animation.

## MARQUEE Attributes

The <MARQUEE> element has a number of attributes to control the speed, direction, and behavior of the marquee.

- ▶ bgcolor: The background color is set in the same way you would choose a background color for the body of the Web page.

- ▶ height, width: You can set the height and width of the box that appears around the marquee in pixels.

- ▶ loop: Setting the value of loop to −1 or infinite means that the marquee element will scroll continuously. Setting the value of loop to the number n means that the marquee element will scroll n times.

- ▶ scrolldelay: Setting the value of scrolldelay to n means that the marquee will pause n milliseconds between each step of the animation.

- ▶ scrollamount: Setting the value of scroll amount to n means that the marquee will jump n pixels between each step of the animation.

- ▶ behavior: Setting behavior to alternate means that the text will first appear on the left of the screen, move to the right, and then start over again on the left. Setting behavior to slide means that the text will scroll across the screen, right to left, only once (whether you have a loop set or not). Setting behavior to scroll means that the text in the marquee moves from one side to the other and then disappears.

- ▶ direction: This attribute only applies if you have set behavior=scroll. Set direction equal to right if you want the text to move from left to right, and set direction equal to left if you want the text to move from right to left.

*Continued*

**CROSS-REFERENCE**
Chapter 10 has more information on using Internet Explorer.

**FIND IT ONLINE**
Microsoft's free SiteBuilder Network (**http://www.microsoft.com/sitebuilder/**) has information on the company's proprietary tags.

## Listing 9-1: A MARQUEE Element —ⓐ

```
<MARQUEE BGCOLOR=red HEIGHT=40 ◀—ⓑ
  WIDTH=200 LOOP=INFINITE SCROLLDELAY=5>
Breaking News! Man clones dog!
</MARQUEE> ◀—ⓐ  ⓒ
```

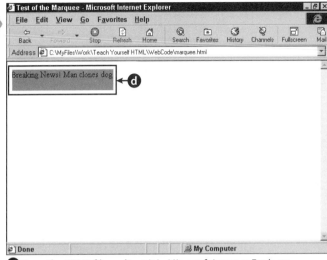

ⓐ Add the <MARQUEE> element and its attributes to your Web page.

ⓑ Decide on your marquee's attributes. How high, how wide, what color, and how should it scroll?

ⓒ loop=infinite means the marquee will repeat.

ⓓ Save the HTML file and test it in Microsoft Internet Explorer.

ⓔ If you test it in another browser, all you will see is the plain text.

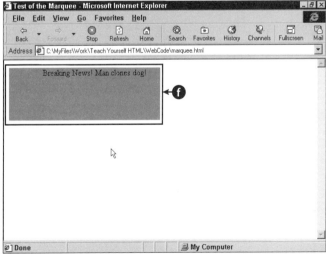

ⓕ An example of a taller, thinner marquee. The text still only scrolls horizontally.

# Using Elements from Other Programs *Continued*

Two nifty elements developed by Netscape are `<LAYER>` and `<MULTICOL>`. But neither element has become part of the HTML 4.0 specification, and Microsoft has decided not to support them. Thus, using these elements will limit your audience.

The `<MULTICOL>` element can be used to set up columns of text. Although somewhat more convenient for setting up newspaper columns than tables, more users will be able to see the text properly if you do set up the text as a table. You can also use style sheets to achieve the columnar effect.

`<LAYER>` elements are used to place objects such as images, embedded multimedia files, and text on top of each other. These effects can now be achieved with style sheets and JavaScript, and since style sheets and scripting languages are supported by HTML 4.0, using the `<LAYER>` element is discouraged.

The `<BGSOUND>` element causes selected background music to be played when a user visits the Web page, but it only works for Microsoft Internet Explorer. If you do decide to use a background sound, place it at the beginning of the `<BODY>` element so that it will begin to load before anything else on the page does. Supported file formats include WAV, which is a Windows sound format; MIDI, which is a synthesized musical format; and AU, a sound format created by Sun Microsystems.

`<BGSOUND SRC="soundfile.wav" LOOP=n>`

Setting `loop` to `-1` or `INFINITE` results in the file being played over and over, while setting `loop` to n causes the file to be played n times.

Both Netscape and Internet Explorer users can achieve a similar effect by using the versatile `<META>` element. This element must be placed inside the `<HEAD>` element:

`<META HTTP-EQUIV=REFRESH CONTENT="n; URL="http://www.somesoundsite.com/pathname/soundfile.mid">`

The n value determines how many seconds it will take for the user's browser to begin loading the file.

A more considerate method, if less sophisticated, is to link a sound file to a graphic. The picture will display in the Web page, and the sound will play if the user clicks on the picture.

`<A HREF="pathname/soundfile.mid"><IMG SRC="picture.gif" ALT="MIDI File"></A>`

## TAKE NOTE

### ▶ AUDIO FILE FORMATS

MIDI files are generally the smallest sound files that you can use in a Web site. MIDI files are often no more than about 10K, whereas WAV files of a shorter length may be about 500K. WAV files are not recommended unless you know your Web site visitors have very fast connections.

**CROSS-REFERENCE**

Refer to Chapter 5 for tips on adding extra features like background sound to your site.

**FIND IT ONLINE**

Check out **http://www.midi.com** for a comprehensive list of MIDI resources.

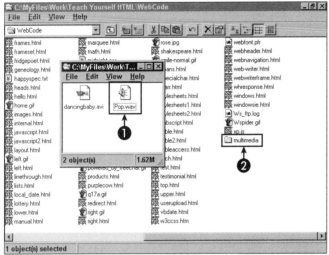

① Find a public-domain music file to add to your site.

② Copy the file into a suitable directory, depending on how you want to structure your files. You may want to make a separate directory for sounds.

## Listing 9-2: Using <META> for Multimedia

```
<HEAD>
<META HTTP-EQUIV=REFRESH ◄①
  CONTENT="10; URL=mybonnie.mid">
<TITLE>My Bonnie Lies Over the Ocean</TITLE>
</HEAD>
```

① This file will begin playing in the background 10 seconds after the page begins to load.

■ When you upload your files to your Web server, be sure the sound file is placed in the right directory.

## Listing 9-3: An Embedded File

```
<BODY>                                    ①
<EMBED SRC="pop.wav" ALIGN="CENTER" BORDER="0"
  HEIGHT=50 WIDTH=50 ALT="Double-click to
  hear the sound!">                    ◄②
<NOEMBED>POP.AU</NOEMBED>
</EMBED>
<H1>An Embedded File</H1>
<EMBED SRC="dancingbaby.avi">
</EMBED>
</BODY>
```

① To embed an object such as an audio file, use the height and width attributes to make an object icon appear on the page.

② Embedded objects often need to be double-clicked in order to run correctly.

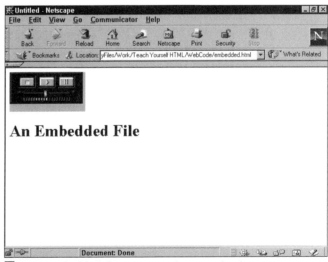

■ Some embedded objects may use browser plug-ins to open the file.

# Indexing Your Site

Do you want people to be able to find your site? Of course. But just how are people going to find your site among the tens of millions of Web pages out there? The <META> element provides one aspect of a solution to this problem. If you want your site to stand out from the great mass of mediocrity available on the Web, you have to organize and index your work on the Web.

HTML now supports the <META> element, which has several standard attributes. The attributes for <META> are customizable — you can create and use whatever ones you wish. In practice, you probably would have little use for creating your own <META> element attributes, but browser companies have included several ways to make special use of the <META> element. As you've seen, the <META> element can be used to play background sound files.

You can also use <META> tags to index your site. Many search engines give special weight to the text contained in the <TITLE> and heading (<H1> - <H6>) elements. Choose headings carefully, and make them as descriptive as possible so the index listing will reflect the topics you cover in the page. Remember that headings are a structural element, not a visual one.

Next, use <META> elements to describe the content of your Web pages. You can use the <META> element to add keywords to your Web page that do not appear in the body or the title of your page. Search engines look at keywords in the <META> tag, as well as the content of your pages, when they index and categorize Web pages. If you have a Web site that deals with the restoration of old violins, and you add the keyword "Stradivarius" to your site, people who search for "Stradivarius" will find your site, even if you do not include the term visibly on your page. You want people who search for closely related terms to find your site, even if you don't use those terms in your text.

```
<META name="keywords" content="Stradivarius,
Stradivari, old musical instruments,
restoring, fiddle, antique musical
instruments">
```

Similarly, if you are creating a frames page, it will have no content except for a little bit of code and the URLs that link to the pages. Use <META> tags to help users find the frames page as an entry point to your overall Web site.

## Search-Engine Considerations

Different search engines have different requirements and specifications as to how the <META> elements should be constructed. Check out your favorite search engine to look for detailed instructions about the specific way it indexes your site.

**CROSS-REFERENCE**

Refer to Chapter 1 to learn how to organize your site with heading tags.

**FIND IT ONLINE**

See AltaVista's indexing help:
http://altavista.digital.com/av/content/addurl_meta.htm.

### JUDICIOUS USE OF META TAGS

Please do not try to "load the dice," so to speak, by overusing <META> tags. Don't try to increase your hit counts by using irrelevant terms. For example, if your site is about gold mining, putting "Bill Clinton" in your <META> tag content does not help interested users find your site, and users will be irritated rather than pleased.

### USING META TAGS FOR SITE DESCRIPTION

You can also use the <META> element to add a description of your site. Some search engines index this description, and use it when displaying the URL for a site. If you include a <META> element as in the following example, the actual content of your page will not be displayed when you find your site on certain search engines, but the content description will be.

```
<META  name="description"
content="Violin Restoration in the
Pacific Northwest">
```

As with other <META> elements, this <META> tag must be placed in the <META> of a document.

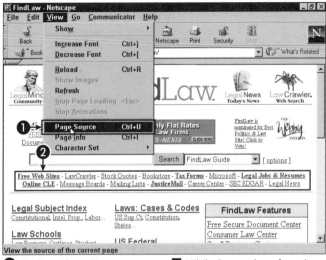

**①** FindLaw (**http://www.findlaw.com**) provides a large collection of legal resources.

**②** View FindLaw's keywords in the <META> element by clicking View ➪ Page Source.

■ While the number of words and phrases is very large, the choices are reasonable for a legal site.

**Listing 9-4:  FindLaw <META> Keywords**

```
<meta name="keywords" content="law, lawyer,
  lawyers, legal, law and lawyers, Law,
  Lawyers, Legal, law and economics,
  employment, FCC, GATT, NAFTA,
  administrative, admiralty, antitrust,
  arbitration, attorney, attorney client
  privilege, attorneys, banking,
  bankruptcy, barrister, business law,
  California law, supreme court, 9th
  circuit, circuit, circuit court, district
  court, cases, civil litigation defense,
  civil rights, commercial, communications,
  congress, constitutional, consumer,
  public interest organizations, consumer,
  commercial, code, case law, class
  actions,copyright, corporate, court">
```

▲ Here are just some of the <META> keywords on FindLaw's Web site.

# Using <META> Tags for Internet Content Selection

The <META> elements can be used to provide your site with a rating. If you use a standardized ratings system, Web surfers will be able to tell if your site is acceptable before they actually click on it. Increasingly, parents and teachers are concerned about children gaining access to a site that is inappropriate. Internet Explorer supports a ratings system for which you can choose settings in the browser options, but Netscape does not. However, you can also buy proprietary software for both browsers that blocks unrated sites and those with particular set ratings.

Many Web users, particularly those outside of North America, use proxy servers to browse the Web. This often means that users are not getting the latest news about a subject, since they may be reading an older version of a page. If you have a site that is updated frequently, you will probably want to set expiration dates for your pages.

You can use the <META> element to help the user's browser know when a page should be reloaded. Add the following code to the <HEAD> element of your Web page:

```
<META HTTP-EQUIV = "Expires" CONTENT = "Tue,
20 Oct 1998 23:00: GMT">
```

When a user's browser attempts to load this page from a proxy server or from a user's cache, it will look at the current date. If the time is later than that shown in the <META> element, the user's browser will reload the page directly from the Web site rather than relying on the cache. Of course, not all users will have browsers that do this, but most probably will.

HTML 4 provides many features that are not implemented by the most common browsers. However, you may still want to use them to aid you in indexing your site. The <LINK> element provides a way for you to organize your site, and may in time (when more browsers support it) help users navigate your site. The <LINK> element has been fully described by the World Wide Web Consortium in its HTML 4.0 specification, but unfortunately the most commonly recognized browsers ignore it. However, you may want to use the <LINK> element on your Web pages even though there is little support for the <LINK> element at this point. You can specify precise details of how various pages relate to each other. For example, you can specify whether a page is a table of contents, or a glossary. Although it won't help most of your Web users, using the LINK element can be a handy way to keep your pages organized.

**CROSS-REFERENCE**

Chapter 14 shows how HTML is a structural markup language and why organization really matters.

**FIND IT ONLINE**

Learn how the element is implemented at http://www.htmlhelp.com/reference/html40/head/link.html.

## Listing 9-5: An Expiration <META>

```
<HEAD>
<META HTTP-EQUIV="Expires" CONTENT-"Tue, 20
Oct 1999 23:00: GMT">
<TITLE>Breaking News</TITLE>
</HEAD>
```
❶

## Listing 9-7: <META> Keywords

```
<HEAD>
<META NAME="keywords" CONTENT="current
  news, stock market, economics, economy,
  developing countries, politics,
  president, premier, prime minister">
<TITLE>Breaking News</TITLE>
</HEAD>
```
❸

❶ *Add a <META> element to the <HEAD> so that the page will reload if the time is after 23:00 Greenwich mean time on October 20, 1999*

❸ *Add keywords with the <META> element.*

## Listing 9-6: <META> Descriptions

```
<HEAD>
<META NAME="description" CONTENT="Breaking News
  about Asia, Africa, North and South
  America, and Europe">
<TITLE>Breaking News</TITLE>
</HEAD>
```
❷

❷ *Add a site description with the <META> element. The description should be something other than just the title.*

■ *None of the <META> elements appear onscreen.*

# Using Special Characters and Character Sets

I f you are using English, and only English, when you create your Web pages, you can generally avoid the question of character sets. The default will usually be sufficient, and you don't have to think about it. However, what if you want to do a page in French, or Russian, or Hebrew, or Chinese? HTML has improved to handle this task as well. Even if you just want to add a foreign word or two to your Web page, you may need to know how to use special characters and character sets.

English-language Web pages, and most European-language Web pages, use the ISO-8859-1 character set. The Microsoft Web pages (and those of many other sites) use this text at the top of the source:

```
<META HTTP-EQUIV="Content-Type"
content="text/html; charset=iso-8859-1">
```

This indicates that the content type is HTML, and the character set used is ISO-8859-1. Not all browsers will necessarily respect this usage, but it is helpful for those that do. If your Web page uses a different character set, you could substitute another value for the `charset` attribute.

Most of the time, the characters you need for your Web pages are easily accessible from your keyboard. However, some symbols are used in HTML markup, such as the less-than and greater-than signs, which surround HTML tags. The less-than sign (<) can be represented by `&lt;` and the greater-than symbol by `&gt;` Some characters, like `&copy` for the copyright symbol and `&trade` for trademarks, are not officially part of HTML 4.0, and are not supported by most browsers.

That goes for everything; while HTML 4.0 supports these character entities, your users may be using browser versions that are not up-to-date. If most of your users are using older browsers, you can use GIF images as substitutes for special symbols.

The Unicode character set is the ultimate answer to HTML coding in different languages. This is a character set with over 25,000 different characters, and it is meant to be able to represent all of the world's languages. For more information about Unicode, refer to **http://www.unicode.org/**.

## TAKE NOTE

### INTERNATIONALIZATION IN HTML

Internationalization and Localization are two different terms, with two different perspectives. Internationalization refers to the process of making a product (in this case Web technology, a Web page or a Web site) available to users in other languages, and other cultures. In HTML 4.0, internationalization efforts have focused on finding ways to accommodate right-to-left languages like Hebrew and Arabic, and character-based languages like Chinese and Japanese.

Localization refers to the process of taking a product or technology and adapting it to a specific local market (often this market consists of users who work in a specific language or dialect).

### SHORTCUT
You can copy and paste special characters from another program as long as they use the same character set.

### FIND IT ONLINE
For Macintosh charsets, visit **http://ppewww.ph.gla.ac.uk/~flavell/iso8859/iso8859-mac.html**.

## BiDirectional Override

The <BDO> element (BiDirectional Override) is used to specify the directionality of text on a screen. Thus, it is useful for Web pages written in languages such as Hebrew or Arabic that do not use Western-style left-to-right text. At this point, the major browsers do not support it.

For more information about the <BDO> element, refer to **http://www.w3.org/TR/REC-html40/struct/dirlang.html#edef-BDO**.

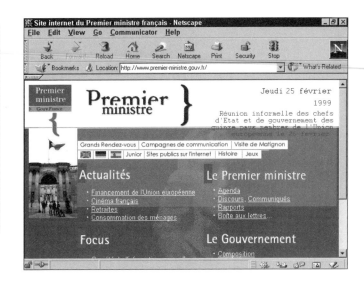

### Listing 9-8: Special Character Codes

```
<P>
    If you want to write a <B>resum&eacute;</B>
    in HTML, be sure to use <B>&lt;META&gt;</B>
    elements to help employers find your
site.</P>
<P>
    <B>&copy;</B> 1998 Stephanie Bryant</P>
```

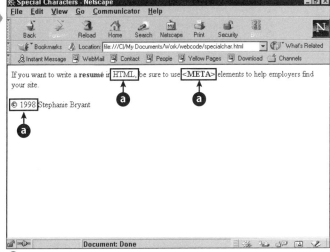

ⓐ *Use special character codes for special words, like résumé, <META>, (c)1998.*

# Displaying Mathematical Notation

The World Wide Web was started back in 1991 to facilitate the transfer of information among physicists. Despite the Web's origins, mathematical and scientific notation has not been well supported by previous versions of HTML. However, HTML 4 includes some very sophisticated methods to attractively and functionally display mathematical equations. In addition, various auxiliary programs offer various ways to display math on the Web.

The simplest way of displaying math on the Web is still sometimes the best, if not the most attractive. You can use text characters to represent mathematical equations. Simple algebraic expressions can be expressed reasonably well with simple HTML. For example, you might write $y = x + 5$, and enclose it with `<CODE>` element. The `<CODE>` element ensures that the equation will be displayed in a monospaced font:

```
<CODE> y = x + 5 </CODE>
```

However, text-based mathematics is unattractive if you have complicated fractions or want to use more advanced mathematical operands.

Another option is to create GIFs or JPGs of the mathematical equations and fit them into the Web page as you would other graphics. You can use a mathematical editor like Microsoft Word's Equation Editor or a program like MathType to create the images. See the figure on the facing page to see how this can look.

Using separate graphic files is a quick and simple solution, but the images cannot easily be saved with the Web page, and the equations cannot be cut and pasted. In addition, it can be a great deal of work to create individual GIFs for each equation if you have a mathematically intensive subject. The appearance can also be variable, depending on the background color you specify in your Web page, or the background color shown by the user.

Various Web experts, mathematicians, scientists, and other interested parties have been working on developing a solution that incorporates mathematical notation into HTML. This is a complicated problem, given that the goal is to develop a structural markup language rather than a page description language. HTML 4.0 provides a very good solution, however, in the form of Math ML, a mathematical markup language, which has been developed from XML. Unfortunately, very few Web browsers currently support Math ML.

## TAKE NOTE

### MATH PLUG-INS AND MATH ML

Perhaps in the future major browsers will support Math ML. Until that happens, however, plug-ins have been created to provide support for this markup language. Math ML is straightforward, although it is, by necessity, complex in order to be able to represent the entirety of modern mathematics. However, editors have been developed so that you can create mathematical equations in a simple, easy-to-use interface, have the editor convert your work, and let the plug-in render the equations without you having to worry about it. In theory, you can code directly in Math ML, just as you can with HTML, but most users will likely find they prefer to use an editor.

## CROSS-REFERENCE

Refer to Chapter 3 for discussion of the `<SUB>` and `<SUP>` elements.

## FIND IT ONLINE

Checkout EzMath, available at **http://www.w3.org/People/Raggett/EzMath/**.

**Displaying Mathematical Notation**

## Listing 9-9: Simple Ways to Include Math Symbols

```
<P>
   Try creating these equations with SUB and
   SUP, using extended characters:
<P>
   x<SUP>2</SUP> + y<SUP>2</SUP>
   &lt; x<SUP>3</SUP> + y<SUP>3</SUP>
<P>
<HR>
4 log<SUB>10</SUB>x = 10000
<P>
This figure was created as a graphic:
   <IMG SRC="q17a.gif">
```

**❶** There are two simple ways to incorporate mathematics into your site: simple text and graphics.

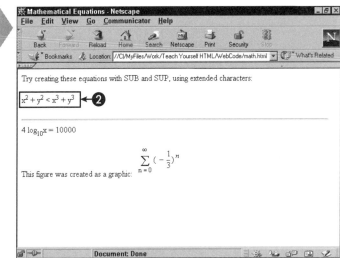

**❷** Try creating the equations shown using the `<SUB>` and `<SUP>` elements.

## Listing 9-10: MathML Example

```
<reln>
  <eq/>
  <apply>
    <fn>
      <ci>f</ci>
    </fn>
    <ci>x</ci>
  </apply>
<!- insert rest of equation here ->
</reln>
```

▲ An example of the MathML code for the equation shown in the figure to the right.

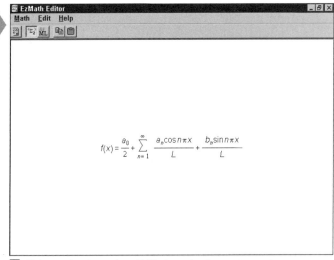

■ Using a plug-in, such as EzMath, makes it easy to create mathematical equations using MathML.

# Using Plug-ins and Multimedia

Suppose you want to use Shockwave animations, or add sound and video to your pages. Maybe you want to show an egg hatching in slow motion, instead of just providing still pictures and text, or provide a corporate video that a prospective client can view with a click of the mouse. You can put a sound clip from your latest musical efforts online, or a MIDI version of a Four Seasons song. If you want to incorporate multimedia into your site, you do not necessarily have to be the one to create the multimedia files yourself. You can use public-domain files (just check to make sure they really are!), or hire someone to make them for you.

One very popular plug-in is Adobe Acrobat Reader, which allows users to read and print documents on the Web that have been formatted for printing. Users can access government legal forms, corporate brochures, and other information. If the appearance of the information you want to present is very important, consider presenting the information as Adobe Acrobat files.

Another popular plug-in is Shockwave, produced by Macromedia to allow users to view sophisticated animations and movies created with Macromedia's Director program. Shockwave is one of the leading multimedia plug-ins available.

Here are a few of the kinds of sights and sounds you might want your user to experience when visiting your site:

- ▶ **Music:** RealAudio, MIDI, WAV
- ▶ **Movies:** MPEG, AVI
- ▶ **Animations:** Animated GIFs, Shockwave, Java applets
- ▶ **Virtual Worlds:** VRML

One factor that can be intimidating to novice Web page builders is actually producing multimedia files. However, computer hardware like video capture boards have become considerably cheaper. Buying a system that records you speaking into a microphone has become increasingly inexpensive as well. You can hire someone to create the files for you and link them to your Web site yourself.

Have you ever been at a Web site, and although your hands were off the keyboard and off the mouse, the Web page still sailed away to a new site? There are two ways for this to happen: either the author used a specially designed <META> tag, or the server was configured to redirect the Web surfer to a new site.

Use a <META> redirect when you have switched servers or set up alternate pages. You can also use <META> if you want to make an interesting slide show with one screen appearing after the other, with a set period of time between slides.

*Continued*

## TAKE NOTE

### ▶ ALTERNATIVES TO CLIENT PULL

Some users find the use of the <META> element annoying. You should provide a hyperlink alternative for users whose browser does not support <META>. If you're using <META> tags to redirect to a new site, also provide the address to which it is moving.

**CROSS-REFERENCE**
You can also redirect Web visitors to another page through a server-side CGI script. Refer to Chapter 19.

**FIND IT ONLINE**
Find more plug-ins for your Web browser at the Plug In Plaza (**http://browserwatch.internet.com/plug-in.html**).

## Listing 9-11: A <META> Redirect

```
<HTML>
<HEAD>
<META HTTP-EQUIV=Refresh
  CONTENT="10; URL=newpage.htm">      ➊
<TITLE>Testing Redirects</TITLE>
</HEAD>
<BODY>
This is the old page, going to the new.
<P>
Or, you can just click this link:
<A HREF="newpage.htm">newpage.htm</A>
</BODY>
</HTML>
```

➊ *Create a* <META> *element to redirect between the current page and the* newpage.htm.

➋ content="10 *means to wait 10 seconds before redirecting the user's browser.*

➌ URL=newpage.htm *tells the Web browser what URL to go to.*

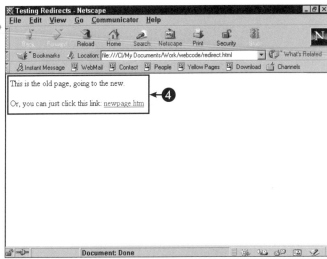

➍ *Test the redirection in your browser by loading* oldpage.htm.

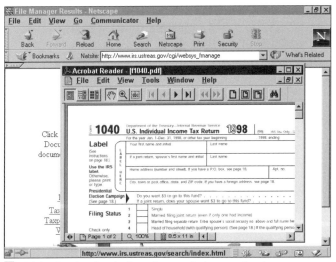

■ *Adobe Acrobat Reader launches as a helper application to open PDF files from the Web.*

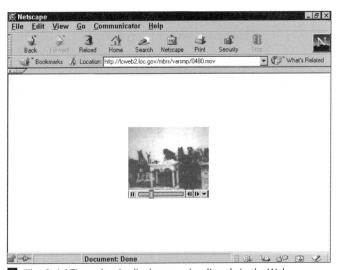

■ *The QuickTime plug-in displays movies directly in the Web browser.*

# Using Plug-ins and Multimedia

*Continued*

The <EMBED> and <OBJECT> elements described next are very complex and highly customizable. <EMBED> is unsupported by HTML 4.0, but <OBJECT> is now a part of the specification.

The <NOEMBED> element is useful for those browsers that do not recognize <EMBED>, since it can be used to provide alternative information. Its function is similar to that of the alt attribute used with the <IMG> element. Netscape 2.0 and later will not render any of the text between the <NOEMBED></NOEMBED> tags. Other browsers will ignore both the <EMBED> and the <NOEM-BED> elements, and just display the information between them as they would any other text.

Here's an example:

```
<EMBED SRC="movie.mpeg".><NOEMBED>Your browser
cannot access this file. Please read this <A
HREF="transcript.txt">
transcript</A> instead.</NOEMBED>
```

As part of the new HTML specification, the <OBJECT> element will eventually handle all instances of nontext content in the Web environment. For example, simple images, movies, and Java applets can all be displayed with the aid of the <OBJECT> element.

The <OBJECT> element is highly versatile. Just as you can use alt text with the <IMG> element to create a text alternative for those users who cannot see images, you can use the <OBJECT> element to create various alternatives for users who cannot view the multimedia you may have in mind. One user may see text, another user may see a still image, and yet another may see a fully featured high-quality video. ActiveX controls can also be embedded in Web pages with the <OBJECT> element.

The World Wide Web Consortium has put forward a specification called the Document Object Model. Currently, <OBJECT> is included in the HTML 4.0 specification, but with time the concept will become more encompassing.

You can use the <OBJECT> and <EMBED> elements together so that all applicable versions of Internet Explorer and Netscape will be able to view the file.

## TAKE NOTE

### ► CROSS-BROWSER COMPATIBILITY

Multimedia can radically improve the Web-browsing experience for many of the visitors to your Web site. However, there are sure to be some who lack the computer capabilities to take advantage of multimedia. If you want to make sure the content of your site is accessible to all users, you will have to make arrangements for those users who lack multimedia capability. If users are required to obtain a plug-in to view certain sections of your site, there is a good chance they won't bother. If you have a business site, make sure they can obtain the information they need in a quick, low-tech fashion. Then, the maximum number of people can enjoy your site!

## CROSS-REFERENCE

The <OBJECT> element can embed Java applets in Web pages. See Chapter 18.

## FIND IT ONLINE

To learn more about Shockwave, see
**http://www.macromedia.com/shockwave**.

## Helper Applications

Helper applications are similar to plug-ins; however, they do not run within the browser itself, but as a separate program. As the Web has matured, plug-ins have become increasingly more popular than helper apps, because they keep all of the action within the browser window. In addition, plug-ins are configured so that they install by themselves, whereas helper applications require some tinkering by the user.

**Listing 9-12:** `<OBJECT>` **Elements**

```
<!- Microsoft Internet Explorer (version 3.0
or later) uses the OBJECT element, and
Netscape 4 supports both OBJECT and EMBED ->
<OBJECT CLASSID="clsid:numericID"
  CODEBASE="URL "
  WIDTH=width HEIGHT=height ID="IDname">
<PARAM NAME="SRC" VALUE="filename.dcr">
<PARAM NAME="BGCOLOR" VALUE="backgroundcolor">
<PARAM NAME="PALETTE" VALUE="background">
>
<!- Netscape 2.0 and 3.0 uses the EMBED
element ->
        <EMBED WIDTH=width HEIGHT=height
SRC="filename.dcr"
        BGCOLOR="backgroundcolor"
PLUGINSPAGE="http://www.macromedia.com/shockwa
ve/download/"
        Start="true" ALT="Shockwave">
<!- Users with browsers that don't support
either OBJECT or EMBED will see the text
inside the NOEMBED element ->
<NOEMBED> If you don't have Shockwave, you can
<A HREF="http://www.macromedia.com
/shockwave/download/">get it here</A> if you
want to view this colorful animation.
        </NOEMBED>
        </OBJECT>
<!- The OBJECT and NOEMBED elements have end
element, but the EMBED element does not. ->
```

▲ *Your browser may not use* OBJECT *or* EMBED *elements, depending on the version.*

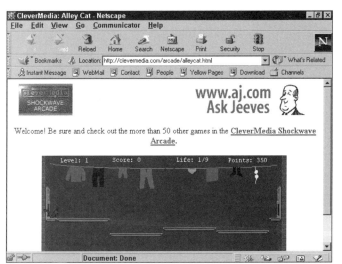

■ *You can see an example of a Shockwave file embedded with this type of code at the Web page shown in the figure.*

# Personal Workbook

## Q&A

**1** What are three uses for the  element?

_____

_____

_____

**2** When and why do you need special character entities?

_____

_____

_____

**3** Name three ways to incorporate sound files into your Web page.

_____

_____

_____

**4** Name two popular plug-in programs.

_____

_____

**5** Name three ways to incorporate mathematical notation into your Web page.

_____

_____

_____

**6** Name at least one possible disadvantage to incorporating multimedia into your site, and how to overcome it.

_____

_____

_____

**7** What is internationalization, and what is localization? How do they differ?

_____

_____

_____

**8** How do you automatically redirect a user from one Web page to another?

_____

_____

_____

ANSWERS: PAGE 439

## EXTRA PRACTICE

**1** Download an ActiveX control from **http://www.activex.com** and incorporate it into your Web page with the `<OBJECT>` element.

**2** Create an `<OBJECT>` so that multimedia-enabled users will see a movie.

**3** Now make it so that users with only graphical capabilities will see an animated GIF, and text-only browsers will see descriptive text.

**4** Create a direct hyperlink to a video on CNN's **http://cnn.com/video_vault/.**

**5** Show the HTML code for your multimedia object onscreen using `<CODE>` elements, `&lt;`, and other special characters.

## REAL-WORLD APPLICATIONS

✔ You've designed a Web site about elephants and you want people who enter the word "pachyderms" into a search engine to be able to find your site.

✔ You want to provide a graph of elephant mortality statistics. This graph will be a Java applet for those users who have systems that support that.

✔ You want to provide an algebraic equation that involves exponents to calculate incremental growth in an elephant population in your Web site.

✔ You want a loud sound file of elephants thumping in the background on your Web page. What are the pros and cons?

## Visual Quiz

Try creating a `<META>` element with keywords for the site shown in the figure using standard `<META>` tags. Then, check the site on the Web and view the actual keywords used.

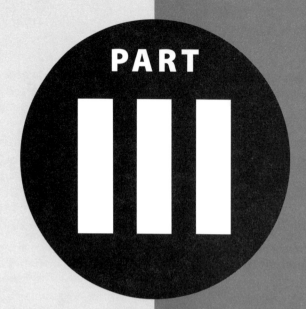

# PART

# III

# Web Tools

In this part, you learn about the two major Web browsers and how to use them. Skip these chapters if you're already familiar with Web browsers, but they provide useful information if you think you've only scratched the surface of what your browser can do. You also learn about the many Web development tools.

As you develop your Web site and learn more about HTML, you'll probably find a lot of software that does what you want. From HTML authoring tools to HTML validation, there are hundreds of available programs and packages. Chapter 12, "Web Tools," discusses HTML editors in particular, but it also touches on graphic editing tools, link verification tools, and HTML validators. Finally, you learn a bit about scripting tools for both server-side and client-side scripts.

By the time you're done with this part, you'll know what tools are available and how to choose one to do the job.

CHAPTER **10**

MASTER
THESE
SKILLS

▶ **Installing Internet Explorer**
▶ **Using Internet Explorer**
▶ **Setting Internet Options**
▶ **Using Internet Channels**
▶ **Using the Favorites List**
▶ **Examining the Active Desktop**
▶ **Exploring Mail and News**
▶ **Checking Out the "Cool and Drool" List**

# Microsoft Internet Explorer

In this chapter, you'll learn about the most widely distributed commercial Web browser, Microsoft Internet Explorer (or IE for short). You'll learn how to install and upgrade it, how to use it for the basics, and how to access other Internet resources with it. There's also an IE 4 "Cool and Drool" list; a comparison of what's good and bad about IE 4, entirely subject to my opinion, based on my experience.

IE is the Web browser included with Windows 95 and Windows 98. If you're using Windows 98, IE is already part of the operating system. If you're still on Windows 95, then you have the option to install higher versions and upgrades.

Market competition between Microsoft and the other leading Web browser manufacturer, Netscape, has caused what's termed the "browser wars." The "browser wars" are basically attempts by Microsoft and Netscape to outdo each other in software features. Through this competition, Web developers have gained frames, tables, JPEGs, image maps, JavaScript, style sheets, ActiveX, Dynamic HTML, and similar one-time cutting-edge technologies. In other words, the "browser wars" have helped push Web technology farther than it would have gone without competition.

By the time this book actually goes to press, Internet Explorer 5.0 will probably be the current version of Internet Explorer. Internet Explorer 5 supports a simpler form of Dynamic HTML, one that is supposedly easier to use for nongeeky Web developers. Limitations of CSS positions were reduced, the `currentStyle` object was introduced to make it easier to script style sheets, and you can use more than one class on an element. Also, IE 5 introduces something called fixed layout tables, which supposedly make it easier to control page layout and column widths with tables.

Internet Explorer 5 is also the first widely available Web browser to support XML, the eXtensible Markup Language. XML is a superset of HTML, and probably the next big thing in Web development. XML is a developing standard, so Internet Explorer won't be the only Web browser to support it. But it is one of the first to do so in a graphical environment, which makes Microsoft one of the early adopters of this exciting new technology. XML is also discussed in depth in Chapter 14.

# Installing Internet Explorer

Microsoft Internet Explorer 5.0 has an unorthodox method of installation. In fact, you may not need to install it at all. IE is "part of the operating system" in Windows 98, and ships with later versions of Windows 95.

However, you might be using a Macintosh, UNIX, or an older Windows computer without IE. If you want to install IE, you'll need to download the installer, at **http://www. lmicrosoft.com/windows/ie/download/.** Although the Web site claims that you can download and install Internet Explorer, you're really only downloading the installation program (about .4MB). Save the installer to your hard drive. (Hint: I keep a special folder on my hard drive just for downloaded programs and files.)

When you install Internet Explorer, most of the installation is automated. You really only have to read the instructions and click the OK button. However, there are a few options you should know about, especially when it comes to installing Active Desktop.

If you have Windows 98, Internet Explorer is preinstalled, and you can skip ahead to the next lesson.

## TAKE NOTE

▶ **ACTIVE DESKTOP INSTALLATION**

When you go to download the product, you'll be asked if you'd like to install the Active Desktop. Active Desktop basically integrates the Internet Explorer browser with your operating system. You'll use IE when you browse your file directories, and your entire Windows desktop will be replaced by Active channels. Active Desktop cannot be removed, so be sure to read the section on Active Desktop before you install it!

▶ **DESKTOP UPDATE INSTALLER**

You can, however, install the Desktop Update from Microsoft. After you install IE, go to the Add/Remove Programs control panel and select Microsoft Internet Explorer. At the Microsoft Internet Explorer Component Site, you can download and install any component you may have wanted, including the Desktop Update (a version of Active Desktop that can be uninstalled in Windows 95 and Windows NT). Follow the instructions to automatically download and install IE component programs.

**CROSS-REFERENCE**

The CD-ROM has Internet Explorer on it if you don't want to wait for the download.

**FIND IT ONLINE**

Go to Microsoft's Web site (**http://www. microsoft.com**) to download Internet Explorer 5.0, updates, and other information.

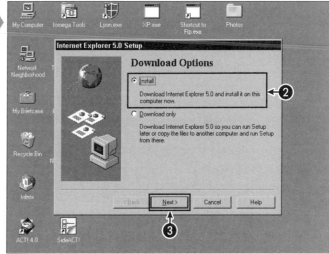

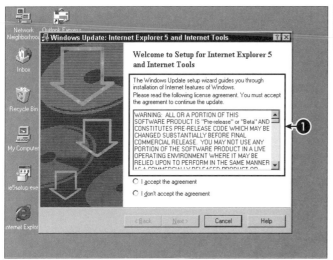

**1** Double-click the installation program and agree to the license agreement to install the software.

**2** Decide if you want to just download the program or install it right away.

**3** Click Next to continue.
■ IE takes over half an hour to download using ISDN.

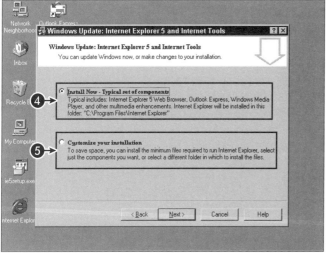

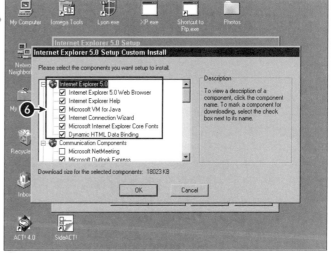

■ The Installation Options are Typical or Customizable.

**4** Standard Installation adds mail and news readers, and multimedia.

**5** Choose Customizable to select.

**6** You can choose to install individual components in Internet Explorer.

# Using Internet Explorer

To start Internet Explorer, double-click the big blue "E" on your desktop, or browse to the Internet Explorer group on your Start Menu. The first time you start IE, you'll go to Microsoft's site. You don't have to enter any information if you don't want to, and you won't return to that page the next time the browser starts.

The menus available in Internet Explorer are File, Edit, View, Go, Favorites, and Help. There are also shortcut buttons on the toolbar, and an address window for the URL.

To follow a hyperlink, place your mouse button over the link. It should turn into a hand, with the pointer finger up. Click once with the left mouse button to follow the link. Click once with the right mouse button to see some optional ways to follow or save the target page.

IE also offers a file browsing feature, in which you can access all your hard drive documents from your Web browser. In Windows 98, this has replaced the Windows 95 Windows Explorer.

Make sure you have the standard toolbars showing. There should be a toolbar with some standard navigation buttons, an address bar, and the status bar (at the bottom of the window). You can change the toolbar settings in the View ⇨ Toolbars menu.

For Web designers, an important part of using Internet Explorer is viewing the source code of Web files. Viewing the HTML source has several advantages. If a page isn't showing up correctly, you might find a syntax error by viewing the original source code. In Internet Explorer, the View ⇨ Source feature shows you the source code in Notepad, which lets you edit the HTML, save it to your hard drive, and upload it or view it later.

You can also browse Internet Explorer in the "full screen" mode by selecting View ⇨ Full Screen. Browsing IE in full screen mode removes the standard toolbars, leaving you with just the button bar. It also prevents you from switching between programs quickly with the standard Windows Alt+Tab keyboard shortcut. However, if you're surfing content-heavy sites, or will be reading onscreen text, this is a handy way to use all available screen "real estate."

## TAKE NOTE

### ▶ MULTIMEDIA IN INTERNET EXPLORER

Many sites have sound, video, and other multimedia files embedded into them. Older Web browsers required plug-ins to handle these multimedia files. Internet Explorer has built-in multimedia programs, so you can listen to music while surfing the Web, watch embedded video files online, and enjoy the full multimedia capabilities of the Internet.

### ▶ URLS

Microsoft Internet Explorer automatically fills in URLs when you enter them, by adding **http://www.** to the front, and **.com** to the end. So, you can type **yahoo** to go directly to **http://www.yahoo.com.** This also works for .gov, .edu, and similar top-level domains.

**SHORTCUT**
Press F11 to switch to Full Screen View and back again.

**FIND IT ONLINE**
IEWorld (**http://www.clubwin.com/clubie/ieworld/**), an online magazine, offers tips, articles, and information on Internet Explorer.

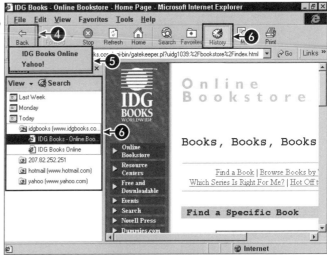

**1** To follow a hyperlink, click it. Hyperlinks are often shown in blue, underlined text.

**2** You can also enter the URL directly into the address bar.

**3** Or, you can select File ⇨ Open and type in the URL or browse to a local file.

**4** Click the Back or Forward buttons to move between pages you've already visited.

**5** Click to the right of the Back or Forward buttons for a drop-down list of sites.

**6** The History button opens the History panel, which lists files you've visited recently.

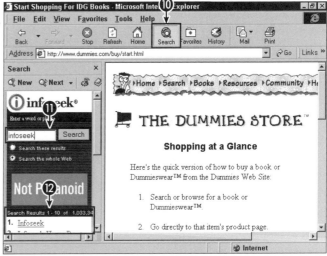

**7** The Home button takes you to your home page.

**8** Stop immediately stops the page and all graphics from loading into your browser.

**9** Refresh requests the document from the server again, and reloads it even if it hasn't changed.

**10** Click the Search button to open the Search panel.

■ Choose from five major search engine sites.

**11** Enter a keyword to search, or browse by selecting a category.

**12** Search results are in the Search panel, but their hyperlinks are in the main frame.

# Setting Internet Options

The Internet Options are user preferences that help control the behavior of your Web browser. By changing them, you alter how IE will look when you surf the Web, and what information it stores about you.

There are six tabs in the Internet Options window: General, Security, Content, Connection, Programs, and Advanced. Most of the changes you'll need to make are in General, Content, and Connection.

In the General tab, you can change the home page location, set up your disk cache and set up or clear the document history. You can also alter the colors, fonts, languages, and accessibility options used in browsing the Web. These options are shown on the next page.

The Security tab lets you change security "zones," as well as security levels for those zones. You can customize your security zones with the Custom button. Custom security lets you decide what technologies you want to let run on your computer: ActiveX, Java, scripting, downloading, user authentication, and miscellaneous features such as unencrypted forms, software channels and installation, and drag-and-drop files. Remember that Internet Explorer can also be used to browse the hard drive; that flexibility makes it easy for dangerous programs to end up on your hard drive by accident. Some of these security features protect you from malicious programs and scripts.

The Connection tab lets you set your networking options. You can use the Connection Wizard to help figure out your networking options, or you can configure it yourself. If you connect to the Internet from a dial-up connection (usually at home), select the "Connect to the Internet using a modem" option.

If you connect to the Internet through a permanent connection, such as an office network, select "Connect to the Internet using a local area network." If you're behind a firewall, select the proxy server and ask your network administrator how to set it up.

*Continued*

## Overriding Design Elements

In the General tab, you can choose to override the Web designer's font, color, and even style sheet choices by clicking the Accessibility button. If you override the fonts or colors, then the designer's graphics will be less attractive, and certain design features may be lost in translation. That's fine — if you don't want a designer's features in *your* Web browser, you don't have to have them.

Beware of using your own style sheet, however. Unless you've spent an extensive amount of time developing a style sheet that you really like, let the designer apply his or her own. Any elements not defined in your style sheet will be defined by the designer — with potentially disastrous results!

**CROSS-REFERENCE**

See Chapter 20 for more security information.

**FIND IT ONLINE**

See **http://www.icomnet.com/~jcarley/index1.htm** to set up the browser, Outlook Express, and Active Desktop.

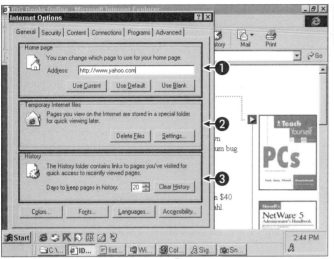

**1** In the General tab, type in the URL for your preferred home page.

**2** You can manage the temporary Internet files (also called a cache) from here.

**3** Finally, change your History settings (or delete your history) here.

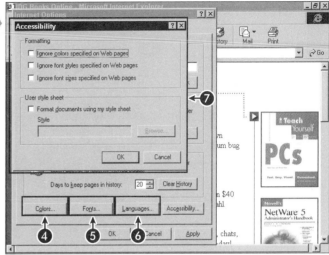

**4** Click the Colors button to change the default colors for your Web browser.

**5** Change your font settings with the Font button.

**6** Language encoding is done with the Languages button.

**7** The Accessibility button changes how font sizes and colors behave, and the default style sheet.

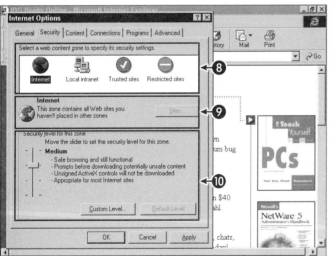

**8** Internet Explorer sets up different security "zones" for you to control.

**9** You can add sites to any zone.

**10** Change your security settings for any zone; potentially damaging content includes client-side scripts, ActiveX, and Java.

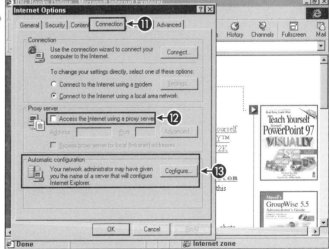

**11** Use the Connection tab to change your Internet dial-up or network settings.

**12** If you connect through a firewall or proxy server, click the Proxy server checkbox.

**13** The Automatic configuration option may not be available; check with your network administrator.

# Setting Internet Options
*Continued*

In the Content tab, you'll find a Content Advisor section (for parental control of Web sites), a Certificates section (for positive identification of yourself and the Web servers you visit), and the Personal information section.

The Internet is an adult medium. It contains millions of adult-oriented sites that may not be appropriate for children. If your kids are on the Internet, you can use the Content Advisor to help control what information they can access, based on their age. You can also use the Content Advisor to block out materials you find personally offensive. For example, I'm not fond of violent images; the Content Advisor warns me if I'm entering a site that could offend me. That gives me the chance to prepare for the content I'm about to see, or to choose not to view it at all.

Click Edit Profile in the Personal Information box to change your user identity. You can create an electronic "business card" that can be shared with Web sites, other users, and other programs (such as email and newsgroups). Web sites can then use cookies to retrieve this information, and you can choose to refuse those requests, or to encrypt the information before it's sent.

In Programs, you can select your default email, newsgroup, conferencing, calendar, and contact information management programs. When Internet Explorer is asked to open or create a file in any of these protocols, it will open the program listed here.

Oddly enough, the Programs tab doesn't offer a choice for your HTML editor. If you've got FrontPage installed, that seems to be the automatic default. You can edit the current page by selecting Edit ⇨ Page.

Finally, the Advanced tab offers a quick rundown of other options. Here, you can change your Accessibility options, Browsing options, decide if you want to have hyperlinks underlined, which multimedia files to automatically play, and more security features. In addition, there are Java Virtual Machine (Java VM) options, printing options, Search options, Toolbar settings, and HTTP settings. You'll need to change the HTTP setting if you connect through a proxy or firewall server.

## TAKE NOTE

### ► CONFERENCE CALLING PROGRAMS

Conference calling programs, such as NetMeeting, are also called *real-time chat* programs and *voice chat* programs. The main difference between chat and conference calls is that conference calls are usually used in business environments. There's usually a file-sharing option, with a whiteboard (so you can mark up the document), a voice option to offer a telephone-like experience, and the ability to connect to multiple users on the Internet.

### ► PARENTAL CONTROLS

You can control what content your kids can use with the RSACi ratings system under the Content tab. Press Enable to set it up. If you have another ratings system such as NetNanny installed, you may also use that rating system by clicking the Advanced tab.

**SHORTCUT**
Use the Content Advisor to go straight to RSACi and learn how to rate your own site.

**FIND IT ONLINE**
Use Win95? Check out PowerToys for IE 4.0 (**http://www.microsoft.com/ie/ie40/powertoys/main.htm**).

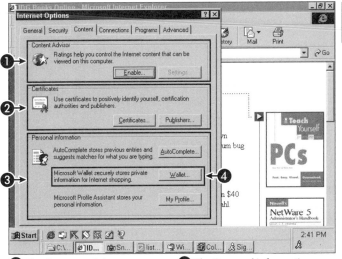

❶ The Content tab lets you enable the Content Advisor.

❷ Certificates are used to verify the identity of other Web sites.

❸ The Personal information section lets you change your user identity.

❹ Microsoft Wallet stores encrypted credit card information.

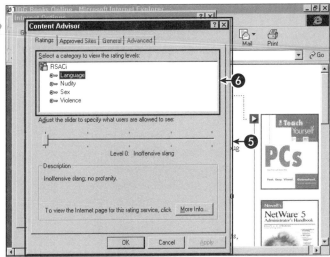

❺ Use the Content Advisor to control what levels of Language, Nudity, Sex, and Violence to allow to be displayed.

❻ Sites are rated by ratings agencies, such as RSACi.

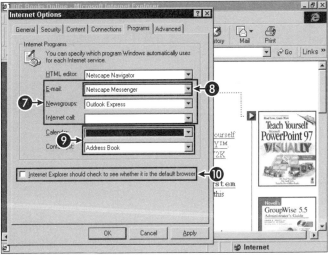

❼ In the Programs tab, choose your mail, news, and conference call programs.

❽ Drop-down boxes offer options for these programs.

❾ Choose contact management and calendar programs.

❿ The "default browser" is used when you double-click an Internet file.

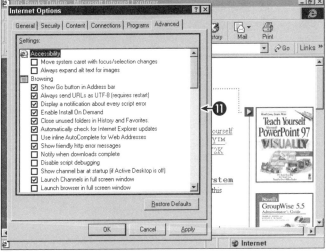

⓫ The Advanced tab lets you set some fairly specific options, like whether to notify you when a file finishes downloading.

# Using Internet Channels

Internet Explorer's Channels use "push" technology to send content to your computer whenever it's updated — which could be as frequently as every minute (for stock reports), to as seldom as once a month (for a newsletter).

An Internet Explorer channel uses ActiveX controls to update the content directly into your browser as often as you wish. You can choose to have it refresh your content whenever it's updated on the server or to just notify you when the content has been changed.

Because channels allow you to identify specific areas of interest, and have those areas automatically updated, this can be a real benefit to people lacking time or knowledge to search the Internet for this information.

Unfortunately, most channels are run by commercial sites, so expect advertisements and a biased viewpoint. Even on the Mercury Central channel, the Internet channel for the *San Jose Mercury-News*, an animated advertisement serves as a constant distraction to users trying to read the articles. My experience has been that a 3   5 index card solves the trick; I tape mine to the side of my monitor and flip it over the animated advertisement when it gets annoying.

You do need to subscribe to a channel to use it. For example, I had to subscribe to the Mercury Center and decide which news sections to read each day. Eventually, Channels may be able to provide part of the newspaper at a reasonable subscription price. So, if you only read the business section, you would only have to pay for that section. For now, a subscription to Mercury Central (and most other online news channels) is free.

**CROSS-REFERENCE**

Channels use DHTML; read more about it in Chapter 15.

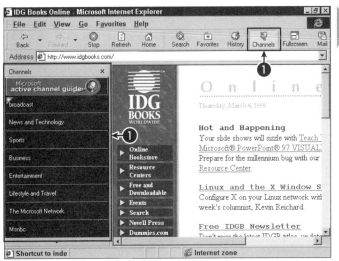

**❶** The Channels button opens the Channels bar in the Web browser, shown at the left.

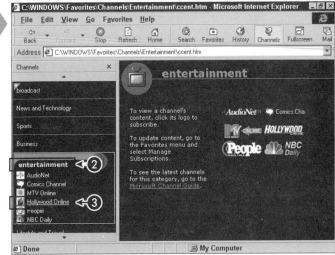

**❷** Click any channel topic to display a list of channels in that topic.

**❸** Click the channel name to go to a channel and learn more about it.

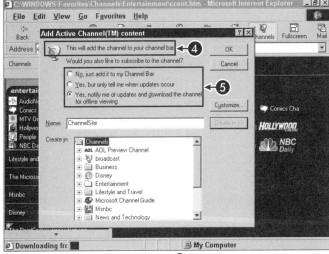

**❹** To subscribe to a channel, click the "Add to active channels" button on the channel's site.

**❺** You can choose to be notified when the channel is updated, or automatically update it now.

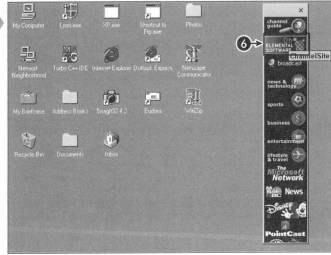

**❻** Channels can have any kind of content, including Dynamic HTML.

# Using the Favorites List

The Favorites list is an old concept. Because it's very hard to keep track of the URLs of all the cool sites you visit, and it's kind of a pain to retype them each time you want to visit, there's a file or directory that your Web browser can access to instantly link to those pages.

In Windows 95 and Windows 98, there's also a Favorites directory in the File Manager. There's another aspect of Internet Explorer and the operating system integration; Internet Explorer uses that directory for your Favorites list. So if you have several programs, files, or directories in that Favorites folder (like me), you'll discover that they're also accessible from the Web browser.

In the Favorites menu bar, you can add a page to the Favorites list, organize your Favorites list (by organizing them into folders and subdirectories), manage and update your subscriptions, and go directly to any item in the Favorites list.

If you installed Internet Explorer over an existing version, or after installing Netscape Navigator, any bookmarks or favorites from the other Web browser programs will be automatically imported to the Favorites list.

When you have several items in your Favorites list, you should organize them. You could organize them by date, topic, user (if more than one person uses your computer), work/personal, or any other organizational system you prefer. The third figure on the next page shows you how to organize your Favorites list using directories and hierarchies to help manage your files. Notice that the list is always alphabetized, regardless what order you put it in.

You can also manage your subscriptions here. That means you can add and delete subscribed channels and update them. Update your channels whenever you want Internet Explorer to request the channel content and inform you if there have been updates.

## TAKE NOTE

### ▶ FAVORITES SUBSCRIPTIONS

You can also subscribe to a favorite item, just as you subscribe to channels. When you update your subscriptions, you'll be notified of any changes to that favorite page.

### ▶ FAVORITES FILE SIZES

You may notice, if you go into your Favorites directory in Windows, that there are many files there; one for each favorite item. And each item is 1KB in size.

Internet Explorer creates these favorites the same way you'd make a shortcut to a file or program. Unfortunately, there's a minimum file size in Windows, usually 1KB in size. That means, if you have a lot of favorite items, your hard drive can actually fill up.

Don't worry too much, though. It takes over 1,000 favorite items and folders to fill 1 MB of your hard disk.

**CROSS-REFERENCE**

Chapter 11 discusses how Netscape handles bookmarks.

**FIND IT ONLINE**

WebOBJ's Bookmark Importer (**http://www. webobj.com/bookmark/**) converts Netscape bookmarks for IE.

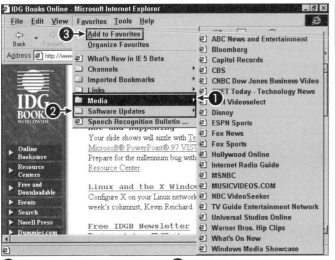

**①** To open a favorite item, select Favorites, then the folder or favorite item.

**②** Your Windows favorites are also shown in the Favorites menu.

**③** To add a favorite item, open the page in the Web browser and select Favorites ➪ Add to Favorites.

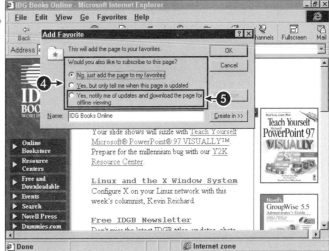

**④** You'll be prompted to subscribe to the page.

**⑤** Page subscriptions mean Internet Explorer will check that page often and notify you when the page changes.

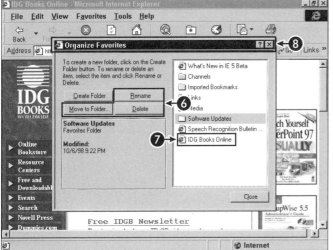

**⑥** To rearrange your favorites, select File ➪ Organize Favorites.

**⑦** Select the favorite to change and click Move, Rename, or Delete.

**⑧** You can also open the favorite item from the Organize Favorites window.

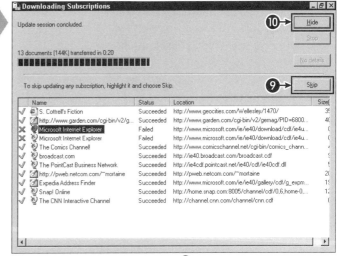

**■** Select Favorites ➪ Update all Subscriptions to check your subscribed channels and favorite pages.

**⑨** Skip subscribed items by selecting them and clicking Skip.

**⑩** Hide the update window by clicking Hide. Subscription updates run in the background.

# Examining the Active Desktop

The Active Desktop is probably Internet Explorer 5's most controversial feature. Users either love it or they despise it, and it makes a big difference in how they perceive the Internet Explorer (and Windows 98) experience in general.

Active Desktop turns your windows desktop wallpaper into a Web page and lets you drop Active Desktop items — such as other Web pages (and sites), images, video files, ActiveX controls, and channels — onto the desktop. Those Active Desktop items appear as borderless windows on your desktop. Channels are updated automatically, and you can click and use any Web page on the desktop, or as the desktop wallpaper itself.

The second figure of the next page shows an alternative desktop wallpaper. It's a Web page with a Yahoo! search form included. The search form is part of the HTML page, which is stored locally. The search form itself runs off of Yahoo!'s site on the Internet. When a user enters a search query in the desktop, Internet Explorer launches the Web browser and opens the results.

Active Desktop also changes the way you browse your hard drive, the Windows Explorer. Gone is the familiar (for most of us) Windows Explorer interface; a simple window with folders and files. Instead, that window appears inside Internet Explorer itself, which may be a little irritating if you don't want to wait for the browser to load. Fortunately, Internet Explorer's integration into the operating system means it takes very little time for the Explorer to launch.

In the Display Control Panel, there's a new tab called Web. In addition to being able to change your background wallpaper to any HTML file in the Background tab, the Web tab lets you change settings for the Active Desktop.

Basically, every Active Desktop item you install is put on this list, and you can add, change, delete, or hide individual desktop items from the Web tab. You can also change the behavior of the background; click "View my Active Desktop as a Web page" to turn on or off the Active Desktop.

## Desktop Update

If you have Windows 95 or Windows NT, you can install the Desktop Update instead of Active Desktop. After you install Internet Explorer (without Active Desktop), go to the Control Panel and select Add/Remove Programs. Select Microsoft Internet Explorer 5.0 and click Add/Remove. You'll be prompted to install the Desktop Update.

Desktop Update and Active Desktop are identical components. The main difference seems to be in the integration with the operating system. Desktop Update also integrates with the OS, but it's able to be removed. Because Windows 95 and Windows NT are complete operating systems without it, it can be removed from those OSs. Windows 98 is too dependent on Active Desktop; it has become the main operating system interface.

The advantage to using Desktop Update over Active Desktop is that you can remove it later. Active Desktop cannot be uninstalled, but Desktop Update can be uninstalled using the Add/Remove Programs Control Panel.

**CROSS-REFERENCE**

Chapter 18 has information on client-side scripts, which you can use in your Active Desktops.

**FIND IT ONLINE**

WinFiles.com has many downloadable Active Desktops; visit **http://www.winfiles.com/apps/98/ wallpaper-misc.html**.

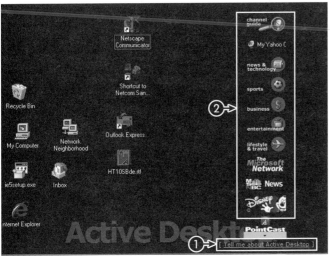

① *The default desktop has a black background and a hyperlink to the Active Desktop tour.*

② *The Channels Bar is an Active Desktop item; an ActiveX control that launches the Active Channels.*

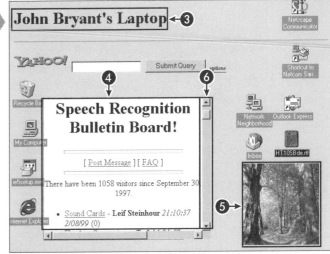

③ *Change the background wallpaper to any HTML page.*

④ *Add Web pages from your hard drive or from the Internet to the desktop.*

⑤ *Graphics, pages, and ActiveX controls float on your desktop.*

⑥ *Click the item's border and move it for drag-and-drop positioning.*

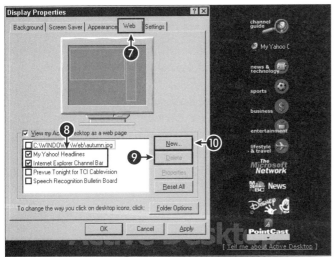

⑦ *You can view desktop items in the Web tab of your Display Control Panel.*

⑧ *Check the item's checkbox to include it on the desktop.*

⑨ *To delete an item, select it and click Delete.*

⑩ *To add an item, click New.*

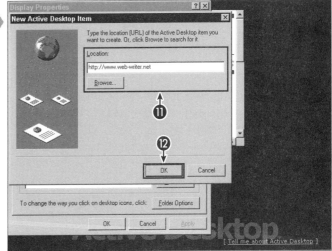

⑪ *At the dialog box, type in the URL of the new item, or browse your hard drive to find it locally.*

⑫ *Click OK to add the item to your desktop.*

# Exploring Mail and News

Like any decent computer program, Internet Explorer comes with email and news readers, bundled together in a package called Outlook Express. Outlook Express is rapidly becoming one of the more popular email clients, because it's included in Internet Explorer, and because it's fairly easy to use.

If you chose standard or full installation when installing IE, then Outlook Express is already installed, or you can install it from the Components site. When you first start Outlook Express, you'll be prompted for information on your email account. You'll need to provide your real name, email address, your email username and password, the POP server (that's the one you retrieve email from), your SMTP server (the one you send mail from), and a "friendly name" to help you access your account.

You can also search for individuals using one of the various 411 email search engines. These search engines keep a database of user's real names and their email addresses, which you can search from Outlook Express. So, if you can't remember your high school best friend's email address, look it up and drop her a line!

With Outlook Express, you can compose messages using special email "stationery," templates that send your email using HTML with graphics and colors. Not everyone can read HTML, however, so only send stationery email when you know the recipient will have Outlook Express, Netscape Navigator, or a similar, HTML-enhanced email client. If you're a member of a mailing list, it's crucial that you post in plaintext, because 75–80 percent of the people reading the mailing list won't have an HTML-enhanced mail client. On a list of 1,000 people or more, that's a lot of people to get annoyed at you. To change the default composition type, select Tools ➪ Options and go to the Send tab. Select "Plain Text" and click OK.

You can also add Usenet newsgroups to Outlook Express. When you first try to use the newsgroups, you'll be prompted for information on your news server and your identity. A professional tip: spammers harvest email addresses from newsgroups, so make your email address something like `me@NOSPAMdomain.com`. Downloading the newsgroup names takes a while, but once done, you can subscribe to just the newsgroups you want.

**CROSS-REFERENCE**

Chapter 23 has information to help you set up mail and newsgroup options and signature files.

**FIND IT ONLINE**

A list of public-access news servers is available online at **http://home1.gte.net/docthomp/servers.htm.**

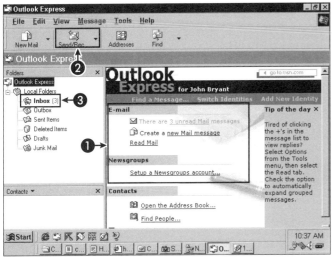

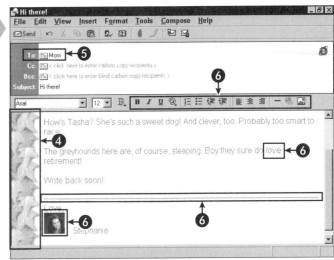

❶ From the Outlook Express startup screen, you can read mail and news, and compose email easily.

❷ The Send and Receive button checks your email and news servers for new messages.

❸ Select the Inbox to view new email messages.

■ To compose mail, click "Create a new Mail message" in Outlook Express.

❹ You can use special electronic stationery.

❺ I used the nickname "Mom" from an entry in my Address Book.

❻ Use HTML elements in the WYSIWYG mail editor to format your email!

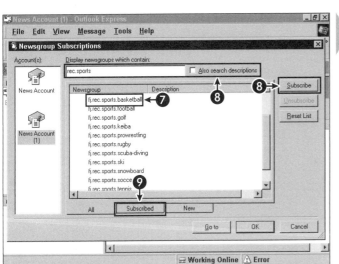

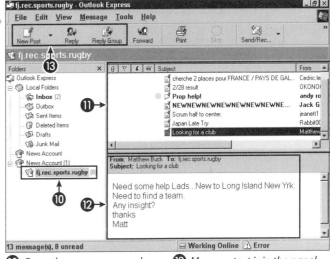

❼ After you download the list of newsgroups, search by keyword, or browse the newsgroups.

❽ Select a newsgroup you'd like to read and click Subscribe.

❾ You can view subscribed groups in the Subscribed tab.

❿ Open the news server and select the newsgroup to read.

⓫ Message subjects (or headers) are shown in the upper-right panel.

⓬ Message text is in the panel below.

⓭ To post new messages, click New Post or Reply to Group.

# Checking Out the "Cool and Drool" List

This section is designed as a quick rundown of what I've found to be the strengths and weaknesses in Internet Explorer. Remember that these are completely my opinions, although they are based on my experiences with Internet Explorer as compared with other Web browsers. I did not grade components I hadn't used, such as Microsoft Wallet or some of the multimedia components.

The next page shows a table of my "Cool and Drool" list for IE. Some Internet Explorer features are very cool — they don't have any real drawbacks and should probably be implemented by everyone. Others, on the other hand, are just ways for Microsoft to make money on support calls and MSDN subscriptions. MSDN, the Microsoft Developers' Network, is a restricted part of their Web site for which you must register — and at higher levels, pay — to access; it includes most of the crucial information on authoring for their browser-specific technologies.

On the next page, you'll see my "grading sheet" for IE. Cascading style sheets, implemented best in IE, still have a long way to go. But CSS-P (positioned CSS) works fabulously.

Dynamic HTML got high grades; Microsoft has made long strides in the Dynamic HTML front, and is the de facto standard when creating DHTML sites.

ActiveX, Microsoft's programming/scripting object language, earned high grades for a number of reasons. Mostly, though, I like the fact that they're extremely fast to use. And, anyone successfully using an ActiveX site uses Internet Explorer, and I can design for that audience specifically. Sometimes, proprietary technology isn't 100 percent bad.

Microsoft's Java implementation was graded poorly — not on performance, but on reputation. The whole point of Java was a cross-platform programming language, and Microsoft's implementation of it invented new Java classes that could only be used on Windows computers. Granted, those Java classes can do some really awesome things, but I think it sort of missed the point.

I have to admit, I like the Active Desktop, so I graded it fairly high. But the Desktop Upgrade option is too confusing: new users won't know they have that option when they first download and install IE. Microsoft should offer Windows 98 and the entire Internet Explorer package with a removable Active Desktop. There's apparently no reason they can't do that — Desktop Update works just like Active Desktop, and is not normally system-critical.

## TAKE NOTE

### ► STANDARD VERSUS PROPRIETARY TECHNOLOGY

It's my experience that open standards (like HTML 4.0) make life easier for everyone. Web designers don't stress over whether or not something will look right, and Web users don't crash their computers trying to use a Web site (I've had this happen, many times). However, there's something to be said for being innovative, and whatever Microsoft's motives have been in developing proprietary technologies, they've certainly helped expand the boundaries of Web.

**CROSS-REFERENCE**

For a similar browser breakdown of Netscape Navigator, see Chapter 11.

**FIND IT ONLINE**

See CNET's review of Internet Explorer at http://www.cnet.com/Content/Reviews/Compare/Browsers4/ss07.html.

## Table 10-1: IE 4 — WHAT'S COOL, WHAT DROOLS

| Feature | Grade | Comments |
| --- | --- | --- |
| Cascading style sheets | B | Good implementation, but text properties — especially borders and background colors — fill the entire line, not just the element. |
| Style sheets with positioning | A | Very fine control over element positions. |
| Active Desktop | B | I really like Active Desktop. It's customizable, and puts any Web page I want onto my desktop. Unfortunately, it lost an entire grade point for not being removable! |
| Outlook Express | A | Very simple, easy to use. The stationery is attractive, but not enough information on HTML vs. plaintext for email. |
| Address Book | A | Everyone should use the Address Book, if only for its "plaintext only" option! You can specify if a particular email address accepts plaintext only or not. Outlook Express won't let you compose an HTML-enhanced message to an address marked "plaintext only." |
| DHTML | A | Great implementation. Serious applications are possible. |
| Java | B | Microsoft implements Java pretty well, but goes too far and makes classes that won't work on other platforms. |
| JavaScript (JScript) | A | IE 4 fixes many previous problems (such as not supporting many of JavaScript's important features) with Microsoft's JavaScript implementation. |
| Active channels | B- | They're convenient, and use an open standard for push, but they can be a little too bandwidth-intensive and don't offer many serious channels. |
| HTML 4.0 | A | Good implementation of HTML 4.0, including style sheets and accessibility. |
| Price | A | I like anything free. |
| Favorites | B | Individual Favorites files eat hard drive space. On the other hand, that makes it easier to add favorite items to the Active Desktop. |
| Tables | A | Tables render faster in Internet Explorer 4 (vs. Netscape Navigator). |
| Cache | C | The minimum size for the cache is 1 percent of your hard drive; on large drives, that's as much as 60MB! |
| Content Advisory | B | With the RSACi rating system, sites can be rated based on Sex, Violence, Nudity, and Language. |
| Security zones | B | I like the idea of grouping security settings, but there's no really fast or easy way to set them up. |
| Profile Editor | C | It really scares me to have a centralized source of my personal contact information shared with Web sites. |

# Personal Workbook

## Q&A

**1** How do you install additional Internet Explorer components?

_____

_____

_____

**2** What's the History button and what does it do?

_____

_____

_____

**3** What's the quickest way to enter the URL for Yahoo!'s site?

_____

_____

_____

**4** What search options are built into Internet Explorer and Outlook Express?

_____

_____

_____

**5** What is an *active channel*?

_____

_____

_____

**6** How do you change the background wallpaper in Active Desktop?

_____

_____

_____

**7** Where do you add, delete, or hide your Active Desktop items?

_____

_____

_____

**8** How or why would you change from HTML to plaintext for composing email?

_____

_____

_____

**ANSWERS: PAGE 439**

## EXTRA PRACTICE

**①** Install Internet Explorer 5.0. Install Desktop Update or Active Desktop. Add an Active Desktop item, such as a Web page or image.

**②** Open your home page in a Web browser and view its source code.

**③** Set up your browser to use the Content Advisory to prevent violent or offensive material.

**④** Subscribe to an active channel and view the available content.

**⑤** Add your home page to the Favorites list. Subscribe to your home page, and have the program automatically update it when you change that page.

## REAL-WORLD EXAMPLES

✔ You've designed a site using Netscape Navigator. You install Internet Explorer and test your site in it. You fix any problems, and have a cross-browser Web site!

✔ Your company is upgrading to Windows 98. Suddenly, your desktop looks completely different! Fortunately, you know how to write a new wallpaper Web page, and how to add items that make your Active Desktop a useful tool.

✔ You exchange email with friends and family using Outlook Express. Some of your friends have HTML-compliant email clients, and some don't. You use the Address Book to distinguish between plaintext-only addresses and HTML message addresses.

## Visual Quiz

Write out the code for this wallpaper. What Active Desktop items do you see here? What should happen when the search query is entered?

_____

_____

_____

_____

_____

CHAPTER

**11**

# Netscape Communicator

Netscape Communicator is one of the most popular Web browser packages on the market today. It's inexpensive and available on nearly every platform (including UNIX and Linux), and Netscape Navigator (the Web browser program itself) was one of the first commercially available Web browsers to gain popular appeal.

In this chapter, you learn how to install and use Netscape Communicator, how to send and receive email and newsgroup messages, bookmarking sites, Web page editing in Communicator, and what I think about each of Netscape's features.

Netscape does certain things better than others. For example, the Composer component isn't as versatile as some of the other WYSIWYG (What You See Is What You Get) editors available. But Netscape originally developed JavaScript, and its implementation of the language has been incomparable. Unfortunately, because Netscape and Microsoft haven't been able to agree on a Document Object Model (DOM), Dynamic HTML has had to rely heavily on complex JavaScripts instead of using DOM features to streamline it.

Netscape Navigator is a descendant of Mozilla, a noncommercial browser originally developed by the NCSA (National Center for Supercomputing Applications) for the World Wide Web. Mozilla was one of the first graphical Internet browsers, meaning it could show text and graphics in the same page. Because it was originally a very graphics-oriented program, the background color was gray. Pictures generally look best on a neutral background, and gray is about as neutral as you can get. However, the legacy of Mozilla's gray background has been that Netscape's default background is also gray.

In 1998, Netscape released the Netscape Navigator source code, the underlying instructions for the program itself. Because the source code is now freely available, anyone can download it and create a new Web browser based on Netscape's original design. As a result, Mozilla has taken on a new meaning. No longer does it refer to an ancestor browser of Netscape's. Now, Mozilla also refers to any Web browser derived from the Netscape Navigator source code, including (but no longer limited to) Netscape Navigator. Although Netscape's browser will still be called Netscape Navigator, it is not a part of the larger group of Mozilla browsers.

Server logs often record the name of each Web browser that surfs your site. If you read those server logs carefully, you won't find "Netscape" mentioned at all. But you will find "Mozilla4.0" listed; that indicates a Navigator-based 4.0 browser.

# Installing Communicator

To install Netscape Communicator (which includes the Navigator Web browser), first download the installation program from Netscape's Web site and save it to your hard drive. For your convenience, Netscape Communicator is also included on the CD-ROM accompanying this book.

When you run the installation program in Windows and Macintosh, you'll be prompted to close all programs and then to read and agree to the license agreement. Next, you'll have the choice between a Typical or Custom installation, as shown in the first figure. The Custom installation options are shown in the second and third figures on the next page.

If you're installing Netscape on Linux or UNIX, you probably know what you're doing, or have a friend to help you. If you don't, uncompress the installation program using gzip and tar, and read the "read me" file enclosed. Since each UNIX and Linux distribution is different, the installation instructions vary widely.

When you install Netscape, you'll have several choices about which components to install on your computer. If you're in the United States or Canada, you'll be able to install strong encryption (128-bit), for use with secure Web servers. Outside the U.S. and Canada, you can only install 40-bit encryption, which is still fairly secure for most applications.

Netscape comes with several optional components. The most important is the Communicator program itself. Communicator comes with the Web browser (Navigator), email client (Messenger), newsgroup client (Collabra), Web authoring program (Composer), and the AOL Instant Messenger program. You can choose to install the optional Netcaster program for receiving Netcaster channels, and an email importer for the popular Eudora mail client (to copy your Eudora mail and settings to Communicator).

When Netscape finishes installing, it will prompt you to restart your computer. Click OK to restart, or finish installation by restarting later. Once you've installed Communicator, you can quickly upgrade it and add plug-ins and other tools with the SmartUpdate feature. Some of the tools available include synchronization tools for the PalmPilot, Netscape Calendar (for coordinating meetings via the Internet), VRML and multimedia viewers, and Internet monitoring software like Net Nanny.

## AOL Instant Messenger

After you restart, you'll be given the option to set up AOL Instant Messenger. Instant Messenger is an Internet paging and chat service that lets you keep track of when your friends are available online. It's a notification tool, as well as a chat program; when one of your friends becomes available, you can use AOL Instant Messenger to page them and start a chat session. A similar program called ICQ (I Seek You) has become very popular, especially among the "chat" crowd.

You don't have to use AOL Instant Messenger if you don't want to. When the Setup screen starts up, simply click the "No" button. Later, whenever AOL Instant Messenger starts, you can click "No" and "Don't Ask Again." to stop it from returning.

**CROSS-REFERENCE**

The CD-ROM includes a copy of Netscape Communicator.

**FIND IT ONLINE**

View the latest Netscape products at **http://home.netscape.com/download/index.html**.

■ *Double-click the installer program to start the installation process.*

❶ *Choose between the Typical and Custom installations.*

❷ *The Typical setup installs the Communicator package, Netcaster, and an email import utility.*

❸ *The Custom installation allows you to choose which options to install.*

❹ *Install the import utility if you already use Eudora and would like to transfer your mailboxes and settings.*

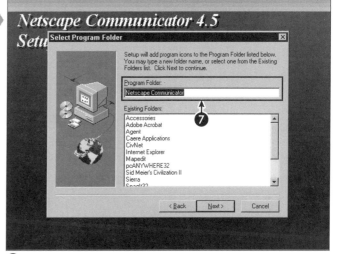

❺ *The extensions dialog box sets up which file types will automatically open Netscape.*

❻ *Each file extension you check will be recognized as a Netscape-compatible file type.*

❼ *Choose a folder to place the Netscape Communicator program icons into, or use the default.*

# Using Navigator

Netscape Navigator may well be the most popular, widely used browser in the world, and with good cause. It's a descendent of one of the first Web browsers ever programmed — Mozilla — and it continues to fill the need for a powerful, independent Web browsing program.

Netscape Navigator has three toolbars at the top of the window: Navigator, Personal, and Location. The Navigator toolbar has the standard navigation buttons: Forward, Back, Stop, Reload, Home, and Search. It also has buttons for Guide, Print, and Security. The Guide button provides quick links to portions of the Netscape Netcenter site. Security gives you important encryption information regarding the current Web page.

The Location toolbar offers two sections. One is the Bookmarks menu, a drop-down menu of bookmarked sites from your bookmark file. The other is a text field for you to directly enter a Web site's URL.

The Personal toolbar contains buttons you set in the "Personal Toolbar Folder" in your bookmark file. You can change the toolbars with a simple mouse click. Place the mouse on the little down arrow next to the toolbar and click it to roll the toolbar up. Clicking its remaining right arrow will roll it back down for you to use. This is a fast and easy way to increase the available reading area in your browser window. To completely hide a toolbar, select "Hide Navigation Toolbar" (or whichever toolbar you wish to hide) in the View menu.

At the bottom of the Navigator window is the status bar, component bar, and an additional Security icon. The status bar provides information about the current Web page and hyperlinks on it. The Security icon indicates if the current Web page is encrypted or not. And the component bar offers a quick way to open the mail, news, and HTML editing programs included with Communicator.

## TAKE NOTE

### ▶ VIEWING SOURCE CODE

To view the source code of the current Web page in Navigator, choose View ⇨ Source from the menu bar. The source code will pop up in a separate Navigator window with a gray background. The source window cannot be edited (unlike Internet Explorer), but HTML element tags are color-coded and formatted in bold for easier reading. Elements appear in purple, attributes are black, and values are blue. Comments appear in italicized text.

### ▶ RIGHT-CLICKING IN NAVIGATOR

Right-clicking has an almost magical effect in Navigator. On Web pages, it lets you send the page, create shortcuts and bookmarks, and quickly navigate the history list. On images, you can also save it as your desktop wallpaper, and view the image alone (useful for large graphics). Right-clicking a hyperlink offers the most options; it's discussed in the third figure on the next page.

## CROSS-REFERENCE

Chapter 10 shows you how to use the other major Web browser, Microsoft Internet Explorer.

## FIND IT ONLINE

See Netscape's Security Docs at **http:// developer.netscape.com/docs/manuals/ index.html?content=security.html**.

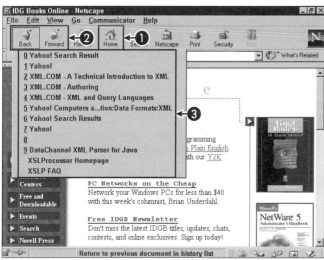

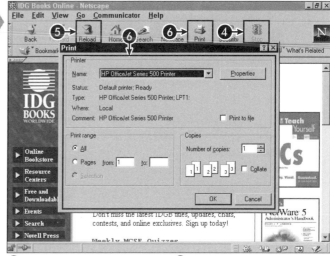

❶ The Home button takes you to your current home page setting.

❷ Back and Forward move you through the sites you've already visited.

❸ Click the little arrow on the Back or Forward button to navigate directly to a page in your browser history.

❹ To stop a page while it's loading, click the Stop button.

❺ The Reload button requests the page from the Web server and displays it in the browser.

❻ Print calls up the Print dialog box and lets you print out the page.

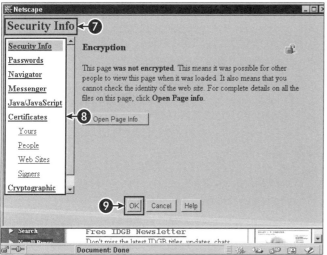

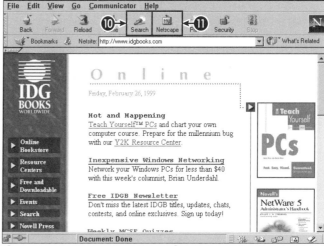

❼ The Security button opens the page's security and encryption information.

❽ You can change security settings with the options on this page.

❾ When you're done, click OK to continue.

❿ The Search button takes you to the Net Search to use six major search engines for the Web.

⓫ The Guide takes you to Netcenter, or use the drop-down menu to choose a directory service.

# Setting User Preferences

Netscape Navigator lets you work the Web however you want. You can change how the browser behaves and looks, what colors and fonts to use, and what programs to run when encountering multimedia files. You can also disable Java, JavaScript, Cookies, and Images (for faster Web browsing). Preferences is also where you can set up your mail and newsgroup information, as well as your Web editing settings.

The most important settings on your Web browser involve security. The settings that affect security the most are found in the Advanced Preferences window, shown in the last figure on the next page. Only a couple of these settings are potentially dangerous: Java, AutoInstall, and Cookies. As a powerful programming language, Java has as many potential security problems as any programming language, including those used in CGI programs. In general, however, the risks are minor, and every time one is caught, it is quickly fixed by Sun, the company that originally developed Java.

AutoInstall (sometimes called SmartUpdate) allows Netscape to update your version of Communicator automatically over the Internet. This is a useful feature, but if you don't necessarily wish to upgrade to every new version of Navigator (and there is no law that says you must upgrade), then disable AutoInstall.

Cookies and JavaScript have had security problems in the past. Previously, it was possible to snag each visitor's email address using an automatic JavaScript program, without the user's knowledge or permission. Now, JavaScript cannot read any information not provided directly by the user, via a form or similar input device. Similarly, cookies have been a useful way to track visitors, but some users dislike them because they gather informa-tion about users without explicit permission. In any case, no server should be able to read another Web server's cookies, and you should check that option just to be sure. You can also insist on being warned before accepting cookies; that gives you the option of rejecting cookies from any untrusted server.

## TAKE NOTE

### ▶ HTML MESSAGES

Netscape Messenger can send and receive HTML pages as email (as can Internet Explorer). However, other users may not be able to receive HTML pages as email, and most news clients are not HTML-compliant.

If you want all outgoing email and news messages to be sent as HTML, check that option in the Mail & Groups ➪ Messages window. Remember that you can change that option for individual messages, and you should never send HTML messages to newsgroups or mailing lists.

### ▶ COOKIES AND GEOCITIES

Since cookies are written and read by Web servers, not individual pages, massive Web hosting services like Geocities or AOL could (and do) track visitors to literally millions of pages. Given how many users keep home pages on these services, these companies have the opportunity to gather usage information from a very large proportion of the Internet community.

**SHORTCUT**

The access the history list of all the Web pages you've visited in the last several days, press Ctrl+H.

**FIND IT ONLINE**

See the Netscape Preferences tutorial at **http://w3.aces.uiuc.edu/AIM/2.0/tutorial/ prefs/prefs.html.**

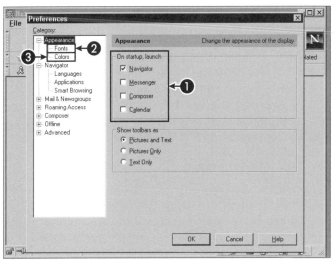

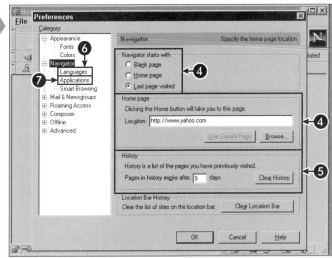

❶ *The Appearance preference lets you change the startup programs and toolbar options.*

❷ *Click Fonts to choose the default fonts and language encoding for Navigator.*

❸ *Choose Colors to specify default colors and whether or not to override the document colors.*

❹ *Navigator lets you change the startup and Home pages.*

❺ *You can also change the History settings.*

❻ *The Languages option lets you specify which languages to display.*

❼ *The Applications option lets you change which programs to launch.*

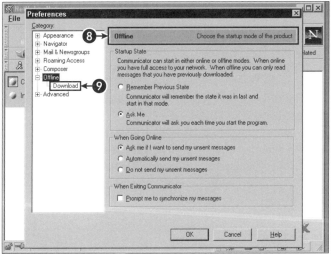

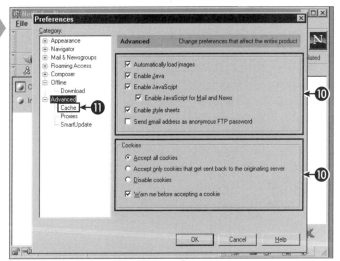

❽ *The Offline options let you set up your system to optimize your modem and connection times.*

❾ *The Download preferences lets you selectively download email and newsgroup messages.*

❿ *Use the Advanced preferences to set up Java, JavaScript, cookies, style sheets, and other options.*

⓫ *Check your Cache to be sure it's not using all your resources, and to clear it out on occasion.*

# Exploring Mail and News

Netscape Communicator comes with mail and news programs, called Messenger and Collabra, respectively. Messenger is shown in the top two figures on the next page, and Collabra is shown in the bottom two figures.

In order to set up Messenger and Collabra, you'll need to know your email username and servers (POP and SMTP), as well as a newsgroup server (NNTP) if you plan to use the newsgroups. You can usually obtain this information from your Internet service provider.

In Communicator, you can also set up folders to store email messages in when you're through downloading them. You can also set up mail filters, which screen incoming messages and move them to specific folders, delete them, mark or flag them, or otherwise manipulate them however you specify in your filters preferences. I usually use a combination of folders and filters to manage all the email I get in a day. If you subscribe to several electronic mailing lists, or are unfortunate enough to be on every unsolicited marketing list, filter your mail into folders for easier reading.

There are literally thousands of newsgroups on the Internet. Hobbies, computers, lifestyles, graphics, jobs — just about every topic you can imagine is available on the newsgroups somewhere. From the Collabra Message Center, you can add newsgroups, subscribe to them, retrieve and read new messages, and post to the newsgroups.

Newsgroups are a worldwide phenomena, and an entire culture has sprung up from their existence. You can find newsgroups that are one giant hugfest, and newsgroups where flame wars erupt daily. However, there are four basic credos of newsgroups:

▶ Don't post the same message to more than one newsgroup. Most people read more than one related newsgroup.

▶ Don't post commercial messages to any newsgroup unless the FAQ says it's OK.
▶ Don't post unrelated messages to any newsgroup.
▶ Read the newsgroup for three weeks to get a "feel" for the group before posting your first message.

## TAKE NOTE

### ▶ THE VCARD FILE

In the Mail and News Identity Preferences, you can make the program automatically attach your address book card to messages. Don't. No one likes to receive a bunch of `vcard.vcf` (the name of the card file) files, or any attachment unless they know it's coming. Set up a signature file in the same window, and only attach your address book card when the recipient is also using Netscape, and you know they want to receive it.

### ▶ THE ADDRESS BOOK

Seems like every program has an address book these days. Netscape's address book is fairly standard. As with the Internet Explorer Address Book, you can specify whether or not individual addresses should receive email messages in HTML or plaintext.

When composing a message, click the Address Book button to choose email addresses, or type the user's nickname to automatically look it up.

**SHORTCUT**

Ctrl+Shift+1 instantly opens the Netscape Message Center, where you can access both mail and newsgroup messages.

**FIND IT ONLINE**

Deja News (**http://www.dejanews.com/**) lets you search past Usenet articles and postings.

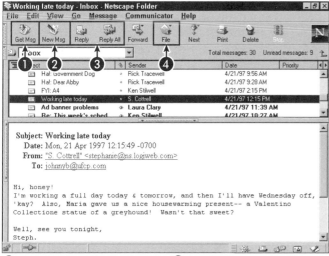

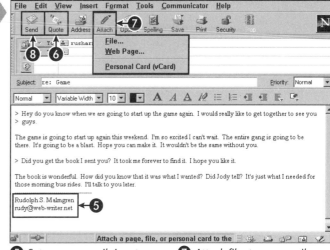

**1** To retrieve messages, click the Get Msg button.

**2** To create a new message, click New Msg.

**3** The Reply button lets you reply to the sender, or to everyone.

**4** To put the message in a folder, click the File button.

**5** Set up your email signature file in Preferences.

**6** To paste a quotation from another source, click the Quote button.

**7** Attach files to any email address with the Attach button.

**8** The Send button mails the message immediately.

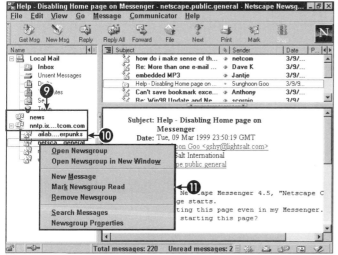

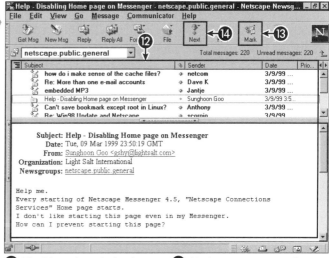

**9** Each news server you use has its own entry. Click it to see your subscribed newsgroups.

**10** Newsgroups with unread messages will appear in bold.

**■** To read a newsgroup, double-click it in the newsgroup list.

**11** Right-click the newsgroup for additional options.

**12** The Discussion window lets you read the message headers and message bodies at the same time.

**13** Mark messages as read or unread by clicking the Mark button.

**14** The Next button moves you to the next unread message in the newsgroup.

# Using Bookmarks

As a chronic Web surfer (incurable, perhaps?), I find myself getting lost pretty easily among all the Web sites I visit. Did I find those amaryllis plants at *garden.com* or *gardens.com*, or *gardens.net*? Is there any way to bypass that login screen? I can't possibly remember a long URL that starts with something like *http://schools.k12.svalley.ca.us*!

A bookmark file is a single, centralized place to put your URLs so you can refer to them later. Netscape Communicator includes a very handy Bookmark menu for you to use. With it, you can add bookmarks, delete them, file them, use them as hyperlinks, and generally organize them any way you want. New installations of Communicator include a preset list of bookmarks, so you'll already have a few good places to go.

The bookmarks in Communicator can be organized any way you like. You can drag and drop them into any organization scheme, or make them automatically sort themselves using the Edit Bookmarks window. You can add folders and put your bookmarks into folders, which could also be organized by name, subject matter, or even date or location. Finally, you can add special dividers that act as a horizontal rule in the bookmark file. That gives your bookmark list a visual cue, to more easily find what you're looking for.

There's a special folder in your bookmarks called the Personal Toolbar Folder. Any item inside the Personal Toolbar Folder will appear as a button on the Personal toolbar in Netscape. That toolbar can be hidden or shown using the View menu, but it can provide quick shortcuts to your most commonly used URLs. On my own toolbar, I've put my Dilbert Zone, ZD University, the HTML 4.0 Specification, and My Yahoo!, because I use them several times a day. If you put folders inside the Personal Toolbar Folder, it will act as a drop-down menu when you click on the corresponding toolbar button.

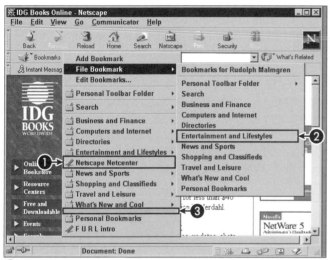

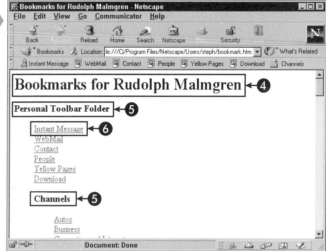

① Go to a bookmark by selecting it in the Bookmark menu.

② To file a page in your bookmarks, select the Bookmark menu, click File Bookmark, and choose its new location.

③ Dividers appear as horizontal rules in the Bookmark menu.

④ The `bookmark.htm` file has a top-level header.

⑤ Subheadings correspond to folders and subdirectories in the file.

⑥ Hyperlinks are the titles of bookmarked pages; clicking them will send you to that page.

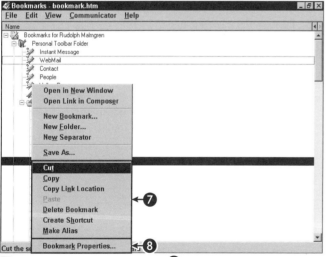

■ You can move bookmarks easily by dragging and dropping them wherever you like.

⑦ Right-click a bookmark to cut, copy, or delete it.

⑧ You can change the bookmark's properties (including its URL and title) with the Bookmark Properties option.

⑨ The View menu lets you sort your bookmarks quickly.

⑩ Click View ⇨ Update Bookmarks to check all bookmarks for recently changed files.

⑪ Set any bookmark folder as the Personal Toolbar Folder by selecting View ⇨ Set as Toolbar Folder.

# Editing Pages in Composer

Netscape Communicator comes with Composer, a WYSIWYG HTML editor that lets you create and edit simple Web pages and automatically upload them to your site. One way to create a Web page in Composer is to use the Composer editor, which looks like a simple word processing program, but with special Web-related formatting options. Netscape offers several Web page templates, available by selecting File ➪ New ➪ Page From Template. Templates are basically pre-created Web pages that you can edit for your own purposes. They come with some graphics, but you can change them to use your own graphics and icons.

Finally, you can use Netscape's Web Page Wizard, available by selecting File ➪ New ➪ Page From Wizard. That takes you to Netscape's Web site, where a Web-based program will help you build your page, complete with colors, graphics and icons, and hyperlinks. You save the page locally, and can then edit it in Composer or upload it directly to your Web server.

When Composer's limitations become barriers to good design, directly edit the page's source using an external HTML editor, such as HomeSite. Set up the default HTML source and image editors in the Composer Preferences window. You may find that a combination of the HTML source editing and Composer works best; it's hard to get a page to look "just right" with a WYSIWYG editing program like Composer, but text-based editors don't always have a preview mode for you to see what you're doing.

One of the things Composer does really well is insert and format images. You can decide how to wrap text around the images (if at all), what to put in your `alt` attribute, whether you want the image to be a background, and what kind of padding around the image there should be. You can also set an alternate low-resolution image, useful for those low-bandwidth connections.

You can also add HTML tags directly into Composer. Select Insert ➪ HTML Tag from the menu bar, and type in the HTML tag you want to include. That's useful for when you want to add a comment, a server-side include, form elements, or any element not normally available in Composer. You can also add HTML attributes to images and to hyperlinks when you add those elements to your page.

## TAKE NOTE

### ▶ COMPOSER LIMITATIONS

You might think that a Web page editor designed by Netscape would support technologies and HTML extensions that Netscape helped create. Unfortunately, it doesn't. Composer won't edit framesets, style sheets, forms, JavaScript, or anything much more advanced than tables.

### ▶ UPLOADING WITH COMPOSER

You can automatically and instantly upload files to your Web server using Composer. When you're done editing the page, click the Publish button to open the Publisher window and upload it to your server of choice. You can also preview the page in Navigator with the Preview button, but it must be saved locally first.

**CROSS-REFERENCE**

Chapter 12 has information on choosing a Web authoring program.

**FIND IT ONLINE**

View Netscape Composer's Web Page Wizard at **http://home.netscape.com/home/gold4.0_wizard.html**.

① *Select the element style from the toolbar, or edit the font style.*

② *Format with Bold, Italic, and Underline buttons.*

③ *You can also add images, horizontal rules, tables, and hyperlinks.*

④ *Be sure to save before you publish or preview the page.*

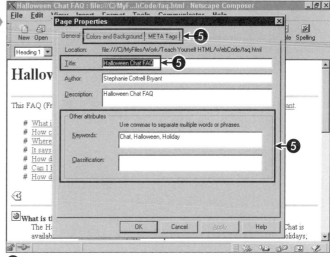

⑤ *Select Format ➪ Page Colors and Properties to change the <HEAD> information for your page. You can add a title, change the description, edit the colors, and add custom <META> elements to your page.*

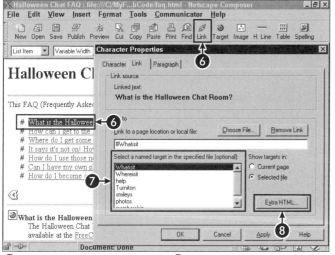

⑥ *To create a hyperlink, select your text and click the Link button.*

⑦ *Bookmarks in the selected page will be displayed by name.*

⑧ *You can add additional attributes with the Extra HTML button.*

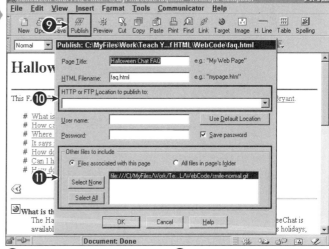

⑨ *Click the Publish button to upload your page.*

⑩ *Type in a URL to publish the page to, and enter your username and password.*

⑪ *Any additional files (such as included images, scripts, and sound files) will also be uploaded.*

# Checking Out the "Cool and Drool" List

Netscape Communicator comes with several programs as one bundled package, and my personal experience with it has been, overall, very good. In the spirit of sharing a piece of my mind, and possibly helping you see where Netscape's strengths and weaknesses are, I'm going to share with you my report card on Netscape Communicator 4.0. Please remember that these are my opinions only, and that other people wildly and vehemently disagree with me, based on their own experiences.

Netscape gets high marks for everything they developed themselves; the JavaScript is well integrated, the user interface itself is intuitive and easy to use, and it's my absolute favorite way to do bookmarks. I'm not quite as keen on the Composer and the Virtual Cards. Because it lacks support for frames, style sheets, and pretty much anything more complicated than Chapter 5 of this book, Composer just isn't up to current WYSIWYG editor standards, and I think that's because Netscape just stopped developing that part of their product.

I lament the fact that Netscape hasn't really pushed Netcaster and made the right marketing relationships. Unfortunately, they have to put all their resources into their browser and into establishing standards for the Web. I'm glad they've made it so easy for developers to create Netcaster channels, but I think they should really encourage developers to use the Netcaster channel features. They should also fix whatever bug they've got in their "More Channels" page; the Dynamic HTML used there doesn't quite work, and results in a pretty inconsistent experience for Netcaster users.

The most perplexing part of Communicator, for me, is the Messenger Mailbox/Collabra/Message Central confusion. The Message Central and Collabra have identical interfaces, so there's no reason to have two separate shortcuts and menu items, nor two separate names. I don't totally understand why newsgroups are called "Collabra Discussion Groups" — I know there's a Collabra Server somewhere (a Netscape news server), but I dislike the way the naming scheme is so confusing for new users.

Similarly, you'll never see "Email" in the menus — everything is a "message." Again, it's confusing to not have a clearly named item that matches the common jargon. I gave Messenger Mailbox a fairly high score, because it's easy to use and doesn't confuse new users with advanced options (like Mail Filtering, which is available) right away. However, when I wanted to send a Web page message to a user who I've set up in my address book as preferring them, I had to change my Mail Preferences to "Send as HTML by Default," even though it was just one message.

Overall, I really love Netscape, and I will continue to use and develop for it in the future. But if you're in the market for a fully integrated product, stick to MSIE. Netscape is more of an à la carte browser.

## TAKE NOTE

### ▶ SMART UPDATE IS SECURE

SmartUpdate is a pretty cool feature that was also available (using ActiveX) in Microsoft Internet Explorer. The potential security problems with being able to install software over the Internet are a nightmare, but Netscape uses certificates to assure users of their identity.

**CROSS-REFERENCE**

For a similar report card of Internet Explorer, see Chapter 10.

**FIND IT ONLINE**

View a comparison of Netscape Navigator and Microsoft Internet Explorer at **http://www.browserwars.com**.

## NETSCAPE COMMUNICATOR: WHAT'S COOL, WHAT DROOLS

| Feature | Grade | Comments |
|---|---|---|
| Cascading Style Sheets | B | Good implementation, but there's no user-defined style sheet, and positioning doesn't always work. |
| Dynamic HTML | B- | Netscape's DHTML doesn't allow scripting of every element in a Web page. |
| JavaScript | A | JavaScript is usable, well developed, and an accepted industry standard. |
| Messenger Mailbox | A- | A decent interface, but there's no way for the program to remember your password. |
| Message Central | B | It's identical to the Collabra interface, and therefore redundant. Each double-click opens a new window, cluttering the desktop. |
| Address book | A | A nice usable interface, and a plaintext option. |
| Virtual Cards | C- | I'm probably just tired of removing them from my attachment directory, but why are they sent by default? |
| Collabra | B | Seems like a fancy name for "newsgroups." I dislike any interface that automatically marks a message as read the minute I focus on its header. |
| Composer | C | As far as Web page editing tools go, it's pretty far behind. It also hasn't changed in three or four years. |
| Netcaster | C+ | Not enough channels shows that "push" is dying. The "More Channels" page has very buggy scripting. The only thing worth saving is the Webtop Channels. |
| SmartUpdate | B- | It makes me very nervous to let anyone install software on my hard drive. On the other hand, it's no worse than Microsoft's site. |
| AOL Instant Messenger | A- | A little annoying because it keeps coming back, but you don't have to install it with Communicator. If you like instant messaging, it's pretty cool. |
| Bookmarks | A+ | One of my favorite parts about Netscape is the bookmark file. |
| Component bar | A- | It's dockable, it's undockable. I guess options are nice. |
| Security | A | A solid A for offering an easy way to see a site's security information, and for offering that information on any Communicator page. |
| Price | A | I love free stuff. |

# Personal Workbook

## Q&A

**1** What installation options are available in Netscape Communicator?

_____

_____

_____

**2** How do you view the source code in Communicator?

_____

_____

_____

**3** Name three ways to open a page in Netscape Navigator.

_____

_____

_____

**4** How do you change the home page URL?

_____

_____

_____

**5** How do you set up your preferences to not send HTML messages by default? By user?

_____

_____

_____

**6** How do you file a new bookmark into a folder?

_____

_____

_____

**7** How do you delete a bookmark?

_____

_____

_____

**8** How do you make a hyperlink in Composer?

_____

_____

_____

**ANSWERS: PAGE 441**

## EXTRA PRACTICE

**1** Create a basic email template using Composer. Include a letterhead with your name, company logo, hyperlinked URL, and email address.

**2** Put the same information into a signature file. Send a default message to yourself.

**3** Set up Communicator to download your mail from your mail server, and retrieve that message. View it in the Messenger Mailbox.

**4** Double-click the URL from your email message and go to your URL.

**5** Set the URL as your home page, or add it to your Personal toolbar.

**6** Add your home page to Netcaster. Update it and view it in Webtop mode.

## REAL-WORLD APPLICATIONS

✔ Your company has an intranet for its 300 employees. Everyone's using Netscape to pick up their mail. You use the virtual cards to exchange contact information instantly, and can freely use HTML in interoffice email.

✔ You've been looking for your best college buddy, but have had no luck. You use the Guide button to quickly search online resources to find him.

✔ Your bookmark file looks like a Rorschach test; there are unrelated links all over the place. You neatly organize them by date and topic, and can quickly surf to the sites you need the most.

✔ Every morning, you check CNN.com for the latest news. You add a Netcaster channel to check for updates overnight, and no longer have to wait for it to download in the morning.

## Visual Quiz

What elements do you see in this message in Composer? Is there a way to send the same information without using HTML? Do you think the sender knows if the recipient can receive HTML mail? What are some ways you would use HTML in mail most effectively? When would you not use it?

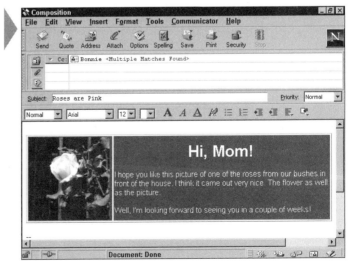

CHAPTER **12**

# Web Tools

All professionals must have certain, specialized tools to do their jobs. The plumber wouldn't dream of trying to fix a leaky pipe without a wrench, and the attorney is nothing without legal papers and briefs.

Web designers are no different. They use specialized tools — mainly consisting of software — to help them in their craft. There are tools for raw HTML coding, tools for graphic design, animation, Java and JavaScript, even tools to help Web designers write server-side scripts.

Because Web designers may come from nearly any background — marketing, graphic design, technical writing, systems administration, or even programming — they may use a variety of tools to get the job done. A Web designer specializing in graphics may stress having a superior drawing program over a Web editor with precise layout control. Depending on the Web designer's own depth of knowledge, they may want to have their HTML code viewable and editable on the screen, or hidden neatly away so they can manipulate the effect of that code instead.

As a professional Web designer, I've looked at many different tools for my own and others' use. I've come to the conclusion that a Web editing program is an individual preference, but that there are certain things to look for in such a program. This chapter will help you identify your own, customized needs, and how to choose a program based on those needs.

# Choosing a WYSIWYG Editor

WYSIWYG (What You See Is What You Get) is a misnomer in HTML design. As you already know, Web pages look different across browsers and platforms. User preferences can also change the appearance of your pages. So what does a WYSIWYG editor do?

Mainly, it shows you how your Web pages will look in a particular Web browser. The editing screen looks a lot like a word processing program; you can type directly into it, using certain shortcuts to insert text formatting and hyperlinks, and you generally never have to see the underlying code that makes it a Web page.

You've already seen one WYSIWYG editor; Netscape Composer. Composer's limitations illustrate the problems inherent in a WYSIWYG editor. Because custom HTML can't be rendered in the WYSIWYG editor, the program must have some way to deal with those customized elements. In Composer, the tags remain in the Web page, but are indicated with arrows in the editing program to show unrecognized HTML. In other WYSIWYG editors, the unrecognized elements may be edited, altered, or removed entirely.

When choosing a WYSIWYG editor, ask yourself how much HTML you really know, and how much you care about. Since WYSIWYG editors don't offer as much control over HTML elements, they're not generally used by "hard-core" Web programmers. On the other hand, they're often preferred by layout designers, who try to control the appearance of a Web page more than the cross-compatibility of the Web really allows.

If you've read this far, you know that HTML is more than just layout, and that good Web design requires you to be involved in the elements themselves. However, there are times when WYSIWYG editors provide excellent shortcuts for Web designers. When you have a long table that you need to enter, nothing beats a WYSIWYG table editor for making it easy to enter data and proofread long technical tables. Similarly, entering a large portion of text is easier with a WYSIWYG editor, although most texts can now be converted electronically.

## TAKE NOTE

### ► WYSIWYG BUNDLES

Many WYSIWYG Web editors come as a package deal. FrontPage Editor is part of FrontPage (including Web site management and server tools), and Netscape Composer is a component of Netscape Communicator. Because of the way these bundles work together, you may find yourself with more tools than you bargained for. For example, FrontPage Editor is really not intended to be used as a separate product; it inserts FrontPage-specific elements when you edit pages using Editor.

### ► ADVANCED WYSIWYG

Some WYSIWYG editors, like Microsoft InterDev and Allaire's Cold Fusion, are designed to work with server tools to develop Web-based applications. InterDev lets you design ASP (Active Server Pages) Web sites, and Cold Fusion uses the Cold Fusion server API.

**CROSS-REFERENCE**

For more information on why WYSIWYG is a misnomer on the World Wide Web, see Chapter 1.

**FIND IT ONLINE**

A brief article on WYSIWYG is at "WYSIWYG: What does it mean on the Web?" (http://home1.gte.net/paulp/wysiwyg.htm).

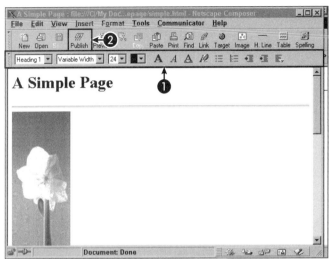

**❶** *Netscape Composer is a WYSIWYG editor that lets you quickly format text using shortcut buttons.*

**❷** *You can also upload files to your Web server with the Publish button.*

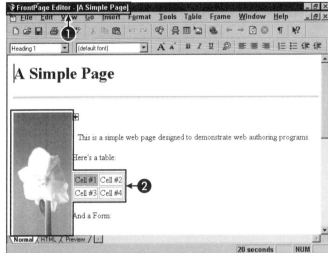

**❶** *FrontPage 98 supports more HTML elements and attributes, such as image alignment and table colors.*

**❷** *You can view the HTML directly, and preview it as it would appear in a Web browser.*

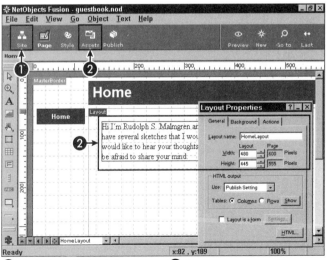

**❶** *NetObjects Fusion helps you manage not only page elements, but entire site elements.*

**❷** *In an unusual way of approaching the Web, NetObjects Fusion sites make each object (including lists and images) into separate Web site elements.*

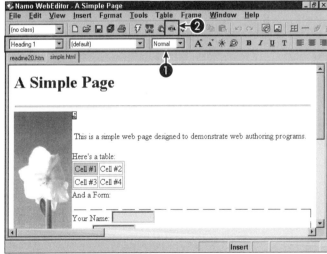

**❶** *Namo Interactive's Web Editor has a simple interface; toolbar buttons allow quick access to common HTML formatting elements.*

**❷** *You can view the HTML source by clicking the little HTML button.*

# Selecting a Tag Editor

Tag-based editors are similar to text-based editors, but they specifically support HTML elements. They usually have a toolbar that you can use to quickly insert HTML elements, and you may or may not be able to directly edit the attributes of a tag.

The advantages to using a tag-based editor are that you have finer control over the HTML generated, you don't have to remember every HTML element to use it, and there's usually a preview mode to see what the Web page would look like in a standard Web browser.

Tag-based editors offer a limited amount of control over the generated HTML code, which varies depending on the program. Part of it is stylistic; some editors insert code in uppercase or lowercase only. Some may not allow you to directly edit an attribute or add HTML 4.0 specific attributes. Still others may not support client-side scripts, style sheets, or embedded files. However, there are a few good "gems" that allow you to do anything with the underlying HTML, offering just shortcuts to elements, and color-coding your code for easier searching and reference.

When you research your tag-based editor, look for an easy-to-use interface. One of the strengths of the WYSIWYG editors is that they often resemble popular word processing programs, such as Microsoft Word and Corel WordPerfect. Tag-based editors are a whole other ball of wax. It can be very confusing to see the elements onscreen without seeing their effects, or to have a toolbar of strange HTML elements instead of the common bold, italic, and underline that most word processors feature.

## TAKE NOTE

### ▶ AUXILIARY PROGRAMS

Many tag-based editors (and HTML editors in general) come with built-in auxiliary programs. These might include an FTP client to instantly upload your Web pages to your server. Or, they might have a built-in color picker, an image map utility, or even a link verification tool. Some programs offer HTML verification, to check your code for "valid" HTML. Those auxiliary programs may be a boon, or they may just be a useless tool that you don't ever use. Don't base your decision on whether or not there are built-in programs; if you need that kind of tool, chances are there's a standalone program you can use instead.

### ▶ PREVIEW AND WYSIWYG MODES

Some tag-based editors also offer Web preview and WYSIWYG editing modes. These additional views allow you to see how your Web page will look in a browser. Sometimes, you'll be able to edit your page directly in the WYSIWYG view. So, what makes a tag-based editor different from a WYSIWYG editor if it has such a view? Control over your code, and the fact that the program's default view (and perhaps most useful view) is the tag-based editor, not the WYSIWYG one.

## CROSS-REFERENCE

The CD-ROM includes two good tag-based editors: CoffeeCup HTML Editor++ and Allaire's HomeSite.

## FIND IT ONLINE

The TUCOWS site has many Web editing programs available, for any operating system: http://www.tucows.com.

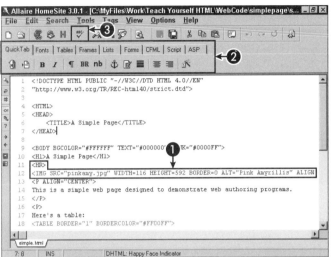

① *Allaire HomeSite, included on the CD-ROM, color-codes your HTML elements for you.*

② *Toolbars offer shortcuts to all HTML elements.*

③ *A built-in spell checker checks the spelling of your Web documents.*

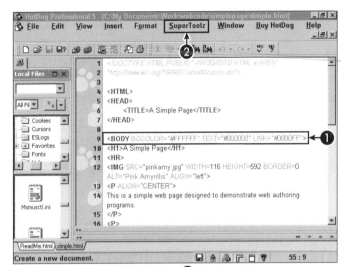

■ *Sausage Software's Hot Dog Pro provides a complete HTML element list for easy reference.*

① *Color-coded tags are easy to read.*

② *The SuperToolz menu consists of several wizards and code snippets to include in your Web pages.*

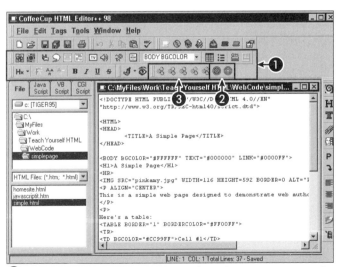

① *CoffeeCup's HTML Editor++ is another tag-based editor with toolbars and shortcuts.*

② *A Preview button automatically lets you view* the Web page in an external browser.

③ *You can set up additional programs to launch from the*

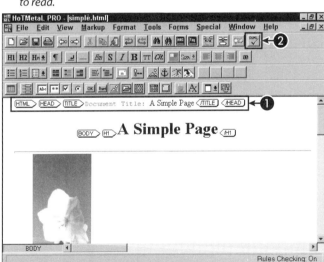

toolbars as well.

① *SoftQuad's HoTMetaL PRO offers a very rich tag-based editing environment, with WYSIWYG and text editing*

capabilities.

② *HoTMetaL PRO supports SGML authoring.*

■ *Site management capabilities are available for advanced developers.*

**211**

# Choosing a Text Editor

Text editors are the most basic of HTML editing tools. Windows Notepad, Macintosh SimpleText, UNIX's vi, or any basic word processor can be used as an HTML text editing program. They provide the most control over your Web document because you edit the HTML directly, without tag "shortcuts" or similar helping tools.

Of course, not all text editors are created equal. Windows Notepad may be a decent text editor, but it wasn't designed to be used for HTML. As a result, you must carefully save your documents as *.html* whenever you edit a page, or risk having your .html file appear as plaintext. Other text editors have been modified or written specifically for Web page editing. Their default document type is HTML, and they may have additional programs to check for valid HTML, or to upload files to a Web server. BBEdit, Emacs, Notepad, WordPad, and SimpleText are all text editors for various platforms and operating systems. On the next page, you can see a few basic text editors, editing a simple Web page.

If you host your Web site on a UNIX-based server, you may need to edit your page using the UNIX text editor, called *vi* (vee-eye). Vi is one of the least user-friendly text editors I've ever encountered, but it's also one of the most popular ones for serious Web designers. Its popularity is mainly due to its speed (because you don't have to upload the file when you're done) and its functionality. If you know vi really well, you can make it do things that only an advanced word processor program can normally do.

To use a text editor, simply open your HTML document, or create a new file. Start typing in your HTML elements, starting with the <HTML> and <HEAD> elements first, as discussed in the first two parts of this book. You can capitalize the elements and attributes if you wish; I find it's easier to locate them later if you do.

## TAKE NOTE

### ▶ COPY, CUT, AND PASTE

Ctrl-C is usually used for copying, Ctrl-X for cutting, and Ctrl-V for pasting, but those shortcuts may be missing in a simple text editor. Use the Edit menu to select them instead.

### ▶ WORD WRAP

As you type, you might find that the text scrolls over to the right, and keeps scrolling. Some text editors have a feature called "word wrap." If word wrapping is on, the line of text will automatically continue on the next line on the screen, but a return character (when you hit the Enter key) will not be recorded in the file itself. Some Web browsers interpret returns in unusual ways, and the <PRE> element makes them extremely important for spacing. With word wrapping, you can still see all your text onscreen, without changing how many returns are in the file.

**CROSS-REFERENCE**

To learn how to create Web pages using just text, see Chapter 2.

**FIND IT ONLINE**

A list of HTML-editor reviews is available at **http://homepage.interaccess.com/ ~cdavis/edit_rev.html.**

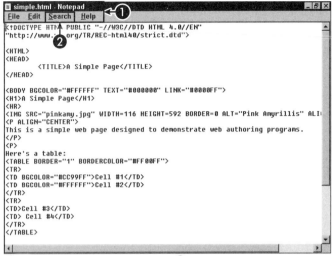

❶ Notepad comes with Windows operating systems, is easy to use, and offers a quick tool for editing Web pages on the fly.

❷ You can search the entire file for a string, and standard editing tools (cut, copy, paste) are also available.

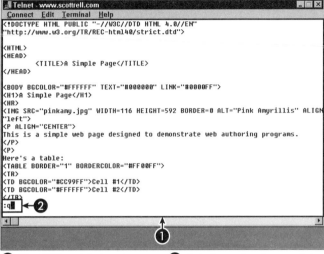

❶ The UNIX tool vi, though not terribly user-friendly, is a potent text editor for Web developers.

❷ A tip for novice vi users: click Esc, then :q to quit editing. Use :q! to quit without saving the changes.

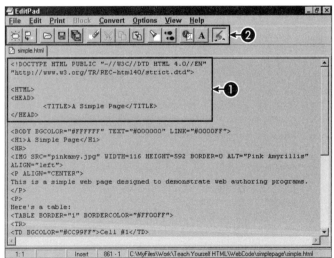

❶ Although simple, EditPad lets you directly edit the code quickly and easily.

❷ Additional toolbars and shortcuts make it more user-friendly than Notepad, without too many confusing features.

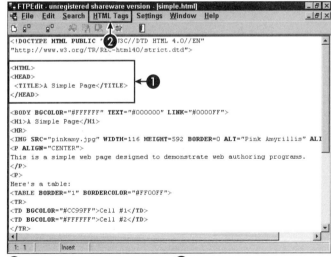

❶ Designed for remote file editing, FTPEdit color-codes your HTML tags.

❷ A drop-down menu offers a shortcut to HTML elements.

# Using Graphics Tools

As you've already seen in Chapter 6, graphics are an integral part of the World Wide Web. They provide visual variety, can help promote products, and may provide crucial information such as technical diagrams and photographs.

You can achieve a variety of effects on the Web with graphics, although only two graphic types are widely supported on the Internet. GIF and JPEG file formats are the two main types of graphics to use, and any decent graphics editing program will be able to create or save as those formats.

Graphics editors tend to come in two types (and price ranges). Shareware programs offer a variety of tools, although they tend to be limited in certain respects. For most Web graphics, however, they work just fine, providing easy access to scanning technology, GIF manipulation, and button and icon creation.

Serious graphic designers, however, use one of the commercial tools, such as CorelDRAW or PhotoShop. These programs offer advanced graphics-editing features, such as layers, additional plug-in programs, and macros, and they usually come with clip art for you to use.

When you use a graphics program to create or edit a Web graphic, be sure to preview it in your Web browser before you use it. Graphics programs optimize the display hardware to show all graphics in the best light. Web browsers, on the other hand, have limited display capabilities, as well as limited color palettes. The color palette restricts the number of colors available to the Web browser, which affects how well your Web graphics look online.

The next page has screen shots from a few common graphics editing programs. The first one, Paint Shop Pro, is a shareware program available on the CD-ROM included with this book. CorelDRAW, shown in the top-right figure, is a commercial software package that comes with a library of clip art images for you to use. The bottom-left figure shows The Gimp, a Linux graphics program that is as full-featured as any commercial program, but under the free GNU license. Finally, MS Image Composer comes with Microsoft FrontPage, a WYSIWYG Web editing package.

*Continued*

## TAKE NOTE

### ▶ GRAPHIC FILTERS

Most graphics programs come with filters you can use to edit photographs and graphics. Some of these filters are designed to correct photographic problems, such as red eyes, and lighting problems. Some are just for fun effects, like swirling, pixelating, and adding blurs. Experiment with filters to produce extraordinary effects with ordinary pictures.

### ▶ IMAGE SCANNING

Scanning a photograph for the Web requires some type of scanner hardware and a scanning program. Most graphic programs and scanners are TWAIN-compliant. That means they use the TWAIN (Toolkit Without An Interesting Name) standard for scanning, but some scanning programs only support one brand of scanner. Make sure your scanner and software are compatible with each other before you spend a lot of money on either.

**CROSS-REFERENCE**
For more information on using graphics to enhance your Web site identity, see Chapter 22.

**FIND IT ONLINE**
Looking for more information on The Gimp? The Gimp home page (**http://www.gimp.org**) has everything you'll need.

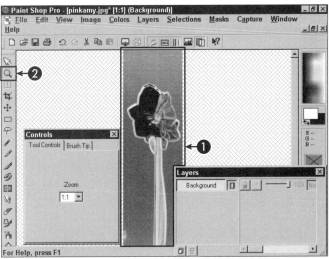

**1** Paint Shop Pro, included on the CD-ROM, offers several filters for unusual effects; this one uses a solarized effect.

**2** You can change the zoom with the Zoom tool.

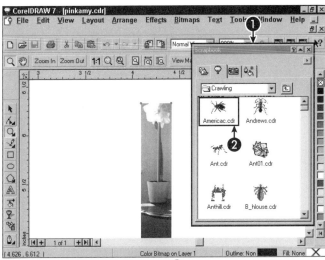

**1** CorelDRAW! 7 comes with a variety of clip art files for you to use.

**2** Drag a clip art image onto the current image to include it in the graphic.

**1** The Gimp is a powerful, free Linux graphics program that offers a number of preinstalled graphics scripts.

**2** You can use the Gimp to create neat Web graphics on a Linux workstation.

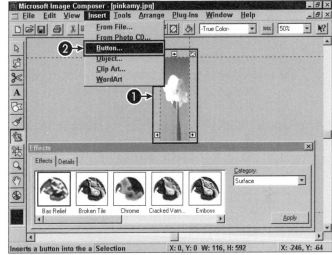

**1** Microsoft Image Composer uses "sprites" instead of graphic layers to create graphics.

**2** A Button Wizard makes it easy to create Web buttons and icons for a sitewide look and feel.

# Using Graphics Tools
*Continued*

There are many other types of graphics tools that enable you to change and manipulate your Web graphics to achieve certain effects, such as image maps, an HTML-specific graphic effect.

On the next page, you'll see two different programs to create animated GIFs. Animated GIFs are basically a series of GIFs that have been "pasted" together into one graphic file. That file can be read as an animated GIF, and it works like a little flip book, running through the graphics as it's instructed to do by the graphic. Netscape Navigator 2.0 and above, and Internet Explorer 2.0 and above, all support animated GIFs, although very early browsers do not.

When you research a GIF animation program, make sure you can create looping animations and timed animations. Loops make the animated sequence repeat as often as you specify. Timed animations can hold one frame for a specified length of time before going to the next image, instead of flipping through the frames in your animation with no delay. Some animators also offer comments that you can include in the GIF image itself, and wizards to help you quickly and easily create animated text GIFs. You should also check the animation program to see how it handles transparent GIFs, and if it has any additional features such as sample animations.

The bottom two figures are image map creation programs. As you learned in Chapter 6, image maps are graphics linked to a series of hyperlinks. When users click somewhere on the image map, they follow a hyperlink, based entirely on where they clicked in the image map.

Image maps can be written in three ways. CERN, NCSA, and client-side (CSIM). CERN and NCSA are server-side image maps, overseen by the W3C and the NCSA (National Center for Supercomputing Applications). They each require a slightly different syntax in the image map file, which must also be separate. In other words, CERN or NCSA image maps are files, called `filename.map` (or something similar), and you link the image map to it with `<A HREF="filename.map"> <IMG SRC="map.gif" ISMAP></A>`. When a user clicks on the image map, the server looks in the `.map` file to find the correct URL to send the user to.

CSIMs are image maps that are executed on the Web browser, or client. When a user clicks on the hyperlink, it's up to the Web browser to look up the correct coordinate and send the user there. The data that would normally appear in a `.map` file can be placed inside the HTML file, often in the `<HEAD>` section of the file. As you can guess, CSIMs are very browser-dependent, but they're quite reliable in the 3.0-and-above browsers.

## TAKE NOTE

### OTHER GRAPHICS FEATURES

Some graphics tools, such as Ulead's SmartSaver and Microsoft Image Composer, let you reduce your graphic's size by minimizing the resolution or compression ratio to something more Internet-friendly. Don't underestimate the value of that kind of feature; smaller graphics download faster on the Internet.

**CROSS-REFERENCE**

For more information on creating image maps, see Chapter 6.

**FIND IT ONLINE**

To convert between server-side and client-side image maps, see **http://www.popco.com/popco/convertmaps.html**.

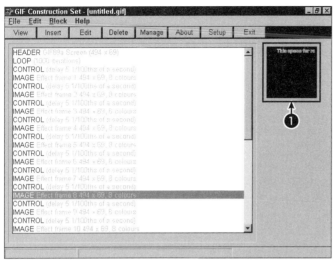

① *Alchemy Mindworks' GIF Construction Set offers a quick preview of your animated graphic.*

■ *Animation wizards let you create transitions from one graphic to another.*

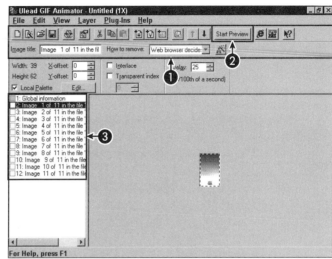

① *ULead's GIF Animator has a more complicated interface, but more options are available from the toolbars.*

② *A Start Preview button starts and stops the animation.*

③ *Change the global information to edit the palette, transparent colors, and similar information.*

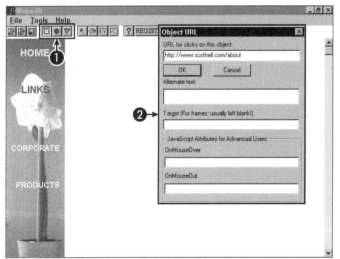

① *Mapedit lets you drag and drop hot spots on an image map using preset shapes.*

② *Test the hyperlinks by clicking on them with the Pointer tool.*

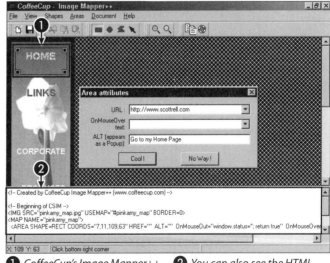

① *CoffeeCup's Image Mapper++ has a similar interface, but hot-spot areas are shown more clearly.*

② *You can also see the HTML image map generated as you work.*

# Examining Verification and Validation

**V**erification and validation tools let you check for valid HTML in your Web pages. You can use an HTML validator to check your HTML for errors, such as open elements, improper syntax, and missing but required elements (such as the `<HTML>` element).

A good HTML validator will look at whatever **DOCTYPE** you declared (if any), and try to use that **DOCTYPE** as the basis for its validation. The **DOCTYPE** refers to the HTML document's DTD, a set of "rules" for how HTML elements should behave, and which attributes belong to different elements.

Some HTML validators don't use the **DOCTYPE** to determine the DTD. They have a built-in DTD that they use instead. Because the standards change so rapidly, using the **DOCTYPE** definition may keep validation tools more up-to-date than using an internal DTD. Since HTML 4.0 specifically supports three separate DTDs (called `strict`, `frames`, and `styles`), it's important to use validation tools that also support those DTDs. With the emergence of XML as a useful markup language, validators may also have to support XML DTDs. Validation tools that support the **DOCTYPE** definition today will be more likely to support XML DTDs in the future.

At the same time, it's important to remember that every Web browser has its own DTD, or its own way of defining how HTML elements behave. One browser may force a default border for hyperlinked images, while another may make the default "0." Not all Web browsers support the **DOCTYPE** definition either, and beginning Web authors are often confused as to why they use the **DOCTYPE** if the Web browser doesn't seem to care. HTML validation programs and other Web tools are the reason; standard Web browsers are not the only programs to access or try to understand Web pages.

Other things to look for in an HTML validator are syntax, spell checkers, and link validation. Most HTML validators do not also check your hyperlinks, but those that do are very powerful indeed. If your validator doesn't include a link checker, you can download a separate program to handle that task for you. Some Web authoring tools, like Allaire's HomeSite and Microsoft FrontPage include these types of tools already. HomeSite comes with the CSE HTML Validator, and FrontPage has an automatic link checker that will help you determine if your hyperlinks are current.

**CROSS-REFERENCE**

For more information on link verification and site management, see Chapter 21.

**FIND IT ONLINE**

See **http://www.cre.canon.co.uk/~neilb/weblint/ validation.html** for more validation and verification tools.

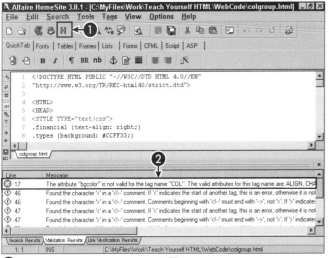

**1** The CSE HTML Validator is integrated into Allaire HomeSite.

**2** Errors are shown with a big red "X", and provide the line number.

■ Because it's an offline validator, CSE HTML Validator checks Web pages very quickly.

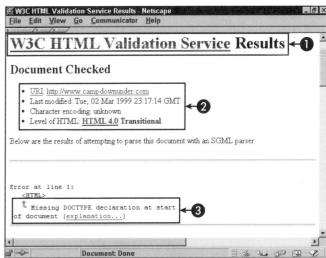

**1** The W3C HTML Validator is a free Web-based validator.

**2** Because it's run by the W3C, you can expect it will be extra picky about valid HTML.

**3** Don't forget your DOCTYPE when using the W3C Validator!

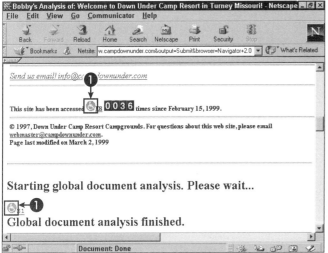

■ The Bobby validator checks for accessibility-related errors on Web pages and offers suggestions.

**1** Accessibility icons indicate potential accessibility issues or errors.

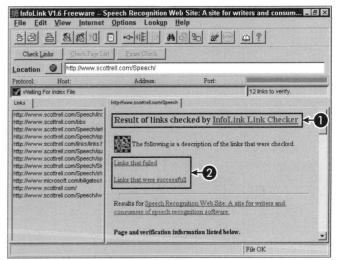

**1** InfoLink Freeware is a free link verification program to check all the links on a page.

**2** Results are generated as an HTML page for you to refer to.

# Exploring Scripting Tools

If you've read this far, you can already create a Web page without much difficulty. You can create graphics to go into it, and you know how to put them in and add hyperlinks. However, what you may not know yet, and will begin to learn in the next two parts of this book, is how to write and use scripts on your Web site.

A script is a short program that takes information from the Web page and performs an action (or series of actions) based on that information. The information is usually the result of a Web-based form, but it could also be user behavior such as mouse movements and clicking on links or images.

Scripts can reside on either the Web server or in the Web browser. Scripts on the Web server are called "server-side scripts," and they're usually run using CGI, the Common Gateway Interface. CGI is a technology that lets you run a program on one machine using input from a client machine. Other server-side scripts include server-side image maps and proprietary server APIs and extensions, such as Active Server Pages, ColdFusion, and FrontPage Extensions.

The other kind of script is called a client-side script. Those scripts are usually written in JavaScript or VBScript, and they require that the user have a Web browser capable of reading and executing whichever scripting language you use. Client-side scripts are therefore very browser-dependent, but they're also a lot faster than server-side scripts. Because the entire program downloads with the Web page, additional requests are not sent to the Web server, and additional files do not need to be downloaded.

Client-side scripting languages are generally fairly easy to learn, and you can use a scripting tool to help you learn one. When the script is generated, look at it using your text editor and try to dissect its contents. Chapter 18 will help you learn more about scripting languages and how to read them.

## TAKE NOTE

### ▶ SOME EXPERIENCE NECESSARY

The scripting tools available do require a certain level of technical knowledge. For CGI tools, you should know if you have a CGI directory, and where it is on the server. For client-side scripting tools, a basic knowledge of client-side scripting languages and the Document Object Model (DOM) is useful. Finally, you should definitely know how to create the HTML parts of your script — forms, buttons, and any elements that will be manipulated through scripts.

### ▶ JAVA APPLET SCRIPTING TOOLS

There are also a number of programs to help you create Java applets quickly and easily. They're usually limited in what the Java applet created can do, but animations, simple games, and Java-driven chat programs are generally possible.

**CROSS-REFERENCE**

For more information on writing server-side scripts, see Chapter 19.

**FIND IT ONLINE**

Create quick JavaScript snippets online at Roller (**http://home.plutonium.net/~pfriedl/roller/roller.html**).

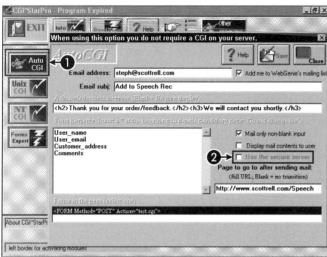

❶ CGIStarPro has an automatic CGI generator that lets you create CGI scripts by just reading an HTML file.

❷ You can use a secure server (if you have one available) if users will be submitting personal or confidential information.

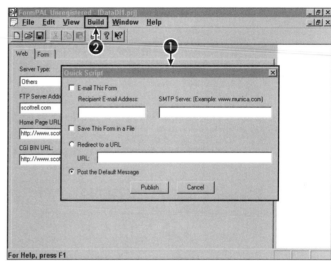

❶ FormPal, included on the CD-ROM, has a Quick Script feature to let you quickly generate server-side scripts to handle forms.

❷ You can also generate a custom script in the Build menu.

❶ Java Script It! automatically generates code and inserts it into your Web page as desired.

❷ The Quick Steps window prompts you to enter information as you create your client-side script.

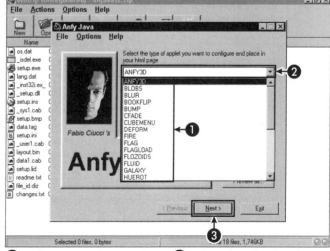

❶ Anfy Java is a collection of Java applets you can customize for your own Web sites.

❷ A drop-down box lists the applets available.

❸ Select one and click Next to customize the applet.

# Personal Workbook

## Q&A

**1** What are some important features in a WYSIWYG editor?

_____

_____

_____

**2** What are the drawbacks to using a WYSIWYG editor?

_____

_____

_____

**3** How important is a preview mode in tag-based editors?

_____

_____

_____

**4** What other types of programs would you expect to find in a Web editing package?

_____

_____

_____

**5** How do commercial graphics programs differ from shareware programs?

_____

_____

_____

**6** Name one advantage of a shareware program over a commercial graphics program.

_____

_____

_____

**7** Why is the DOCTYPE so important to HTML Validation tools?

_____

_____

_____

**8** When creating server-side scripts, what information will you probably need to provide?

_____

_____

_____

ANSWERS: PAGE 442

## EXTRA PRACTICE

① Evaluate the programs you currently use for applications outside of Web design.

② Visit the Web sites of at least four Web editing programs. Look at the screen shots of those programs, or download available demos.

③ Download and install an evaluation version of a Web editor. Try creating a simple page with a header, a graphic, a table, and a form.

④ Now look at the generated code using a text editor, like Notepad. Make sure the editor created your Web page using the tags you requested.

⑤ Validate the HTML generated using an HTML validator program or online validation service.

⑥ Use a link checker to check the hyperlinks in your home page or main Web site.

## REAL-WORLD APPLICATIONS

✔ You find it's time-consuming to use Notepad for HTML coding. You use an HTML editor to make the job go faster.

✔ Your boss wants to create an image map using the company logo. You edit the logo graphic by adding some text to refer to the hyperlinks, and use an image map program to create the map itself.

✔ You keep your links pages up-to-date by checking them frequently with a Web spider or link checker tool.

✔ You need to do just one thing with client-side scripts, but you don't know any scripting languages. You use a JavaScript generation program to create a quick script to include on your pages.

## Visual Quiz

What kind of HTML editor is shown here? How would you create a new Web page using it? How would you include HTML elements and images? What do you like and dislike about this kind of Web editing program?

_____

_____

_____

_____

_____

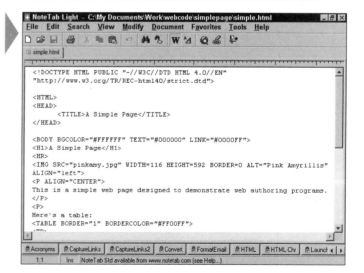

PART

# IV

# Other Technologies

In this part, you discover advanced technologies that make the Web exciting for Web designers. Style sheets, which are an integral part of the HTML 4.0 specification, help designers and users compromise on the look and layout of Web pages. They also solve many compatibility problems, although, as this section reveals, they can cause other problems as well.

Many are heralding EXtensible Markup Language, or XML, as the "next HTML." It is possible that HTML will become a subset of XML. XML enables designers to create their own elements and use them in the same syntax as HTML. Although not fully implemented yet, XML is a potentially powerful tool for serious Web designers.

Finally, Dynamic HTML (DHTML) has been the most recent battleground in the browser wars. DHTML uses scripts and built-in document objects to provide a more interactive, dynamic experience, without using Java or server-side scripts. Microsoft and Netscape seem unable to agree on how to implement Dynamic HTML — their browsers use different technologies to implement it. However, because the Web is a dynamic medium, it is only a matter of time before this becomes standardized.

Plug-ins and Java applets are used to enhance Web sites and create an interactive user experience. By the end of this part, you'll know how to use these technologies to create an effective Web site.

CHAPTER **13**

# Style Sheets

At the heart of HTML 4.0's formatting issues lies the nebulous specification known as style sheets. Style sheets started in Microsoft Internet Explorer 3.0 as Cascading Style Sheets. They were later turned into a W3C specification, CSS1. CSS1 has been replaced by CSS2, but few Web browsers fully support the style properties outlines in CSS1, much less CSS2.

You may have noticed that many layout and visual formatting issues in this book have mentioned style sheets as a solution to the browser incompatibility issue.

In fact, style sheets do not solve browser incompatibility; rather, they make it less important when designing the site. Essentially, style sheets provide a guideline for Web browsers: display this element this way, or use whatever default is available. Web browsers generally do that anyway; any unrecognized element is simply ignored. With style sheets, however, designers have more options for specifying how each element should be displayed.

There are other good reasons to use style sheets. One reason is that, especially with external style sheets, only one page needs to be changed to reformat the entire look and feel of the whole site. You can also change the way an entire element acts in a Web page without editing the element itself. This can be useful if you're using a common site template but want just one page to look different.

# Creating Style Sheets

A style sheet is nothing more than some text that tells the Web browser how to interpret your HTML code. It basically expands the standard elements; if the element `<P>` indicates a text paragraph, then the tag `<P style="color: green;">` indicates a text paragraph in green. Style sheets take HTML one step further in the HTML specification.

Styles are made up of properties and their values. In the green text paragraph, the property is `color`, and its value is `green`. You can also use hexadecimal values (discussed in Chapter 2) to specify colors.

There are three ways to include styles in your Web document. First, you can use the style attribute in virtually any element. That's useful for when you want to change the style of an individual element without affecting the rest of the document. The syntax for this method is `<ELEMENT style="property: value ;">`. Note the semicolon between the property and the value, and the semicolon after the value. There's some debate over whether or not there should be a space between the semicolon and the value. Since there's only a problem when there's no space, I usually put one in.

You can also put style sheet information inside the `<HEAD>` element. To do this, use the `<STYLE>` element. The syntax for this kind of style sheet is `<STYLE> ELEMENT { property: value ;} <STYLE>` Again, notice the punctuation. The curly braces are crucial to style sheets. You can include more than one element inside the `<STYLE>` element. An example of using the `<STYLE>` element in the `<HEAD>` section is shown in the second and third figures on the next page.

The third way to include style sheets is to create a style sheet separate from the HTML page. You can then link this external style sheet into your HTML document. Linking an external style sheet is discussed later in this chapter.

## TAKE NOTE

### ▶ INHERITED STYLES

Styles are inherited from one element into another. Basically, any element that is contained by another element will inherit that element's styles unless the style is overridden in the style sheet. For example, most elements are contained by the `<BODY>` element. If the `<BODY>` element has been specified with red text and blue background, then all elements within the `<BODY>` element will have red text on a blue background. Even if a particular element, such as `<H1>`, is also specified in the style sheet, it will inherit the `<BODY>`'s properties unless `color` and `background` properties are specified for it in the style sheet as well.

**CROSS-REFERENCE**

Centering and similar text styles are also discussed in Chapter 3.

**FIND IT ONLINE**

Visit Webmonkey's tutorial style sheets:
**http://www.hotwired.com/webmonkey/stylesheets/.**

## \<DIV\> and \<Span\> Elements

Most HTML elements already have some formatting "built in," so to speak. A text paragraph will start a new line before and after the paragraph, and will use a different font than other elements in some browsers.

Because style sheets are supposed to combine structural markup with visual markup, neutral elements had to be created. The \<DIV\> element is a block-level element — meaning it will have a line break before and after it — that otherwise has no visual formatting assigned to it, and content inside this element will appear in the default text unless otherwise specified.

\<SPAN\> works the same way, except that it's an inline element, like \<EM\> or a hyperlink anchor. Both elements accept the style attributes, and can be specified in a style sheet like any other element.

As a result, you can use these elements to insert styles based entirely on the structure of the page rather than on design elements. For example, if the first section of your document contains the most important information, enclose it in a \<DIV\> element and give it a style, such as a special font color or family, or even italicized text. All the content — including headings and images — will inherit the \<DIV\>'s style.

### Listing 13-1: Two Style Definitions

```
<HEAD><STYLE>
P {text-align: left; text-indent: 15pt;        ←─ a
  border-width: 3;}
SPAN {font-family: arial; text-decoration:
  underline; }
</STYLE></HEAD>                    b
<BODY><H1 style="background-color: #00CCFF;
  text-align: center; border-width: 4;
  border-color: 66FFFF;">Style Sheet        c
  Examples</H1>
<HR>
<P>This is an example of using style sheets
  <SPAN>inside</SPAN> the HEAD element. The
  Header uses an in-line style definition.
</P></BODY>
```

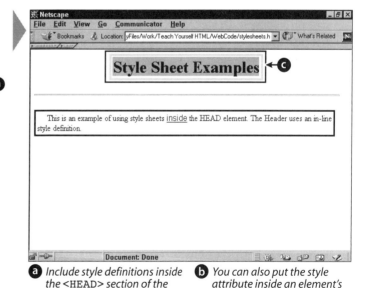

**a** Include style definitions inside the \<HEAD\> section of the Web page using the \<STYLE\> element.

**b** You can also put the style attribute inside an element's opening tag.

**c** To center a text element, use `style="text-align: center;"`

229

# Changing Fonts with Styles

As you recall, the `<FONT>` element has been problematic for Web designers since it was first invented. It doesn't degrade to older browsers well, and it occasionally conflicts with the `<BODY>` element.

Style sheets answer the `<FONT>` problem, and they do it fairly well. In the future, users will be able to specify a default style sheet for the Web browser to use, which will specify not only the font colors and sizes, but spacing elements, borders, and indentation. Right now, all those design elements can be set with style sheets.

To change the color of a section of text, use the `color` property. For example, `<P style="color: #990000 ;">` will make the paragraph dark red (#990000). You can change a single word or phrase with the `<SPAN>` element: `<SPAN style="color: #990000 ;">`. Be sure to close all your elements when using styles, or the styles will continue to be used in the next element. To change the background color, use `background-color`: `<P style="color: #990000 ; background-color: #66FFFF ;">` for a dark red text on light blue background (background colors in text will appear to highlight the text).

The `font-family` property changes the font type used in a page. You can define a specific font, such as Arial or Helvetica, or you can use a generic family name, such as sans-serif or serif. You can also specify more than one font family to use. The Web browser will try each font family in order, and will use the first one it can understand. So, if you have `font-family: Arial, Helvetica, sans-serif ;` as your style, the Web browser will first try the Arial font (which is installed on most PCs), then the Helvetica font (which is installed on most Macintoshes),

and finally the sans-serif generic family, which includes any font that does not use serifs (such as Arial and Helvetica). Other generic families include serif, cursive, fantasy, and monospace. Font families are separated with commas, but make sure there's no ending comma before the semicolon.

Table 13-1 shows a list of properties for text and fonts. You can "shortcut" those properties by including them all in one property definition. For example, to define an element's font as italicized, bold, small, in the Arial or sans-serif font, you could specify each individual property: `{font-style: italic ; font-weight: bold ; font-size: small ; font-family: Arial, sans-serif ;}`.

## TAKE NOTE

### FONT SHORTCUTS

You can also use the `font` property to specify all the properties that have to do with fonts. To do that, you must specify each font property in its correct order. Leave out the property names, and just use the values. The order for the `font` property is `font-style font-weight font-size font-family`. So, for the previous example, you would use `{font: italic bold small Arial, sans-serif ;}`. The advantage to these shortcuts is that it takes less room. Individual properties are separated by spaces, and multiple values within a property (such as the `font-family` values) are separated with commas.

## CROSS-REFERENCE
Older methods of formatting fonts and text are discussed in Chapter 3.

## FIND IT ONLINE
Web Review has a CSS guide available at http://webreview.com/wr/pub/guides/style/style.html.

## Table 13-1: STYLE SHEET PR

| Property | Values |
|---|---|
| background-color | *hexadecimal color* |
| color | *hexadecimal color* |
| font | font-style font-weight font-size font-family |
| font-family | *any font name*, serif, sans-serif, cursive, fantasy, and monospace |
| font-size | *size in points*, xx-large, x-large, large, larger, medium, small, smaller, x-small, xx-small |
| font-style | normal, italic, oblique |
| font-weight | *increments of 100 (not implemented)*, normal, bold, bolder, lighter |
| text-align | left, right, center, justify |
| text-decoration | none, underline, overline, line-through, blink |
| text-indent | *length in points*, *length in percentage* |

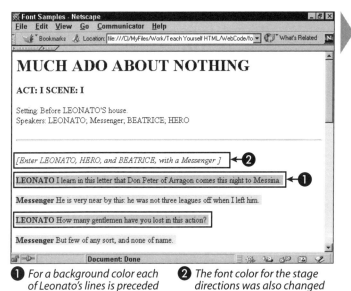

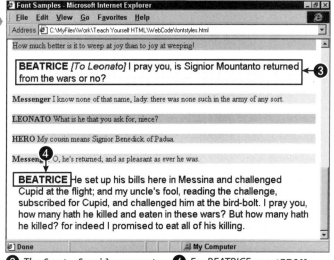

❶ *For a background color each of Leonato's lines is preceded by* <P style= "background-color: #99CCCC; "> <B>LEONATO</B>.

❷ *The font color for the stage directions was also changed with a style:* <P style="font-style: italic; color: #000080;">.

❸ *The* font-family *property lets you set a specific font or font style:* font-family: Arial, Helvetica, sans-serif;.

❹ *For BEATRICE, use* <SPAN style="font-weight: bold;"> *to bold the name. Increase the size with the* font-size *property:* font-size: 14pt;.

# Positioning with Styles

You've already learned about block-level elements and how they position themselves onscreen. Using tables, you can even shift those elements around a bit, although it takes a lot of "tweaking" to get it just right. Until now, there's been a fundamental conflict between the cross-compatibility of HTML and its ability to display information graphically.

Style sheets provide a compromise between your own layout needs and your audience's wishes. You can define block-level HTML elements in CSS box properties and determine where and how the element will be displayed. The first figure shows a diagram of how these properties control layout.

There are three basic parts to a box property: the `margin`, the `border`s, and the `padding`.

The outermost property is the `margin`, a transparent space between the edge of the screen (or other elements) and the current element. You can specify the width (or height) of each margin, or of the entire margin around the element. For example, `{margin: 1pt ;}` places a pixel-wide margin all around the block element. That's a very thin margin; the affected element will appear to fill the space provided. `{margin-top: 1pt ; margin-right: 10pt ; margin-bottom: 1pt ; margin-left: 10pt ;}` gives the affected element a top and bottom margin of 1 pixel (still very small), and left and right margins of 10 points, about half an inch on a 17" monitor running 640 480 resolution.

Borders have the following available properties: `border-top-width`, `border-right-width`, `border-bottom-width`, `border-left-width`, `border-color`, and `border-style`. Widths can be specified in values of `thin`, `thick`, `medium`, or a width in points.

The `border-color` property is similar to the `color` property for an element, and is used the same way.

`Border-style` can specify a specific style for the border, although this property is not implemented in all browsers. Possible values for the `border-style` are `none`, `dotted`, `dashed`, `solid`, `double`, `groove`, `ridge`, `inset`, and `outset`.

Finally, the `padding` property uses the same syntax as the `margin` property, including shortcut syntax. It's a transparent property defining whitespace around an element inside the border.

*Continued*

## Shortcuts

Just like the `font` property, box property definitions also have shortcuts. To shortcut the `margin` property definition, put the `margin` values in the following order: `{margin: margin-top margin-right margin-bottom margin-left ;}`. Notice that only spaces separate the individual values. The previous example, with a 1-point margin at the top and bottom and the 10-point margin at the left and right, could also be written `{margin: 1pt 10pt 1pt 10pt ;}`.

Shortcut border widths with the `border-width` property: `{border-width: thin thick 10pt thick ;}`. To shortcut all border properties, use the border-top (or right, bottom, or left) property: `{border-top: border-top-width border-style color ;}`. The border property itself will apply the same property values to all borders of the given element, using the same syntax and property order: `{border: . border-width border-style color ;}`.

**CROSS-REFERENCE**

Positioning can also be dynamically controlled using JavaScript. Scripts are discussed in Chapter 18.

**FIND IT ONLINE**

Microsoft's Web site has a paper on CSS positioning at http://www.microsoft.com/workshop/author/css/csspos/csspos.asp.

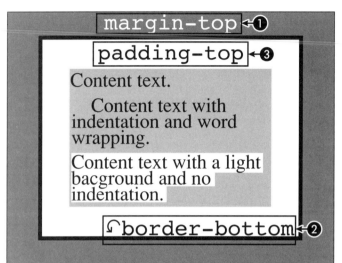

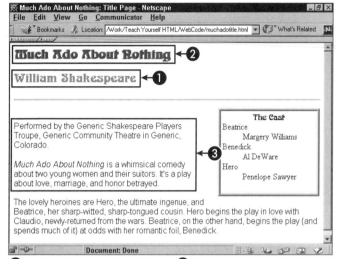

**①** *The margin is the outermost space between an element and other elements on the page (including the edge of the screen).*

**②** *Borders, an optional property, can now appear around any HTML element using styles.*

**③** *The padding is the area between a border and the element itself.*

**①** *To increase the margin around the author's name, use* `margin: 20pt` *for a 20-point margin all around.*

**②** *Use negative margin values for a "shadowing" effect.*

**③** *A margin also provides whitespace between wrapping elements (the text) and floating elements (the list).*

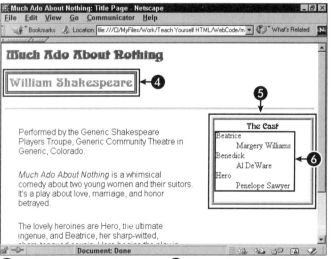

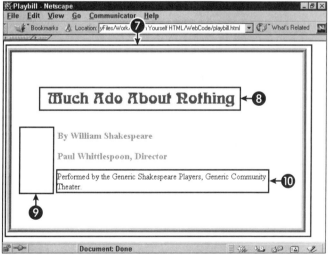

**④** *Add a navy blue border to the author's name:* `border: 4pt double #191970;`.

**⑤** *The floating element also has a styled border.*

**⑥** *When using a styled border on a <DL> element, the text does not wrap; use <DIV> instead.*

**⑦** *This page uses a <DIV> element with a 7-point ridge border and a 50-point padding.*

**⑧** *The title is formatted with fonts, and has a bottom padding of 20 points.*

**⑨** *The rest of the content has a left padding of 15 points.*

**⑩** *This text uses padding so the second line is correctly aligned.*

# Positioning with Styles

*Continued*

There are several other placement properties you should know about. All of the placement properties are implemented in Internet Explorer 4.0 and above, and many of them work in Netscape Navigator 4.0.

The first of these is called `position`. It determines if an element's position is `absolute`, `relative`, or `static`. The default is `static`, which means the element appears in the normal flow order (usually based upon source order). An `absolute` position means the element's position on the screen is immobile, compared to the top and left edges of the browser window. Elements with this kind of positioning can overlap other elements because they are removed from the normal flow of content.

The `relative` position places the element in relation to the parent or previous element. If the parent element uses an `absolute` position, then the `relative` element will appear at the end of that element, and may overlap other elements because it too is removed from the normal flow of content.

The `left` and `top` properties determine where the element is to be positioned in relation to the screen's edge (or, in the case of child elements, the edges of the parent element). They can take percentage or point values. `Height` and `width` are similar to the attributes in that they determine the height and width of the element. Use `overflow` to define what happens if the element's content is larger than the defined space.

The `z-index` property lets you control which element will appear on top of another when absolute properties overlap. `Clip` defines the crop area for the element, and `visibility` lets you determine if the element is shown (a `visibility: hidden;` element takes up space, but cannot be seen).

---

## TAKE NOTE

### ▶ LENGTH UNITS

Eight units exist for positioning elements: em (current font-size), ex (current font-height), px (pixel), in (inch), cm (centimeter), mm (millimeter), pt (point), and pc (pica, or 12 points). Of these, em and ex don't work in all browsers, with ex being the most buggy.

### ▶ NETSCAPE INCOMPATIBILITIES

In Netscape Navigator 4.06, the following "known issues" were listed in the release notes (available by selecting Help | Release Notes in the menu bar):

▶ The padding property of style sheets is not supported. Use topPadding, rightPadding, bottomPadding, and leftPadding instead.
▶ The margins property of style sheets is not supported. Use leftMargin, rightMargin, and bottomMargin instead.
▶ Width, height, and border tags for images in style sheets are not enabled.

---

**CROSS-REFERENCE**

These properties replace many of the table elements and attributes learned in Chapter 4.

**FIND IT ONLINE**

CNet has several articles on CSS positioning at **http://builder.cnet.com/Authoring/CSS/ss07.html**.

## Table 13-2: POSITIONING ELEMENTS

| Property | Value | Example | Effect | Browsers |
|---|---|---|---|---|
| margin | *length, percentage,* or auto | margin: 10pt; | Gives a 10-point margin all around the element | Partial support in all browsers. (Use margin-top, margin-right, margin-bottom, and margin-left for better support.) |
| border-width | thin, medium, thick, *length* | border-width: thin thick thin thick; | Gives a thin border to the top and bottom, and thick borders on the sides. | Netscape and Internet . Explorer 4.0 |
| border | border-width \| border-style \| border-color; | border: 4pt double #000000; | Adds a black 4-point double-lined margin around the content. | Support in Netscape and Internet Explorer 4.0. May be buggy in Netscape 4.0. |
| padding | *length, percentage,* or auto | padding: 10pt; | Adds a 10-point padding between the content and the border. | Supported in Netscape and Internet Explorer 4.0 |
| width | *length, percentage,* or auto | width: 100pt; | Forces the element to a 100-point width (replaces tables for this purpose). | Netscape Navigator and Internet Explorer 4.0. |
| height | *length* or auto | height: 20pt; | Forces the element to a 20-point height. | Netscape Navigator and Internet Explorer 4.0. |
| float | left, right, or none | float: left; | Puts the element in a floating box to the left. | Netscape Navigator and Internet Explorer 4.0. |
| position | absolute, relative, static | position: absolute; | Positions the element, regardless of other elements on the page. | Internet Explorer 4.0 and up. |
| top | *length or percentage* | top: 10pt; | Positions the element 10 points from the top of the document or parent element. | Internet Explorer 4.0 and up. |
| left | *length or percentage* | left: 15pt; | Positions the element 15 points from the left of the document or parent element. | Internet Explorer 4.0 and up. |
| clip | *shape (top-value, right-value, bottom-value, left-value)* | clip: rect (5 10 10 5) | Crops five pixels off the top and bottom, and 10 pixels off the sides. | Internet Explorer 4.0 and up. |
| overflow | visible, hidden, auto, scroll | overflow: scroll; | Gives a scroll bar to the element, whether it needs one or not. | Internet Explorer 4.0 and up. |
| z-index | *integer* | z-index: 1; | Places the element first, layering other on top of it. | Internet Explorer 4.0 and up. |

# Using Special Selectors

Although style sheets let you change the formatting of standard HTML elements, you can only define each element once in a style sheet. Classes and IDs allow you to define elements more than once.

A class lets you apply style properties to any element at any time. For example, you might have formatting for general text paragraphs, and a special formatting option for a highlighted text area, such as the Shakespeare script example. The class will inherit all the properties of the `<P>` element style, but it will override any properties that are set in the `.beatrice` class definition. An example of using a style class is shown in the first two figures.

To define a class by itself, use the syntax `.classname {property: value ; property: value ;}`. Note the period before the class name. In this case, the class takes the place of an HTML element in the syntax. Class names must start with a letter — no numbers, dashes, or symbols.

To define a class as a part of an element, use this syntax: `ELEMENT.classname {property: value ;}`. In this case, the properties defined in the style will only apply to that particular class, and only when it's used in that particular element.

You can specify the same class in several ways using this method. For example, a style sheet could include the following:

```
P {color: #000066 ; font-size: medium ;}
.topics {color: #006600 ;}
P.topics {font-family: sans-serif ;
background: #990066 ;}
```

Here, a simple text paragraph will have blue text in medium size. A topics paragraph (`<P class="topics">`) will have green text (inherited from the class definition), medium size text (element definition), and a light pink background (defined in the `P.topics` style). Other elements using the `.topics` class have the default heading styles or formatting, but the heading text would be green.

IDs are similar to classes, except that they can only be used once in each document, and are preceded in the definition by a pound sign: #. If you have a unique item (such as a page footer or a signature) that will only appear once on any page, you can use an ID to format the item on each page where it appears.

## TAKE NOTE

### ► USING A .FINEPRINT CLASS

You can create a class called "fineprint," and define its style separate from that of a normal paragraph. You can reduce the size of the print, change the color, etc. And if you're using external style sheets, you only have to do it once for the entire site. I recommend using a class definition of `.fineprint {font-size: x-small; font-color; #C0C0C0; }` to format text into small, gray text (used on documents with black text and white background).

**CROSS-REFERENCE**

Chapter 14 has more information on defining elements, in much the same way individual classes and IDs can be defined.

**FIND IT ONLINE**

Microsoft's CSS resources includes the following page on naming your classes and IDs: **http://www.microsoft. com/workshop/author/css/numericclass.HTM**.

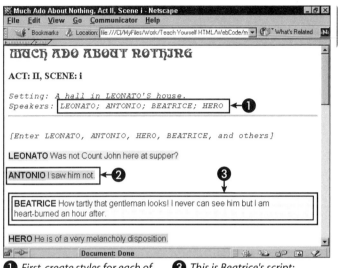

① First, create styles for each of the speakers and the stage direction.

② Next, put each speaker's lines inside a text paragraph using their class.

③ This is Beatrice's script; another actor's script would use a different style sheet.

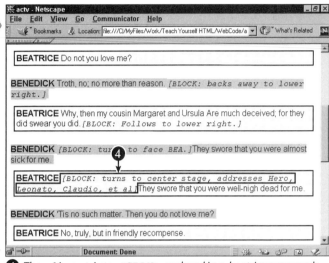

④ The `.direction <SPAN>`, enclosed in a `.beatrice` paragraph, inherits that paragraph's style, except in properties defined by the `<SPAN>`'s class.

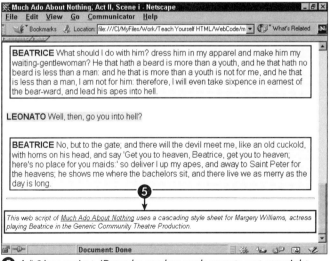

⑤ A `#fineprint` ID can be used on each page to put copyright, ownership, or other "legalese" information. In this case, the ID was defined as: `#fineprint font-weight: light; font-style: italic; font-size: small; }`.

### Listing 13-2: A STYLE SHEET WITH CLASSES

```
BODY {color: #000000; background: #FFFFFF;}
.direction {font-family: monospace;
  font-style: italic; color: #000080; }
.leonato {color: #000000; background:
  #F8E8CB; text-decoration: none; text-
  align: left; }
.antonio {background: #D3D9FA; text-align:
  left; }
.hero {background: #F4CBCA; text-align:
  left; }
.beatrice {background-color: #FFFF66;
  margin: 5pt; font-family: sans-serif;
  font-weight: medium; font-style: normal;
  border-width: 2pt; }
```

▲ This style sheet defines the appearance of the speakers' parts.

# Using Aural Style Sheets

tyle sheets provide special ways to present information to Web users who browse the Web with a nontraditional browser interface. For example, there are style sheet properties for paged media such as a printout. Similarly, the W3C has provided several properties designed for aural, or audio, devices.

An aural style sheet can be used by visually impaired readers, with hands-free Web browsers, and with similar text-to-speech devices. In addition to representing traditional Web content, aural style sheets enable Web designers to use special audio effects, such as cues, multiple speakers, and voice stress.

Unfortunately, at this time there are no style-sheet–compatible text-to-speech Web browsers, although that must change in the future. I cannot imagine that, given a standard way to present audio cues on the Web, text-to-speech manufacturers won't find ways to read and use those styles.

An important speech property is the `speak` value. To "turn off" speech rendering of a particular element, use `{speak: none ;}` as the element's style. The element will not be spoken, although this property can be overridden by speech readers. Use the `spell-out` value to have the words spelled out, and the `normal` value for normal speech mode.

In many text-to-speech browsers, hyperlinks are read as normal text. To give a special audio cue when the browser reaches a hyperlink, use an audio cue. The style sheet property for an audio cue is `{cue: url("pop. au")}`. You can have a cue before or a cue after, using the `cue-before` and `cue-after` properties.

You could also simply include a slight pause before or after the cue. In this case, use `{pause: 20ms ;}` to include a 20-millisecond pause before and after the element. You can also use the `pause-before` and `pause-after` properties, using the same syntax. Finally, the `pause` property has a shortcut: `{pause: pause-before-value pause-after-value ;}`.

As I mentioned above, you can create separate voices with aural style sheets. Using the `azimuth` (direction), `elevation` (height), and `voice-family` properties, you can add dramatic elements to your Web page. Naturally, these properties may or may not be heard correctly by all browsers, but these ambitious properties are the first step in making a universally usable audio Web format.

**CROSS-REFERENCE**

Chapter 5 explains why you'd want to include aural style sheets in your Web page.

**FIND IT ONLINE**

For aural style sheet properties, see:
http://www.w3.org/TR/REC-CSS2/aural.html

## Changing Speech Properties

Use the `volume` property to change how loud or quiet the program renders the speech. A value of `silent` will cause the program to pause for as long as it would take to render the text into speech, but it will remain silent.

Other ways to change the voice properties include the following: `pitch` to make the voice higher or lower; `voice-family` to denote a male, female, or child's voice (or to use a "voice font" that would be browser-dependent); `speech-rate` to speed up or slow down the speech; `richness`; and `stress` to change certain attributes of the voice itself.

**❶** *The style sheet for this page renders the links at the top of the page in normal speech.*

### Listing 13-3: An Aural Style Sheet

```
BODY {color: #000000; background: #FFFFFF;}
.direction {font-family: monospace;
  font-style: italic; color: #000080;
  speak: silent;   ❶
.leonato {text-decoration: none;
  text-align: left; speak: normal;
  voice-family: male; }
.beatrice {background-color: #FFFF66;
  margin: 5pt; font-family: sans-serif;
  font-weight: medium; font-style: normal;
  border-width: 2pt; border-style: double;
  speak: normal; volume: silent;
  speech-rate: slow; }   ❷
.benedick {text-align: left; speak:
  normal; voice-family: male; richness:75;}
```

**ⓐ** *Use* `speak: silent` *to prevent certain elements (such as the stage directions) from being rendered.*

**ⓑ** *I used* `volume: silent` *on* `.beatrice`, *so the*

actress can practice her lines with an aural Web browser.

**ⓒ** *Beatrice's lines still have the visual cues from before, because this script is being used in private rehearsal.*

239

# Linking External Style Sheets

A s I've already mentioned, you can link an external style sheet to any Web document. External style sheets are a good idea for large sites: they provide a single file to change when you need to edit the styles. Combined with a Web page template, they can help organize and standardize your site.

To create an external style sheet, start with a normal text file. You don't need any special elements or tags in the file; just start defining your properties right away, as if you had them included in the `<STYLE>` element of an HTML file.

There are no opening and closing elements for a `.css` document. Comments are enclosed in `/*` and `*/` symbols — a carryover from programming syntax. Make sure you save the style sheet as a `.css` file.

Now that you have your CSS file, how do you link it into an HTML page? Use the `<LINK>` element to include an external style sheet. All style sheet information, including the `<LINK>` element, should be put into the `<HEAD>` section of a Web page, if possible.

To link an external style sheet, put `<LINK rel="STYLESHEET" type="text/css" href="styles.css">` The value of the `href` attribute should be the path and filename of your `.css` file. Unfortunately, absolute URIs are supported sporadically, so use style sheets hosted on your own server.

## Style Sheets and Media Descriptors

You can set multiple style sheets, depending on what media will be used to browse your Web page. Currently, the Web is browsed primarily by interactive Web browsers, or `screen` media. Other recognized media types include `aural`, `braille`, `emboss`, `handheld`, `print`, `projection`, `tty`, and `tv`. Some of these types are considered "paged" media, meaning the user navigates them in pages, and paged styles should be recognized. The media might be visual, aural, or tactile, and it might use either a grid system of display (such as ASCII text), or a bitmap. Finally, media types can be either static or interactive, or both. Static media means the user cannot change the content or respond to the media. Useful for projection and paged media, these media types would not render forms or interactive scripts very well.

To link your style sheet by media type, use the `media` attribute in your `<LINK>` element: `<LINK rel="stylesheet" type="text/css" media="print, handheld" href="styles.css">`. You can also use the `@media` rule within a style sheet to provide separate media type information in the same sheet:

```
@media print {
    BODY { font-size: 10pt }
}
@media screen {
BODY { font-size: 12pt }
}
```

**CROSS-REFERENCE**

`@import` and external style sheets are a little bit like server-side Includes, discussed in Chapter 19.

**FIND IT ONLINE**

Be sure to read the W3C's specification on inheritance rules at **http://www.w3.org/TR/REC-CSS2/cascade.html**.

## Listing 13-4: An External Style Sheet ⓐ

```
BODY {font: normal normal light medium serif ;}
   /* normal style, normal weight (not
   smallcaps), light font (vs. bold), medium
   size, 10 point line height, serif font
   family as default for entire document
   body.*/
P {font-family: Arial, Helvetica, sans-
   serif ; font-size: small ; color: #880000
   ; }
   /* sans-serif font, size small, color
   red for text paragraphs*/
.fineprint {font-size: x-small ;}  ◀ⓒ
   /* decreases the font size for the
   fineprint class */
```

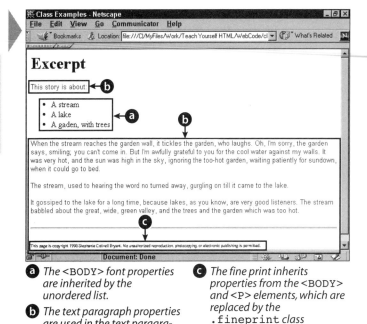

ⓐ The <BODY> font properties are inherited by the unordered list.

ⓑ The text paragraph properties are used in the text paragraphs, and the fine print.

ⓒ The fine print inherits properties from the <BODY> and <P> elements, which are replaced by the .fineprint class properties.

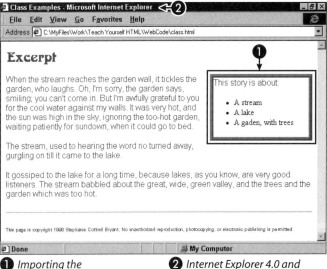

❶ Importing the muchado.css style sheet and placing the unordered list into a <DIV> element blended the two styles into one sheet.

❷ Internet Explorer 4.0 and higher recognizes the @import rule in style sheets, but Netscape Navigator does not.

### Table 13-3: MEDIA DESCRIPTORS

| Media Descriptor | Intended for |
|---|---|
| **screen** | Nonpaged computer screens |
| **tty** | Media using a fixed-pitch character grid, such as teletypes |
| **tv** | Television-type devices |
| **projection** | Projectors |
| **handheld** | Handheld devices |
| **print** | Paged, opaque material and documents viewed onscreen in print preview mode |
| **braille** | Braille tactile feedback devices |
| **aural** | Intended for speech synthesizers |
| **all** | All devices |

# Using Cascading Style Sheets

With as many ways to include styles and style sheets, it's no wonder that someone had to come up with a way to order them around. If you have an external style sheet, an internal style sheet (in the `<STYLE>` element), and a style within an element itself, which one actually gets displayed?

In general, inheritance rules are very simple: start from the outside (external style sheets) and work your way in. Elements that are enclosed in other elements inherit the properties of the outer element unless they also have a style defining that property, too. An external style sheet is overridden by an internal one, and internal style sheets are overridden by element-level styles.

In addition, child elements override their parent elements. So, an `<H1>` element contained by a `<DIV>` element will take the properties of the `<DIV>` element, and replace any `<DIV>` properties that are defined by the `<H1>` element definition.

Inheritance list:

▶ User-defined style sheet properties of current element

▶ External style sheet properties of parent element

▶ Local style sheet properties of parent element

▶ Inline styles of parent element

▶ External style sheet properties of current element

▶ Local style sheet properties of current element

▶ Inline style properties of current element

## Cascades and User-Defined Sheets

The *cascading* part of cascading style sheets originated with the rules on whether or not to use a user-specified style sheet (which is referenced by the Web browser with user preferences), or a designer-specified style sheet (referenced by the Web page, with the `<LINK>` element).

At the present time, only Microsoft Internet Explorer 4.0 and up supports user-specified style sheets. When IE 4 finds a site that specifies a style at the same or higher priority, it displays content in favor of the Web designer's style sheet.

**CROSS-REFERENCE**

More information on Internet Explorer can be found in Chapter 10.

**FIND IT ONLINE**

The W3C has created several "core styles" to use on Web pages: see **http://www.w3.org/ StyleSheets/Core/**.

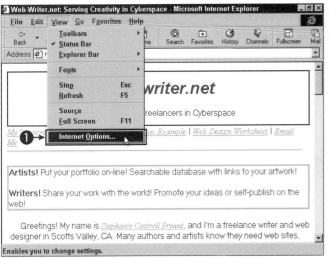

**①** To set the user style sheet in Internet Explorer 4.0, open it and click View ➪ Internet Options.

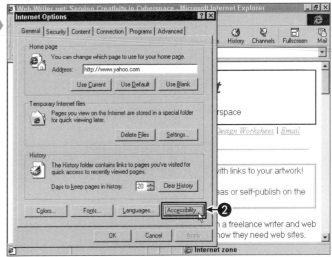

**②** In the General tab, click the Accessibility button.

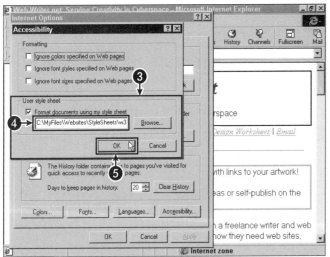

**③** Select the "Format documents using my style sheet" checkbox.

**④** Put the style sheet path and filename in the dialog box.

**⑤** Click OK to exit the Accessibility options, and again to save your Internet Options settings.

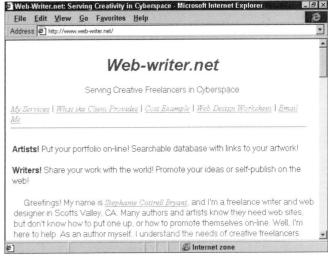

**■** This site incorporates both a user and a designer style sheet.

# Personal Workbook

## Q&A

**1** How do you create a local style sheet?

_____

_____

_____

**2** Replace the following using inline styles: `<FONT COLOR="#8B008B" SIZE=4 FACE="Arial">`

_____

_____

_____

**3** What part of the box is defined by `padding`?

_____

_____

_____

**4** What kinds of border styles can you use?

_____

_____

_____

**5** How do you use a floating element?

_____

_____

_____

**6** How many times can you use an ID in a given document?

_____

_____

_____

**7** How do you include an external style sheet?

_____

_____

_____

**8** What values does the `speak` property accept?

_____

_____

_____

**ANSWERS: PAGE 442**

## EXTRA PRACTICE

**1** Take a page where you've used <FONT> elements and layout tables. Convert all the <FONT> elements using style sheets.

**2** Replace the tables with positioning styles.

**3** Use float for any sidebars.

**4** Create a heading with a dropped shadow using positioning (not font properties).

**5** Now, make an external style sheet to format your page. Link it in to the page.

**6** Write a new external style sheet and replace the linked one. See how it changes the appearance of the page without altering the content.

## REAL-WORLD APPLICATIONS

✔ You're editing the company's financial report for online publication. You put the executive summary of the report findings in a floating box at the top of the page for easy reference. Later, if your boss tells you to change the report's font size, you can do so in one central place.

✔ You've written a how-to article on bicycle maintenance. You used a style sheet and <SPAN> elements to highlight important points in the manual.

✔ Because your monitor resolution is so high, you have a hard time reading standard text on the Web. You create and use your own user style sheet to increase the font size of Web pages without detracting from the designer's choices.

## Visual Quiz

What font and color properties do you see used in this page? What positioning properties? Could you produce the same effect with other layout and color elements? How?

_____

_____

_____

_____

CHAPTER **14**

MASTER
THESE
SKILLS

▶ **Learning About XML**

▶ **Creating an XML Document**

▶ **Using Element Declarations**

▶ **Examining Attribute Declarations**

▶ **Declaring Entities**

▶ **Discovering Other XML Topics**

▶ **Using XML in an HTML Document**

▶ **Exploring XSL and CSS**

▶ **Using XML on the Web**

# XML

When the Web first started expanding and corporate and personal Web sites began cropping up, HTML was a boon to developers. Reasonably simple to learn, HTML allowed people to add content to the Web. Like any new set of clothes, we have started to grow out of HTML and are in need of more power. This power can be delivered by XML: eXtensible Markup Language.

Mastering SGML, another powerful markup language, is a difficult task: developing document type definitions (DTDs) that define the structure of a document and finding tools for developing content has restricted the adoption of SGML. HTML found no such restriction. Tools abound, and documents can be knocked together with relatively simple HTML tags. There are areas of HTML that are deeper and require more skill and understanding, but the core of HTML can be learned quickly and used immediately.

HTML has some inherent restrictions. The structure of the language restricts its expansion. Browsers implement the HTML standard inconsistently.

XML provides more structure and more flexibility to Web developers. Where HTML's limitations have led to poorly coded sites, XML requires developers to create well-formed documents that provide content within a clearly defined semantic structure.

The XML DTD is not as difficult to develop as the SGML DTD, and authors can begin with a simple DTD and develop it over time, adding complexity and flexibility. The Web community of Web developers has participated in the discussions, and a number of XML parsers are already available. A parser reads in the DTD information and any style information that is available and begins the process of rendering the XML content.

Style information can be created using a separate XML document, called an XSL document. XSL stands for eXtensible Style Language. This complements the DTD and content, providing rendering information for the browser. The style language is based on the formatting languages currently in use.

Channel Definition Format (CDF) is a proposed extension to XML. Microsoft has submitted this extension and set up the methods for using it.

You can begin right away with XML development. Internet Explorer 5.0 already displays XML documents, and parsers exist that can transform your well-formed XML and XSL documents into HTML documents. You can load these documents up on your Web site, maintain the source in XML, and be ready for the next wave on the Web.

# Learning About XML

Now that you are familiar with HTML, you can look at the next wave in markup languages, XML. With HTML, you can create a Web page using a predefined set of tags understood by most browsers. The tags don't say much about the content of your Web page, and you can use tags any way you want. XML allows you to create a set of tag definitions for your information that define the context of the content.

With HTML, you don't have to worry about a browser understanding your page. As long as you are using standard HTML, the browser can render your page. The browser doesn't care if you use <DD> and <DT> tags for making lists that have a different format than the <UL> or <OL> <LI> tag options. With XML, you are defining the purpose of the information more than you are defining its presentation.

Like HTML, you can define a style sheet for formatting the information in your XML document. These style sheets associate the presentation elements with the contextual elements. Unlike HTML, because your tags are specific, you don't need to create a series of classes for each tag to accommodate its different uses within the document.

There are a number of DTDs already defined and available. You can use one of these or create your own. If you create your own, you can share it with others. This has the benefit of allowing you to create, share, and preserve information independent of the tool used to view the collected information. Even if you didn't have the DTD for an XML document, if the tags in the DTD are explicit enough, you don't need the DTD to understand the content of the page.

This feature alone could make your information presented on the Web much more accessible. Robots that traverse the Web, seeking out information, don't understand the structure of what they are reading. If you are using the <DT> and <DD> tags to create a list of contacts, the robot doesn't recognize the purpose of the list — it can only read in the content and index it. If the tags for the list expose the purpose of the list, the robot can index more effectively and make your information more readily available to the people looking.

## TAKE NOTE

### GETTING YOUR XML ONTO THE WEB

Microsoft's Internet Explorer 5 supports XML browsing. There are tools — such as Lark, DXP, NXP, and MSXML — available that help you to convert your XML documents into HTML documents.

**SHORTCUT**

Convert HTML to XML by identifying the structure and replacing the tags with XML structure tags.

**FIND IT ONLINE**

For basic XML information, visit **http://www.textuality.com/xml/**. For links to tools, check out **http://www.xmlsoftware.com/**.

## Table 14-1: PIECES OF AN XML PUZZLE

| Document | Description | Optional/Required |
|---|---|---|
| XML content document | This is the document that contains the information you have collected. The information is organized using tags. | Required |
| DTD | This is one or more documents that describe the structure and tags used in the XML content document. A DTD need not be a separate document, but can be embedded in a DOCTYPE declaration in the XML content document. It is also possible to use both internal and external DTDs; the declarations written into the XML content document take precedence over the tag declarations in the external DTD. | Required |
| XSL style sheet | This document describes formatting associated with the various tags in the DTD and XML content document. If this document is not present, the XML content document is rendered as an ASCII stream. Also, if you are converting to HTML, the parser will have no information about the correlation between the XML tags and the HTML tags. | Optional |

### Listing 14-1: An XML Page

```
</xml version=1.0" standalone="yes"?>
<COURSE>
<NAME>JavaScript Basics</NAME>
<NUMBER>500</NUMBER>
<INSTRUCTOR>
  <NAME>
  <Family_surname>Bryant</Family_surname>
<First_personal>Stephanie</First_personal>
  </NAME>
  <EMPLOYEE_CODE>100</EMPLOYEE_CODE>
  <EMAIL>steph@scottrell.com</EMAIL>
</INSTRUCTOR>
<DESCRIPTION>This course covers basic
  JavaScript concepts</DESCRIPTION>
<COST>$100</COST>
</COURSE>
```

▲ *XML documents offer a conceptual structure for document content. The structure is defined in a DTD, which describes the arrangement of elements in the document.*

### Listing 14-2: An HTML Page

```
<!DOCTYPE HTML PUBLIC "-//W3C//DTD HTML
  3.2 Final//EN">
<HTML>
<HEAD></HEAD>
<BODY>
<IMG SRC="writelogo.gif">
<H1>JavaScript Basics</H1>
<H2>Stephanie Bryant</H2>
<P>$100</P>
<P>This course covers basic JavaScript
  concepts</P>
</BODY></HTML>
```

▲ *In contrast, HTML documents don't reveal the meaning of content. HTML is limited in creating a specific structure. Instead, you must arrange your content to fit into the tags defined in the HTML DTD.*

# Creating an XML Document

Like an HTML document, an XML document is a text document. You can use any text editor, making sure to save the document without formatting. When you create an XML document, you also need to include structure information that gives meaning to the content that you provide.

The first is the declaration, identifying this as an XML document:

```
<?xml version="version number"
encoding="character set name"
standalone="state"?>
```

When you create the XML declaration, you must include the version and you can also include the following:

▶ `encoding=`, which can equal one of the recognized character sets

▶ `standalone=`, which can equal **"yes"** for XML documents that are complete in themselves and **"no"** for XML documents that use external DTD elements

The declaration identifies the document as an XML document, and in the example on the next page, it uses version 1 of the XML standard.

The example includes the statement **standalone="yes"**, which indicates that it does not use tags defined in an external source. In the sample document, all the tags are defined within the document. If you are using tags that are defined outside of the document, you would use **standalone="no"**.

If you do not include an encoding definition, the default encoding, UTF-8, is used. Whatever encoding information you include here constrains what character set encoding can be used in any included entities.

Once you have added the basic required XML elements, you can save the document. If you are using a text editor, be sure to save your document as a text-only file with the `.xml` extension.

## TAKE NOTE

### ▶ WELL-FORMED XML

The XML standard calls for XML documents to be well formed. This means if the document does not use an external DTD, it contains the `stand-alone="yes"` declaration in the header. It also means the document contains one or more elements and those elements conform to these rules:

▶ There must be a root element and all other elements must nest properly within the structure.

▶ All text elements are enclosed in balanced tags, as in HTML's `<H1></H1>`.

▶ All attribute values are enclosed in quotes, as in `standalone="yes"`.

▶ All empty tags must either close with `/>` or a closing tag, as in `<IMG attributes />` or `<IMG attributes></IMG>`.

▶ The document cannot use markup characters, such as the ampersand (`&`), greater than (`>`) or less than (`<`) characters, in the text stream.

### ▶ DECLARATION SYNTAX

The document declaration starts with `<?` and ends with `?>`. These identify the information for the browser, indicating that this tag contains processing instructions.

## CROSS-REFERENCE

What I've discussed here is XML syntax. If you're still confused by HTML syntax, see Chapter 1 for more information.

## FIND IT ONLINE

See **http://www.isi.edu/in-notes/iana/assignments/character-sets** for common character sets used for the `encoding=` option.

## Listing 14-3: Creating a Basic XML Page

```
<?xml version=1.0" standalone="yes"?>
<COURSES>
<COURSE>
<NAME>JavaScript Basics</NAME>
</COURSE>
</COURSES>
```

❶ To create an XML document, type the XML declaration.

❷ Add the element tag `<COURSE></COURSE>`.

❸ Add the course name inside the `<NAME>` element.

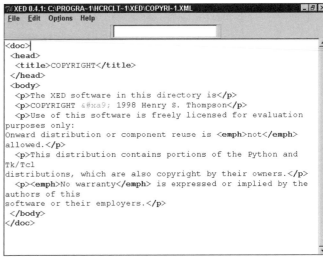

```
<doc>
 <head>
  <title>COPYRIGHT</title>
 </head>
 <body>
  <p>The XED software in this directory is</p>
  <p>COPYRIGHT &#xa9; 1998 Henry S. Thompson</p>
  <p>Use of this software is freely licensed for evaluation
purposes only:
Onward distribution or component reuse is <emph>not</emph>
allowed.</p>
  <p>This distribution contains portions of the Python and
Tk/Tcl
distributions, which are also copyright by their owners.</p>
  <p><emph>No warranty</emph> is expressed or implied by the
authors of this
software or their employers.</p>
 </body>
</doc>
```

■ A variety of editors are being developed for XML, including XED, as displayed here. The XML standard and concept are widely supported.

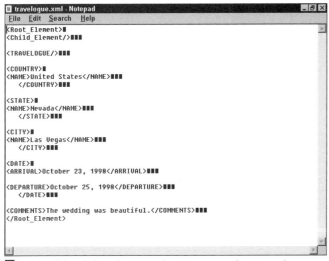

■ Be careful with the editor you choose, as some do not produce clean copy. XMLNotepad adds nonprinting characters that may be misinterpreted by some parsers.

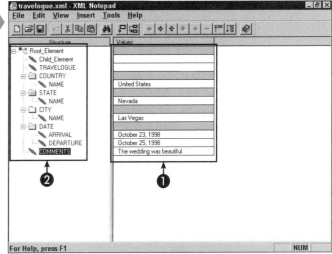

❶ XML Notepad lets you create your XML document using an outline of values.

❷ The left-hand panel provides the structure of your XML document.

# Using Element Declarations

The first thing you need to do is create a structure for your content. You do this with a DTD for your document. The DTD can be either inside the document or an external file. It may be easier, if you are developing your own DTD, to add the declarations in your document initially. Later, when you want to expand the use of that work, move the DTD into its own document to be referenced in other XML documents that you or others author.

To create an element declaration, you need to understand the structure of your document and the context of the elements you expect to use. You also need to understand the structural requirements of XML.

Using the course catalog example, we can expand the definition to include a course name, instructor, cost, description, list of prerequisites, and requirements. For the DTD, you need to define each element. The declaration includes both information about the relationship between the elements and some basic information about the element, such as its name.

## The Element Declaration

The element declaration consists of the notation identifying it as an element declaration, the name of the element, its data type, and its children, if any.

```
<!ELEMENT tag_name tag_contents>
```

Each element declaration uses the `<!ELEMENT>` identifier and includes the content type for the element. The content type can be `ANY` if the element being defined is the root element. This works for simple, unstructured documents, but is not ideal. It is important that the element declarations be detailed and precise.

The content type can also be `#PCDATA` (parsed character data) for text, `EMPTY` for tags that do not directly contain data, or a list of the element's children. The types `ANY`, `#PCDATA`, and `EMPTY` are case-sensitive keywords and must appear in all caps if used.

If the element has children, the child elements must be defined in their own element declaration. The parent element declaration can include markup to indicate whether the children are optional or repeatable.

In the example, the instructor can be used one or more times in each classroom element.

**CROSS-REFERENCE**

Chapter 2 discusses DOCTYPE declarations in HTML.

**FIND IT ONLINE**

The XML specification can be found at
http://www.w3.org/TR/PR-xml.html.

## TAKE NOTE

### CASE-SENSITIVE XML

XML is case-sensitive. Your element declarations must include the tag name exactly as you plan to use it. You cannot declare a tag <classroom> but use <CLASSROOM> in the document; this would result in <CLASSROOM> appearing as an undeclared element.

### ELEMENT NAMES

Each element is defined once, although its name may appear in another element declaration if it is the child of the other element. The root element is assumed to be the parent of all other elements and does not require the iteration of child elements in its declaration.

### MANAGING RELATIONSHIPS

► No indicator means the child element is required and occurs only once.

► ? indicates the child element is optional but may only occur once if used.

► * indicates the child element is optional and may appear more than once.

► + indicates the child element is required and may repeat.

## Listing 14-4: A DTD Listing

```
</xml version=1.0" standalone="yes"?>
<!DOCTYPE COURSE [
<!ELEMENT COURSE ANY>
<!ELEMENT TITLE (#PCDATA)>
<!ELEMENT NUMBER (#PCDATA)>
<!ELEMENT INSTRUCTOR (NAME,EMAIL?)>
<!ELEMENT NAME
   (Family_surname,First_personal)>
<!ELEMENT Family_surname (#PCDATA)>
<!ELEMENT First_personal (#PCDATA)>
<!ELEMENT EMAIL (#PCDATA)>
<!ELEMENT DESCRIPTION (#PCDATA)>
<!ELEMENT COST (#PCDATA)> ]>
```
◄─❶

❶ *Beginning with your basic XML page, add the DTD information, defining each element included in the document.*

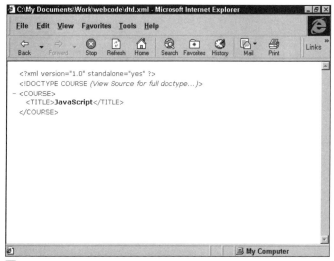

■ *When the DTD has been created, the page renders correctly in XML-enabled browsers.*

# Examining Attribute Declarations

You've now defined information about the structure of the elements to be included in your document. You can add attributes to those elements, informing the browser or parser about what is required, what default values are available, and other information about the element. Although this information is intended for use by the application interpreting the XML document — not for the person viewing the document — some of the information can be used to help people author documents using the DTD.

You can define the attributes within each tag as it is used, or you can create an attribute list in the DTD and assign attributes to the various elements in the DTD. You can override the DTD attributes with the information embedded in specific tags, but this information affects only the element identified, not all other elements of the same name.

What you are working with is not necessarily the content of the element, but the content of the tag for the element. For example, if you want to include the instructor's employee number but don't want to publish that information for the students, you can embed the information in the tag and make it a required part of the element.

## Defining Attributes in the DTD

The attribute definitions in a DTD are declared using the `<!ATTLIST>` tag. The declaration looks like:

```
<!ATTLIST element_name attribute_name
attribute_type default_value>
```

▶ The `element_name` is the unique name you've given to the element. The attribute list does not have to be defined before or after the elements in the DTD, but any element that you assign attributes for must be defined in the element list.

▶ The `attribute_name` is the name you are giving to the attribute. This helps you identify and use the attribute later.
▶ The `attribute_type` is one of the three kinds: `string`, `tokenized`, or `enumerated`.
▶ The `default_value` is a setting that allows you to give the element a value that users can use or change. If, for example, you require an instructor for the course you are listing, you can use the attribute to assign a default instructor name to the element.

You can use a single attribute declaration to assign multiple attributes to an element.

```
<!ATTLIST instructor name CDATA #REQUIRED
                empcode CDATA>
```

It may be easier to list a series of attribute declarations for the tag, rather than trying to format the perfect line spacing to put all the element attributes into a single declaration. The above declaration could more easily be made using two statements:

```
<!ATTLIST instructor name CDATA #REQUIRED>
```

```
<!ATTLIST instructor empcode CDATA>
```

**TAKE NOTE**

▶ **SINGLE DECLARATIONS**

You must format the declaration carefully if you use a single declaration for a series of attributes assigned to an element. It is simpler to have a series of attribute declarations.

**CROSS-REFERENCE**

Appendix C lists the items on the book's CD-ROM.

**FIND IT ONLINE**

View **http://www.w3.org/TR/WE-xml-names/** to read the XML namespaces working draft, which is subject to change.

## Attribute Default Values

▶ #REQUIRED for elements that must have a value for each occurrence of the element
▶ #IMPLIED for elements that may have a value for each occurrence of the element
▶ #FIXED to assign a specific value to the element

### Listing 14-5: Attribute Definitions

```
</xml version=1.0" standalone="yes"?>
<!DOCTYPE COURSE [
<!ELEMENT EMAIL (#PCDATA)>
<!ELEMENT DESCRIPTION (#PCDATA)>
<!ELEMENT OPTIONS (RECOMMENDED_READING*,PRE-
   REQUISITES*,REQUIREMENTS)>
<!ELEMENT COST (#PCDATA)>
<!ATTLIST INSTRUCTOR CODE CDATA #REQUIRED>
]>
```

▲ Note that the employee code is no longer a separate element, but is now an attribute of the <INSTRUCTOR> element. This is similar to identifying the size (height and width) of an image in an HTML document.

**Table 14-2: ATTRIBUTE TYPES**

| Type | Definition |
|---|---|
| String | CDATA for string data (alphanumeric characters) |
| Tokenized | ID, which contains a unique identifier for an element |
| | IDREF, which allows the element to reference content used elsewhere |
| | IDREFS, which allows you to list the references to other elements |
| | ENTITY, which allows you to reference external information in binary format, such as images |
| | ENTITIES, which allows you to reference a list of external sources |
| | NMTOKEN, which assists you by restricting the attribute value for handling the XML data programmatically |
| Enumerated | NOTATION, which allows you to define the helper used for displaying external data |
| | Enumerated NOTATION for listing the extensions of external sources and their helper applications |
| | Enumerated for a list of possible data |

# Examining Attribute Declarations

*Continued*

In the attribute declaration in Listing 14-5 above, the keyword `#REQUIRED` appears. This is a tool that you can use in your attribute declarations to ensure that information that your DTD requires appears in the document. When the document is parsed, the processor parsing the document will look for data in the elements with the `#REQUIRED` attribute and return an error if the element exists but does not contain data.

You can also use `#IMPLIED` for data that may, in some circumstance, not be available. The course catalog, for example, could extend the instructor element to include more information. Some of that information could be `#REQUIRED`, such as the instructor's name, and some could be `#IMPLIED`, such as a contact email address.

The next option allows you to set a list of options. This allows you to constrain the contents to a selected list of data. If you extend the course catalog to include an element for the area of study and declare the element attributes to be a list of options, with a default value, the processor parsing the document warns if the element does not contain the proper data.

```
<!ELEMENT area (#PCDATA)>
<!ATTLIST area (web|writing|technology)
"writing">
```

This element declaration assigns the default value of `"writing"` to the element area (of study) and validates the contents of the element against the list of options:

Web, `writing`, and `technology`. The XML document author cannot use any other description for the area of study.

The final type of value validation that you can use is for a `#FIXED` data value for the element. This type of declaration forces the XML author to use a specific data value for the element. If the DTD for the course catalog includes a tag for an element describing the organization sponsoring the course, and that organization is always Write Livelihood, then that element could be declared as a `#FIXED` element with the data value in place.

```
<!ELEMENT sponsor PCDATA>
<!ATTLIST sponsor #FIXED "Write Livelihood">
```

The processor will not accept any data other than `"Write Livelihood"` in the sponsor element.

You can combine these element attributes to force an additional degree of consistency on the documents using this DTD. If an element has multiple attributes and there is a conflict, the parser uses the first attribute declaration. In some circumstances, you can also reset the attribute in the tag.

In the first situation, if you have a fixed attribute declaration that sets the sponsor to `"Write Livelihood"`, you cannot later override that attribute with another declaration setting the sponsor to another name.

In the second situation, you can set the area of study to `web`, overriding the default value of writing.

**CROSS-REFERENCE**

Appendix B includes a list of HTML attributes, which will help you understand XML as well.

**FIND IT ONLINE**

A number of DTDs and information about DTDs is available at **http://www.schema.net/**.

# Adding Attributes in a Tag

When you declare attributes in an `<!ATTLIST>` tag, you define the attributes for all elements of that name. You can also set the attributes of a single occurrence of an element by including the declaration in the start tag or empty element tags in the body of the XML document.

```
<!ATTLIST description language CDATA
"English">
...
<description language="Francais">Les etudients
etudier la description du documents pour
distribue par...
```

This change of language from the declared English to a single occurrence of French can be done at the tag level.

Generally, `<EMPTY>` tags are used for external data, such as images, sound, or video that is included in the document.

```
<!ELEMENT logo EMPTY>
<!ATTLIST logo src CDATA #REQUIRED>
...
<logo src="writelogosmall.gif"/>
```

This occurrence of the `<logo>` element in the body of the XML document uses the file `writelogosmall.gif`. If it were a movie or sound clip, it would be reasonable to include a list of possible helper applications in the attribute list.

> **EMPTY ATTRIBUTES**
>
> When you declare attributes for an `<EMPTY>`, you establish the settings that can be made within individual tags. You can include information, such as a list of helper applications, in your attribute list.

> **USING ATTRIBUTES TO CONTROL CONTENT**
>
> The `AUTHOR` attribute of the `<OPTIONS>` element allows you to have the name of the person who added the course prerequisites, reading material, and requirements. The `#IMPLIED` keyword indicates that this is optional.
>
> The `CODE` attribute of the `<INSTRUCTOR>` element requires the instructor's employee code to be included.
>
> The `CURRICULUM` attribute of the `<TITLE>` element is required and can be one of a list of three predefined curriculum streams.

### Listing 14-6: Defining Attributes with Keywords

```
<!ELEMENT TITLE (#PCDATA)>     ◄—❶
<!ATTLIST TITLE CURICULM
(writing|design|production) "design">   ◄—❷
<!ATTLIST TITLE CURICULM CDATA #REQUIRED>
                            ❸
```

❶ Define the element to add an attribute to.

❷ Insert the attribute definitions. Specify required attributes with the `#REQUIRED` keyword.

❸ Set the possible values in parentheses, separated by pipe bars (|).

# Declaring Entities

An entity is a source of content. It generally refers to an external file, such as the image file used in the previous section. It could be a text file. It could be boilerplate text (the same text that is used repeatedly) such as your copyright or contact information.

An internal entity can be used to replace frequently used text such as copyright, ownership, or contact information. This type of general entity declaration includes the following:

```
<!ENTITY name "replacement value">
```

The name is the name of the entity; this is how it is referenced in the document. The replacement value is the text that appears where the entity is used. The course catalog, for example, could include an entity for a standard footer:

```
<!ENTITY endnote "Copyright 1998 Write
Livelihood. Solving Problems.">
```

This would then be used in the document:

```
<footer>&endnote;</footer>
```

This type of internal entity could be also be used to define terms that are not yet available, such as product names during development. It could also be used for changing information such as instructor names, course numbers, or room locations.

You can also use entities to reference external files, such as sound or image files, that you plan to use in your document.

Not all XML processors can handle the external binary files, and you may have to create an entity to point to the data.

```
<!ELEMENT image EMPTY>
<!ATTLIST image source ENTITY #REQUIRED>
<!ENTITY branding SYSTEM
"writerlogosmall.gif">
```

This would then be used in the document:

```
<image source="&branding;"/>
```

If you are using a data type that XML does not recognize or process, referred to as an "unparsed entity," you can use a notation to identify the content by name and possibly type. You cannot use the MIME type for the content because the forward slash (as in `image/gif`) is not a valid character.

## TAKE NOTE

### ▶ XML SYNTAX

Note that the reference in the body uses the ampersand (&) to precede the entity name and follows it with a semicolon (;).

**\*SHORTCUT**

You can create an internal entity for repeating information in your DTD, such as the list of attributes for images.

**FIND IT ONLINE**

To view DTD development, check out **http://www.xmlinfo.com/examples/**.

**Table 14-3: ENTITY DECLARATIONS**

| Entity Type | Declaration | Sample |
|---|---|---|
| Internal | `<!ENTITY name "text">` | `<!ENTITY signoff "Brought to you by Write Livelihood.">` |
| | appears in the document as: | `<docend>&signoff;</docend>` |
| External | `<!ENTITY name URI>` | `<!ENTITY signoff SYSTEM "/corp/notice.txt">` |
| | appears in the document as: | `<docend>&signoff;</docend>` |
| Parameter | `<!ENTITY %name "content">` | `<!ENTITY %loc "http://62.59.132.189/standard/"` |
| | appears in the document as: | `<!ATTRIBUTE home "%loc">` |

## Listing 14-7: Entities in XML

```
<!ELEMENT INSTRUCTOR (NAME,EMAIL)>    ←❶
<!ATTLIST INSTRUCTOR CODE CDATA #REQUIRED>
<!ELEMENT TITLE (#PCDATA)>←❶
<!ATTLIST TITLE CURRICULUM
   (writing|design) 'design'>
<!ATTLIST TITLE CURRICULUM CDATA #REQUIRED>
<!ENTITY LAST "Copyright 1999, S. Bryant">
<!ENTITY EMAIL "steph@scottrell.com">
```
                    ❷

## Listing 14-8: Using Entities

```
                ❹
<FOOTER>
  <CPY>&LAST</CPY>
❸  <MAIL>&EMAIL</MAIL>
</FOOTER>  ❺
```

❶ Add the element definitions.

❷ Insert the `<ENTITY>` definitions.

❸ Add the elements to the bottom of the course element.

❹ `&LAST` displays the copyright notice.

❺ `&EMAIL` is replaced by the email address.

# Discovering Other XML Topics

Although you can add an image to your document using entities and attributes, you'll notice that so far there has been no mention of links. How can a markup language be more powerful than HTML if you take the linking out? In fact, XML has a superior linking system and grants you some power that HTML cannot.

Linking from one HTML document to another is a pretty straightforward affair. Using the `<A>` or `<IMG>` tags you can link external sources up to your page. This has some limitations. First, you may not control the external document that you're linking to, and are therefore forced to simply open a single document at its top location. And then you have to rely on the browser to remember its way back to your page.

XML allows you to have these simple links; in fact, they're called "simple links." You can add information about the link's purpose and destination. These links will probably be the first available, as they are close to the HTML links we're familiar with.

XML goes beyond these simple links and allows you to have multiple destinations identified for a link. You can control the behavior of the link without adding scripting of any sort. You can create a group of links, and you can even store the links in a separate document.

XML also has XPointers, which replace the HTML anchors. Unlike anchors, XPointers can access a particular occurrence of an element.

The simple link is an attribute of an element. If you wanted to connect the reading list to the bookstore listing for the book, you could include a link attribute for the `<RECOMMENDED READING>` element.

Using a simple link, you could identify the element as a link element with the form `"simple"`.

```
<!ATTLIST element_name
xlink:form data_type link_type
(#REQUIRED|#FIXED|#IMPLIED)
href data_type (#REQUIRED|#FIXED|#IMPLIED)>
```

If you use the `FIXED` for the `xlink:form` attribute, you do not need to declare the link form in the tag. Otherwise, you need to indicate in the element tag what form of link you are using. Putting the `FIXED` attribute in the DTD attribute declaration saves you work developing and maintaining your information.

This simple link goes to a single target, which could be any external data. The location is given in the familiar URI/URL format.

You can add information to this link, enhancing the reader's understanding of the link. How this information is rendered is up to the browser, but it's likely that the information will be presented to the user through tips or status bar messages.

*Continued*

## TAKE NOTE

### ▶ XML GLOSSARY

The *element name* identifies which element can be used as a link. The *form* identifies whether the link is simple or extended. *Simple links* are more likely to render properly, as they most closely resemble the existing `<A>` tag in HTML. The `href` is the location of the URI, familiar from HTML.

**SHORTCUT**
Create internal entities for links; then, you can simply apply the link types by referring to the entities.

**FIND IT ONLINE**
Cafe con Leche (**http://sunsite.unc.edu/xml/**) has a comprehensive collection of XML information.

**Table 14-4: COMPARING XML AND HTML**

| XML | HTML |
|---|---|
| Author-defined tags | A collection of predefined tags |
| Document structure and content semantics associated with tags | No connection between tags and their semantic content |
| Document structure is implied through a hierarchy of tags | |
| Developed after the Web has matured | Developed to create the Web |
| Strict rules for parsing documents | Few strict rules for displaying documents |
| Public DTDs available and under construction | Templates available |
| Tools for developing and displaying documents not widely available | Tremendous number of editors and browsers available |
| Can include links to locations within a document using a variety of methods | Can link to locations within documents if the location is properly tagged |

### Listing 14-9: Hyperlinks in XML

```
<!ATTLIST RECOMMENDED_READING
  xlink:form CDATA #FIXED "simple"
  href  CDATA #REQUIRED          ◄—❶
  content-title CDATA #IMPLIED
  content-role CDATA #IMPLIED>
]>
<COURSE>                    ❷
<RECOMMENDED_READING href="http://www.web-
  writer.net/books/book1.html">Advanced
  Web Topics</RECOMMENDED_READING>
```

### Listing 14-10: Adding Content to Hyperlinks

```
<RECOMMENDED_READING href="http://www.web-
  writer.net/books/book1.html" content-
  title-"Recommended Book Title" content-
  role="Link to bookstore review">Advanced
  Web Topics</RECOMMENDED_READING>
```
❶

❶ Insert the attribute declaration.

❷ Change the <RECOMMENDED_READING> tags to include the link destination information.

❶ You can also add content to the link.

# Discovering Other XML Topics

*Continued*

The information you can add includes the content and role of the information in the link element. This does not describe the destination, but rather explains what the link element represents.

The keywords `content-title` and `content-role` allow you to identify what the link element is. For the recommended reading list, the `content-title` attribute could state: `"recommended book title"`. The `content-role` could include information such as: `"link to the school bookstore's book review and ordering page"`. The `content-title` attribute states what the element is and the `content-role` attribute states what it does.

If you want to also describe the destination, you can do that with two other attributes: `title` and `role`. The `title` attribute could match the title of the destination page, and the `role` is similar to the `content-role` — describing the purpose of the destination page.

## Controlling the Link

You now have a simple link element in place — some text to help the reader understand where the link goes. You can now extend the attribute declaration further to include instruction on how the destination should display and how the link should behave.

You can use three keywords here:

▶ `show`, to control how the new document is loaded
▶ `actuate`, to control which link destination is selected when there is more than one destination
▶ `behavior`, to add data to the link

With `show`, you have three options. You can replace the current document with the new document in the same window. You can open a new window for the destination document. You can also embed the new document into the calling document.

The first option, `replace`, is pretty familiar. This is how <A> links work in HTML, unless someone has written code to force it to do something else. The reader clicks on the link and the page is replaced with the linked document.

The second option, `new`, is something that you may have seen on the Web already — accomplished, generally, with some JavaScripting. When the reader clicks on the link, a new instance of the browser is launched and the linked document is loaded into that window.

The last option, `embed`, is a new idea. This allows you to open a document and place it inside the original, calling document. How this will be implemented is yet to be seen.

These cover the basics that are most likely to be available to you if you convert to HTML or find an early XML browser.

There are many more options that you can explore in advanced linking.

**SHORTCUT**

You can have a DTD listing entities you use frequently. Include a reference to that DTD in your documents.

**FIND IT ONLINE**

A working draft of the XLink language is available at http://www.w3.org/TR/WD-xlink.

### IMPLIED ATTRIBUTES

If the attribute is #IMPLIED, it is optional. If you don't have an adequate description for the link, you don't need to add the attributes.

### SHOW ATTRIBUTE OPTIONS

▶ embed — The external data should be inserted into the calling document at the link location.

▶ replace — The external data replaces the calling document in the browser window.

▶ new — The external data is displayed in a new window.

### ACTUATE ATTRIBUTE OPTIONS

▶ auto — Retrieve specific external data whenever a part of a link group is selected.

▶ user — Enable the user to identify which members of a link group are retrieved.

### COMBINED OPTIONS

▶ show="embed", actuate="auto" — Automatically insert the external data into the document.

▶ show="replace", actuate="auto" — Load external data without user intervention.

**Listing 14-11: Internal Entities**

```
<!ATTLIST RECOMMENDED_READING
    %link-info;    ◄─❸
<!ENTITY % link-info
    xlink:form  CDATA  #FIXED 'simple'
    href        CDATA  #REQUIRED
    content-role   CDATA  #IMPLIED
    content-title  CDATA  #IMPLIED
    title CDATA  #IMPLIED
    role CDATA  #IMPLIED
    show CDATA('new'|'replace'|'embed') 'new'>
```

❶ *Insert an ENTITY declaration with the range of link attributes you want. Use the percent sign (%) to indicate that it is an internal entity.*

❷ *In the link attribute declarations, replace the content with the name of the link attribute entity.*

❸ *The entity name must be preceded by the percent sign and terminated with a semicolon.*

# Using XML in an HTML Document

One interesting use for XML that doesn't require a lot of extra work is the CDF proposal that Microsoft has put forward. This proposal allows for small documents that define a Web channel for pushing content updates to readers.

In this case, the XML document is referenced by the HTML document. This allows you to work with CDF now, since most browsers in use do not support XML parsing.

If you have a site that you update regularly — like the course catalog — with CDF, you can allow readers to register themselves with the site and receive notices when the site changes. If you add a course, change an instructor, or modify the description of courses, a message is sent to readers who have activated the channel using Microsoft Explorer.

If you decide to use the CDF channel push, it is well worth your while to explore Microsoft's Site Builder Network, where you can find the code for linking the CDF file to your page and the CDF Generator, which simplifies your work.

The first element that you define in a CDF document is the <CHANNEL>. This is how you define what page is associated with the channel. The primary attribute of the <CHANNEL> element is its HREF, in which you identify the URL or location of the page. This can also include the following attributes:

- ▶ BASE, which is the URL for relative addressing.
- ▶ LASTMOD, which is the date on which the channel content was last updated.
- ▶ PRECACHE is an instruction to the browser to download the page contents for viewing offline.
- ▶ LEVEL, which identifies how far down the hierarchy of the channel the cache should go if the PRE-CACHE attribute is on.

You can also include a <TITLE>, <ABSTRACT>, <LOGO>, <SCHEDULE>, and <LOGTARGET> element within a basic channel:

- ▶ <TITLE> names the channel.
- ▶ <ABSTRACT> is a text field for information about the channel.
- ▶ <LOGO> allows you to include graphics for the channel.

The <SCHEDULE> and <LOGTARGET> elements are a bit more advanced. The <SCHEDULE> element dictates a timetable for updates to the channel. Use this if you make regularly scheduled changes to the page, as it facilitates the notification process. If you use the <LOGTARGET> element, you have to identify a location for the log file, the type of activity that is logged, and how the log file is updated.

## TAKE NOTE

### ▶ CDF CHANNELS

Essentially, the CDF channel push allows you to create a subscription service for readers. When they click on the CDF Subscription icon and select a notification method, they have single-click access to your page and automatic notification of changes to your page.

### ▶ CHANNEL CHILDREN

A channel can have children that are also channels. These children identify pages that also belong in the channel and create a hierarchy of the channel.

**CROSS-REFERENCE**

Some of these features can also be accomplished using scripting tools, discussed in Chapters 15 and 19.

**FIND IT ONLINE**

CDF documentation is available at
http://www.microsoft.com/presspass/press/1997/Mar97/Cdfrpr.htm.

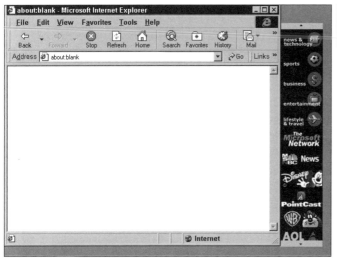

■ *Readers can use channels and XML in Microsoft Explorer to access your XML Web site with a click of a button.*

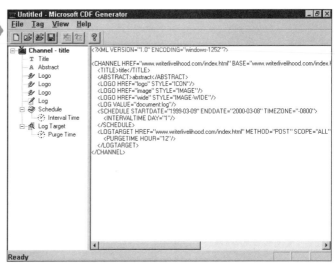

■ *You can create a simple CDF file using the CDF Generator available on Microsoft's Web site.*

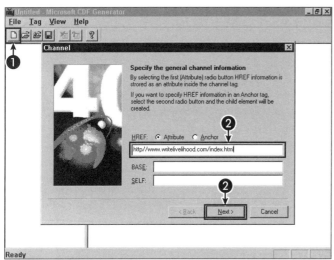

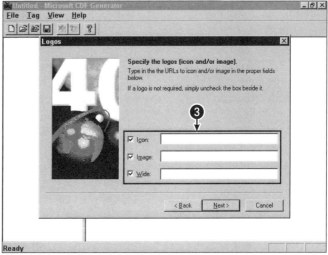

① *In the CDF Generator, click the New Document button to start a new CDF file.*

② *Identify the location (URL) of the Web page associated with the CDF file and click Next.*

■ *Identify the title of the CDF link and give a brief description of the page, and click Next.*

③ *Identify any logos you have available and click Next.*

■ *You can also enter the schedule information for scheduled updates, as well as the log file's destination and posting instructions.*

# Exploring XSL and CSS

Just as XML is derived from SGML, so is XSL, the style language based on the Document Style Semantics and Specification Language (DSSSL). Again, as XML is more powerful than HTML and simpler than SGML, XSL is more powerful than cascading style sheets (CSS) and simpler than DSSSL.

The first step, then, is to work out what can currently be done with an XSL document, work with that, but keep your mind open to how browsers develop and interpret the XML standard.

The XSL document is an important part of the process of getting your XML into HTML and onto the Web using current technologies. This document includes the information that the parser requires to associate your XML tags with HTML tags for rendering.

The XSL document is more than just a road map for the HTML rendering. It is also a source of the CSS information that is included in the resulting HTML document. The CSS information is integrated into the HTML tags — not the prettiest HTML you've ever seen, but as long as the sources are well formed, you'll be able to automatically generate the HTML for viewing. The coding is all done in your XML and XSL documents.

The XSL document is an XML document of a particular type. It must be a well-formed XML document that contains the rules necessary to parse the XML data provided in your document. In the XSL document, you declare rule elements that have a target and an action. The target is the elements declared in your XML document and the actions are the instructions for processing and rendering your content.

## Creating an XSL Document

The first element is the root element <xsl></xsl>. All rules fall between these two tags, just as the XML document DTD and content are bracketed by the root tag and HTML documents are bracketed by the <BODY></BODY> tags.

The primary rule is the root rule that generates the HTML structure tags <HTML></HTML> and <BODY></BODY>. This is the only tag that is handled in this way. The root rule inserts the necessary HTML structure around your output.

This first rule doesn't need to identify the element by name, but by role.

Each element in your XML document can have a single rule applied to it. This rule tells the processor how to handle the content in the element. The element in your XML document is the target, and the action is the HTML tag and style information.

```
<rule>
   <target element type="tagname"/>
   action
</rule>
```

**CROSS-REFERENCE**

For more information about style options in HTML documents, see Chapter 13.

**FIND IT ONLINE**

A collection of sample XSL files is available at
http://Xmlu.com/Experimental/.

**Table 14-5: STYLE CONSIDERATIONS**

| Style Attribute | Considerations | Options |
|---|---|---|
| Font | Font families are not a universally available attribute. The font families that work well on one machine may be replaced, in the course of rendering the CSS information, with another family on another machine. What is available across platforms does not render the same across platforms. | Avoid detailed specifications of fonts in your styles. |
| Color | Like fonts, you cannot count 100 percent on the rendering of color choices. There are palettes available on the Web that list various cross-platform colors. You must also consider that not all readers will have high end monitors that can render millions of colors. | Avoid using complex backgrounds or incompatible color combinations (such as red text on a black background) |
| Styles | Keep in mind that styles are not rendered by all browsers, and are not rendered the same by the different browsers. | Keep your style selections to a minimum, using only those that make your page more readable. Test on a variety of machines. |

## Listing 14-12: XSL

```
<xsl> ◄①
  <rule> ◄②
    <root/>
    <html>
    <body>
    <children/>
    </body>
    </html>
  </rule> ◄②
</xsl> ◄①
```

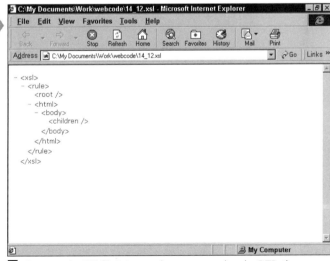

① Type the `<xsl></xsl>` root element tags.

② Insert the rule for the root element in the XML document.

■ Be sure to save the document as "filename.xsl".

■ Because the XSL file is incomplete compared to the DTD, the results consist of empty tags and no content.

# Exploring XSL and CSS

*Continued*

To generate paragraph tags around the course description, the XSL document would include the following rule:

```
<rule>
  <target-element type="description"/>
  <p><children/></p>
</rule>
```

This generates HTML code that encloses the content of each description element in HTML paragraph tags.

If you then wanted to add some style attributes to the HTML output, you could include the information in the HTML tag.

```
<p style="font-size: 14pt; font-family:
Helvetica, sans-serif; text-align:
center;"><children/><p>
```

You can use the CSS style sheet information to add the style content.

Each rule is applied to at least one element in the XML document. The same rule can be used on multiple elements, and multiple rules can be applied to an element. If you have a series of rules that target the same element, the more specific rule is used. The output can be recursive if there are child elements defined, as in the instructor element that includes the instructor's name and employee code.

The target for a rule can be a specific occurrence of an element. For example, if the instructor element repeated, allowing for more than one instructor in a course, you may format the first instructor's name differently to indicate that he or she is the primary source of information for the course.

To format the first instructor, include the position attribute in the rule declaration. You can apply the rule to

any of the following positions: `first-of-type`, `last-of-type`, `first-of-any`, or `last-of-any`.

The first two depend on the type, such as the instructor names. So, you could highlight the lead instructor using a rule such as:

```
<rule>

  <element type="instructor" position="first-
of-type">
    <target-element type="name">
  </element>
  <SPAN style="font-weight: bold; color:
#0000FF">
    <children/>
  </SPAN>
</rule>
```

This rule formats the first occurrence of the instructor name in bold blue text.

## TAKE NOTE

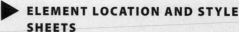

### ELEMENT LOCATION AND STYLE SHEETS

The context of the element can be a facet in its selection for the application of a rule. You can select an element based on where it occurs. If it is the child of a particular element, it is formatted in one way. If you are sharing the style sheet amongst a number of DTDs, you could create rules that leverage on the dependencies.

**CROSS-REFERENCE**

Chapter 13 covers cascading style sheets and the formatting options that you can use.

**FIND IT ONLINE**

Visit the XSL parsers at
http://www.w3.org/XML/#software.

## Listing 14-13: Parsing XSL for Internet Explorer 5

```
<xsl>
<rule>
<target-element type="classroom">
<attribute name="area" value="web"/>
</target-element>
<SPAN style="color: #0000FF">
<children/>
</SPAN>
</rule>
<rule>
<element type="instructor"
position="first-of-type">
Led by: <target-element type="name">
</target-element>
</element>
<SPAN style="font-weight: bold;" >
<children/>
</SPAN>
</rule>
<classroom>
<class>Creating an XML Document</class>
<area>web</area>
<instructor>
<name>WandaJane Phillips</name>
</instructor>
</classroom>
</xsl>
```

◄—➊

◄—➋

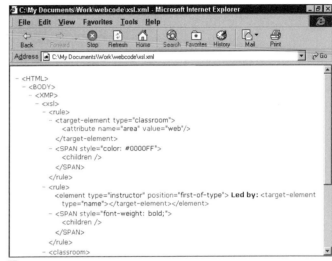

■ *This is an XSL page in Internet Explorer 5.*

➊ *You can use attributes in a style sheet. This rule takes the classroom area elements with the value of "web" and presents them as inline text blue.*

➋ *This rule adds the* Lead *by in front of the instructor's name.*

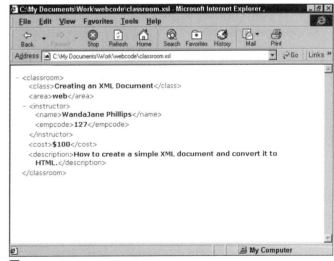

■ *Here is an XML page without parsing tags.*

# Using XML on the Web

With this taste of XML, you can build a small project. This section walks you through creating a simple XML document.

This example creates a list of your video tapes. The first step is deciding what each record in your inventory could have. You want to use the most extensive definition you can manage, giving yourself flexibility in the design stage.

Each video has some basic elements:

▶ Name of the movie
▶ Director
▶ Actors in the movie
▶ Synopsis of the plot

To this you can add

▶ A rating for the movie, or ratings if you want to include your own and those of the critics
▶ Awards the movie has won
▶ Lending information (if you lend your collection to friends)
▶ Information about the actors in the movie

In this case, the relationships are fairly clear. You could organize the information differently, but we'll go with a simple structure.

You could also test your structure before you commit yourself to developing a DTD along these lines. Try filling out several movie records, not necessarily in an XML document. If you want to put it into the XML format, you could use Microsoft's XMLNotepad. This product produces the XML file but does not support DTD development. You can play around with your content until you're satisfied, and then use the tree view of the records to develop your DTD.

Once you have the basics decided, you can start to build the DTD for the document. It is simplest to take your basic structure and create a series of element declarations for each element you identified in your design. The core of the XML DTD is the element definition. All else flows from the description of the document structure.

This will be a simple DTD, there are only three elements with children: DIRECTOR, ACTOR, and LENDING. If you were planning on sharing this information and DTD with others, you could add an element called OWNER, which would have information about the person in possession of this movie. This information could be more involved, including the name, address, and contact information.

*Continued*

*Continued*

## TAKE NOTE

### ▶ CONTENT DETAIL

You can take this information down to the smallest level of detail. The more detailed you can get, the better your design will be. In developing a DTD, detail gains you flexibility. Once you have the granularity of information at the smallest unit you can, then you need to decide what structure the information has and what kinds of attributes each element needs.

### ▶ DTD BUILDING IN NOTEPAD

The XMLNotepad does not support DTD building. If you look at the structure you have developed in XMLNotepad, you can open a simple text editor, such as Notepad, and create a DTD based on the XMLNotepad tree view.

### SHORTCUT

Create your draft structure using an Outline tool. You can see and move elements, while working in a familiar environment.

### FIND IT ONLINE

View Internet Explorer 5 beta tutorials at **http://www.microsoft.com/xml/tutorial/author_element.asp**.

## Table 14-6: VIDEO INVENTORY ELEMENTS

| Element | Contents | Attributes |
|---------|----------|------------|
| movie_title | Name of the movie in the language of the copy | language, alternate_language_title |
| subtitles | Language spoken in film | yes \| no, language visible if yes |
| remake_of_movie | Name of original film | yes \| no, visible if yes |
| number_in_series | Number of the film in a series | yes \| no, visible if yes |
| director | Name and information about the director | This is a container element and does not have attributes of its own |
| director_name | The name of the director | #PCDATA |
| director_info | Other films by the director | #PCDATA, repeatable |
| Actors | Names and roles of actors in the film | This is a container element and does not have attributes of its own |
| actor | Names of the lead actors in the film | #PCDATA, repeatable |
| roles | Roles played by the actors named | #PCDATA, repeatable |
| synopsis | A brief plot line summary | #PCDATA, repeatable |
| rating | Any critic ratings given | #PCDATA, repeatable |
| awards | Any awards won | #PCDATA, repeatable |

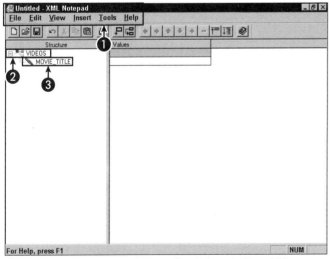

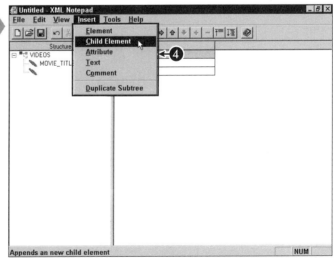

❶ *Launch the XMLNotepad.*

❷ *Click on the root element and name the document VIDEOS.*

❸ *Click on the first child element. Change its name to MOVIE_TITLE.*

❹ *Select the <VIDEOS> element and choose Insert ➪ Child Element.*

■ *Continue until you have all the elements entered.*

# Using XML on the Web
*Continued*

Now you can begin to add the attributes for the elements that you have defined. Table 14-6 represents the first impressions on what attributes each element needs. If you have experimented with filling out records using the structure described for the video collection, you may have already altered the elements included. The first element, the movie name, has two attributes: the movie's language and the name of the alternate language version of the movie.

```
<!ATTLIST MOVIE_TITLE language CDATA #IMPLIED>
<!ATTLIST MOVIE_TITLE alt_lang_title CDATA
#IMPLIED>
```

Combined, these two attributes enable you to create movie titles that handle movies in a language you understand, movies in a foreign language with subtitles, and movies that have another version in another language.

```
<MOVIE_TITLE>The Wild Boys</MOVIE_TITLE>
<MOVIE_TITLE language="German">Zwei
Kinder</MOVIE_TITLE>
<MOVIE_TITLE language="Spanish"
alt_lang_title="Si Mia">Yes, My
Dear</MOVIE_TITLE>
```

Once this code is processed and displayed, readers will not see any difference between the three:

```
The Wild Boys
Zwei Kinder
Yes, My Dear
```

If you want the information about languages visible, create child elements to contain the information. The synopsis and rating elements include an attribute called `source`. This identifies where the information originatecd. This does not have to be displayed, but it may be important to track.

```
<RATING source="Siskel and Ebert">2 Thumbs
Up!</RATING>
```

If you want to link the actors, the movie, or the director to Web pages or other documents, you can add links to the attributes for the elements.

```
<!ATTLIST MOVIE_TITLE
  xlink:form     CDATA  #FIXED "simple"
  href           CDATA  #IMPLIED
  content-title  CDATA  #IMPLIED
  content-role   CDATA  #IMPLIED
  title          CDATA  #IMPLIED
  role           CDATA  #IMPLIED>
```

This declaration allows you to include a link using the `href` attribute. You can also include information about the link.

```
<MOVIE_TITLE
href="http://www.movieland.com/reviews/472839.
htmlcontent-role="link to a great site with
reviews and other news">
The Banished</MOVIE_TITLE>
```

To make XML documents cross-browser compatible, you'll have to generate HTML from the XML code. To generate the HTML for your document, use an XML parser such as expat. Identify the input file (`videos.xml`), your style sheet (`videos.xsl`) and the output file (`videos.html`).

## TAKE NOTE

### ▶ XML AND WEB BROWSERS

Because all the tags in XML documents are built for that document or suite of documents, browsers cannot process the document directly, but require a map from you telling them what rules to apply to the XML document.

## SHORTCUT
Try a couple of different editors, such as the XMLNotepad and Notepad.

## FIND IT ONLINE
Look for XML parsers at
http://www.w3.org/XML/#software.

## Parsing XML

A parser interprets your instructions, much as browsers will in the future. Following your instructions, a parser attempts to create an HTML-tagged version of your document.

There are a number of parsers available. Some of the parsers validate your documents as they interpret. Look around for a parser that has an interface you feel comfortable with and that produces messages that you can understand.

### Listing 14-14: Simple XSL Sheet

```
<xsl>
<rule>
  <root/>
    <html>
    <body>
    <children/>
    </body>
    </html>
</rule>

<rule>
  <target-element type="ALTERNATE_LANGUAGE"/>
  <SPAN>
    <children/>
  </SPAN>
</rule>

<rule>
  <target-element type="SUBTITLES"/>
  <CITE>
    <children/>
  </CITE>
</rule>

<rule>
  <target-element type="REMAKE"/>
  <P>
    <children/>
  </P>
</rule>
</xsl>
```

❶

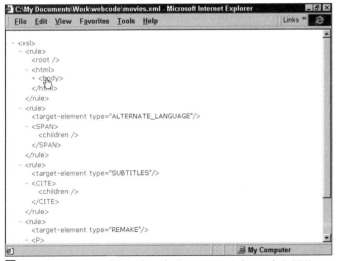

■ *XML files can be published on the Internet as-is, but only in XML-enabled browsers*

❶ *Associate your XML tags and HTML elements. Later, you can add styles to the HTML tags using CSS.*

# Personal Workbook

## Q&A

**1** What are the key components of a well-formed XML document?

_____

_____

_____

**2** What is an *element declaration*?

_____

_____

_____

**3** How does a DTD work?

_____

_____

_____

**4** How do you get XML onto the Web?

_____

_____

_____

**5** What is a *channel*?

_____

_____

_____

**6** What is an <EMPTY> element?

_____

_____

_____

**7** Identify the documents used to render an XML document.

_____

_____

_____

**8** What is the difference between a parsed and unparsed element?

_____

_____

_____

**ANSWERS: PAGE 443**

## EXTRA PRACTICE

1. Outline the elements that you would use for an email DTD.

2. Download a DTD and create the XML content for it.

3. Create a basic style sheet for your XML content.

4. Create a channel definition for your Web page.

5. Create simple links to an image and another document.

6. Create an image tag, defining which attributes are required for displaying images.

## REAL-WORLD APPLICATIONS

✔ You use boilerplate comments, such as contact information, for your Web site. You create entities for each comment, and when the information changes, you can change it in a single DTD location.

✔ Other people add content to your Web site. Your DTD controls some input, ensuring it is consistent and complete.

✔ You get involved in a genealogy project. You find DTDs on the Internet, learn what information you should collect, and have a predefined format for storing the data. The source XML is a text file, so you share information on your Web site.

✔ Your information contains multiple languages and scripts. Your XML DTD defines the default language as English, but you can easily override the attribute and include information in all the languages required.

## Visual Quiz

Create a DTD for the document shown on the right.

_____

_____

_____

_____

_____

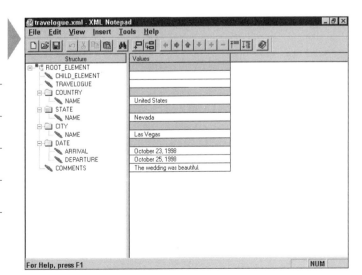

CHAPTER **15**

**MASTER THESE SKILLS**

- ▶ Writing to Cookies
- ▶ Using JavaScript
- ▶ Examining VBScript
- ▶ Installing a Java Applet
- ▶ Learning Scripting Languages

# Client-Side Scripting

Client-side scripting is one of the fastest-developing features of Web browsers right now. JavaScript, VBScript, and Dynamic HTML have forced Web browsers to compete more aggressively than ever before for developer attention. The latest battle in the browser wars is Dynamic HTML (DHTML). Netscape and Microsoft have differing implementations of the underlying technology for DHTML, and they continue to pursue each other competitively — each refusing to compromise and come to a standard.

Because of this, Web sites are becoming more and more fragmented as they implement more and more DHTML features. Want to include one feature of DHTML, but not another? Use a script to identify the Web browser, and split your audience into "those who are using the same version of the same browser that I am," and "those who are using any other browser."

As you can probably tell, I'm not too fond of browser wars. While I do believe in improving our Web browsing platforms, I think anything that requires Web designers to make a decision on which platform to design towards has completely ignored the entire theology behind the Internet and the World Wide Web. The original idea was to share ideas and information, regardless of computer platform, operating system, or application.

This chapter deals with one area of the browser wars that seems to be settling down: client-side scripting (not DHTML). Starting with the most "standardized" client-side technology — cookies — I'll show you the fundamentals of JavaScript, the most widely implemented client-side scripting language (JavaScript is implemented as JScript in Microsoft browsers). Then, I'll examine VBScript, Microsoft's Visual Basic–based scripting language, Java applet installation, and the basic concepts you should focus on as you try to learn a scripting language. This chapter won't teach you JavaScript, or VBScript, any more than the server-side scripting chapter will teach you Perl. Those subjects are beyond the scope of this book, and I encourage you to learn about them in other books and online tutorials. For now, just learn the basics so you have a preliminary understanding when you go to learn the scripting languages later.

# Writing to Cookies

Cookies are little pieces of information that remain on the user's machine after the connection has been disconnected. Because HTTP is a single-state protocol, each individual request sent to the Web server is independent of the previous requests. In other words, the Web server has no way of knowing if you're the same person who just requested page one when you request page two.

A cookie file is the plaintext file where your cookies are stored. In Netscape, cookies are stored in your user profile directory, and each user has their own cookie file (just as each user has their own set of bookmarks).

In Internet Explorer, cookies are stored in the `C:\Windows\Cookie` directory on the hard drive. Each cookie is an individual file, but because of minimum file sizes, it can add up to a lot of storage space on your hard drive (the favorites list has this same problem).

Users don't generally do much with their cookies, and they're not really supposed to. Although many cookie management utilities have made cookies more accessible to the average user, they're really designed to provide information to a Web server, and to keep a consistent state while browsing the Web.

Cookies sometimes store important information, such as usernames and passwords, which many Web users would be uncomfortable sharing with anyone other than the site those passwords were intended for. As a result, one of the cookie's limitations is that it can only be read by the Web server that issued it. So, if you have a Web server at **http://www.mydomain.com**, and you set a user cookie that gave the user's name and telephone number, only scripts running on www.mydomain.com would be able to read that cookie and get your telephone number from it.

Cookies can be used to store data a user inputs into a Web form, or similar online input device. They can also be used to record behaviors, such as hyperlinks followed, or images displayed. That's useful for tracking advertisements, and for understanding which navigation features are most effective on your site, and which items attract individual users in which ways.

## TAKE NOTE

### ▶ WHAT COOKIES CAN'T DO

Cookies can do a lot, but they are definitely limited in their scope. They cannot run other programs on your hard drive, download or install viruses, force your computer to send email without your knowledge, read anything you don't choose to provide in a Web form, or otherwise make changes to your system. A cookie can store a single line of information in the appropriate place on your hard drive (the cookies.txt file in Netscape, or the `C:\Windows\Cookies` directory in Internet Explorer). That's it. The information it gets can only come from the Web server, using data that you provide in a form or other online input device.

**CROSS-REFERENCE**

More information on <META> elements can be found in Chapter 23.

**FIND IT ONLINE**

The Unofficial Cookie FAQ is at **http://www. cookiecentral.com/unofficial_cookie_faq.htm**.

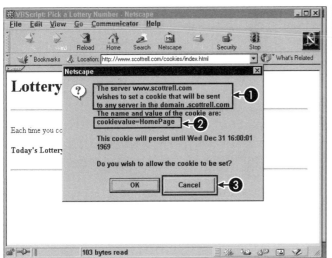

① Users can opt to accept or reject cookies, as they wish.

② This cookie sets the cookie name as `cookievalue`, and the value as `HomePage`.

③ The domain is `.scottrell.com`; only servers in that domain will be able to read this cookie.

④ The cookies.txt file has the cookie I set, and many others!

⑤ You can set multiple cookies, which can be used at the same time.

### Listing 15-1: Setting a Cookie

```
<HTML>           ❶
<HEAD>
<META HTTP-EQUIV="Set-Cookie"   ❷
   content="cookievalue=HomePage;expires=Saturday,
   30-Nov-98 23:00:00 GMT; path=/cookies;
   domain=.scottrell.com"    ❸
<TITLE>The Cookie Page</TITLE>
</HEAD>
<BODY BGCOLOR="#FFFFFF">
<H1>I WANT COOKIES!</H1>
</BODY></HTML>
```

① Use a <META> element to set the cookie.

② This cookie has a name of `cookievalue`, which is set to `HomePage`.

■ You can have multiple cookies under `cookievalue` with different values.

③ Use semicolons between each cookie header.

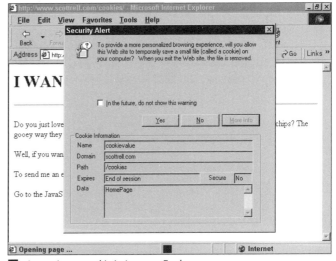

■ Accepting a cookie in Internet Explorer.

# Using JavaScript

JavaScript was developed by Netscape to enable Web developers to run short programs on the Web browser instead of on the Web server (hence the term client-side scripts). It's a client-side scripting language, which means it doesn't require a Web server to work.

You've already gotten a taste of JavaScript in previous chapters, and in the previous section. Although this book just isn't long enough to teach you everything there is to know about JavaScript, I can teach you the fundamental syntax and basic vocabulary — the building blocks to learning JavaScript on your own.

JavaScript is now the most ubiquitous scripting language on the World Wide Web. Microsoft recently implemented JScript, their own version of JavaScript, as of Internet Explorer 3.0. It's also becoming an international standard (ECMA-262 and ISO-10262), which makes it one of the few Internet nonprotocol technologies to obtain standardization from a worldwide standards organization (even HTML never gets beyond a W3C standards recommendation).

JavaScript can customize the appearance of HTML documents, open and close pop-up dialog boxes, manipulate cookies, run calculations, and dynamically generate and manipulate content in the HTML page itself. JavaScript can be a part of Dynamic HTML, as it uses the Document Object Model to dynamically change Web pages.

*Continued*

## TAKE NOTE

### ▶ JAVASCRIPT FUNCTIONS

JavaScript's usefulness to authors of dynamic Web pages is its ability to use functions. A JavaScript script can be a single line of code to input a bit of text or the current date and time, for example. Once the page is loaded, there's no way to update the time without using a Refresh <META> element, or asking the user to reload the page. But if the script to include the time is in a JavaScript function, you can have the function run any time the user performs a certain action (such as moves the mouse over an image or clicks a button.)

### ▶ JAVASCRIPT LIMITATIONS AND SECURITY

JavaScript, like cookies, is limited in its abilities. JavaScript cannot format your hard drive, run programs on your system, or install viruses. There are JavaScript viruses out there, but the worst they can do is cause your browser to crash (which might crash Windows 95/98, but that's not a problem with the browser or JavaScript) or steal some personal data.

Unfortunately, JavaScript has been able to exploit certain browser-specific security flaws, such as the ability to read your Netscape Preferences (this was solved as of Netscape Communicator 4.05), or the ability to browse and copy certain commonly known files from your hard drive in Internet Explorer 4.0 (a patch is available). Check your Web browser manufacturer's Web site at least once a month to see if any security updates or fixes have become available.

## CROSS-REFERENCE

Chapter 20 has more information on security on the Web.

## FIND IT ONLINE

You can find thousands of JavaScript scripts at **http://www.javascripts.com**.

# Client-Side Scripting

## Using JavaScript

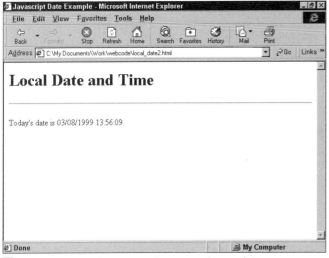

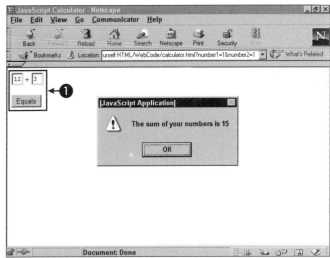

A JavaScript clock, reporting the current date and time.

This JavaScript calculator adds two numbers and produces the result.

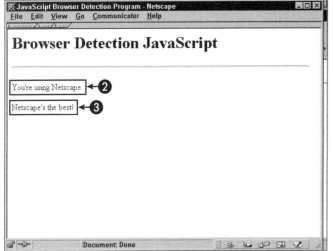

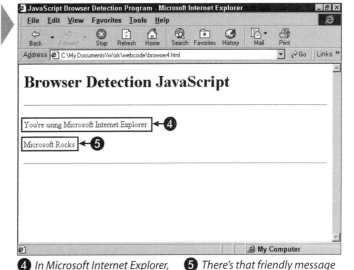

② The browser detection script writes the browser name into the document.

③ A cheerful message is also added, depending on which browser you're using.

④ In Microsoft Internet Explorer, the browser name shows up correctly as well.

⑤ There's that friendly message again!

# Using JavaScript

*Continued*

JavaScript syntax is a little different from HTML, but it's not horrible. The first thing you need to know is that JavaScript is case-sensitive. That means that if you create a function called `tickingClock`, you can't call it using `tickingclock`, `TICKINGCLOCK`, or `TickingClock`. You can only call it with `tickingClock`. That may be a big switch if you're used to HTML, which is not case-sensitive.

JavaScript pays little to no attention to line breaks, like HTML. That's especially important when you need to "hide" your code from older browsers. A typical JavaScript script would appear as plaintext in a browser that didn't support JavaScript. By putting a comment opening after the opening `<SCRIPT>` tag, you'll hide the JavaScript from older browsers but still make it available to more recent ones.

JavaScript comments are a little different than HTML comments. JavaScript comments start with two forward-slashes (`//`). When you close the comment to hide your JavaScript, make sure you comment it out from JavaScript, or you'll get errors in your code.

```
<SCRIPT>
<!- (hides JavaScript from older browsers
[script contents]
// ->
</SCRIPT>
```

On the next page, you'll see an example of a basic JavaScript script. This little script does one simple thing. It prints "Today's date is" followed by the current local date and time. That's not tremendously useful, but it is a basic building block in building a clock function, for example.

The first line of a JavaScript program is the `<SCRIPT>` element. That element takes one attribute: `language`. Note that the `language` attribute's value is case-sensitive. "JavaScript" is different from "Javascript", "Javascript 1.1", and "JScript". So far, the `language` attribute has been optional; VBScript just isn't widespread enough for too much confusion, and the browser generally defaults to JavaScript when it encounters a `<SCRIPT>` element without a `language` attribute.

JavaScript also uses semicolons (`;`) to show the ends of programming lines. Although not required, those semicolons are useful for JavaScript authors to know when that particular line is supposed to end. They're part of the punctuation of JavaScript, like periods at the end of your sentences.

Finally, there are parentheses `( )` after all functions. When you call a function in JavaScript, you sometimes want to send it a variable to work with. Later on, I'll show you how to send a variable to a script function using those parentheses.

*Continued*

## TAKE NOTE

### ▶ ARRAYS

JavaScript also lets you use arrays in your scripts. They're set up using brackets [ ], and let you do things like choose random sayings or dynamically change images.

### ▶ JAVASCRIPT AUTHORING PROGRAMS

There are some software programs available to help you code JavaScript. Some of them are just a bare-bones text editor with a few JavaScript tags included. Others are more fully featured, letting you create entire scripts without ever seeing a docu-ment.write or a function at all.

## CROSS-REFERENCE

CGI scripts can also read cookies; read about them in Chapter 20.

## FIND IT ONLINE

A JavaScript FAQ is available at
**http://idm.internet.com/faq/js-faq.shtml**.

## Listing 15-2: Local Date/Time Script

```
<SCRIPT LANGUAGE="JavaScript">
<!--
  today = new Date();  ← ❶
  document.write("Today's date is " +
❷━today.toLocaleString() + ".");
// -->               ❸
</SCRIPT>
```

■ *This JavaScript prints the local date and time.*

❶ *This sets a new variable, today, to use the global method, Date().*

❷ *document.write means to print the information in parentheses.*

❸ *toLocaleString() is another JavaScript object for using local dates and times.*

## Listing 15-4: Reading Cookies in Javascript

```
function readcookie(){  ← ⓐ
var cookieList = document.cookie;
if (cookieList == "") document.write("No
 cookies for you!");
var position = cookieList.indexOf("cookievalue=");
if (position != -1) {
  var start = position + 12;
  var end = cookieList.indexOf(";", start);
  if (end == -1) end = cookieList.length;
  var value = cookieList.substring(start, end);
  if (value == "HomePage")
  document.write("You've been to the cookie
  page!");
    }
}
```

## Listing 15-3: The Browser Detection Program

```
<SCRIPT LANGUAGE="JavaScript">
//<!--          ❹
function browseDetect(){
document.write(navigator.appName + ".");  ❺
  if (navigator.appName == "Microsoft Internet
Explorer")document.write("<P>Microsoft Rocks!</P>");
if (navigator.appName == "Netscape")
  document.write("<P>Netscape's the
best!</P>");      ❻
}
//-->
</script>
```

❹ *This finds what browser you're using and prints it.*

❺ *navigator.appName is a document object for the browser's name. Netscape and MSIE both support it.*

❻ *This uses a function to print the browser's name.*

ⓐ *The readcookie() function reads the cookies (document.cookie) for this server and checks for the HomePage cookie.*

ⓑ *If the script finds the cookie, it returns a message.*

283

# Using JavaScript

*Continued*

Like any good language, JavaScript has a "vocabulary" consisting of individual words which, when combined into functions, instruct the Web browser to do something. Some of the words in this vocabulary are shown in Table 15-1.

JavaScript can basically be broken down into objects, methods, and events. Objects are like the nouns of the language. They'll be discussed later on, in the Dynamic HTML chapters, because the set of objects available to the scripting languages is determined by the Web browser, using the Document Object Model (DOM). The DOM has yet to be standardized, and Microsoft and Netscape have highly divergent implementations of it.

Methods are like JavaScript verbs. In the previous example, `document.write("Today's date is " + today.toLocaleString() + ".")` uses the method `write()` to insert some text into the `document` object, and make it appear in your Web browser. Unlike an English sentence, the object comes before the verb, so `document.write("Today's date is. . . .")` means "Write 'Today's date is. . .' inside the document," to the Web browser.

Finally, events are how you call functions into play. If a function is a series of JavaScript instructions that will run when you say the magic word, events are the magic words to make them go. If our example script were a function called `todaysDate`, I could have called it using an event like `<BODY onLoad="todaysDate()">`, which would have run the script. `onLoad` is the event; it tells the Web browser when to call the function and run the script.

## TAKE NOTE

### ▶ OTHER RESERVED WORDS

There are many other "vocabulary" words used in JavaScript in addition to the objects, methods, and events discussed here. There are also arrays, statements, and operators. Arrays are basically a list or collection of objects or variables grouped together under one variable name. Some statements use reserved words, like `if`, `else if`, and `switch`. Each of those statements has a conditional meaning to the JavaScript. For example, `if` means to check to see if one statement is true, and do something if it is. While there are many types of operators, the most basic do mathematical computations or compare items (such as in an `if` statement.)

### ▶ DOCUMENT OBJECTS

Document objects, such as `document.cookie`, are a part of both JavaScript and the Document Object Model (DOM). JavaScript has several objects built in, such as the cookie object, which you can use automatically as part of the document object. As mentioned before, Netscape and Microsoft have incompatible implementations of the DOM, making life very difficult for most Web designers. You don't have to use Dynamic HTML to use the DOM, but you can't get away from the different implementations of the DOM in DHTML, which is why DHTML is split between the browsers.

## CROSS-REFERENCE

For more information on targeting links in other windows, see Chapter 7.

## FIND IT ONLINE

A longtime JavaScript resource is at http://www.webreference.com/javascript.

## Table 15-1: JAVASCRIPT DOCUMENT PROPERTIES

| Property Name | Usage |
|---|---|
| alinkColor | document.alinkColor.#CC0000 is the equivalent of \<BODY alink="#CC0000"\> |
| bgColor | document.bgColor.#FFFFFF is equivalent to \<BODY bgcolor="FFFFFF"\> |
| cookie | document.cookie gets the value of any cookies associated with that document |
| fgColor | document.fgColor.#000000 is equivalent to \<BODY text="#000000"\> |
| lastModified | document.lastModified gets the date of the most recent change to the current document |
| linkColor | document.linkColor.#0000CC is the same as \<BODY link="#0000CC"\> |
| location | document.location gets the URL of the document (similar to \<!—#echo var="DOCUMENT_URI"\>) |
| referrer | document.referrer reads the URL of the referring document (the Web page that linked to the current one) |
| title | document.title gets the TITLE element for the current document |
| URL | See location |
| vlinkColor | document.vlinkColor.#CC00CC is the same as \<BODY vlink="#CC00CC"\> |

## Listing 15-5: Launching Another Window in JavaScript

```
<SCRIPT LANGUAGE="JavaScript">
<!--                   ➊
function makeRemote(){
 remote = windowopen("","remotewin",:width=125,height=175);Ł
 remote.location.href = "remote.html";Ł
 if (remote.opener == null) remote.opener = window;Ł    ◄ ➋
 remote.opener.name = "opener";Ł
}
//-->
</SCRIPT>
</HEAD>Ł
<BODY onLoad = "makeRemote()" BGCOLOR="#FFFFFF">
```

➊ This pop-up menu uses a JavaScript function to launch a "remote control" navigation window for the site.

■ A navigation bar at the bottom of the site offers an alternative for older browsers.

➋ Links in the remote controller target the main browser window.

# Examining VBScript

VBScript is Microsoft's scripting language based on their Visual Basic programming language. VBScript was not originally designed as a scripting language for the Internet; because of that, it has a firmer programming base to work from. In addition, Visual Basic was designed for nontechnical users, and VBScript uses a lot of Visual Basic syntax. Thus, it is sometimes easier for nontechnical users. In my opinion, if you see enough of any scripting language, you'll get accustomed to its syntax, no matter what programming language it's based on.

VBScript is very similar to JavaScript, but it uses a slightly different punctuation syntax. Comments start with an apostrophe, and certain operators use a different character symbol (& instead of +, for example). VBScript is not case-sensitive; `document.write`, `document.Write`, and `Document.Write` are all the same thing.

As in JavaScript, your code should be set off inside a `<SCRIPT>` element, using a comment line to hide it from older browsers. You can also use a `<NOSCRIPT>` element to display some text or a link for users without VBScript installed.

On the next page, you'll see some examples of VBScript in action. The first example shows a simple VBScript that displays the local time, similar to the JavaScript you saw earlier. The remaining figures are a random lottery number generator that uses a VBScript method to pick three numbers (0 through 9) for you when you click the button.

## TAKE NOTE

### ▶ VBSCRIPT AND ACTIVEX

The main thing that VBScript handles so much better than JavaScript is ActiveX. Not surprising, since both VBScript and ActiveX are Microsoft technologies. VBScript may also be a little faster at processing DHTML in Internet Explorer. Right now, if you design a site using VBScript, you can use any Internet Explorer feature you want; it's the only Web browser available that supports VBScript and ActiveX. Of course, I don't have to remind you to include an alternate site for your non-MSIE users.

### ▶ VBSCRIPT LIMITATIONS

VBScript has many of the same limitations as JavaScript; it can't run programs, write, or change anything on your hard drive, and it cannot install anything on your computer. ActiveX can install and run programs, but Internet Explorer will warn you that it is a high-risk action, and that you should verify that the programs are legitimate before running them.

**CROSS-REFERENCE**

If you don't know how to write a form yet, they're discussed in Chapter 8.

**FIND IT ONLINE**

More information on VBScript is at http://msdn.microsoft.com/scripting/vbscript/default.htm.

## Listing 15-6: VBScript Clock

```
<H1>The Local Time is. . .</H1>
<HR>
The local time is now
<SCRIPT LANGUAGE="VBSCRIPT">
<!--
Document.write Time() & " on " &
MonthName(Month(Now), False) & " " & Day(Now) & ",
" & Year(Now)
'-->
</SCRIPT>
```

❶ The Time() object
automatically inserts the
current local time.

❷ The other objects are for the
month's name, date, and year.

■ VBScript uses Y2K-compliant
date schemes.

## Listing 15-7: VBScript Lottery Number Generator

```
<SCRIPT language="VBScript">
<!--
Function GetLottery()
  Dim NumberOne, NumberTwo, NumberThree
  Randomize
  NumberOne = Int(Rnd() * ((10-1) + 1))
  NumberTwo = Int(Rnd() * ((10-1) + 1))
  NumberThree = Int(Rnd() * ((10-1) + 1))
  GetLottery = NumberOne & NumberTwo &
  NumberThree
End Function
' -->
</SCRIPT>
```

❸ GetLottery prints the three random variables NumberOne,
NumberTwo, and NumberThree in that order.

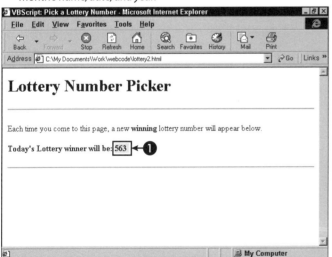

❶ I used a style to highlight the lottery number.

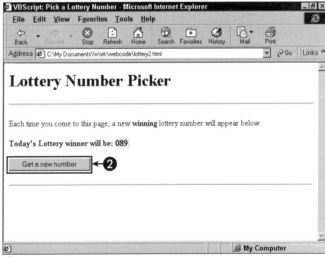

❷ In a more complex script, users can click the button to generate a
new lottery number.

# Installing a Java Applet

When Sun Microsystems released Java in 1995, they took the world by storm. Suddenly, everybody wanted Java in their Web sites. Java was used to solve problems it wasn't even designed for, and you could create an entire online arcade based on the Java game applets you could find.

Java was so popular because it provided two things that the Web hadn't had before. First, it let you create cross-platform, fully functional applications and run them on the Web in real time. Second, it provided an entirely dynamic way to control and manipulate Web content in real time. The fact that you could run these programs in real time made Java more popular than the coffeemaker on Monday morning.

Dynamic HTML promises to take some of the air out of Java's tires. With DHTML, you can dynamically control and manipulate Web content in real time, and it generally takes less time to download. However, DHTML is not currently cross-browser, let alone cross-platform, and I imagine it will be a long time before all DHTML elements are implemented in all browsers and platforms.

This book is on HTML, so you won't learn how to code Java here. However, you can use HTML to plug in a Java applet to your Web page using the `<APPLET>` and `<PARAM>` elements. Because Java applets are partially compiled, you can't view the source code the way you can with HTML, JavaScript, and VBScript. That's important for developers who want to keep their Java applets secret.

To insert a Java applet into a Web page, use the `<APPLET>` element. The typical HTML code for an applet is `<APPLET code="classname.class" width="100" height="100"></APPLET>`. The code attribute is the name of the Java class that serves as the main file of the applet itself. Between those `<APPLET>` tags, you might put one or more parameters in `<PARAM>` elements. `<PARAM>` elements send certain variables and controls to be used by the applet. Most good Java applets that you can download and use for free have documented which parameters you should set up and what kinds of variables to use.

## TAKE NOTE

### ▶ JAVA APPLETS

Java applets, which most people think of when discussing Java, are only the smallest part of Java's capabilities. Java can be used to write any kind of application, from a word processing program to a Web server. An applet is a very small Java program designed to run on the Web, using a Java Virtual Machine (such as the one inside your Web browser), and constrained by the standard restrictions put upon Web documents and programs.

### ▶ JAVA SECURITY RISKS

Java's original security flaws allowed it to manipulate and even change files on your computer system. Sun quickly remedied that problem, but Java applets can now request additional permissions, and applets from untrustworthy sources may contain malicious viruses and programs.

**CROSS-REFERENCE**

The CoffeeCup Applet Marquee Wizard is included on the CD-ROM.

**FIND IT ONLINE**

Many more Java resources, including applets, are available at **http://www.gamelan.com**.

## Table 15-2: COMMON <APPLET> ATTRIBUTES

| Attribute | Value |
|---|---|
| align=value | Aligns the applet, similar to the align attribute in the IMG element. |
| alt=value | Provides alternative text for non-Java browsers. |
| class=value | Applies a cascading style sheet class to the applet (not the same as a Java class)! |
| code=value | A required attribute that specifies which class to use for the applet (similar to the src attribute in an IMG element). |
| codebase=value | The base URL for the Java class. |
| height=value | The height, in pixels, of the applet. |
| Mayscript | Allows the applet to use JavaScript. |
| name=value | Gives the applet a name (useful for JavaScripts) |
| title=value | Gives the applet a title. |
| width=value | The width, in pixels, of the applet. |

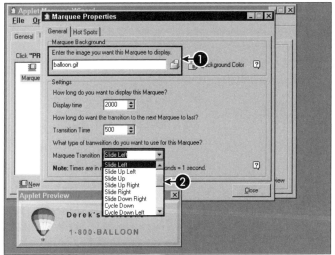

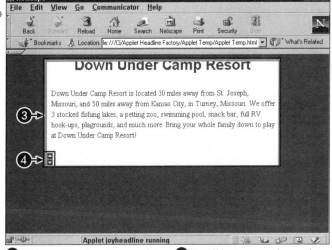

■ CoffeeCup's Applet Marquee Wizard lets you create animated applets.

❶ Enter a marquee graphic to use.

❷ Choose a transition to make your marquee move across the applet!

❸ This scrolling headline applet lets you put any text you want into a scrolling text box. It can provide attention-getting headlines, directions, or news information.

❹ Scroll buttons on the applet let users control how fast the text goes by.

# Learning Scripting Languages

Scripting languages aren't easy to learn, and there are many things that will seem confusing or unusual when you first try to pick them up. Just remember that HTML was a little strange at first, too, but look how far you've come with that!

Seriously, remember the basics of learning any new language. Start with the syntax — it's the basic grammar of computer languages, programming, scripting, or markup. Once you know the syntax, learn the vocabulary — the reserved words and names. What does "frame" mean in JavaScript, and why is it different from **FRAMESET** in HTML? As soon as you learn the vocabulary, you're already learning the built-in functions and calls, and are fast on your way to programming in the language.

You can learn scripting languages using the same methods you used to learn HTML. You can buy a book like this one, view the source code in your Web browser, and check out the mailing lists and newsgroups. There are several good online resources, including the sources of the scripting languages themselves: Netscape's DevCenter for JavaScript, and Microsoft Developer's Network (MSDN) for VBScript.

Start small — don't overwhelm yourself by trying to write a word processor (or HTML editor) in JavaScript your first time around. Try creating a few simple scripts, like the one to display the current date, or validate a form input field. Any good scripting book will start you out with the basics, and don't be afraid to try them out at first. As you gain proficiency, you'll move on to more advanced programs. You didn't start out writing complex Web pages with forms, frames, and client-side scripts; don't hesitate to start small in scripting either.

## TAKE NOTE

### ▶ REUSING CODE

You may have noticed that I reuse a lot of HTML in this book. There are certain snippets of code that are just plain useful, like a drop-down box with all the U.S. states in alphabetical order. It takes time to write that form input, and it's a multipurpose piece of code. So, I save it and reuse it whenever I have a form that requires an address. Reuse your script snippets to save time and programming headaches. If a function or subroutine works, use it in other appropriate scripts and save yourself the trouble of writing it again. After all, why reinvent the wheel? Many individual scripters share their work with everyone, encouraging people to use and reuse their scripts in whatever Web pages they like.

### ▶ USING COMMENTS IN SCRIPTS

Remember to use comments in all your scripts. They're crucial for figuring out problems and coming up with solutions. If you can't figure something out, comment out everything nonessential, then slowly add functions back into the script until it doesn't work again. Whatever you last added will probably contain some sort of error, and you can go through the script and fix it.

**CROSS-REFERENCE**

Learn how to write server-side scripts in Chapter 19.

**FIND IT ONLINE**

Many scripting resources are available at
**http://www.irt.org/**.

## Scripting Resources

For basic tutorials, start with A Beginner's Guide to JavaScript at **http://jsguide.simplenet.com/**, the Wired Webmonkey JavaScript Tutorials at **http://www.hotwired.com/webmonkey/javascript/**, or the Website Abstraction JavaScript Tutorials (**http://www.wsabstract.com/javaindex.htm**).

Be sure to check out the "official" JavaScript resources at Netscape, too: **http://developer.netscape.com/tech/javascript/index.html** for Developer Central, **http://developer.netscape.com/docs/index.html** for the all-important documentation.

There are dozens of sites that just provide JavaScript snippets and code samples. One such is at **http://tanega.com/java/java.html**, the "Simple Little Things to Add to Your Pages" JavaScript resource. Internet World's JavaScript Source is at **http://javascript.internet.com/**. Yahoo! even has an entire directory devoted to JavaScript applications (**http://dir.yahoo.com/Computers_and_Internet/Programming_Languages/JavaScript/Applets/**). HotSyte (**http://www.serve.com/hotsyte/**) is a JavaScript-only resource with several other scripts you can download.

Don't forget other learning resources, either. The Usenet newsgroup **comp.lang.javascript** offers a good source for asking questions and reading the latest information on JavaScript. There are also several email mailing lists; a search at **http://www.liszt.com/** returned seven different JavaScript lists to subscribe to (follow the instructions at Liszt to subscribe).

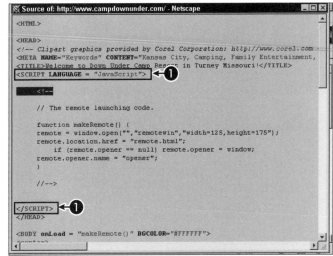

■ Select View ➪ Source in the menu bar to view the page's source code.

❶ Most scripts will be inside <SCRIPT> tags in the <HEAD> section of the document.

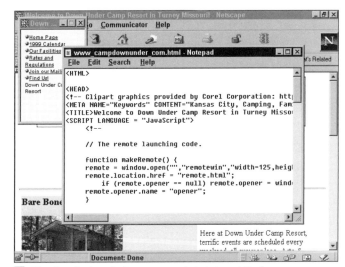

■ Viewing the JavaScript source code in Internet Explorer.

# Personal Workbook

## Q&A

**1** How do you use <META> elements to create a new cookie?

_____

_____

_____

**2** What security restrictions are there for cookies?

_____

_____

_____

**3** Name two limitations of JavaScript, deliberate or otherwise.

_____

_____

_____

**4** What method do you use to display the current date in JavaScript?

_____

_____

_____

**5** What is a *script function*? How do you call one in the document body?

_____

_____

**6** How do you access cookies with JavaScript?

_____

_____

_____

**7** Name two differences between JavaScript and VBScript.

_____

_____

_____

**8** What attribute is required in an <APPLET> tag?

_____

_____

_____

**ANSWERS: PAGE 444**

## EXTRA PRACTICE

❶ Using your Web server to test, create a cookie that contains your favorite color. Make it expire on December 31 of this year.

❷ Use JavaScript to read that cookie and print the value of your favorite color in the form of "Your favorite color is …."

❸ Now, use either JavaScript or VBScript to add the current date and time to your page.

❹ Write a script to launch a new window containing your site's navigation menu. Have all links in the new window target the main browser window.

❺ Use JavaScript to set the navigation bar's background and hyperlink colors.

## REAL-WORLD APPLICATIONS

✔ You've designed your site using a few platform-dependent features. You can use a scripting language to detect the user's browser and send him or her to the appropriate version of the site.

✔ Your site's navigation menu has become quite complex. You create a floating navigation bar that serves as a remote controller.

✔ You have an order form on your site, but many of the order fields come back as invalid. You can use a client-side script to check the form fields to be sure they're valid.

✔ An upcoming event that your company is hosting has users looking on your site for current information on the event. You use a JavaScript to change the content based on the current date, so users can have a daily update for the event.

## Visual Quiz

What scripting elements do you see in this example? Which scripting language is this script probably written in? How would you rewrite this script to make it more user-friendly?

_____

_____

_____

_____

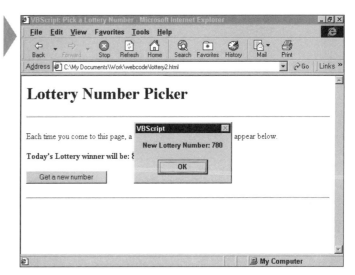

CHAPTER  **16**

MASTER ▶ **Learning About DHTML**
THESE
SKILLS ▶ **Creating Dynamic Content**

▶ **Using DHTML and CSS**

▶ **Dynamic Positioning**

▶ **Data Binding and Scripts**

# Dynamic HTML in Internet Explorer

In this chapter, you'll learn about Dynamic HTML (DHTML), as it's implemented in Internet Explorer. Although authoring with DHTML is far beyond the scope of this book, you'll see how to create dynamic content, set dynamic style sheets, position design elements, and access database information to create database-driven material. You'll also learn where DHTML fits in with HTML 4.0, and with style sheets.

Dynamic HTML, or DHTML, is a submitted (but not recommended or accepted) standard that hopes to bring about some agreement in the "browser wars" on how the Document Object Model (DOM) will work. The DOM is basically the idea that every item in an HTML page — every paragraph, `<DIV>` element, image, video clip, and form — is a scriptable object that can be manipulated. Which means that, under the DOM, Web designers can create sites in which users can move, change, and manipulate every piece of information on the site. Although this has largely been used for mere presentation value, some applications include creating floor plans and custom layout plans for design sites.

This chapter deals with the DOM as implemented in Internet Explorer. Unfortunately, the DOM isn't a finalized standard yet, and Microsoft and Netscape have completely different ways of using it in their Web browsers. Chapter 17 deals with DHTML in Netscape Navigator.

I should also mention in passing that IE 5 implements Dynamic HTML differently from IE 4. For one thing, it's easier to use common, premade scripts in IE 5, such as highlighting, drop-down directories, and more advanced applications. Unfortunately, Internet Explorer 5 had not been released by press time, so all the examples in this chapter are for IE 4. Never fear: IE 5 uses and displays IE 4 applications correctly. It just has additional shortcuts to make things easier for Web designers.

# Learning About DHTML

DHTML is really a collection of technologies, as implemented in various browsers. Internet Explorer has given the Document Object Model the greatest flexibility, by allowing nearly every element to be scripted. Add to that the scripting languages (JavaScript and VBScript), HTML 4.0, and cascading style sheets, and you have Dynamic HTML.

As you know, HTML 4.0 isn't totally implemented in any browser, including Internet Explorer. However, the parts of HTML 4.0 that are used in DHTML — `name` attributes, scripting, and the Document Object Model — have been incorporated into MSIE. If you're designing DHTML for MSIE, chances are you'll be able to do what you want, how you want.

The main difference between DHTML in Internet Explorer and DHTML in Netscape Navigator is their use of the Document Object Model (DOM). This chapter deals with Internet Explorer, so that's the DOM implementation I'll be talking about here.

The Document Object Model is an Internet standard proposal, meaning it isn't a universal standard, or even a recommendation, like HTML. In fact, the committees haven't even agreed on what objects will be included in the DOM, which is the primary split between Internet Explorer and Netscape Navigator. Each browser uses its own DOM, with different objects.

JavaScript and VBScript use DOM objects, such as `document.forms` to dynamically apply scripting elements to the HTML elements in the document.

Document objects are named from the top down. In other words, the first word in the document object name is the highest level in the object hierarchy, `window`. Next, you'll use a `frame` object, a user-specific object, like `history`, `navigator`, or `screen`, or the `document`.

The `document` object is the one that really gets into the HTML in the Web page, and it has a few preset objects within it, such as `body`, `links`, and `images`. In Internet Explorer, it also has the `all` object, to allow you to script any element based on its HTML `id` attribute: `window.document.all.elementid.property.value`. An example of this naming scheme is shown in the top-right and bottom-left figures.

## TAKE NOTE

### ▶ BOOKS TO READ

Even though it sounds like a shameless plug, *Dynamic HTML for Dummies* is one of the best books for new DHTML authors to learn about coding DHTML for Internet Explorer browsers. It doesn't cover Netscape's DOM, so when you advance to the point where you want to make your applications cross-platform, you'll need to do a little more research.

### ▶ THE WINDOW OBJECT

When using document objects (like `document.forms`), you don't need to include the `window` preface to the object. The Web browser will assume that you're talking about the current window. If you want to refer to an object inside another named window, you would preface the document object with the window's name — `windowname.document.forms`, for example.

**CROSS-REFERENCE**

Read about Netscape's implementation of the DOM in Chapter 17.

**FIND IT ONLINE**

The DOM Level 1 specification is available at **http://www.w3.org/TR/REC-DOM-Level-1/**.

## Document Object Model

```
window
    event
    frame
    history
    navigator
    location
    screen
    script
    document
        all         frames
        anchors     images
        applets     links
        body        plugins
        embeds      scripts
        filters     selection
        forms       styleSheets
```

■ *The Document Object Model (DOM) names all the scriptable objects in a Web page.*

## Document Objects

```
window.document.all              <HTML>

window.document.all.title        <HEAD>
                                     <TITLE>DOM PAGE</TITLE>
                                 </HEAD>
window.document.all.body         <BODY>
window.document.all.head1            <H1 id=head1>DOM page</H1>
window.document.all.hrule            <HR id=hrule>
window.document.all.text             <P id=text>
                                     This page is dedicated to
                               ❶     learning about DHTML in
                                     Internet Explorer.
                                     </P>

window.document.images[0]            <IMG src="dom.gif">
window.document.applets[0]           <APPLET code="dom.class
                                         width=100 height=10>
                               ❷     </APPLET>
                                 </BODY>
                                 </HTML>
```

❶ *Document objects must be called by their names;* `window.document.all.objectID`.

❷ *Note that some elements, such as images and applets, also have special arrays for scripting.*

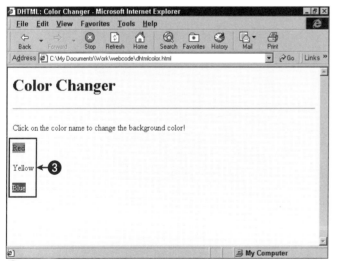

❸ *This simple Dynamic HTML application changes the <BODY> colors.*

### Listing 16-1: DHTML Color Changer Code

```
<SCRIPT LANGUAGE="JavaScript">
<!--
function colorred() {              ❶
    document.body.bgColor = "red";
    document.body.text = "black";
}
function colorblue() {
    document.body.bgColor = "blue";
    document.body.text = "white";  ❷
}
//-->
</SCRIPT>
```

❶ *The* `document.body.bgcolor` *is the same as* BODY bgcolor *for purposes of scripting.*

❷ *Writing* document.body.text = "white"; *means to change the value of the text attribute of the <BODY> element to "white."*

# Creating Dynamic Content

This next section will take you step by step through creating a Dynamic HTML application. I call it an application because, unlike a static Web page, DHTML pages usually do something (that's why they're dynamic), and whatever they do is based on user input, in the form of mouse clicks and movement, or following hyperlinks.

The first thing to do is write a spec sheet. The spec sheet is a holdover from programming days, but it's a great idea when you're planning a DHTML document. It contains the name of the application, the date, the author's name, and a simple description of what the DHTML application is supposed to do — and how. My spec sheet is shown in the top-left figure on the next page. Notice that I also included information on the due date, other people who might work on the program, and the names of the files to be used in the application. This spec sheet will serve as a blueprint for the rest of my program design, as well as tell me when I need to back up and create other files (such as images, sound clips, static Web pages, etc.)

The next step is to decide which browser I want to design DHTML for. This chapter is on DHTML in Internet Explorer, so the decision is easy. I'm going to use the Microsoft implementation of the DOM, which means I've already pre-selected my audience. Everyone in my audience will be using Microsoft Internet Explorer 4.0 and above.

That gives me a lot of freedom in making my next choice — which scripting language to use. I've decided to write my application in JavaScript, so I can convert it over to Netscape Navigator more readily and because I know the language better than I know VBScript. Because I'm not using any ActiveX controls on this Web page, JavaScript will suit my purposes just fine.

As you build your DHTML applications, you'll need to test them in the browser frequently. Error messages will pop up. Use them to help identify the script errors, and to fix problems.

## TAKE NOTE

### SPECIFICATION SHEETS

Most companies have done away with the specification sheet for Internet application development. This is a much-lamented fact among most programmers; the spec sheet was once a vital part of knowing what you were supposed to write, and how.

### NAMING ELEMENTS

In HTML, every element can take the `name` and `id` attributes. That's important for DHTML. The DOM uses an object's name to provide a shortcut. In the example on the next page, `document.moodGetter` is a shortcut for `document.all.forms[0]`, which stands for the first form out of all the forms on the page. The `all` in between `forms[0]` and `document` is the Internet Explorer-specific part of the DOM, which allows all elements in the document to be scripted.

**CROSS-REFERENCE**

For more information on writing JavaScript, see Chapter 15.

**FIND IT ONLINE**

http://www.irt.org maintains a DHTML resource for developers.

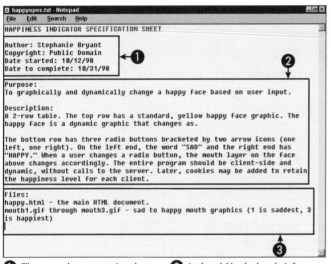

① The spec sheet contains the program's name, author's name, manager, and start and completion dates.

② It should include a brief description and the program's purpose.

③ The Files list tells you what to name the files you create.

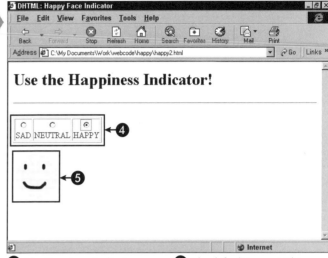

④ The Happiness Indicator page has a smiley face graphic and three radio buttons.

⑤ The default image is the smiling happy face.

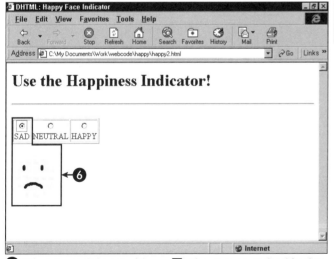

⑥ When a user clicks one of the radio buttons, the graphic changes automatically.

■ There's no server load for this kind of application.

### Listing 16-2: DHTML Mood Indicator

```
<SCRIPT Language="JavaScript">
function happyFaces() {
  if (document.MoodGetter.mood[0].checked)
    document.images[0].src = "face1.gif";
  if (document.MoodGetter.mood[1].checked)
    document.images[0].src = "face2.gif";
  if (document.MoodGetter.mood[2].checked)
    document.images[0].src = "face3.gif";
}
//
</SCRIPT>
```

① This DHTML application uses the document.images[] array to change the image.

② The user's mood is determined by the document.moodGetter object, created by the form named moodGetter.

# Using DHTML and CSS

One of the more popular uses of DHTML is changing and applying styles to Web pages "on the fly." Remember that cascading style sheets may or may not be viewable by Web users, or the user may not particularly like the styles used. You can write a DHTML page that will let people view your site with whatever style sheet they like. With some advanced scripting, you can save the style sheet as a cookie and refer to it the next time that user comes to visit.

In the following example, I'm just going to change the entire style sheet based on the mood of the user. That means I've had to write three separate style sheets: one for "happy," one for "neutral," and one for "sad." Each <STYLE> element has a name, and selecting one of the moods changes the style sheet accordingly.

You can also change the individual style for a particular element. If I just wanted to change the style of the table, for example, I would first name the table (I'll call it layout), then script it using the object `document.all.layoutTable.style`.

You can also call individual style properties within an object, or overwrite the style with the **cssText** property: `document.all.layoutTable.style. cssText = "border: 5pt groove grey; font-family: Times New Roman, Times, serif;"`. To change an individual style property, such as changing just the table's background color, use `document.all.layoutTable.style. backgroundColor = #FFFFFF`.

## TAKE NOTE

### THE DISABLED ATTRIBUTE

In this section, I'm introducing some new attributes of the <STYLE> element. These attributes are only used when you script style sheets. In particular, the `disabled` attribute, which takes a value of "true" or "false", helps scripts determine if a style sheet is currently active.

If you want to apply the style sheet to the document by default, do not insert a `disabled` attribute. However, when you want a script to dynamically apply several different style sheets, the nondefault style sheets should have `disabled=true` to turn them "off" before the script starts running. When you run the script, it will overwrite the default style sheet and enable the disabled styles.

### ARRAYS IN DHTML

Some objects are actually collections of objects in the page. For example, the `document.images[]` object is really a collection of all the images in the page. There are many preset arrays, including `forms[]`, `applets[]`, `images[]`, `styleSheets[]`, `anchors[]`, `embeds[]`, `frames[]`, `links[]`, `scripts[]`, `classes[]`, and `ids[]`. The value inside the brackets [ ] in the array should be the number of the array item. For example, the first anchor in the page would be `document.anchor[0]`. Arrays start counting with 0, not one.

**CROSS-REFERENCE**
Cascading Style Sheets are covered in Chapter 13.

**FIND IT ONLINE**
The W3C Style Sheets Specification is available at http://www.w3.org/TR/REC-CSS2/.

## Listing 16-3: DHTML Style Sheet Selector

```
<SCRIPT Language="JavaScript">
function happyFaces() {
  if (document.MoodGetter.mood[0].checked) {
  document.images[0].src = "face1.gif";
  document.styleSheets[2].disabled = true;
  document.styleSheets[1].disabled = true;
  document.styleSheets[0].disabled = false;
  }
  if (document.MoodGetter.mood[1].checked)
{
  document.images[0].src = "face2.gif";
  document.styleSheets[0].disabled = true;
  document.styleSheets[2].disabled = true;
  document.styleSheets[1].disabled = false;
  }
  if (document.MoodGetter.mood[2].checked)
{
  document.images[0].src = "face3.gif";
  document.styleSheets[2].disabled = false;
  }
}
//

</SCRIPT>
```

❶ *When a user clicks the Neutral face, the look of the entire page changes.*

❶ Use the `document.`
`styleSheets[]` *object to change the style sheet.*

❷ The `document.`
`styleSheets[i].`
`disabled` *object changes the style sheet disabled attribute.*

❸ *Style sheets must be set to document.styleSheets[1]. disabled = false to be active.*

❹ *Note that the styleSheets array starts at 0.*

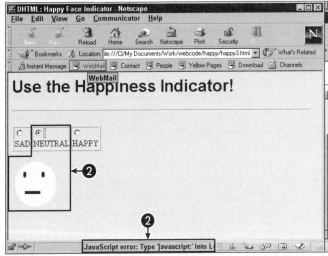

❷ *Dynamic style sheets do not work in Netscape 4.5 and below.*

# Dynamic Positioning

Perhaps the hottest thing in DHTML right now is positioning elements. Style sheet positioning properties allow you to specify where an item will be on the screen. Dynamic positioning lets you write scripts to allow the user to specify where the item will be, or to create animation, slide shows, and drag-and-drop interfaces.

This isn't just useful for dragging a simple graphic around; you can use dynamic positioning to create whiteboards, interior and exterior design plans, recipe books, and all sorts of graphically enhanced DHTML applications.

A typical application for dynamic positioning doesn't use user-entered positions. Instead, you click a button or select an image, and it animates or moves around the screen. That might be a little irritating, especially if you don't like animations. However, on the next page, the Shakespeare Notebook is a good example of an application with preset positions that reposition based solely on being clicked by the user.

It's good to start this with a strong understanding of style sheets and positioning in general. Unfortunately, this is one area where online documentation is scarce, and trial and error is the primary way to figure out what works and how.

On the next page, the Shakespeare Notebook example uses dynamic positioning to hide or show the Shakespearean selections. You can achieve the same effect using a style sheet property called `visibility`, but this section is on positioning, not visibility properties.

Each Shakespearean selection is actually contained in a `<DIV>` element, which is then scripted and called like any other HTML element. Because the `<DIV>` element is a block-level element, you can also apply block-level style sheets to it. All `<DIV>` elements start out with a style of `left: -350px;` or 350 pixels to the left of the leftmost edge of the screen. Since the `<DIV>` elements are also 350 pixels wide (from the `width` style property), I know they'll be safely hidden. When a user clicks one of the selections, it appears to the right of the paragraph text, with a left value of `250px`.

The last part of the Notebook application hides all the pages, effectively resetting the script. This is done with a simple function that repositions each `<DIV>` object back to its original starting place, 350 pixels to the left of the screen.

## TAKE NOTE

### Z-INDEX STYLES

You can create dynamically positioned objects and use the `z-index` property to place them in front of or behind other objects. For example, you can have an advertisement that flips in front of and behind another object or element, or a pop-up window that obscures other elements on the page.

### USING DREAMWEAVER

Macromedia's Dreamweaver is one of the few authoring tools for creating dynamic positions and animated Web pages. You can create time lines and layers to keep track of object behaviors and positions. More information is available at Macromedia's Web site (**http://www. macromedia.com**).

## CROSS-REFERENCE
More information on basic layout can be found in Chapter 4.

## FIND IT ONLINE
Several DHTML positioning tutorials are available at **http://www.dansteinman.com/dynduo/**.

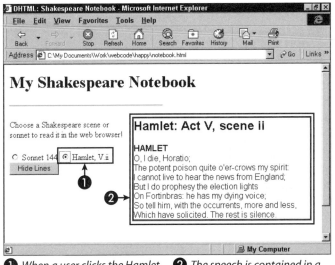

① *When a user clicks the Hamlet radio button, a speech from Hamlet pops up.*

② *The speech is contained in a <DIV> element, which uses style sheets for visual effect.*

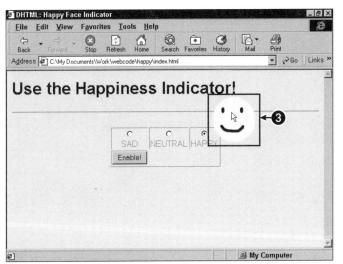

③ *Another application of dynamic positioning; the Happiness Indicator lets you drag and drop the smiley face graphic.*

## Listing 16-4: DHTML Positioning

```
<HEAD><SCRIPT LANGUAGE="JavaScript">
<!--
function moveLines() {  ①
  if (document.forms[0].lines[0].checked) {
document.all.sonnet144.style.left="250px";
document.all.hamlet.style.left="-350px";
  }                              ①
  if (document.forms[0].lines[1].checked) {
document.all.hamlet.style.left="250px";
document.all.sonnet144.style.left="-350px";
  }            ③
}
function hideLines() {
document.all.sonnet144.style.left="-350px";
document.all.hamlet.style.left="-350px";
}
//-->
</SCRIPT></HEAD>
<BODY><FORM>
<INPUT TYPE="Radio" NAME="lines"
VALUE="sonnet144"  ②
  onClick=moveLines()> Sonnet 144
<INPUT TYPE="Radio" NAME="lines"
VALUE="hamlet"      ②
  onClick=moveLines()> Hamlet, V.ii<BR>
<INPUT TYPE="RESET" VALUE="Hide Lines"
  onClick=hideLines()></FORM>
                 ③
```

① *The main function, moveLines, uses the DOM and if statements to move the selections around.*

② *Each radio button of the form uses onClick=move Lines() to call the moveLines function.*

③ *The hideLines function is only called by the reset button, which also deselects both radio buttons.*

# Data Binding and Scripts

Data binding is basically a way to get database entries into a Web page quickly and without using a server-side script or CGI. Data binding only works in Internet Explorer 4.0 and above, and it seems that Microsoft is continuously making changes to its data-binding implementation.

The basic idea behind data binding is that the scripts that request a database field are now embedded into the browser as an ActiveX control. That's important; any browser that supports ActiveX and has the Tabular Data Control (TDC) installed (IE comes with it) should be able to use data-binding Web pages.

You can create a basic database in a text editor. When you create your database, be sure to separate each field in the database with a special character, like commas or the pipe symbol (|). Also, have some sort of character that will surround text strings, such as & or %. A typical database entry could have three columns, separated by pipes. Each column contains a text string, which is set off with percent signs:

`%Stephanie%|%Bryant%|%steph@scottrell.com%`

Because you don't want to have the pipe character in that text string to incorrectly create a new column, surround all text strings with special characters.

After you create a basic database, bind it to the Web page with the data binding attributes. The most important of these is the `<OBJECT>` element. Use `<OBJECT id=objectID classid= "CLSID:333C7BC4-460F-11D0-BC04- 0080C7055A83">` Note that the value for `classid` must be typed in exactly; that's the ActiveX control you'll be using in Internet Explorer. Start by creating a simple page that displays the data, as shown in the top-right figure. In this case, you're not doing anything to the data except displaying it — you're not sorting it or anything. To sort data records, add `<PARAM NAME="SortColumn" VALUE="ColumnName">` to the `<OBJECT>` element. Add `<PARAM NAME="SortAscending" VALUE="True">` to sort data in the `SortColumn` from A-Z or 1-10.

At this point, you've used data binding to create a basic display of the records in a simple text database. The facing page shows how to create a simple script that dynamically moves through the records in your database.

## TAKE NOTE

### BEGINNING AND END OF FILES

The beginning and end of the database files are special to data binding scripts. When you hit the end of a file, an error may be generated unless you have some way of handling it. In the bottom-left figure, the possible error is avoided with an `if` statement.

### OTHER TYPES OF DATABASES

There are many other types of databases, including SQL, MS Access, and ODBC databases. Data binding with more advanced databases is a complex subject beyond the scope of this book.

**CROSS-REFERENCE**
Learn how to communicate between the Web browser and Web server databases in Chapter 19.

**FIND IT ONLINE**
For more information on advanced databases, see
**http://www.microsoft.com/workshop/
c-frame.htm#/workshop/author/default.asp.**

## Listing 16-5: A Text Database

```
%firstName%|%lastName%|%eMail%     ◄①
%Stephanie%|%Bryant%|%steph@scottrell.com%
%John%|%Bryant%|%johnnyb@scottrell.com%
%Bill%|%Gates%|%bgates@microsoft.com%
%TechSupport%||%support@scottrell.com%
        ②              ③
```

## Listing 16-6: Data Binding

```
<OBJECT ID=email CLASSID="CLSID:333C7BC4-460F-
11D0-BC04-0080C7055A83">
<PARAM NAME="DataURL" VALUE="data.txt">
<PARAM NAME="UseHeader" VALUE="True">      ◄①
<PARAM NAME="TextQualifier" VALUE="%">
<PARAM NAME="FieldDelim" VALUE="|">
</OBJECT>                    ②
<TABLE DATASRC=#email BORDER=1>
<TR>                         ③
<TD><SPAN DATAFLD="firstName"></SPAN></TD>
<TD><SPAN DATAFLD="lastName"></SPAN></TD>
<TD><SPAN DATAFLD="eMail"></SPAN></TD>
</TR></TABLE>
```

■ This database has three columns and four records.

① The first line contains the column names, which you can refer to later in the data binding.

② Data fields are separated with | symbols, and text strings are surrounded by % symbols.

③ Records without fields omit the field data.

① The <PARAM> elements specify to the database file, columns, text symbols, and field separators.

② The datasrc attribute calls the <OBJECT> by its id — in this case, #email.

③ datafld pulls in data, using the column name, or Columnx if the columns are unnamed.

## Listing 16-7: Data Binding with Sorting

```
<SCRIPT language=JavaScript>
function goForward() {
  if (email.recordset.AbsolutePosition < email.recordset.RecordCount) {
    email.recordset.MoveNext();  ◄④
  }
  else {
    email.recordset.MoveFirst();  ◄⑤
  }
}
function goBack() {    ⑥
  if (email.recordset.AbsolutePosition > 1) {
⑦    email.recordset.MovePrevious();
  } else {  }  } </SCRIPT>
```

④ This uses a function to move the record shown forward.

⑤ At the end of the database, the user is taken back to the first record.

⑥ The goBack function goes to the previous record in the database if the current record number is greater than 1.

⑦ Otherwise, the script does nothing, though you could script an error message.

305

# Personal Workbook

## Q&A

**1** What's the biggest different between Microsoft and Netscape's DHTML?

_____

_____

_____

**2** What's a *spec sheet*, and why would you create one for DHTML?

_____

_____

_____

**3** What are the `name` and `id` elements used for in Dynamic HTML?

_____

_____

**4** How do you dynamically change an element's style properties?

_____

_____

**5** What array would you use to switch between style sheets?

_____

_____

_____

**6** Name two arrays in Dynamic HTML.

_____

_____

_____

**7** How do you change the position of an object in DHTML?

_____

_____

_____

**8** What parameter do you use for sorting columns in data-bound DHTML?

_____

_____

_____

**ANSWERS: PAGE 445**

## EXTRA PRACTICE

① Write a spec sheet for a DHTML program.

② Create a Web page with your name, address, and email address. Create a script to highlight your email address whenever the user moves his or her mouse over it.

③ Create a DHTML application that changes a navigation graphic when a user right-clicks on it.

④ Make a Web page that lets a user preview a list of style sheets.

⑤ Write and implement a script to allow a user to click between one or more overlapping objects to bring it to the front.

## REAL-WORLD EXAMPLES

✔ You've designed a site with a multimedia presentation of your product on it. The presentation uses embedded ActiveX controls, and you use DHTML for an interactive experience.

✔ The company intranet contains the company phone book. You create a dynamic Web page to quickly sort and filter through the entries.

✔ An interior design business wants to offer a "pick-and-choose" application to their clients. They provide you with a series of graphics, and you create a dynamic Web page that lets potential customers design their own draperies, carpet colors, and wallpaper.

## Visual Quiz

What DHTML elements are evident in this figure? What would you expect to happen if you put a different name in the text field? How many functions do you think this application has?

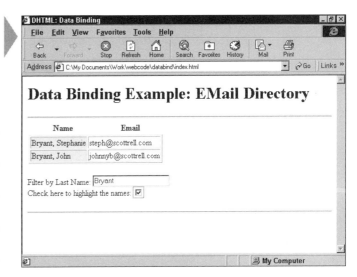

CHAPTER **17**

# Dynamic HTML in Netscape Communicator

I n this chapter, you learn the differences between how Netscape and Microsoft implement the Document Object Model (DOM). You also learn how to create and manipulate layers, and how to provide a dynamic font for your users.

Writing Dynamic HTML applications for Netscape Communicator is a little different from writing them for Internet Explorer. The main difference is in how the two companies use the DOM. Put simply, Internet Explorer has made it possible to dynamically manipulate any HTML or JavaScript element in a Web page. Netscape is a little more limited in its implementation; there are specific items that can be scripted, mainly having to do with layers.

Netscape uses the `<LAYER>` element to allow designers to create scriptable levels of a Web page. A layer can be any size — it can contain a heading, an image, or even a Java applet. The layer can be moved around the screen or hidden, and its styles can be manipulated with scripts. Although you can't change the entire style sheet for a Web page, you can change the styles for individual layers.

Finally, Netscape enables Web designers to provide downloadable fonts. These are fonts that can be included in the dynamic Web page, which will download and be used on the fly by the Web user. In this way, you can force users to use the font you designed for. That's especially important for international sites, which may need to use a separate character set for different languages.

# Examining Differences in the DOM

As I mentioned before, there are some major differences between Microsoft's DOM and Netscape's DOM. Both companies support the first few levels of the object hierarchy: `window`, `frame`, `history`, `navigator`, `location`, `script`, and `document`. Below the `document` object, some serious differences appear.

The number one difference is that Netscape doesn't have a `document.all` object, and it's limited in the other objects available for scripting. So, you can't call just any HTML element with the DOM; there has to be a pre-existing object in place. The document objects available in Netscape are shown on the next page. Pay particular attention to the `layer` object: it's the most important object to Netscape's DOM implementation.

You can think of layers as being a little like `<DIV>` elements in DHTML for Internet Explorer. They're essentially containers for other HTML elements and objects. They can be manipulated with JavaScript, but they have limitations on how much they can be manipulated and which parts can be moved or changed.

Individual layers are considered to be separate documents for purposes of arrays (such as forms, images, and applets). All the objects you might have in any HTML page will be called through the `layer` object when they appear inside a `<LAYER>` element: `document.layerName.document.forms[0].property`.

Another major difference in the DOM is the ability to change elements on the fly. For the most part, very few properties are "on the fly" dynamic in Netscape Navigator. Most need to redraw the entire screen in order to take advantage of dynamic properties, and they generally use JavaScript to do so. Layers are the most dynamic part of Netscape's implementation of DHTML. Unfortunately, layers don't allow much else in terms of scriptability, although you can embed a scripted Web page into a Netscape layer to create several levels of JavaScript.

The DOM has become a W3C recommendation, and that hopefully means that Web designers will start seeing more cross-browser compatibility between the two implementations. Right now, you can barely write anything in DHTML without having to rewrite it for another browser.

## TAKE NOTE

### SOME USEFUL DOCUMENT OBJECTS

The `document.forms[]` array has perhaps the most useful document objects in Netscape Navigator, provided you're not trying to reposition elements (in which case, `layers` are more useful). The elements in a form are called by their names or by the element's name: `document.forms[0].radio[0].checked = true` says the first radio button on the first form is checked. You can also replace the `radio[]` part of the object with the radio button's `name` attribute.

### ARRAYS IN THE DOM

As you may already know, a few important arrays were originally introduced as JavaScript objects. They've now been incorporated into the Document Object Model. The following arrays are supported in Netscape: `document.anchors[]`, `document.applets[]`, `document.classes[]`, `document.embeds[]`, `document.ids[]`, `document.images[]`, `document.images[].areas[]`, `document.layers[]`, `document.links[]`, `document.plugins[]`, and `document.tags[]`. `Document.tags[]` isn't the same as `document.all`: it's an array of the elements to be scripted into a JavaScript style sheet.

## CROSS-REFERENCE

Chapter 16 has information on DHTML in Internet Explorer.

## FIND IT ONLINE

Netscape's Developer's site is at **http://developer.netscape.com**.

**Table 17-1: NETSCAPE DOCUMENT OBJECTS**

| Object | HTML Element or Attribute | Properties and Methods |
|---|---|---|
| document.anchors[] | `<A>` | `hash, host, hostname, href, name, pathname, port, protocol, search, target` |
| document.applets[] | `<APPLET>` | `length` |
| document. classes[] | class | `elementname.propertyname` |
| document.embed | `<EMBED>` | `name` |
| document.form | `<FORM>` | `action, elements[], encoding, handleEvent(), length, method, name, target, reset(), submit(),` |
| document.ids[] | id | `elementid` |
| document.images[] | `<IMG>` | `areas[], border, complete, height, width, hspace, vspace, lowsrc, name, x, y` |
| document.links[] | `<A>` | `length` |
| document,plugins[] | `<PLUGIN>` | `description, filename, length, name, refresh()` |
| document.tags[] | All HTML elements | `All element names` |

```
       Netscape DOM
window.document.
   anchors[]    ids[]
   applets[]    images[].areas[]
   classes[]    layers[]
   embeds[]     links[]
   forms[].     plugins[]
    button      tags[]
    checkbox
    fileupload
    hidden
    password
    radio
    reset
    select.options[]
    submit
    text
    textare
```

■ The DOM, as implemented in Netscape's browser, names the scriptable objects in a page.

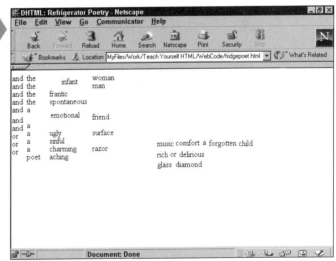

■ An example of Dynamic HTML at work; you'll learn how to create this kind of application later in this chapter.

# Creating a Layer

To create a layered document, start with a standard HTML Web page. Create a `<LAYER>` container to add each layer to the document. There are two basic types of layers: inline and standard. A standard layer uses the `<LAYER>` element, and the in-line layer uses the `<ILAYER>` element. In-line layers are a lot like inline frames in that they're embedded into the Web page as a scrollable, sized document. Unlike inline frames, however, inline layers have dynamic positioning, allowing you to move them around. For now, concentrate on standard layers, as inline layers are neither widely used nor widely supported, and their applications are limited at best.

On the next page, there's an example of a Dynamic HTML page for Netscape Navigator, using simple layers and some JavaScript to make it all dynamic. The application is fairly simple: switch between two layers of text when the user clicks on a visible part of a layer. That's not unlike switching between two windows when you click on the window's edge in Windows or Macintosh operating systems.

As you create your layers, keep focused on your specification — that short document that describes what the application is supposed to do. In this example, the specifications are to use a document called windows.html with two layers, yellowlayer and greenlayer, which overlap each other on the screen. When the user clicks on the visible part of a layer, bring it in front of the other one.

This application doesn't really demonstrate the full dynamic capabilities of DHTML in Netscape, but that's all right for now. The simplicity of this example just shows that there are some things in Netscape that are that much easier to do than in Internet Explorer.

You can include another file as your layer with the `src` attribute. For example, you could include a layer containing your photograph, which you use as a background for another layer directly on top of it. Your layer source files can use JavaScript and style sheets to alter their appearances; by hiding or showing those files, you'll be able to change the style sheets of the visible content.

## TAKE NOTE

### ► BACKGROUND COLORS IN LAYERS

Layers can take the attribute `bgcolor`, as well as the corresponding style sheet and JavaScript properties. Layers without a set `bgcolor` are effectively transparent; the contents will still show up, but any layers behind it will show through the background.

### ► LAYERS LIMITATIONS

Naturally, layers have many limitations. For example, they don't support all the cool HTML elements that they could. You can't really change or manipulate the content of a layer with scripts, although you can apply certain style information to it. Finally, layers are only partially supported by Microsoft's Web browser, making them a significant barrier to cross-browser compatibility.

## CROSS-REFERENCE

Be sure to read Chapter 5 to learn about issues in designing for various Web audiences.

## FIND IT ONLINE

A layer example is available at **http://www.kics.bc. ca/services/help/html/taglist/ LAYER1.html.**

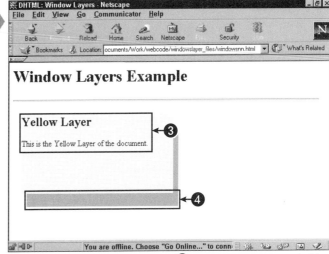

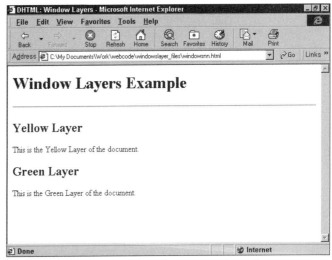

**①** In the windows layers example, the green layer is on top by default.

**②** The yellow layer is hidden behind it.

**③** When you click the visible part of the yellow layer, it moves forward.

**④** The green layer is now hidden behind; clicking its visible border will bring it forward.

## Listing 17-1: DHTML with Layers

```
<LAYER ID="yellowlayer" HEIGHT="150" WIDTH="300"
  BGCOLOR="#FFFF33" LEFT="25" TOP="100"  ②
  ABOVE="greenlayer"
  onFocus="moveAbove(greenlayer)">
<H2>Yellow Layer</H2>  ①
<P>This is the Yellow Layer of the
document.</DIV>
<LAYER ID="greenlayer" HEIGHT="150" WIDTH="300"
  BGCOLOR="#66CC33" LEFT="35" TOP="125"  ②
  onFocus="moveAbove(yellowlayer)">
<H2>Green Layer</H2>
<P>This is the Green Layer of the
document.</DIV>
```

**①** This example uses the `moveAbove()` method to switch the layers' z-index position.

**②** Built-in positioning methods make JavaScript unnecessary in this application.

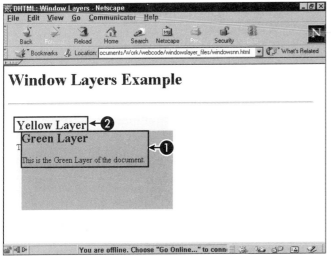

**■** Cross-browser compatibility, of course, remains an issue, as you can see when this example loads in Internet Explorer.

# Positioning a Layer

One of the best and easiest things to do with a layer is positioning. In fact, layers have a few built-in methods developed by Netscape to allow you to move them more easily. With these built-in methods, and a little knowledge of JavaScript, you can more easily create mobile applications, animated pages, and drag-and-drop interfaces.

In the top-left example on the next page, I'll show you how to create an animated Web page. This dynamic page is fairly simple. It uses an `onload` method in the `<BODY>` element to cause one of the layers to move across the page. As the dynamic layer moves, it encounters other layers and must move either above or below those other layers.

Being able to move in front of or behind another layer is very important in Dynamic HTML. If a layer uses the `bgcolor` attribute or `bgColor` property, its background becomes opaque, covering up the layers beneath it. So, you need to know if other layers will be hidden or revealed by a moving layer. In the example, a hidden layer behind the moving layer becomes visible as the mobile layer passes over it. This makes it look like the moving layer has "left behind" a message.

There are a couple ways to achieve this effect. The easiest is completely unsupported in Internet Explorer; use the `z-index` or `above` or `below` attributes of the `<LAYER>` element. In the previous example, I used `above` to place the yellow layer below the green one. That's a little confusing, but important: the values of `above` and `below` are the `ids` of the layers that are above and below the current layer.

The `z-index` attribute corresponds to the style sheet property of the same name; it uses a number to show where the current layer is in the general scheme of things. The lower the `z-index` value, the further back the layer will be. If two layers have the same `z-index`, the first one to appear in the HTML code will be laid down first, followed by the next (which will appear to be on top of the first one), and so on.

*Continued*

---

## TAKE NOTE

### ► POSITIONING METHODS

The built-in methods `moveTo()` and `moveBy()` take a pair of coordinates for parameters. The first coordinate is a number representing the value to move horizontally, while the second coordinate is the value of vertical movement: `moveTo(5,100)` means to move the layer to 5 pixels from the left border, and 100 pixels down. `moveBy(-5, -5)` moves the layer 5 pixels up and right from its current position.

### ► LAYER POSITIONING AND CSS POSITIONING

You may have noticed that many of the layer positioning properties are similar or identical to CSS positioning properties. That's no coincidence. Although there are a few bugs to be worked out, you can use CSS to position a layer or similar element that you also dynamically change with DHTML and JavaScript.

---

**CROSS-REFERENCE**

CSS-Positioning is also discussed in Chapter 13.

**FIND IT ONLINE**

Cross-browser Dynamic HTML tutorials are available at http://www.dansteinman.com/dynduo/.

### Listing 17-2: An Animated Heading

```
<SCRIPT LANGUAGE="JavaScript">
<!--
function moveHeadlines() {
  if (document.moving.left <=200) {
    document.moving.moveBy(3, 0);
    document.stationary.moveBy(3, 0);
    }
  else {
    document.moving.moveBy(3, 0);
    }
  setTimeout("moveHeadlines()", 1);
}
// -->
</SCRIPT>
</HEAD>
<BODY>
<LAYER ID="moving" bgcolor="#33CCFF"
  TOP="25"  LEFT="-250" WIDTH="250">
<H1>Mobile Header</H1>
</LAYER>
<LAYER id="stationary" WIDTH=250 TOP="25"
  LEFT="-250" WIDTH="250" ABOVE="moving">
<H1 ALIGN="CENTER">Heading One</H1>
</LAYER>
<SCRIPT LANGUAGE="JavaScript">
<!--
  moveHeadlines();
// -->
</SCRIPT>
```

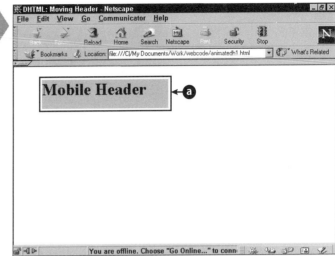

**ⓐ** *The* moving *layer starts out offscreen and gently scrolls in from the left.*

**ⓑ** *The* stationary *layer is hidden behind the moving layer when they start out.*

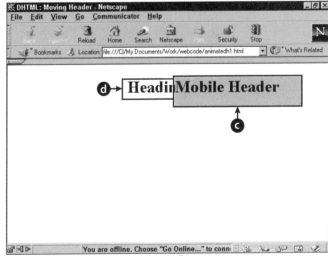

**ⓒ** *As the* moving *layer passes the 200-pixel mark, the* stationary *layer stops moving.*

**ⓓ** *The* moving *layer continues offscreen and out of sight, leaving the* stationary *layer behind.*

315

# Positioning a Layer
*Continued*

As you can see, positioning layers can be fairly easy, even for a novice. Naturally, you could use this code to create surprising effects with transparent backgrounds, images, and so forth. You can also use the positioning properties to move the layers around the screen less predictably, or to create more traditional blinking or animated GIF-like effects.

However, there's a lot more you can do with DHTML than this, and the next example shows you how to use these simple layers to create an effective drag-and-drop interface. Drag-and-drop may be one of the less enjoyable aspects of computer use (who hasn't had a case of "mouse arm"?), but it's one of the best ways to manipulate drawing and graphics programs.

The typical example would be a Mr. Potato Head-type of application, which allows the user to drag and drop graphics onto a face template of some sort. Java applications of this type sprang up like wildfire shortly after Java began to gain popularity. They're easy to code, require very little more than a knowledge of drag-and-drop, and are generally fairly simple.

Well, I've always been more of a literary person, and not such a great artist. So, my drag-and-drop example will use words instead of graphics. Words take less bandwidth than pictures, and if you can do the job with text, then do it. This application is a simple "refrigerator poetry" application. I've created a list of objects, which are basically poetic words, that the user can drag and drop into position onscreen.

One of the main advantages to using Dynamic HTML for this kind of application is the download time. This file is only 4KB in size, which means it loads into a Web browser fairly quickly. The browser itself may take a moment to render all the layers onscreen, but the bandwidth transfer is reduced to an absolute minimum. A similar program written in Java has a file size of 9KB and takes about twice as long to load and render onscreen.

## TAKE NOTE

### ▶ DHTML TOOLS

There are a few Dynamic HTML authoring tools available. The most notable is Macromedia's Dreamweaver (**http://www.macromedia.com**), which does try to create cross-browser Web pages.

Another one is the Visual DHTML application (still in beta), available at **http://developer.netscape. com/docs/examples/dynhtml/visual/index.html**. The Visual DHML program lets you create Netscape-specific dynamic Web pages using widgets and layers. A screen capture of Visual DHTML is shown in the last figure on the next page.

### ▶ SCRIPT SOURCE FILES

The basic code for this example comes from a Netscape drag-and-drop component, available at DevEdge Online. This basic component, which can be linked into the page using a <SCRIPT src=dragable.js> tag, enables you to create a layer on the fly a nd make it dragable to any location on the screen.

**CROSS-REFERENCE**

Chapter 12 has other suggestions for useful Web design tools.

**FIND IT ONLINE**

The Electro-Magnetic Poetry Java applet is at **http://prominence.com/java/poetry/wordMagick**.

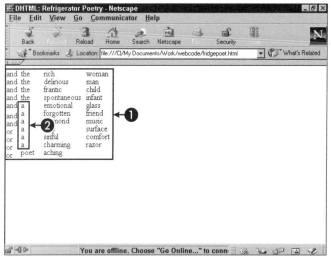

❶ *The fridgepoet DHTML application starts out with all the words placed onscreen.*

❷ *Multiple words appear onscreen multiple times.*

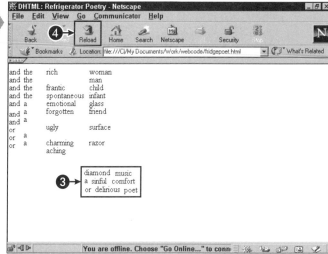

❸ *Users can drag-and-drop words into position.*

❹ *Clicking the "Reload" button resets the poetry application to its original.*

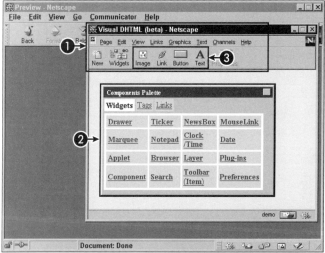

❶ *Use the Visual DHTML program to create dynamic Web pages in Netscape.*

❷ *Premade widgets let you add small DHTML snippets to your Web pages.*

❸ *You can also add standard HTML elements, such as links, text, and images.*

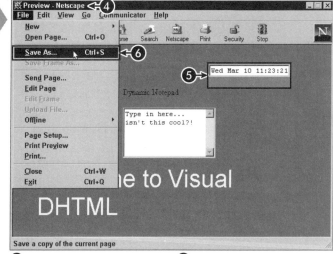

❹ *The Preview page lets you view the page as you create it.*

❺ *You can also move items around on the dynamic page.*

❻ *Save the page with File ⇨ Save As on the menu bar.*

■ *The saved page will open as a dynamic Web page in Netscape Navigator.*

# Using Dynamic Fonts

Ever since the Web became a tool instead of a novelty, people have been trying to read more and more text onscreen. Unfortunately, computer screens can strain the eyes, and only a limited number of fonts are actually easy to read in an electronic form.

In addition, many Web designers long to be able to use special symbols and characters without resorting to a Unicode character or worse, thousands of little images, to use an alternate font. The old rule "Don't send a graphic to do the job of text" has been broken so many times, it's hard to remember why you wouldn't create graphics to show specific fonts. But just because a rule is broken doesn't mean it isn't a good one.

Fortunately, Netscape has created the dynamic font (also called a *downloadable font*) for Web designers to use. It's not really dynamic in the sense of being able to change after the Web page has loaded, but you can embed a font into a Web page, and it will install itself into the user's browser and appear in the Web page as the page is loaded into the browser.

One of the elegant things about dynamic fonts is that you can now send text to do the job of a graphic. If you have a font that consists mainly of images or symbols, you can include images from that font in your Web page without using a GIF file. Because the image is basically included as text, you can apply style sheets to add color, increase or decrease the sizes, and generally make them more usable for your site.

To create a dynamic font, you need to create a font definition file, using some program to convert a standard TrueType font on your system into a PFR file. PFR files are the actual font definition files; they can contain one or more fonts, and reside on the Web server. Unlike other Web content, dynamic fonts that have been "burned" into PFR files cannot be copied onto users' systems and used later.

For the examples on the next page, I created the PFR files using Typograph 2.0, from HexMac (**http://www.hexmac.com**).

## TAKE NOTE

### ▶ FONT COPYRIGHT

Just because you have a font installed on your computer doesn't give you the right to embed it into a Web page and use it. Like graphics and text, you must have explicit permission to distribute a font on the Internet, and embedded fonts are certainly being distributed. Although there are many fonts available for free, make sure the copyright owner of the font you want to use has given permission to do so.

### ▶ DYNAMIC FONT SECURITY

Worried about font viruses that might piggyback onto your fonts? Don't. Fonts are like graphics and simple text; they don't execute a program, and therefore can't run a virus on your computer.

**CROSS-REFERENCE**

Chapter 9 has information on rendering special characters in HTML.

**FIND IT ONLINE**

Bitstream's Dynamic Font site is at **http://www.truedoc.com/webpages/intro/**.

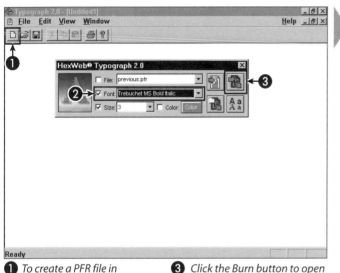

❶ To create a PFR file in
Typograph, start with a new
file.

❷ You can select a font for your
<FONT> element.

❸ Click the Burn button to open
the PFR creation window.

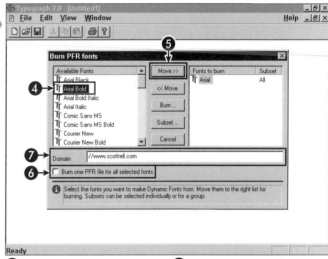

❹ Choose the fonts to embed in
your document.

❺ Click the Move button.

❻ For multiple fonts, check the
"Burn one PFR" box to add
multiple fonts to a PFR file.

❼ Be sure the domain name is
correct!

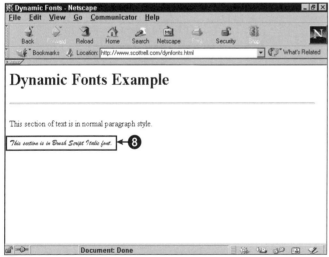

❽ Even though this computer doesn't have the font installed, it shows
up anyway using a <LINK> to a dynamic font.

## Listing 17-3: Dynamic Fonts

```
<HEAD>
<LINK HXBURNED REL="fontdef"
SRC="webfont.pfr">
   <TITLE>Dynamic Fonts</TITLE>
</HEAD>
<BODY>
<H1>Dynamic Fonts Example</H1>
<HR>
<P>
This section of text is in normal paragraph
style.
</P>
<P><FONT FACE="Brush Script MT
   Italic,Helvetica,Arial" SIZE="3">
This section is in Brush Script Italic font.
</FONT>
```

▲ This code generated the figure to the left of this listing.

# Personal Workbook

## Q&A

**1** How does Netscape implement the DOM?

_____

_____

_____

**2** What arrays are available in Netscape's DOM?

_____

_____

_____

**3** How would you create a layer?

_____

_____

_____

**4** What element should you use for sites that don't display layers correctly?

_____

_____

_____

**5** How do you change the style of elements inside a layer?

_____

_____

_____

**6** How do you move a layer to the right?

_____

_____

_____

**7** How do you change which layer is on top of other layers?

_____

_____

_____

**8** How do you include a dynamic font in a Web page?

_____

_____

_____

ANSWERS: PAGE 446

## EXTRA PRACTICE

**1** Create a Web page with one layer. Insert a graphic in the layer, and name the layer "picture1."

**2** Create a second layer that contains the name of the subject of the picture. Name it "caption1." Give this layer a transparent background.

**3** Position the caption and picture layers so the two layers overlap. Make the caption appear on top of the picture layer.

**4** Reposition the caption below the picture layer. Make sure it can't be seen beneath the picture.

**5** Use an onmouseover event to bring the caption forward when a user moves his or her mouse over the picture layer.

**6** Finally, add a scripted button that will separate both layers, making each one separately visible.

## REAL-WORLD EXAMPLES

✔ An online florist uses drag-and-drop DHTML to give customers a quick, customizable bouquet preview picture for their orders.

✔ Your company's Web site calls for an animation, but bandwidth is already a company concern. You use Dynamic HTML to create a fast, animated banner for your users.

✔ An electronic library has its books split into HTML pages. A DHTML page makes the contents accessible from one Web browser, with a minimum of download time.

✔ The corporate logo is, in fact, a specialized font that can't be easily duplicated. You use dynamic fonts to shortcut the need for graphics and control access to your logos.

## Visual Quiz

What DHTML elements do you see present in this figure? How would you expect this page to behave? What other ways can you think of to present this information?

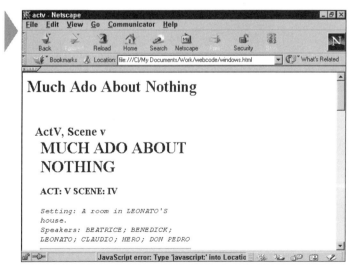

_____

_____

_____

_____

_____

PART

V

# Are You Being Served?

This part teaches you about Web servers and scripting for them. You learn how to choose a Web server, employ JavaScript and VBScript, install a Java applet, and use cookies to enhance your site. You also learn how to install and write a CGI script, and modify an existing script for your server. Finally, you learn about server security, a crucial aspect of Web design that is too often overlooked.

Nothing is quite as important to the success of your Web site as is its Web server. It runs everything your site does, from displaying graphics to multimedia to downloadable files. Every form you install must communicate with the server. Basically, your entire Web site depends on a hardware and software system about which you may know nothing.

There may be no reason to go into this. Setting up and maintaining a Web server is hard work, and it may not be what you need right now. However, sooner or later you're going to want to install a custom program or use an uncommon plug-in. At that time, you can refer to this part as a guide to dealing with Web servers (and server administrators!).

CHAPTER 18

MASTER
THESE
SKILLS

▶ Choosing a Web Server
▶ Selecting a Web Hosting Company
▶ Finding Collocation Facilities
▶ Choosing Not to Use Your ISP
▶ Publishing with FTP

# Web Servers

Whenever you try to do something really neat with a CGI script, or even certain plug-ins, you get the old "Ask your server administrator" advice. Why? What's so great about the server administrator? What's so great about the server?

A basic concept behind all networks is called the client-server relationship. Essentially, it's a relationship between machines in which one machine (the client) requests information from another machine (the server) and receives it. There are several types of servers on the Internet: network servers (for LANs), SMTP servers (for email), FTP servers (for FTP), and HTTP, or Web, servers for the World Wide Web. On any given server computer, there could be one or more of these servers running. Thus, a server is a composite of hardware and software that delivers data to authorized clients. I say authorized because some Web servers use security features to control who accesses their documents. Most Web servers on the Internet are open to the public; anybody is an authorized user.

The client, of course, consists of a user's hardware and software. Netscape Navigator is a Web client, and Netscape Communicator also includes email and Usenet (newsgroups) clients as well.

This chapter focuses specifically on Web servers, the hardware and software that delivers your Web site to authorized clients (your Web-using audience). Web servers are also called HTTP servers, named after the protocol that transfers Web documents over the Internet.

In this chapter, you learn how to choose a Web server based on the features available in most server packages. I also show you how and where to find a good, inexpensive Web hosting company for your Web site. If you decide to set up your own Web server, including hardware, you might want to have it inside a protected environment with a high-speed Internet connection. Therefore, I also discuss collocating your server (renting a space in a Web server facility). And I tell you some good reasons why you would or would not want to host with your ISP.

Finally, I cover one of the most important and useful skills for any Internet user, Web author or not. File Transfer Protocol (FTP) is one of the most reliable ways to transfer information over the Internet, and it's the most common way to upload your Web files to your Web server.

# Choosing a Web Server

The first step in setting up your Web server is choosing the server hardware and software package. A Web server is typically quite expensive: upward of $5,000 for an enterprise-level system, not including the server software. For most Web sites, including many businesses, that's beyond the available resources, and not an option. These businesses often collocate or host their Web server on someone else's computer, leaving the hardware and Internet connection in someone else's hands. Later in this chapter, I help you pick a Web hosting company and tell you what to look for in a collocation facility.

There are four basic types of server hardware. You've probably heard of two of them: Macintosh and Intel-based (or PC-compatible). Each hardware platform has its strengths as well as its weaknesses. While the Macintosh is a good graphically oriented environment, it hasn't been shown to have the stability for long-term heavy network usage. Intel, Sun, and the DEC-Alpha are all hardware platforms that have proven reliable network architectures, provided the other required components are adequate to the task: memory, hard drive, and (most important) operating system.

The operating system is a program that serves as an interface between the hardware and the software. Windows 95, Windows NT, Mac OS, O/S 2, UNIX, and Linux are all different operating systems available on the market today. Because they interface with the hardware directly, your operating system must be compatible with your hardware architecture.

Finally, the Web server software is usually dependent upon both the operating system and the underlying architecture. If your server machine uses an Intel or Intel-compatible CPU, then your options are limited to Web servers that work in Intel-compatible operating systems, such as Windows NT, Windows 95, OS/2, and Linux. Sun, DEC

Alpha, and SGI all use separate chip sets. Web servers written for one operating system may not be available on another.

*Continued*

## TAKE NOTE

### ▶ PERSONAL WEB SERVERS

If you're using Windows 95 and just want a Web server so you can test your site, check out Microsoft's Personal Web Server (available at **http://www.microsoft.com**), O'Reilly's WebSite Professional (at **http://website.oreilly.com**), and the Apache Win32 build (at **http://www.apache. org**). They're all small Web servers that easily run on Windows 95. Personal Web Server and Apache are completely free, while WebSite has a 30-day demo version available.

### ▶ A POPULAR CHOICE

Although every Web server manufacturer claims their option is the most popular, independent studies show that the least expensive combination seems to also be the most popular (go figure). That combination is the Linux operating system (free), running the Apache Web server (also free) on some type of Intel server (prices keep dropping, and can be as low as $1,000 for a midlevel Pentium-based system, at the time of this writing). Because Linux is not as "resource-greedy" as Windows, it's gaining popularity as a client operating system as well, and can easily run on a low-end or otherwise obsolete machine.

### CROSS-REFERENCE

Some of the authoring environments mentioned are also discussed in Chapter 12.

### FIND IT ONLINE

You can find several less-expensive Web servers at Tucows (**http://tucows.tierranet.com/**).

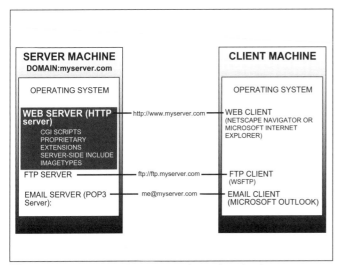

■ *This diagram shows client/server relationships for the various Internet protocols, including HTTP (Web), FTP, and POP3 (email).*

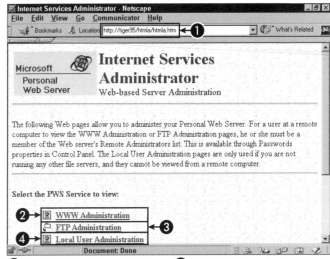

❶ *To administer Microsoft's Personal Web Server, open the administration page.*

❷ *Change the Web server configuration by clicking the WWW Administration link.*

❸ *FTP Administration lets you configure the FTP server.*

❹ *Local User Administration lets you add and delete authorized users and groups of users for the server.*

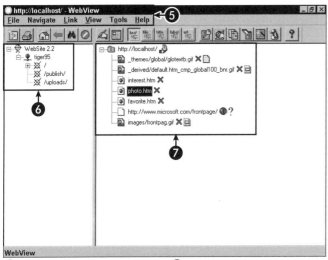

❺ *O'Reilly's WebSite Professional offers a WebView program to help you manage your documents.*

❻ *See servers and directories running on the current machine.*

❼ *Notice the individual pages and documents, linked to other pages.*

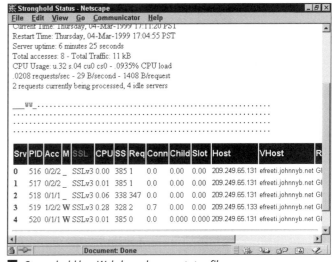

■ *Stronghold has Web-based server status files.*

# Choosing a Web Server
*Continued*

As you look at the Web servers available, ask yourself a few honest questions. What's your level of technical expertise? Are you a quick learner? Can you remember a bunch of esoteric commands? Or, do you work better in a graphical environment, using visual clues to manage your account?

Network operating systems seem to fall into two broad categories: Windows NT, and UNIX. Windows NT is a Microsoft product that only runs on Intel and RISC platforms.

If you decide to use a Sun server (hardware), you'll probably be using a version of UNIX called Solaris. With Digital, you have the choice between a Windows NT system or their DEC AlphaServer, with UNIX or VMS as the operating system.

In Windows NT, 95, and 98 (commonly called "Win32" systems), a few commercial options are Microsoft's Internet Information Server, Microsoft's Personal Web Server, O'Reilly and Associates' WebSite, and Netscape FastTrack Server (and other Web servers from Netscape). There are also many less popular servers, many of which are freely available on the Internet.

However, the real powerhouse of Internet servers has been the UNIX operating system, including all the many "flavors" of UNIX available (such as BSDI, Linux, and Solaris). Most Web servers run Apache on the Linux operating system; it's inexpensive, stable, and, with several thousand developers worldwide, you can always find a Linux guru on the Internet, no matter what the hour.

However, Apache isn't the only Web server that runs on UNIX. Others include Solaris Web Server (which runs on Sun Solaris servers), Java Web Server, Netscape's servers, NCSA HTTPd, Open Market, SPRY Web Server, and W3C httpd (or CERN httpd).

Each Web server has its advantages, its disadvantages, and its quirks (known as bugs, if they're quirky enough). Some servers — such as Netscape and Apache, which are available on more than one operating system — may not have the same quirks on all architectures. Some servers emphasize one feature over another. If you think that feature's important, check to make certain that it's available on whatever server platform you choose.

## TAKE NOTE

### ▶ PROPRIETARY PROGRAMS

There's another consideration when discussing Web server hardware. Are you going to use a proprietary authoring package, such as Cold Fusion, Active Server Pages, or FrontPage? Although FrontPage extensions are now available for more Web servers on most platforms, they aren't available for all of them. Similarly, Active Server Pages only work on Microsoft Web servers. And Cold Fusion is only available for Sun Solaris and Windows NT platforms. If you plan to use additional authoring or scripting environments, double-check the system requirements before you buy a Web server system.

**CROSS-REFERENCE**

Chapter 19 has information on CGI programming languages and scripts.

**FIND IT ONLINE**

WebCompare (**http://webcompare.internet.com/**) compares different Web servers.

## Table 18-1: WEB SERVER FEATURES

| Features | Apache | Microsoft IIS | Netscape FastTrack | O'Reilly WebSite Professional |
|---|---|---|---|---|
| Operating systems | Linux, UNIX (all flavors) Windows 95, Windows NT | Windows NT Server | UNIX Windows 95 Windows NT | Windows 95, Windows NT |
| GUI/Web-based interface | Under XWindows | Yes | Yes | Yes |
| SSL | In commercial version (Stronghold) | Yes | Yes | Yes |
| Shopping cart/ commerce software | No | No (upgrade to Site Server) | No | iHTML Merchant |
| APIs | CGI, Apache API, Java Servlets | CGI, ISAPI, Java Servlets | CGI, NSAPI, Java Servlets | CGI, WSAPI, ISAPI, Java Servlets |
| Scripting | Embedded PERL, PHP, SSI | ASP, VBScript, JScript | Server-Side JavaScript, LiveWire, SSI | ASP, iHTML, Embedded HTML |

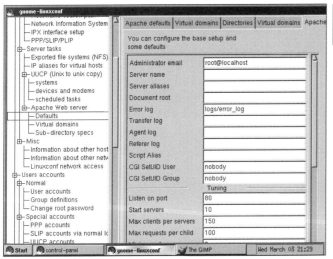

■ *The Apache GUI is available under XWindows, a windows manager program for UNIX-based systems.*

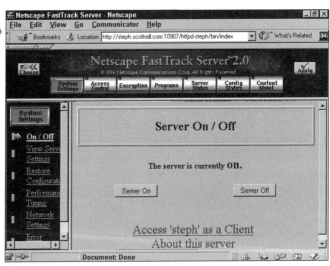

■ *An example of Netscape FastTrack Server's user interface.*

# Selecting a Web Hosting Company

I'm going to jump ahead a bit here and suggest that you may have decided not to buy your own system after all. Maybe the hardware was just too expensive, or the software too difficult to install. More likely, you're really just looking to put up a small commercial site for your business. You don't anticipate heavy traffic yet; that will come later.

One solution for the entrepreneur is to host your Web site on someone else's computer. They set up all the software and hardware and maintain the Internet connection, and all you have to worry about is the site's content and maintenance. What a deal! Better yet, you have worldwide competition to choose from, because your Web server can be literally anywhere in the world.

This next section deals with choosing a Web hosting company. What features are important? How much should you pay? What do SSI, SSL, and FrontPage Extensions mean? Does it matter if it's Windows NT or Linux?

First, start with the basics. Most people never look beyond hard drive space and transfer rates. Hard drive space means how much storage space you have available on the server. That usually includes any stored email, FTP space, as well as your Web space. If you keep your graphic sizes down to a reasonable size, a typical Web site won't take more than 5–10MB of hard drive storage space.

Then, there's the transfer rate. You'll probably see between 500MB and 2,000MB per month. That's how much data you can send back and forth through their network before they start charging you extra. I know of no hosting companies that will absolutely prohibit you from sending more; they just like to get more money for it. If you find yourself going over your transfer allotment on a regular basis, switch hosting companies.

There are some hosting companies that allow unlimited transfer, but I prefer to stay off of their networks. Why? If they're giving me unlimited hits, then they're giving the same thing to their other customers. Honestly, my site doesn't need to compete with a bunch of other sites for *bandwidth* (that's the connection speed). Even if they offer unlimited hits, the company still has a speed limit to the Internet. When their connection gets too many hits at the same time, everything slows down.

*Continued*

## TAKE NOTE

### ▶ BANDWIDTH SPEEDS

*Bandwidth* refers to how many bits that can be transferred to and from the Internet in a single second. A 56 Kbps modem has a bandwidth connection of 56,000 bits per second. An ISDN connection is much faster. A T1 is faster than an ISDN, and T3 is the fastest yet. Your Web hosting company should have at least one T1 connection (if it's a small company), or multiple T1s or T3s, to adequately handle the traffic.

## CROSS-REFERENCE

Cut down on transfer rates and server load with client-side scripts, covered in Chapter 19.

## FIND IT ONLINE

FreeIndex.com (**http://www.freeindex.com/**) has a directory of free Web spaces on the Internet.

## Free Web Hosting

What's that? Free Web hosting services? Really?

Yes, really. Free Web space abounds on the Internet. Online communities, search engines, and advertising clearinghouses offer free Web space to anyone who will make it worth their time.

The Web spaces are usually supported through advertising — that's advertising on *your* Web page. Most of them have a bunch of restrictions as well; your storage, bandwidth, content, and advertising may be restricted based on where you put your pages. And very few of them allow you to run your own CGI scripts.

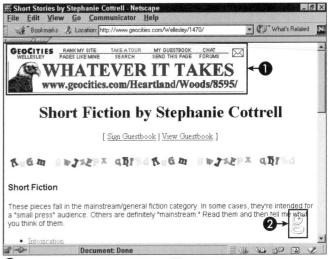

❶ Geocities, a popular free Web space service, requires banner advertisements.

❷ They also use a floating JavaScript logo to identify Geocities sites.

■ Geocities' terms of usage heavily regulate the content as well.

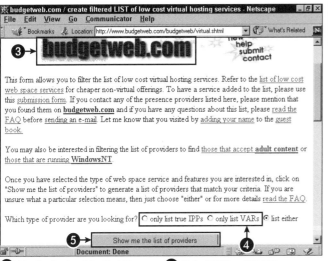

❸ Use budgetweb to find the right Web hosting company for you.

❹ Select VAR or IPP: IPPs maintain their own Web servers, while VARs host space on someone else's server.

❺ Select the options and click "Show me the list of providers."

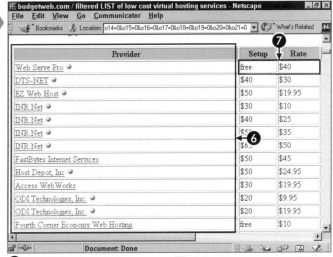

❻ The list has hyperlinks to a report on each hosting company.

❼ See at a glance how much the service costs to set up and maintain on a monthly basis.

■ Other features are provided offscreen to the right.

# Selecting a Web Hosting Company *Continued*

When you've figured out the very basics — how much, how many, how fast — you need to learn about the features available and which ones you'll probably need. The table on the next page has a quick breakdown of some common Web hosting features. However, I'd like to mention a few of them here.

First, CGI scripting is a major feature, and one you probably can't do without. Eventually, you'll want to use a CGI script to handle something on your site: a form, a discussion group, or an image map. Most hosting services offer a few preinstalled CGI scripts, and many allow you to install your own scripts (although there may be limitations on the scripts allowed). One common CGI language is Perl, and it should probably be available in any Web hosting company offering CGI access.

Email, shell, and FTP accounts are features that you probably need to manage your server adequately. You'll probably need at least one POP3 email account so you can send and receive email from your Web site. Additional email accounts are useful for other employees of your company or members of your organization. Similarly, you may want additional FTP accounts for other individuals who will have "write" access (to upload files) to your FTP server. Finally, if you can get one, a telnet, or shell account can be invaluable if the Web hosting company uses UNIX. It's possible to manage your accounts without it, but any serious Web administrator will eventually want the kind of control that only comes with a shell account.

Finally, decide if you want or need your own domain. For a business site, your own domain might be a necessity, but noncommercial sites may find price is more important than vanity.

## Web Hosting Checklist

Be sure to ask yourself the following questions when researching a Web hosting company:

▶ Is the storage space enough? (5MB to 15MB is usually enough to start.)
▶ Will I exceed my monthly transfer rate? (1,000MB to 2,000MB is usually enough at first.)
▶ What bandwidth will be available? (Multiple T1s are almost a minimum.)
▶ Do I need my own domain? If so, will they handle registration for me? (Most will.)
▶ Is a shell account included? What about additional FTP accounts?
▶ Does the account come with preinstalled CGI scripts? What about image maps and server-side includes?
▶ Can I install my own CGI scripts?
▶ How many POP3 email accounts do I get?
▶ Are there any special email features, like redirect, mailing lists, or infobots?
▶ What content or use restrictions are there? Can I put a commercial site on this server?
▶ Is there a built-in statistics program?
▶ Is a secure server available? Does it use Secure Sockets Layer (SSL)? Does it cost extra?
▶ Is there a database available for me to use?
▶ How far off of a major Internet "backbone" is the server?
▶ How much will it cost?

**CROSS-REFERENCE**

More information on Web server security is in Chapter 20.

**FIND IT ONLINE**

BudgetWeb (**http://www.budgetweb.com**) offers an impartial list of low-cost Web hosting companies.

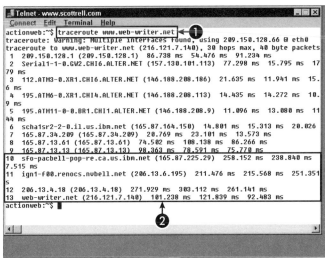

❶ Use the tracert program in MS-DOS or traceroute in UNIX to see how far your Web host is from your local computer.

❷ This server has several large hops! Usually, 10-15 hops of about 7 or 8 ms is normal.

■ Asterisks (*) indicate timed out connections.

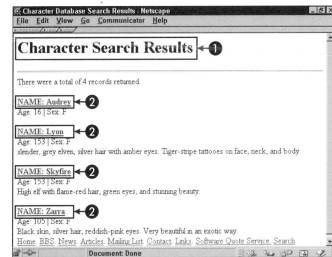

❶ One Web hosting facility offers a searchable, customizable database program.

❷ You could include a URL to the item's home page, and create a hyperlinked list like this one.

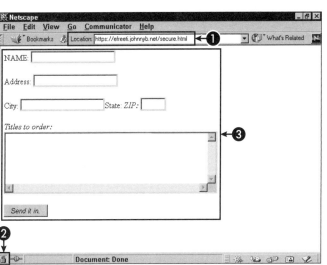

❶ Secure Web servers (using SSL) usually start with https:// in the URL.

❷ They also have a completed lock or an unbroken key for the Security icon.

❸ Use your secure server for sensitive transactions, such as order forms and credit card transfers.

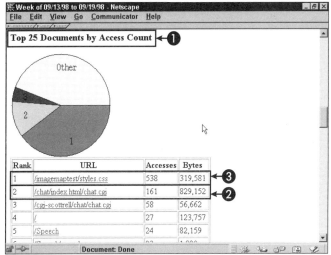

❶ My server statistics report shows the top 25 documents requested.

❷ Although I only ran it for a short time, my chat program took a lot of hits!

❸ An authoring error causes `styles.css` to be requested too many times as well.

# Finding Collocation Facilities

One option for businesses with specialized Web hosting needs is to set up your own hardware and software but rent space in a computer-friendly facility. These facilities usually have several high-speed connections to the Internet, climate-controlled hardware rooms, and fire prevention and security measures not normally available in the typical office.

Renting space at such a facility is known as *collocating* your server. Servers are usually placed in open racks of shelves, which have been specially wired to the Internet for your bandwidth needs. The facility uses special monitoring software to measure the amount of bandwidth you use, and you generally pay by the amount of data transferred during the billing period.

Some collocation facilities also offer network monitoring options, in which they will contact you if your server fails to respond to a client hit, and will send client requests periodically to be sure that your server is responding correctly.

When you collocate, you have more control over what software and scripts you can install on a collocated Web server. You can change anything you want, provide whatever user permissions suit your fancy, and generally "hog" the CPU's resources. When you host with a Web hosting company, you're usually restricted in your permissions, CPU usage, and hard drive storage capacity. With collocation, you can take total responsibility for the hardware and software maintenance and upkeep — a source of pride for many Web administrators.

Most offices are built for the comfort of the people inside them. Computers like dry, cool climates, and a water-based fire extinguisher is literally murder to sensitive hardware components. Most collocation facilities use a type of fire suppression system that effectively removes the oxygen from the area — great for computers, but not the best choice for people.

Finally, your office might not have the kind of security system you'd like to protect your $10,000 system (and the priceless data it contains). Good collocation facilities offer the kind of security features you'd expect from a branch of the military, and they should offer security upgrades for especially valuable systems. (One facility offers private, bulletproof rooms with fingerprint security locks!)

## TAKE NOTE

### COLLOCATION DRAWBACKS

You still have to be responsible for your own hardware and software, and their maintenance. You won't have access to the server at all times. If you need to install new software from a CD-ROM or floppy, you'll have to drive out to the collocation facility to do so.

Finally, not all collocation facilities are equal. Although some are diligent in reporting "downtimes," others may give up if they don't reach you immediately, or fail to report network errors at all until they've become a serious problem. Make sure you check client references at any collocation facility you consider.

## CROSS-REFERENCE

You can often exchange advertising for collocation costs; see Chapter 23 for ideas.

## FIND IT ONLINE

http://dir.yahoo.com/Business_and_Economy/ Companies/Computers/Communications_and_ Networking// has a program for remote configuration.

## Collocations Checklist

Here are some questions to ask when checking out a collocation facility:

▶ Is the bandwidth speed adequate for my needs?

▶ Is the monthly bandwidth allotment enough?

▶ Are there redundant Internet connections to the facility?

▶ Does the facility use multiple peers for backbone access? (Peers are companies like UUNet, Pacific Bell, MCI, AT&T, AlterNet, and others that help build the main Internet backbones.)

▶ Is there a clean, consistent power supply?

▶ Do backup generators provide uninterrupted power?

▶ Is the environment clean, cool, and dry? Is there air conditioning?

▶ Does the facility use a dry fire suppression system, such as FM200?

▶ Is the physical security adequate for my needs? Is there security personnel onsite?

▶ Is the facility accessible 24 hours a day, 7 days a week? Can I work on my server at 3 A.M.?

▶ Does the facility monitor my server connection and response?

▶ How quickly will they contact me if something goes wrong?

▶ Do they offer DNS (domain name service), email, or other servers for companies that use their facility?

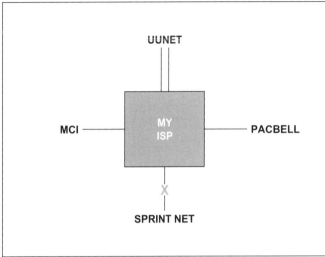

■ *Multiple peers and redundant connections are a must for any full-time colocation facility.*

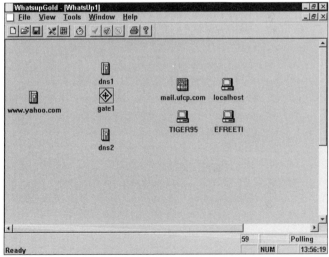

■ *Ipswitch's What'sUpGold software monitors your server, and notifies you immediately if there's a problem. It requires a 24-hour Internet connection to function.*

# Choosing Not to Use Your ISP

An ISP is an *Internet service provider*. Generally speaking, that's the company your computer calls to get your Internet connection, often called a *dial-up connection*. Some companies have high-speed, dedicated lines — a permanent connection to the Internet for the office. (That's why surfing at home is so much slower than surfing at work.) The Internet connection itself is owned by and regulated by the Internet service provider. Typical connect fees are $20 per month for a single-user account, and any ISP you use should have a local telephone number, to avoid long-distance charges.

ISPs generally specialize in providing dial-up connections. Those connections are expensive to maintain, so your ISP might also offer other services to defray their dial-up charges, and provide an all-in-one package for you or your company.

And in some cases, that kind of package is a great deal. If your company needs to have several dial-up lines for telecommuting employees, a dedicated office line, a Web hosting company, and a few additional services, then you should research the packages available from your ISP and compare it to an a la carte Web hosting package, using several different vendors.

However, if you get your Internet connection from a company that doesn't offer Web hosting services, or from a university or government agency, then the ISP hosting packages aren't quite as attractive as those offered by Web hosting companies.

As an example, one California ISP charges $19.95 per month for a dial-up account, a fair price. As with most ISPs, that dial-up account comes with an email address and some Web space on the server. However, the URL will have the address:

`http://www.myisp.com/myusername/index.html` or some similar, long-winded URL.

To get a simpler address, such as `http://www.mydomain.com`, you have to register your domain name (the `mydomain.com` part), and get a virtual hosting account. The next page shows a cost comparison between one ISP's small business virtual domain account (its low-end business hosting account) and a Web hosting company's virtual domain gold plan account (its midlevel plan).

## Registering Domain Names

Some ISPs (and Web hosting companies, too) will charge an extra fee for the convenience of registering your domain name. Domain name registration is done through the InterNIC, or Network Solutions, at **http://www.internic.net** (note: `internic.com` is **not** Network Solutions!). Although you'll need to know the DNS server entries, you can usually obtain those from your ISP or Web hosting company for free.

Be sure to read Network Solutions' policies carefully. This company deals with thousands of requests per day, and they've become quite picky on how your request must be formatted. Make sure your name appears in the Administrative Contact/Agent section; that's who legally "owns" the domain name, should a dispute arise.

**CROSS-REFERENCE**

Chapter 20 discusses security concerns you'll encounter when you have your own Web server.

**FIND IT ONLINE**

For a listing of ISPs around the world, see The List at **http://www.thelist.com**.

| Table 18-2: COST COMPARISON FOR A TYPICAL VIRTUAL DOMAIN ACCOUNT | | |
| --- | --- | --- |
| **Service** | **ISP** | **Web Hosting Company** |
| Setup fee | $75.00 | $24.95 |
| Monthly rate | $25.00 | $15.95 ($13.95 with annual contract) |
| Monthly bandwidth | 1GB | 6 GB |
| Disk space | 20MB | 200MB |
| Domain registration (not including InterNIC fees) | Included | Included |
| Monthly bandwidth charges (over allotment) | $20/250MB | $5/100MB |
| Commercial use OK | Yes | Yes |
| Email accounts | One included, $5 setup/ $5/month additional | Two included, $2/2 additional (monthly) |
| FTP accounts | One included | One included, $1.50 monthly per additional |

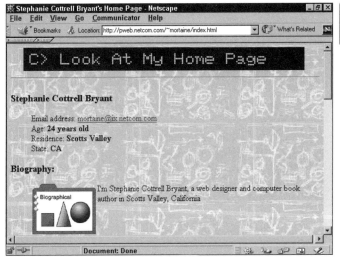

■ *Most ISPs offer Web page creation tools, templates, and wizards to help beginning designers create their Web sites. Here's a page created using an ISP's template.*

■ *The main advantages to virtual domains at a Web hosting company are flexibility and a permanent URL. This site has preinstalled CGI scripts, but the owner of the site can install his or her own if desired.*

# Publishing with FTP

After you've created your Web site, and have a Web server to put it on, the hardest part might seem to be putting your site onto your server. After all, you know how to write the pages, you know how to download, and you even know where it all goes. But how do you get your files from here to there?

File Transfer Protocol, or FTP, is one of the easiest Internet tools you can find. It's also one of the oldest, most reliable protocols on the Net. Some FTP servers even support a "restore" option that resumes a downed connection wherever you left off.

In this section on FTP, I'll show you how to use a basic, graphical FTP program to upload a Web site. Then, I'll show you how to use a command-line FTP program (less expensive, faster) to do the same thing. Finally, I'll show you how to do a little site management with FTP, and how to download your files as well.

Many Web authoring programs, such as Netscape Communicator and Allaire HomeSite, now support some variant of "one-click publishing." That means they've included an easy-to-use FTP program for the sole purpose of managing a Web site. FTP is used for many other applications, especially downloading free software from open FTP servers, such as **cdrom.com**.

A typical graphical FTP program uses "drag and drop" technology to let you move files from your home machine to the server, and vice versa. Most programs will automatically switch between Binary mode (for graphics, compiled programs, and so forth) and ASCII mode (for text files, CSS and HTML documents, and Perl scripts). Be sure that the program you're using recognizes .html, .pl (for Perl), and .cgi as ASCII files!

Be warned, however: drag-and-drop FTP programs can sometimes translate into "drag and destroy." Many users have accidentally deleted entire directories with an accidental mouse click. And on a Web server, there's no "Undelete," and no "Recycling Bin" to retrieve those lost files from; once deleted, they're gone forever.

*Continued*

## TAKE NOTE

### ▶ FTP SOFTWARE

There are literally hundreds of shareware FTP programs available on the Internet. Some are simple "outboxes," providing an upload utility to wherever you want to go. That's useful for Web authors, who often only use their FTP programs to upload a developed site to the server. The FTP program used in this example is WS_FTP, which is included on the CD-ROM in the back of this book.

### ▶ ANONYMOUS FTP

WS_FTP comes with several public FTP sites pre-configured. You can connect anonymously to these sites to download documents, images, and even shareware programs.

If your server has FTP installed, you can also have an anonymous FTP server to deliver documents and files to your audience. It's an easy, low-maintenance way to publish files on the Internet.

---

**SHORTCUT**
You can also change directories quickly by double-clicking the directory name on either the local or remote machine.

**FIND IT ONLINE**
WS_FTP is made by Ipswitch (**http://www.ipswitch.com**).

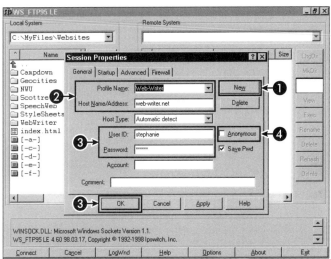

❶ To create a new profile, click the New button.

❷ Type in a name for the profile. Enter the host name.

❸ To connect to your own server, put your username and password in the User ID and Password boxes. Click OK.

❹ If it's an anonymous connection, check the Anonymous box and click OK.

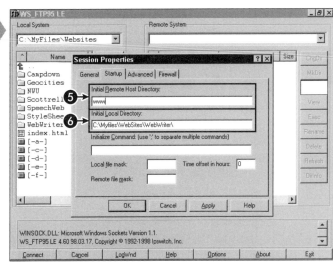

❺ In the Startup tab, change the Initial Remote Host Directory to the Web directory on your server.

❻ Change the Initial Local Directory to start in your computer's document directory for this profile.

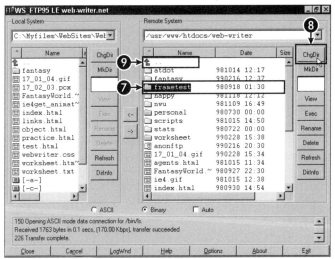

❼ Once connected, you can change directories by selecting the directory in the right-hand pane.

❽ Click ChgDir to open that directory.

❾ The up arrow takes you up one directory level.

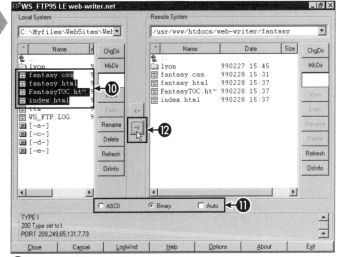

❿ To upload files and directories to the server, first select them in the left-hand pane.

⓫ Make sure the transfer mode is set correctly: ASCII for text, Binary for other files, and Auto for automatic detection.

⓬ Click the right arrow button to upload the files to the Web server.

# Publishing with FTP

*Continued*

Every Windows computer also comes with a command-line FTP client, and this is one of the more popular ways to upload and download files. Maybe because it's free, or maybe because there's little chance of the software getting in the way of the transfer (if you've ever had a graphical program crash without warning, you know what I mean), the MS-DOS-prompt FTP program is a useful tool for uploading your site.

Command-line FTP is not the most intuitive tool to use. There are no special buttons or tip windows to help you figure out what you're doing. In fact, most people have a hard time remembering all the FTP commands, which is why those graphical programs are so popular. However, you're less likely to "drag and destroy" using the command-line FTP client, because you cannot move entire directories all at once.

On the next page is a listing of common FTP commands and how to use them. Be sure to familiarize yourself with them. Fold down that corner of the book so you can get back to that page quickly. If you ever have to transfer a file from one computer to another computer and you just can't seem to get it to work, try the command-line FTP program, which is the underlying program for every FTP transaction. Even graphical FTP programs use those commands, although they hide them behind user-friendly buttons and menus. Command-line FTP is also part of every major UNIX-based distribution.

One great advantage of command-line FTP is that it's available on almost any computer, anywhere. If you know how to use the basic FTP commands, you won't be lost without "your" computer — you'll be able to use just about anyone's system to transfer files.

*Continued*

## TAKE NOTE

### ▶ FTP FOR MACINTOSH

The most common FTP program for the Macintosh is called Fetch, available at **http://www.dartmouth.edu/pages/softdev/fetch.html**. Like most Macintosh programs, Fetch is a user-friendly graphical environment.

### ▶ BINARY VS. ASCII MODE

When you upload or download files, you need to be very careful about how they're being transferred. Basically, there are two types of data: binary and ASCII. ASCII is just like a plaintext file; no special encoding or compiling has been done to compress it into a smaller file, or to make it into a graphic. Web pages, style sheets, Perl scripts, VRML worlds, source code, and text files are usually stored (and transferred) in ASCII mode.

Binary mode, on the other hand, is used to transfer any file that is not plaintext. That includes graphics, programs, ZIP files, encrypted files, word processing documents (such as `.doc` and `.wpd` files), PDF files, and compiled CGI scripts.

To switch between ASCII and binary, type the command `ascii` or `binary` at the prompt. Another feature in graphical FTP programs is automatic detection: the FTP program automatically switches modes depending on the file type.

**SHORTCUT**
To view your local directory's files when in FTP, type `!dir` (or `!ls` for UNIX clients). `!` runs any command following it on the local system.

**FIND IT ONLINE**
The FTP Request For Comments (RFC 959) is available online at **ftp://nic.merit.edu/documents/rfc/rfc0959.txt**.

## Table 18-3: COMMON FTP COMMANDS

| Command | Result |
|---|---|
| open ftp.domain.com | Opens an FTP session with ftp.domain.com |
| close | Closes the current FTP session |
| bye | Closes the current FTP session and the FTP client |
| dir (ls on UNIX) | Lists the current remote directory |
| ascii | Transfers files in ASCII format |
| binary | Transfers files in binary format |
| prompt | Turns on or off verification for uploading and overwriting files |
| !command | Runs specified command on the local directory or system |
| get filename.html | Downloads filename.html to the local directory |
| mput filename.html, other.txt | Uploads filename.html and other.txt to the remote server |
| mget *.html | Downloads all files with an .html ending |
| put graphic.gif | Uploads graphic.gif to the remote directory |
| mkdir directory_name | Creates a directory called directory_name inside the current remote directory |

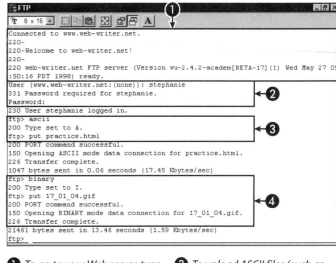

❶ To go to your Web server, type **open www.myserver.com.**

❷ Log in with your username and password.

❸ To upload ASCII files (such as HTML pages), type **ascii** then **put filename.html.**

❹ For binary files (such as graphics), type **binary** then **put filename.gif.**

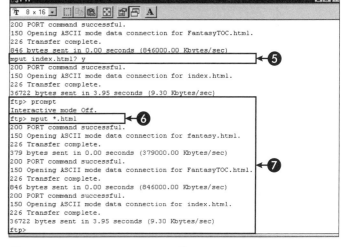

❺ To upload multiple files, use the mput command.

❻ You can upload all files of a certain type by using the * wildcard; *.html means all files ending in .html.

❼ Type **prompt** to turn off the verification mode.

# Publishing with FTP

*Continued*

When you create a complex Web site, you usually organize your files into subdirectories. It's easier to remember which file went where, and you can use the same filename for two different files if they're in separate directories. You can create a new directory in FTP with the `mkdir` command: `mkdir directory_name`. Remove a directory using `rmdir`: `rmdir directory_name`.

Thousands of FTP servers exist where you can download free information, software, graphics, and documents, which you can then open on your computer.

A word of warning: if you download a program, be sure you trust the site you got it from before you install it. Viruses are often spread through freeware and shareware programs, and some of these viruses can be quite damaging to your computer.

To download files from an anonymous FTP server, log in as `anonymous` and use your email address as the password. Most FTP servers recognize this as a standard anonymous login scheme. It's a bit like logging in from the Web; you don't have many permissions, but you can find and get public files on the system.

Most Web browsers handle FTP downloading. Recent browsers (especially recent versions of Netscape Navigator and Microsoft Internet Explorer) also support FTP upload. With those browsers, you just have to go to the FTP site you want to upload to and log in. Some FTP servers allow you to upload anonymously into a directory called `incoming`, for example. However, since most require you to have write permission, you can log in using your username and password in the URL, as shown in the bottom two figures on the facing page.

## TAKE NOTE

### ▶ FTP SECURITY

As you know, Web pages can be encrypted for security purposes, using SHTTP or SSL. Because of its simplicity, however, FTP cannot encrypt pages during transmission or storage. Because most FTP servers accept anonymous connections, anyone can log in and read any file on the FTP server. In other words, don't put anything on an FTP server that you wouldn't mind having everyone in the world reading. If you want to transfer sensitive data over the Internet, use an encrypted email or HTTP program instead of FTP.

### ▶ FTP VS. HTTP-PUT

HTTP-PUT (or HTTP-POST) is a publishing protocol used in Netscape's 1-click publishing. It allows a Web client to upload files directly to the HTTP server without using an FTP server. Because HTTP was traditionally a download protocol, anyone wanting to edit and upload files to the Web had to go through an FTP server first. And because the difference between ASCII and binary was so confusing for so many people, HTTP-PUT was invented.

With HTTP-PUT, you can upload directly from your Web browser, transferring any file that could normally be transferred with HTTP, such as HTML, CGI, Perl, CSS, and graphics files.

## CROSS-REFERENCE
More information on using Netscape and Internet Explorer are in Chapters 10 and 11.

## FIND IT ONLINE
Tile.Net's FTP list (**http://tile.net/ftp-list/**) contains information on FTP servers around the world.

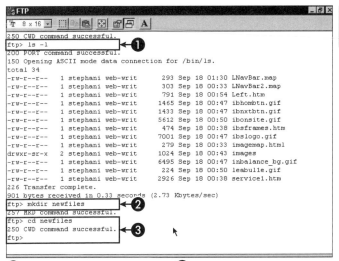

❶ To see the directory listing, type **ls**.

❷ Create a new directory with **mkdir**.

❸ To change directories, type **cd**.

❹ FTP downloading with your Web browser is easy. Point at the file you want, and click.

❺ Save the file to your hard drive. The Web browser will automatically detect the file type (ASCII or binary).

❻ To upload in Netscape, type **ftp://username@Ł domain.com**.

❼ At the prompt, enter your password for this server.

❽ Press OK to continue.

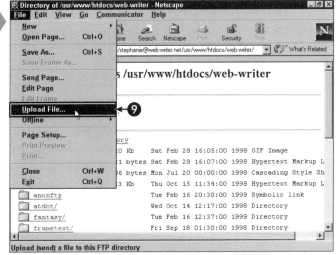

❾ Click File ➪ Upload File.

■ You'll see a Windows Explorer dialog box. Browse to the file, then click Open.

# Personal Workbook

## Q&A

**1** What three things should you determine first about a Web hosting company?

_____

_____

_____

**2** How much storage space will you probably need for a basic Web site?

_____

_____

_____

**3** What's a popular Web server setup that uses only free software?

_____

_____

_____

**4** Name three important features in a collocation service?

_____

_____

_____

**5** What's the major drawback of graphical FTP programs?

_____

_____

_____

**6** How do you open an FTP connection to an FTP or Web server?

_____

_____

_____

**7** How would you upload all the HTML files in a directory to your Web server?

_____

_____

_____

**8** What's the difference between ASCII and binary in FTP modes?

_____

_____

_____

ANSWERS: PAGE 446

## EXTRA PRACTICE

① Write down the features you'd need in a server system, including bandwidth and disk storage.

② Research the cost and benefits of a Web server that has all your required and preferred features.

③ Try to find a collocation facility nearby and check out their prices.

④ Find an inexpensive Web hosting company, or research your ISP's Web hosting prices.

⑤ Use WS_FTP (or another graphical FTP program) to upload your HTML files to the server.

⑥ Use the command-line FTP program to add a directory, delete it, and upload multiple files to the Web.

## REAL-WORLD APPLICATIONS

✔ Your boss tells you to set up a Web site for the company. You must decide between an onsite Web server, collocation, or Web hosting.

✔ You have a high-speed dial-up connection to the Internet and are online several hours a day. You discover that a domain account is less expensive than an a la carte Web site.

✔ You're out of the country and only have a command-line FTP program available. Fortunately, you know the simple commands in FTP and can still work on your files remotely.

✔ You're uploading your files using the command-line FTP program. Unfortunately, you forgot to make a directory before you opened the FTP session; you use mkdir to create it on the fly.

## Visual Quiz

Which of these files is a binary file? Which ones are ASCII files? How do you download a file from this page? How would you go to the previous directory?

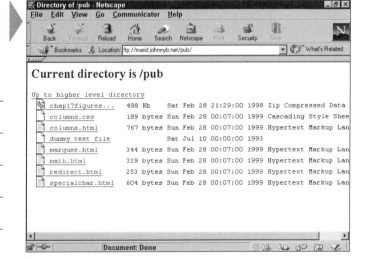

CHAPTER **19**

MASTER
THESE
SKILLS

▶ Discovering CGI
▶ Writing a Script
▶ Modifying Existing Scripts
▶ Working with Programmers
▶ Learning Programming Languages for CGI

# Server-Side Scripting and CGI

As you already know, the World Wide Web consists of a collection of files on the global network known as the Internet. Those files are accessed by users' computers with standard protocols such as HTTP (Hypertext Transfer Protocol). However, the files themselves are stored on Web servers. Just as a user's computer can run a program from the Internet (such as a JavaScript script), Web servers can run programs and scripts on the server side of the transaction.

In this chapter, you learn about server-side scripts and CGI programs. This chapter focuses mainly on CGI, although it also introduces other server-side scripting, such as APIs, SSIs (server-side includes), and server-side image maps.

CGI, or Common Gateway Interface, is a computer interface for starting programs on the Web server using a Web browser or client. It's a method for sending information back and forth between sever and client, and for using that information on either side. Most CGI programs are written in Perl or in C, although Visual Basic, C++, Java, and any program available and usable by the server can be used. Perl is the most popular choice, having been ported to pretty much every server platform out there. Because the program runs on the Web server, users can use Windows, Macintosh, Linux, or any platform or Web browser to access and run it.

When you read this chapter, be sure to refer to Chapter 8 as indicated. A lot of the material covered here is also covered in Chapter 8, so if you're getting a little lost, skip back to that earlier text and reread the sections on installing and running scripts to handle forms. CGI scripts and HTML forms are intricately linked, so a solid understanding of forms will help you understand CGIs.

After you've finished this chapter, you'll understand what goes into writing and modifying a CGI script, and what CGI really is. You'll know when to call in a programmer, and how to make the best use of one when you do. I end by pointing you in the right direction for learning or teaching yourself a programming language for CGI.

# Discovering CGI

In the previous chapter, you learned that a script can run on either the Web browser or the Web server. And, while browser scripting languages have come a long way, they are still limited in what they can and cannot do.

Server-side scripts are more flexible than client-side scripts; you have a full range of programming languages available, and you can change and affect files and data residing on the Web server. In fact, that's the main difference between a client-side script and a server-side script; the server-side script can affect the Web server itself.

The applications for CGI are virtually unlimited. Every time you use an online form, chances are there's a CGI script handling its results. When you set your user preferences, there's a CGI that stores those preferences and recalls them later. Online email services such as Hotmail and Yahoo! Mail use CGI to retrieve your email and show it to you onscreen.

The top-left figure shows how data travels from the Web browser to the server and back again using CGI. The CGI program could do anything with that data; it could throw it away, return an error message, send the user to a new page, add or delete information in a database, send the data by email, or encrypt the data and put it in a secured area for later retrieval (useful for secure services).

Before JavaScript and ActiveX, CGI was the only way to add cross-platform interactivity to your Web sites. It's still the most reliable way to handle cross-platform scripting; while JavaScript is enabled in MSIE and Netscape Navigator, it's not necessarily available in Amaya, Emacs, Lynx, or your cellular phone (which will probably have a tiny Web browser by the year 2000).

## TAKE NOTE

### ► CGI IS NOT A LANGUAGE

Don't get too confused here. CGI is not a programming language. Rather, it's a way to start a program from another place. Think of it as part of a remote control for the Web server. Your remote control needs to have some way to start the VCR when you're across the room, right? Usually, there's a little infrared interface you point the remote control at. Now, no one would say that the infrared interface had made the VCR turn on; you started the VCR by pressing a button on the remote, which sent a signal to the VCR, and it turned on. CGI is an interface for starting programs that already exist on the Web server, not for actually writing, editing, or otherwise authoring those programs.

### ► SERVER SIDE INCLUDES

Server-side includes, discussed in previous chapters, are used to include a file or environment variable into a Web page. When an HTML file ending with .shtml (for SSI-HTML) is requested, the Web server reads it for the SSI, then inserts the file or variable, replacing the SSI code. One great use for SSIs is in inserting a standard header and footer in all Web pages across the site.

**CROSS-REFERENCE**
SSIs are discussed in more detail in Chapter 17.

**FIND IT ONLINE**
An introduction to CGI can be found at CGI: Common Gateway Interface(**http://hoohoo.ncsa. uiuc.edu/cgi/intro.html**).

## Static and Dynamic Pages

When discussing the Web, you'll often hear people use words like "dynamic" and "interactive." These are primarily buzzwords used to describe pages that aren't strict HTML; pages that are created "on the fly" by CGI scripts and SSIs, for example, or pages that take input from users and tailor the site itself to the user's specific needs.

A static page is a strict HTML page, similar to what you learned in the first half of this book. It uses no scripting elements, and is fairly straightforward in appearance and execution. Static pages are great for pages that don't change often, and for pages that need to be written quickly. They also require less processing power from the Web server, so they're especially good for high-traffic pages, such as a home page.

A dynamic page is one that changes often, based on the time or date, or that is generated by a database. A server statistics log page could be considered dynamic; it changes daily (or weekly, in some cases), and provides up-to-date information as requested. CGIs are often used to create dynamic pages.

Finally, an interactive Web page is one that takes user input and returns pages based on that input. A common example is a search engine, but one of my favorite examples is **http://www.garden.com**, which refers to the user's profile when browsing the catalog, and gives shipping information for that area (some plants will not be shipped during certain seasons, depending on your locale).

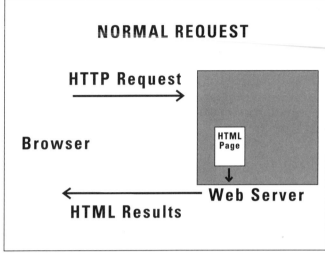

■ *A typical HTTP transaction. The Web browser sends a request to the Web server, and is answered with an HTML page.*

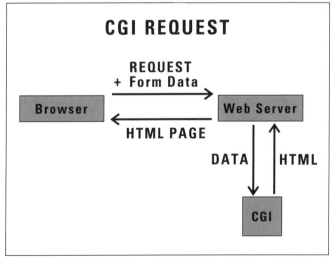

■ *A CGI transaction. The browser sends a request or form data to the Web browser, which sends it to the CGI script. The CGI returns the results (usually in the form of an HTML file), which the browser then forwards to the Web browser.*

# Writing a Script

In reality, you probably won't be writing a CGI script for a long time, unless you already know a programming language like C or Perl. However, this section helps give you an overview of what writing a CGI program is like. Since Perl is the most common language for CGIs, and it's easy to use and to debug, I'll use it in this example.

The first part of writing any program is to decide what it's going to do, and what results it will return. This is called the specification. This particular CGI is going to gather contact information from users and append it to a file. That file can then be added to a database, printed out, or otherwise manipulated by the Web designer using other scripts and programs. The specification, then, is: Gather user name, address, telephone number and email address. Save them to a file called `addresses`.

Because there's now a specific goal, you can move on to the next step: identifying the inputs and the outputs. An input is data that is sent to a program. When you enter information into an accounting program, you're providing input. The program's running total of your checkbook constitutes output: the program takes your information, adds it to previous data, and produces a result.

In this program, the inputs have already been suggested: user name, address, phone number, and email address. An address is usually more than one form field: standard convention provides two fields for the street address (one of which is optional), a field for the city, another for the state, and a fifth for the ZIP or postal code. For international applications, you could also add a field for the user's country. Finally, you need to know which file to append the data to. That could be stated in a hidden field in the form or directly in the script itself. For security reasons, filenames are best when embedded into the script, but a multipurpose script may require the variable to be passed from the form.

*Continued*

## TAKE NOTE

### ▶ CGI LIBRARIES

When using a general-purpose programming language, use CGI libraries, such as `cgi-lib.pl` or `cgi.pm` (for Perl), to help decode the results from your form input. Include the CGI library when you write the code, and you can then use the library's modules, variables, and functions.

### ▶ APPLICATION ENVIRONMENTS

An application environment, such as Active Server Pages (ASP), PHP, server-side JavaScript, and similar server-side scripting environments, creates an embedded program within the Web server, which eliminates the inefficiencies of using CGI. Some environments, such as PHP, can be compiled either as CGI or as an embedded application environment.

Many application environments use the developer's proprietary programming language. For example, ASP pages cannot be used on a nonproprietary Web server (such as Apache, the most popular Web server). However, some application environments, such as PHP and perl-mod (which embeds Perl into the Web server) are openly developed, freely available, and available on nearly every platform.

## CROSS-REFERENCE

Chapter 8 shows you how to create the form to gather the input for this script.

## FIND IT ONLINE

cgi-lib.pl is a Perl library maintained at **http://cgi-lib.stanford.edu/cgi-lib/**.

## Listing 19-1: A Perl Script Header

```
#!/usr/bin/perl ◄❶
############################
# address.pl
# October 4, 1998
#
# Copyright: Public Domain ◄❸
#
# This script may be used, altered, modified,
# or otherwise played with however you like.
#
############################
                              ❷
```

❶ The first line of any Perl script has the location of the Perl program on the server.

❷ Document your program with comments: # comment text.

❸ Document the program's name, creation date, and copyright information.

## Listing 19-2: CGI Programming

```
# Bring in the cgi-lib library
require("cgi-lib.pl"); ◄❹

# Read the form into an array: a function from
cgi-lib
&ReadParse(*form); ◄❺
```

❹ Include any libraries; the cgi-lib.pl library is especially useful for Perl CGIs.

❺ Use the ReadParse function from cgi_lib.pl to turn the form contents into something readable.

## Listing 19-3: Opening and Write

```
open(ADDRESS,">>/$ENV{DOCUMENT_ROOT}/address"); ❻
print ADDRESS <<EndText; ❼
First Name: $form{firstname} ❽
Last Name: $form{lastname}
Address1: $form{address1}
Address2: $form{address2}
City: $form{city}
State: $form{state}
Zip: $form{zip}
Email: $form{email}
---
EndText
close ADDRESS;
```

❻ This line creates a file handle as a reference to the file being affected.

❼ Use the CGI environment variable for the Web directory: ENV{DOCUMENT_ROOT}.

❽ The print ADDRESS statement enters data into the file. <<EndText means to stop printing at "EndText".

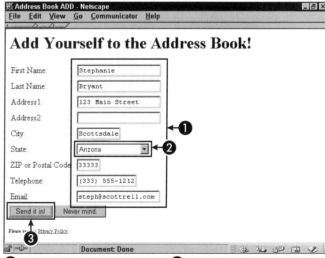

❶ The Address Book ADD form has fields for each piece of contact information.

❷ A drop-down box provides a multiple choice for the state.

❸ Clicking "Send it In!" will send the data to the script, called address.pl.

# Writing a Script

*Continued*

When you've gathered the data and run it through the program, you need to produce an output. There are a few ways you can do this. First, of course, you want to append the data to the end of an existing file, named addresses. You saw how to do that on the previous page; use a file handle to manipulate the file.

Next, you want your users to know that the information has been received. You could have the CGI script produce an HTML page with a simple thank you, and a link back to the home page. You could have it send users to a separate "Thank You" page — an existing HTML file that all users return to. You can even have it send users to a page showing their contact information, and thanking them for their contribution.

In this script, you'll send users to a page that returns their data and thanks them for participating. A link on the page will send them back to the home page. The upper-right and lower-left figures show you how to write the script to create a new HTML page, and how to include user variables and data into that script. Finally, when your script is complete, it should return a Web page similar to the one shown in the bottom-right figure. Remember that this is a normal HTML page, although it's been created by a script. You can edit the HTML in this part of the script however you wish, adding <HEAD> and <META> information, style sheets, or even frames!

## TAKE NOTE

### ▶ CGI ENVIRONMENT VARIABLES

As part of HTTP and CGI, certain variables are pre-defined. For example, HTTP_USER_AGENT is the type of Web browser used by the client, such as Mozilla 4.0 (Netscape), Internet Explorer, etc. In addition, user authentication information (or user login) is stored in the environment variables. You can use environment variables in your CGI scripts to create a customized site for your users.

### ▶ CGI AND APIS

The whole idea behind the APIs is that the CGI interface is slow, because CGI effectively causes the server to launch a program every time a CGI is called. So if it's a really popular page that's CGI-driven, it might overload the machine. So, lots of other application programming interfaces (APIs) were developed, such as ISAPI (Microsoft's), NSAPI (Netscape's), and WSAPI (O'Reilly's WebSite API). These server APIs are a full set of functions for interfacing with the Web server directly, so that the program you write becomes part of the Web server. Since the Web server is already running when the program is called, there's less overhead from starting and stopping the Web program.

## CROSS-REFERENCE

For more information on Web servers in general (including server APIs), see Chapter 17.

## FIND IT ONLINE

For more information on Perl, see **http://language.perl.com/**.

### Listing 19-4: Close and Send

```
print &PrintHeader;
print <<EndHTML;
<!DOCTYPE HTML PUBLIC "-//W3C//DTD HTML 4.0//EN"
  "http://www.w3.org/TR/REC-
html40/strict.dtd">
<HTML>
<HEAD>
  <TITLE>Address Book: Thanks!</TITLE>
</HEAD>
<BODY BGCOLOR=#FFFFFF>
<H1>Thanks for your Address!</H1>
<HR>
Thank you for submitting your information to the
Address Book:
<P>
<TABLE BORDER=0>
<TR>
<TD VALIGN=TOP><B>NAME:</B></TD>
<TD VALIGN=TOP>$form{firstname}
$form{lastname}</TD>
</TR>
<TR>
<TD VALIGN=TOP><B>ADDRESS:</B></TD>
<TD VALIGN=TOP>$form{address1}<BR>
$form{address2}<BR>
$form{city}, $form{state} $form{zipcode}
</TD>
</TR>
</TABLE>
<P>Please visit my <A HREF="index.html">
  Home Page</A> on your way out!
<P style="font-size: x-small;">
Please see the
<A HREF="privacy.html">Privacy Policy</A>.
</BODY>
</HTML>
EndHTML
```

- ⟨10⟩ at `print &PrintHeader;`
- ⟨11⟩ at `print <<EndHTML;`
- ⟨9⟩ at `<HTML>`
- ⟨13⟩ at `<TITLE>Address Book: Thanks!</TITLE>`
- ⟨15⟩ pointing to `<B>NAME:</B>`
- ⟨14⟩ at `$form{firstname}`
- ⟨12⟩ at `EndHTML`

**⑨** The last steps output the results to an HTML file.

**⑩** Add the HTTP header so the resulting Web page will be sent by the Web server.

**⑪** Start writing the output page with another print statement.

**⑫** Notice that the <<EndHTML means to end when the program reads EndHTML on a line by itself, with no whitespace.

**⑬** Include all the normal HTML elements you would include in a Web page of this type.

**⑭** To include a user variable in the HTML page, use the syntax $form(name).

**⑮** Use HTML markup elements to format the names.

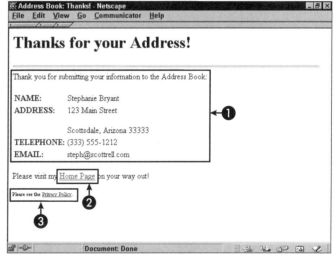

**①** The resulting page says thanks, and verifies the user's information.

**②** A link to the home page provides somewhere else to go.

**③** Always include a link to your privacy policy when asking for personal information!

# Modifying Existing Scripts

There's an odd theory among programmers: It says that there's no program that can't be shortened by at least one line, and no program that does not contain at least one bug. Thus, all programs can be shortened to one line of code that doesn't work.

Whatever the theory, the reality is that there are no perfect programs. Even the coolest CGI script will probably have an error or two; that doesn't make it unusable, but you may eventually have to go through and fix the program. The top two figures and the one in the lower-left corner explain how to debug your program and what kinds of errors to look for.

In addition, you may find a script that does what you want but requires a different configuration for your system. You'll have to modify certain set variables to make them work on your Web server system. These aren't bugs; they're simple problems with using CGIs on your server that weren't written specifically for your application.

Another reason you'd want to modify a CGI is to add, change, or remove a feature. Most of the free CGI scripts available can be modified as you wish, while others are restricted to only changing certain variables. In any case, you'll need to carefully proofread and test your script for errors, and make sure it's doing what you want it to do.

Many programmers make their entire living off of installing, debugging, and enhancing CGI programs for other people. If you find that this is just too complex, work with a programmer to produce the results you desire.

## Free Scripts and Security

Any time you download *any* program, ever, make sure you know who wrote it, what it does, and that you trust the source of the program. It goes without saying that, since CGIs can alter files on your server, there are potential security risks when you run untrustworthy scripts.

In addition to the security risk posed by hackers, there's an even bigger security risk posed by yourself. As the administrator of your site, you can change the permissions of a file or directory fairly quickly and easily. You can also, however, change the wrong file to the wrong permission, and open the doors of your server to whatever errors may come.

In the previous section I showed you how to write a simple script that gathers user contact information. That information is saved to a file on the server. Because the file is in the Web directory (and most servers are set up to prevent CGI scripts from saving to files outside the Web directory), anyone can read it by default. But I don't want anyone to be able to read that file; that's what the privacy policy is about. So, I change the permissions on the file so that only authorized users can read the file. When you have a file that can only be read, not altered, it's called a "read-only" file.

---

**CROSS-REFERENCE**

Chapter 8 has an excellent section on modifying scripts to work with your server.

**FIND IT ONLINE**

For information on debugging CGIs on Apache, see the Apache RTFM at **http://www.jlk.net/apache/debugging_cgi.shtml**.

**①** Check for syntax errors in your Perl script with the `perl -c filename.pl` command.

**②** Any syntax errors will immediately be evident.

**③** You can run the script directly from the command line by typing `./filename.pl`.

■ Although this script cannot accept variables from the command line, the cgi.pm library adds that capability.

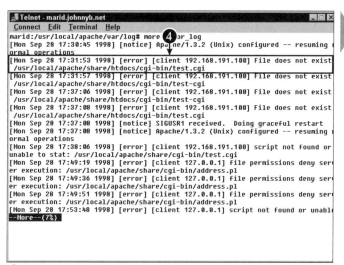

**④** Be sure to check the server's error log for possible problems with your scripts!

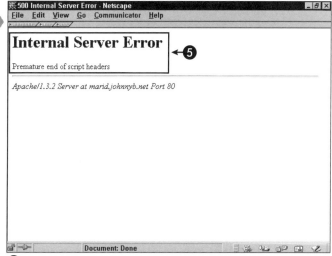

**⑤** If your script has errors, then error messages like this one will result when you try to run the script.

# Working with Programmers

The term "programmer" is applied to everything from hardware to people. In fact, after you finish this book, you might find a few unenlightened folk calling you a "Web programmer" or an "HTML programmer." HTML is not programming, no matter how much you can do with it.

But that's all right. You don't need to know how to write a program to write a Web page, and anyone intimidated by the idea of object-oriented anything should still be able to get along on the Web.

But when you want to have an interactive site, and add CGI scripts to your pages, then you may eventually have to work with a programmer.

Sure, you could just sit down with the guidelines I've provided here and try to alter a free program yourself. You could try to write one yourself. But, again, you'll need to know enough about programming languages or have a well-documented script to start with. Frankly, even the best programmers get stuck by poorly documented scripts. And eventually, you'll find that the modified script just isn't working. You need help.

When you go to hire your programmer, make sure he or she has the experience and knowledge to write your CGIs. Do they know Perl (or C, or whatever language you'd like to use)? Do they have experience with CGIs, and with your Web server? Have they written or debugged programs of this type before?

The chances are, you'll be able to find someone with CGI and Perl experience. Don't ask for more than you need — if your site doesn't use Java, don't ask for Java just because everyone else is asking for or using Java.

Once you've hired a programmer, show him or her your specification and ask for a program. Use the example on the next page as a sample of the types of information to include in your spec sheet.

The programmer may then ask for more information. Do you want to be emailed when someone adds an entry? Will the results be needed for a database? What's the ultimate goal of the project? If you explain the entire goal, the programmer may have an idea or solution that shortcuts a lot of unnecessary work. Because programmers have experience with many types of programming projects, they can often see the shortest way to achieve a project's goal. Some programmers I know just call it laziness, but I prefer to think of it as efficiency.

Once you've given the specification to the programmer, let them work on the program until they considers it almost done. When they bring you the program for testing, or ask you to check it out, find out what version they consider it to be, and then go test it out, understanding that it may not be ready for release yet. Submit any comments or changes to the programmer, then don't be surprised if they implement them.

**CROSS-REFERENCE**

Chapter 21 has more to say on teamwork and coordinating with other members of your development group.

**FIND IT ONLINE**

Check out the Top 16 April Fools' Jokes to Pull on Programmers, at **http://www.proaxis.com/ ~gregerk/humor/16progfool.html.**

### TEAMWORK

I've had jobs where I was instructed to write a script one way, then rewrite it in the exact opposite way by another member of the team. Make sure you and your programmer know who's the main contact for the job, and who will finally decide if the specification has been fulfilled or not.

### VERSION NUMBERS

The life of a program goes through several phases before it's released. There's the `alpha` stage, when it's not even ready for testing. The `beta` stage, when it's ready to be tested (and is sometimes tested by the public in "public beta programs"), and finally, the release stage. Each new version of a product has a version numbering system: 1.0.0 would be the very first build of the very first release of a product. 1.1.0 would be the first build of an updated version. And 2.0.1 is the first build of a second version of the product. Most of the time, build versions aren't used as part of the version number: you might have 3.2, for example, or 4.0, but not 3.2.01.

## Sample Specification Sheet

**Program Name:** `address.pl`
**Project Coordinator:** S. Bryant
**Programmer Name:** John Bryant
**Date Assigned:** July 04, 1999
**Date Due:** July 31, 1999
**Purpose:** To append information from an HTML form to a separate file, and return the results in a Web page.
**Form Fields:**

```
firstname
lastname
address1
address2
city
state
zip
phone
email
```

**Files Provided:**

`add.html` — The input form for the program.
`addresses` — The file to append data to. File should not be readable by Web users.
`results.html` — The results HTML code; insert this code into the script as the output page. Place the field data into the commented field names in this code.

# Learning Programming Languages for CGI

If you've gotten this far, you've probably noticed that there's a lot more to CGI than just a few commands or tags. In fact, programming for CGI is a rich and lucrative field in the high-tech industry, and not something you should undertake to learn lightly. Good programmers command high salaries, but they also tend to work very hard at their jobs, coding those "simple little scripts" to run the multimillion-dollar sites.

As a Web designer, you may wish to add a programming language to your repertoire, with the express purpose of being able to develop CGIs. In that case, you should learn Perl or ASP, depending on what kind of system you're on.

Once you've mastered Perl or ASP, learn the other technology. Then move on to C, server-side JavaScript, PHP, HTMLScript, and iHTML. By the time you've learned two programming languages, you'll find that learning additional ones is a cinch.

You may have also heard of object-oriented programming (or OOP). Some of the more advanced programming languages, such as Java and C++, are object-oriented. Perl can even use object-oriented modules, although it's a far less complex language.

Finally, you'll notice that I recommend learning Perl, which is a programming language, or ASP, an application environment. CGI programs require a lot of processing power from the computer, and application environments and APIs reduce that requirement quite a bit. However, ASP is a proprietary technology. Once you start using it, you may be locked in to a Microsoft product. That may be all right for your needs, or you may prefer an open source

product, such as Perl. Remember, though, that no single company develops Perl and certifies it as "safe." It's up to you to watch out for potential problems in your programs.

## TAKE NOTE

### ▶ SYNTAX

When learning a new programming language, always start with the syntax. What symbols and punctuation do you need to know, and how do you use them? Just as HTML has a syntax you had to learn, so too with programming languages. In fact, programming languages are far less forgiving of syntax errors than the typical Web browser.

### ▶ BREAKING INTO FUNCTIONS AND FLOW CONTROL

The simple script I showed you earlier didn't have any functions. More complicated scripts, however, may have multiple functions, or small script snippets that are pasted together into the script program.

Functions are sometimes hard to understand for beginning programmers. Although the concept is fairly easy to understand, the implementation is much harder. That's because the script needs to know in what order to call each function. Scripts use flow control to decide which function is activated first, as well as which functions will not be activated at all.

**CROSS-REFERENCE**

Chapter 17 details what programming languages come with Web servers.

**FIND IT ONLINE**

You'll find a biased comparison of Perl and other programming languages at **http:// language.perl.com/versus/index.html.**

## Table 19-1: PROGRAMMING RESOURCES

| Language | Resource | URL |
|---|---|---|
| C<br>cprogram/ | C Programming, an Introduction | http://www.cit.ac.nz/smac/ |
| | DevCentral Learning Center | http://devcentral.iftech.com/learning/tutorials/ |
| | C Programming Tutorial | http://www.geocities.com/SiliconValley/Hills/1317/ |
| | CProgramming.com | http://www.cprogramming.com/ |
| | USENET FAQ: comp.lang.c | http://www.cis.ohio-state.edu/hypertext/faq/bngusenet/comp/lang/c/top.html |
| | lcc ANSI C Compiler | http://www.cs.princeton.edu/software/lcc/index.html |
| Java | Sun's Java Technology Home Page | http://java.sun.com/ |
| | Café Java | http://www.cafejava.com/ |
| | Java Coffee Break | http://www.davidreilly.com/jcb/ |
| | The Java Tutorial | http://java.sun.com/docs/books/tutorial/ |
| | Making Sense of Java | http://www.disordered.org/Java-QA.html |
| Perl | Perl FAQ | http://language.perl.com/faq/ |
| | Perl.com | http://www.perl.com/pace/pub |
| | O'Reilly Perl Center | http://www.perl.oreilly.com/ |
| | perl.net | http://www.perl.net/ |
| | Perl: The Swiss Army Chainsaw | http://www.virtualschool.edu/lang/perl/index.html |
| Visual Basic | Chuck Easttom's Visual Basic Page | http://www.redriverok.com/easttom/vb/vb.htm |
| | Jelsoft VB-World | http://www.vb-world.net/ |
| | Microsoft Visual Basic | http://msdn.microsoft.com/vbasic/ |
| | Visual Basic Info Booth | http://www.buffnet.net/~millard/vblinks.htm |

# Personal Workbook

## Q&A

**1** What does *CGI* stand for?

_____

_____

_____

**2** What programming languages are used in CGI?

_____

_____

_____

**3** Why would an API or application environment be preferable to CGI?

_____

_____

_____

**4** Name a CGI environment variable. When or how would you use it?

_____

_____

_____

**5** What's the first step in writing a CGI script?

_____

_____

_____

**6** Where do your script's input variables come from?

_____

_____

_____

**7** Name two things to look for when modifying or adapting a script.

_____

_____

_____

**8** What is a *version number*?

_____

_____

_____

ANSWERS: PAGE 447

**1** Design the home page for a site that would use static pages, dynamic pages, and interactive pages.

**2** Figure out what CGI scripts you would need to run the site.

**3** Write specification sheets for each script you'd need.

**4** Look on the Internet for scripts that would fulfil those specs.

**5** Write the forms pages or other input/output pages needed for your programs.

**6** Find out what Web server your site is on, and what you would need to do to be able to run a CGI script.

✔ You're setting up an online store for your home-based business. A custom script provides an online shopping cart and secure ordering environment for your customers.

✔ As a travelling salesperson, you're away from the office. You use CGIs to access your customer database from the Web, and instantly update their orders.

✔ You're researching your final academic paper for college. You use a search engine (with CGI) to find information quickly.

✔ You store your entire portfolio of photographs on the Internet and use CGI to produce a dynamically generated photo album.

## Visual Quiz

Write a specification sheet for this form. (The field names are shown inside the fields.) What would you want to do with the data? Would you protect the data from unauthorized access?

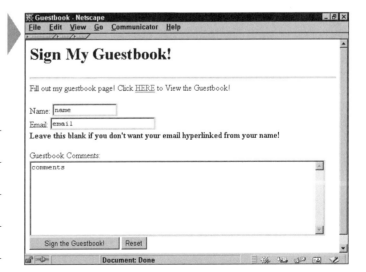

CHAPTER **20**

MASTER
THESE
SKILLS

▶ **Choosing a Server**
▶ **Using SSL Servers**
▶ **Requiring User Login**
▶ **Password-Protected Directories**
▶ **Setting File and Web Permissions**
▶ **Protecting Your Passwords**

# Server Security

**W**eb server security should be one of the most important aspects of your site. If you collect user data or require passwords, or if you accept credit cards orders online, you need to address the security risks involved in transferring sensitive data over a public connection.

Information sent over the Internet may go through several servers before finally reaching its destination. At any point on its journey, the data might be copied, saved, or even tampered with and sent on. Imagine the potential risk for fraud and credit card theft if you accept credit card transactions online. Similarly, passwords can be stolen and then reused to hack into systems.

Most security systems sacrifice convenience for safety. Passwords are inconvenient but necessary. Firewall systems — which protect internal computers from external connections — are an inconvenience some may prefer to do without. A high-security setup encrypts all data, including passwords, and changes user passwords often.

The basic idea behind any security system is fairly simple — use physical validation, like a car key; intellectual validation, such as a password; or biological validation, like a voice print, fingerprints, or even visual identification. For high security, use more than one validation system. A secure Web server uses intellectual validation, in the form of passwords, combined with encryption (which is like doing everything in code) to pass sensitive data across the Internet. Future systems may also validate with biological data, such as voice recognition. The new Pentium III processor provides physical validation; the chip's ID can be transmitted during a transaction to verify that the same person is consistently accessing the account.

Some Web servers are more adept at answering security questions than others, and you need to know how to choose a Web server for its security features. If you run other servers, such as email or newsgroups, on the same server as your Web site, keep your ears open for potential security holes in those server programs as well. Some programs create security problems when installed on the same system as your Web server, databases, or other data systems.

In this chapter, you learn how to select and use a Secure Sockets Layer (SSL) Web server for encrypted Web transactions, how to use login and session management tools to track users on your system, and how to protect your own passwords from being stolen and misused.

# Choosing a Server

The first step in setting up your server security involves choosing a Secure Sockets Layer (SSL) Web server. SSL is the accepted standard for encrypted transactions on the World Wide Web. Previous attempts at Web security included SHTTP (Secure HTTP), but that technology has succumbed to technological Darwinism. Some Web servers support both SSL and SHTTP, but very few Web browsers support SHTTP.

Some of the more popular SSL Web servers include Netscape Commerce Server, Microsoft Transaction Server (on IIS), and Apache/Stronghold (a commercial version of Apache). Because most SSL servers are commercially produced, there are few differences in their implementation of the SSL itself, so most Web developers would choose an SSL Web server based on its other features, such as stability, standards support, and flexibility.

However, if you do decide to install and use an SSL server, take the time to learn about the Web server you're going to use. Poorly installed security is worse than no security, because users have come to trust that the security features will work as they expect them to.

An SSL Web server should offer certain features, which you should also look for in any other Web server you plan to buy. Server-side includes, CGI support, and compatibility are three important aspects of your Web server, and the CGI support is crucial if you're going to be taking orders over the Internet. Basic authentication is a quick way to limit access to certain directories, and a server API can help you build full-featured commerce applications that run quickly and efficiently, using fewer system resources than a CGI script.

## TAKE NOTE

### ▶ 40-BIT AND HIGHER ENCRYPTION KEYS

SSL uses a public/private key system to encrypt data and send it over the internet. Because these encryption schemes are so close to military encryption logarithms, the United States government placed an export ban on all computer encryption programs. Recently, the government determined that it was easy to "crack" a 40-bit encrypted message if one had a high-speed personal computer and a little bit of patience. Thus, the 40-bit encryption export ban was lifted.

Today, there are generally two types of encryption on the Web: 40-bit encryption, and "strong" encryption. The 40-bit encryption is used primarily on overseas sites, and strong encryption is supposedly used only in the United States. Strong encryption includes logarithms using up to 168 bits, far more secure than the 40-bit encryption I've been talking about.

### ▶ CERTIFICATE SERVERS

Another important part of your SSL system is the certificate. Without a valid certificate, users may be hesitant to submit confidential information to you. Certificates are issued by a certificate authority, to verify that you are who you say you are. Some large companies may benefit from having their own certificate server, such as the Netscape Certificate Server, which can be used to issue certificates to individuals or departments within the company.

**CROSS-REFERENCE**

Chapter 19 has information on Web servers and their supported features.

**FIND IT ONLINE**

Find out what SSL server a secure site is running at
http://www.netcraft.co.uk/cgi-bin/Survey/sslwhats.

## Table 20-1: WEB SERVER SECURITY FEATURES

| Feature Required | Function | Technical Expertise |
|---|---|---|
| Basic authentication | Password-protection of directories | Intermediate |
| File permissions | Restrict access to files | Intermediate |
| Secure Sockets Layer | Encrypts transactions between Web browser and server | Advanced |
| Separate Web user permissions, login | Prevents users from logging into the system from an unrestricted computer, such as the World Wide Web | Basic |
| Program execution restrictions | Prevents any Web program or file from running system programs or executables | Basic |
| Server certificates | Third-party validation of site owner's identity | Basic |
| Certificate server | Ability to issue certificates for other Web servers | Advanced |
| PGP Encryption | Public/private key encryption program for general use | Basic to intermediate |

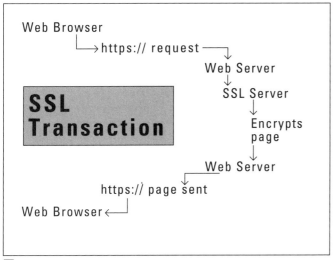

A simplified diagram of an SSL transaction.

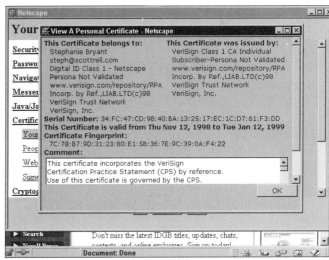

You can get a personal certificate to use in email. A personal certificate is usually not verified by any trusted CAs (Certificate Authorities).

# Using SSL Servers

Once you've chosen and installed a secure server, you need to use it efficiently. For example, some people might wonder why everything isn't encrypted. After all, if you have that expensive secure server, why not use it to encrypt all the pages?

As I mentioned before, SSL uses a public/private key system to encrypt data between computers. If you encrypt everything, it's like locking all the doors inside your house with deadbolt locks. It's effective, but probably not necessary. And opening each door takes extra time. With SSL, each page you keep in the secured section of the server will be encrypted before it's sent over the network; it will be "locked up," and the user's Web browser will also have to unlock it once it arrives.

Now, the extra time is insignificant when compared with the risk of sending unencrypted credit card numbers over the Internet. But it's not so insignificant when you have the SSL server encrypting every page, no matter how trivial the information. The server takes extra time to encrypt the pages, in addition to the time it takes just to download files. If you think your internet connection is slow now, just imagine how bad it would be if your Web browser also had to descramble each page before showing it onscreen.

Most Web sites using SSL also use some form of certification to prove that the secure server is owned and used by the company that claims to be using it. Certificates are issued by a Certificate Authority (CA), such as Verisign,

which verifies that the company or individual is who they say they are (usually by requesting company papers and letters of incorporation, for example). The CA then issues a secret certificate code to the company. That code is installed on the SSL server, which sends its verification to the user's Web browser when a secure transaction is made. The user can then go to the CA's Web site to verify that the certificate was issued to the right person, or to decide if the CA itself is trustworthy.

## TAKE NOTE

### ▶ TRUST ON THE INTERNET

Web security is all about trust. Certificates only work because users trust that the CA will actually verify that the company is who it says it is. SSL only works because users trust the company not to sell their credit card number for fraudulent purposes. Shareware works because users trust software companies not to deliberately distribute malicious software.

Web browsers now come with a list of "trustworthy" certificate authorities, which the Web browser company has decided can be trusted to only issue certificates to valid companies. However, it's up to you to double-check the list of CAs, and to delete those that you don't trust.

**CROSS-REFERENCE**

Chapters 15 and 16 offer more information on using the browser's security features.

**FIND IT ONLINE**

Netscape's Security Solutions can be found at http://www.netscape.com/products/security/index.html.

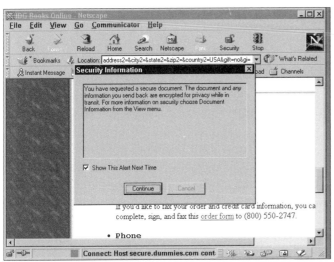

■ *When a user goes to a secured area of a site, the security information box pops up to let him or her know it's safe to send personal information.*

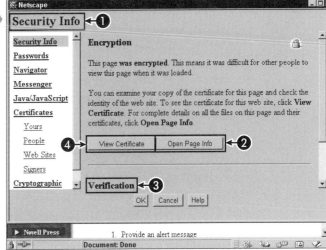

❶ *You can see the encryption and certificates for any page by viewing its Security Info.*

❷ *Check the Page Info for page details, such as its creation date, filename, and size.*

❸ *The Verification section tells you which domain sent this particular page.*

❹ *Click View Certificate to check the server certificate and decide if it's authentic.*

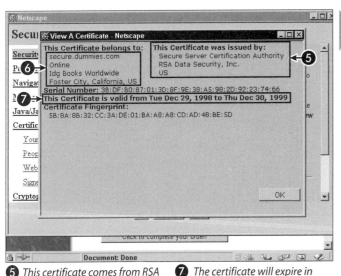

❺ *This certificate comes from RSA Data Security.*

❻ *RSA says that this page was sent by IDG Books Worldwide in Foster City.*

❼ *The certificate will expire in Dec. 30, 1999.*

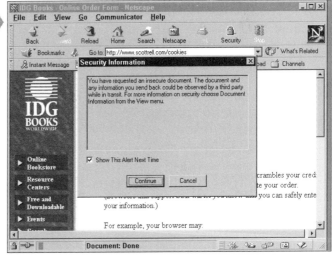

■ *When the user leaves a secured area, a security window pops up to warn them not to transmit sensitive information.*

# Requiring User Login

You might have noticed that many sites now require user registration and login, using a form somewhere on the first page of the site. Some sites won't let you access any of the content at all without logging in, while others wisely provide a Guest Access button to let you surf the site anonymously. Some online communities limit posting to users, while some for-pay sites may restrict guest users from the paid portions of the site.

How the site uses a login to control their content is an issue for the next chapter. To create this kind of login site, start with a CGI script (or similar application environment). The CGI script will use a form to request a username and password from the Web user, and then check the username and password against one stored in an encrypted file on the server.

If they match, the CGI script returns a "cookie" to the user's browser. That cookie tells the browser that this is an authorized user, and assigns the browser a unique session identification number. The cookie might also include the user's name (taken from the password file), and a session timeout to force idle users to be logged out of the system. When the session ends (by closing the browser window, for example), the cookie disappears and the user will have to login again next time.

The cookies sent by the server might also be encrypted to prevent the cookie from being tampered with in-transit, and to add one more level of security to the whole system. When you're dealing with sites that cost money, or that might be targeted by computer hackers, be sure to use every level of security available or reasonable.

## TAKE NOTE

### ▶ OTHER BENEFITS OF USER LOGIN SITES

Session management is a benefit of logging in with a CGI program, and you can use it to great advantages. For example, suppose you have a Web store that caters to cat lovers, and your user registration requests the names of each cat in the household. When the user logs in, the cookie could include their pets' names. DHTML and JavaScript pages can access that cookie information and use it to show customized products, welcome the pets themselves, or have a little fun with your customers.

### ▶ EXPIRATION DATES ON COOKIES

You can provide two types of login cookies. One cookie stays around for a while, and the user doesn't have to login each time he or she visits the site. The other cookie automatically expires at the end of the session, requiring a login each time the browser is closed and reopened. The only difference between those cookies is one ingredient: the expiration date. Cookies without expiration dates expire as soon as the Web browser is closed.

**CROSS-REFERENCE**

Chapter 19 has more information on designing CGI scripts to use on user login sites.

**SHORTCUT**

Use a server API, such as ColdFusion, Microsoft FrontPage, or Active Server Pages to develop login sites; they're faster and more secure than CGI.

■ Users login to garden.com to use specialized tools, like planning diagrams, a private notebook, and the online shopping.

❶ You can personalize garden.com's site.

❷ My physical location is stored in my user profile.

❸ The wheelbarrow is like an online shopping cart, but it saves items in the user profile.

❹ My notebook lets me store notes and comments.

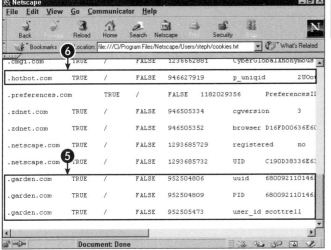

❺ The `cookies.txt` file shows my user ID and session IDs for garden.com.

❻ Other cookies store other information, such as passwords, customer reference numbers, and so on.

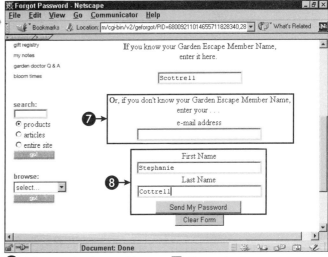

❼ A form on the site provides a password lookup for forgetful users like me.

❽ I fill in my name or email address, and my password is emailed back to me.

■ Be sure to change your password after you receive it by email!

# Password-Protected Directories

A password-protected directory is one that requires a valid username and password to be able to access any files inside the directory. Unless the directory is on an SSL server, the password is sent over the Internet unencrypted, providing only the most basic of server security. Not surprisingly, that's called "basic authentication."

Of course, you could have basic authentication on an encrypted server using SSL to provide an additional level of security to sites that need them. For the most part, basic authentication is used on Web sites that provide a private area for members to exchange information, post ideas, or learn about something that isn't ready for public consumption yet.

If you've ever gone to a site and tried to access a protected area, you might have been prompted for a username and password. The top-left figure shows such a prompt in Netscape; a small dialog box pops up and requests your login information.

As an example, the W3C has a members-only part of their site, which is only for people working on the actual standards projects and committees. Imagine the chaos if the W3C made their speculations and standards development process into a public forum. The members of the committees would spend more time answering questions from the public than they would on their tasks! Uninformed designers and developers would assume that

something posted to the speculations list was what would be in the next standard, and the entire process would get bogged down in confusion and speculation.

You might have wondered how to set up that kind of login on your system. In Windows NT, you need to create a new user, and then restrict the directory to just that user. The new user may have additional user privileges on the server. In UNIX, you create a hidden file, place some important information in that file, and save it to the directory to be protected. The bottom two figures show you how to set up basic authentication in UNIX.

## TAKE NOTE

### ▶ WINDOWS NT BASIC AUTHENTICATION

In Internet Information Server for Windows NT, directory permissions use the same list as file permissions. That's like having an email/Web account on a server, and being able to log in to password-protected directories using your primary password login. Anyone intercepting a basic authentication password under this system can gain access to the entire NT server, not just the Web server.

## CROSS-REFERENCE

Information on controlling content can be found in Chapter 21.

## FIND IT ONLINE

http://www.apache.org/docs/misc/FAQ.html#user-authentication has a good tutorial on Apache basic authentication.

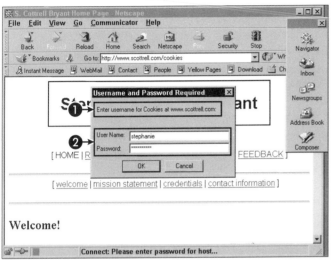

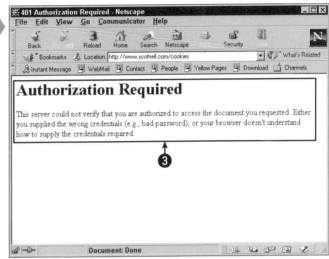

**①** With basic authentication, users fill in a pop-up dialog box with an authorization name.

**②** A username and password are the only fields in this box.

**③** An incorrect username or password lets you try again, or cancel to be sent to an error page.

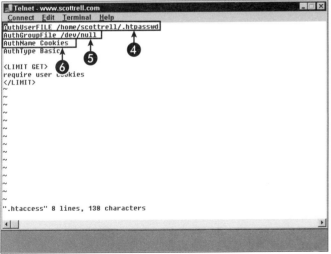

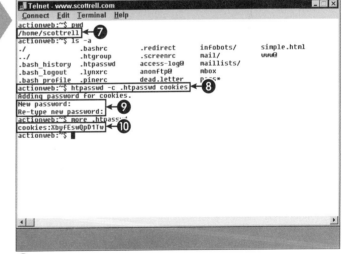

**■** To protect a directory, create a `.htaccess file`.

**④** The `AuthUserFile` is the complete directory path to the file containing user passwords.

**⑤** The group file should remain `/dev/null` for single-user directories.

**⑥** `AuthName` is the Authorization Name.

**⑦** To create the passwords, go to the directory specified in the `AuthUserFile` line of the `.htaccess` file.

**⑧** Type `htpasswd -c .htpasswd username`

to create a new `.htpasswd` file with a single user.

**⑨** You'll be prompted twice for the new password.

**⑩** The password is encrypted.

# File and Web Permissions

File permissions are a part of every system administrator's job. They're one of the trickiest parts of system administration, but they're also the most important. Most computer crimes exploit weaknesses in the way file permissions are set up, usually by systems administrators that didn't understand all the intricacies of permissions.

Network servers have three types of permission: read, write, and execute. There are also three groups of users: the current user (you), current group (usually of system-authorized users), and world (everybody, including anonymous Web connections).

Anonymous users from the Internet belong to the world group. They usually only have read permission on any given file in a Web directory, and they should not have even that permission for files in other directories (like your home directory or email inbox). Scripts in your cgi-bin or script directory should grant "execute" permission to Web users, and chat rooms, discussion boards, and guestbooks should also give Web users "write" permissions (but not necessarily execute permission).

So, how do you know what permissions have been set up? And how do you change them? Because UNIX is still the most popular Web server platform on the Internet, and the one you're most likely to be using, I'll show you how to set up file permissions in UNIX.

To view the permissions of a file, type `ls -l` at the command prompt. You'll see a list, similar to the top-left figure, with a series of letters before the rest of the file information. That series is a 10-character code for the file permissions. The first character tells you if the item is a directory (`d`) or a file (`-`). The next three characters stand for the current user's permissions, read (`r`), write (`w`), and execute (`x`). A character having a hyphen instead of a letter means permission is not granted.

The fifth through seventh characters are the group's permissions, and the last three are the world's permissions. Most UNIX files that aren't on a Web server will grant the "world" no permissions, not even read permissions. Web directories grant read permissions to anybody, so don't put private documents on a Web site.

## TAKE NOTE

### DIRECTORY PERMISSIONS

Directories also have file permissions, even though you can't read a directory or execute it. However, you can read, write, and execute to files within the directory. When you create a new file, the file automatically inherits the parent directory's properties. You can change the permissions for individual files within the directory, or you can use the `chmod` command to change all files in the directory: `chmod -r` (the `-r` stands for recursive; be careful with this!)

**CROSS-REFERENCE**

For more information on server-side scripts, see Chapter 19.

**FIND IT ONLINE**

**http://www.wastenotcomputers.com/web/ perms.htm** has a quick chmod reference.

# Changing File Permissions

To change a file's permissions, first do a little math. There's a three-number "code" to change file permissions. The numbers stand for the current user, group, and world, in that order. Now, here's the math: each permission level has a number — read is 4, write is 2, and execute is 1. To change a file's permissions to grant read and execute permissions only, (for CGI programs, for example), you would add 4 and 1, to get 5. You would use the UNIX program chmod to change the permissions: chmod 555 filename.cgi to change a program to grant those permissions to everybody.

Now, if you wanted to retain permission to write to that file, but not grant that permission to anyone else, you'd use chmod 755 filename.cgi, because the first number (7) is the permissions for the current user, you. For most read-only Web files, you should use chmod 744. You can control access to your files and protect your data fairly simply by limiting the permissions to just what the user needs to use the file effectively.

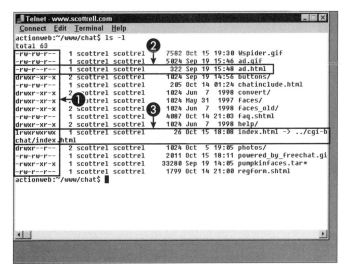

**❶** The leftmost column shows the file permissions for all the files in this directory.

**❷** New files inherit the permissions of whatever directory they're created in.

**❸** Granting full permissions is dangerous—hackers exploit those weaknesses.

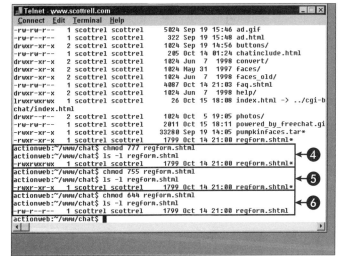

**❹** Allow permissions for everyone: chmod 777 filename.html.

**❺** Limit Web users' access to read and execute or read and write permissions only.

**❻** chmod 644 is a common permission set; it grants read and write permissions to you and your group, and read-only permissions to the Web.

# Protecting Your Passwords

None of the password systems, encryption keys, or security devices you consider using will be at all effective if you can't keep your password secret. What's the point of having a secret word if everyone knows it?

The first step in protecting your password is to pick a password that's easy to protect. Pick a word that isn't in the dictionary, change its spelling, capitalize an unusual pattern of letters (every third letter, for example), and add some numbers. Don't use your telephone number, birth date, or social security number. One of the best passwords I've heard of is that of an amateur astronomer; the otherwise incomprehensible sequence of letters and numbers was, in fact, the stellar coordinates for an obscure celestial body in the winter night sky.

Once you've chosen a password, resolve to change it. Change your password every month, without fail. Some companies have instituted policies that automatically expire all passwords on a regular basis. When a user logs in after his or her password has expired, the system asks for the old password and prompts that user for a new one. You might even generate a list of passwords to use in the future. If you do, keep it in a locked cabinet or similarly protected place.

Use different passwords for different systems, and different levels of security. I have a different password for the main login for each of my four email/telnet accounts. I also keep another password for unsecured Web site logins, and another for encrypted Web site logins. In total, I probably have about 20 or 30 different passwords or pass phrases for all the different systems I log into.

With so many passwords, it's hard to remember them all. Like many computer professionals, I keep my passwords written down, off of my computer system, in a safe place. Here's my secret: I keep a little address book in a locked cabinet in my desk. Each username and password is written down under the first letter of the account, or the Web site domain name.

If you store your password in your head, then keep it there. Don't give it out, email it to anyone, or share it with your coworkers or friends. If you write your password down, store it in a locked cabinet or drawer, and keep the key to yourself. If you don't have a secure place to store your passwords at work, then take them with you at all times.

## TAKE NOTE

### ▶ PASSWORD-MANAGEMENT SOFTWARE

As you might have already guessed, some enterprising programmers and software companies have already addressed the problem of too many passwords. These programs keep a list of your passwords, which you can then open using a single password that you know. Always try before you buy with these kinds of programs, and don't use any important passwords until the program is shown to be secure.

**CROSS-REFERENCE**

For other tools to use in Web development, see Chapter 12.

**FIND IT ONLINE**

You can find more password programs at http://tucows.tierranet.com/security95.html.

## Protecting PGP Pass Phrases

There's one password you should never write down. If you use PGP, or a similar public/private key encryption program, never copy down your private key, and never write down your pass phrase. Because I have a terrible memory, I do write down where I found the pass phrase. Generally, it's something like "Shakespeare, page 25, line 14." With over 30 Shakespeare books in my office, it's a good bet that no one else can find my pass phrase without spending some time and energy inside my office.

PGP can be used to encrypt a list of your passwords, which you can then decrypt using your pass phrase. In that case, you'd only need one pass phrase to access your entire password list, but so would anyone else. Now you see why keeping that secret is so important. Any password or key you use to protect a list of your passwords should be guarded with the strictest of security.

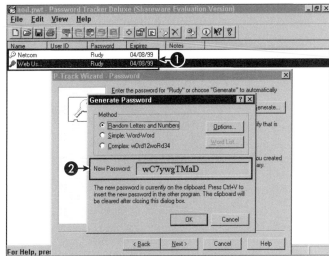

■ Password Tracker, available at **http://www.clrpc.com/ptd/index.html,** lets you store multiple password profiles.

❶ A shortcut option lets you launch the application or Web site associated with that password.

❷ You can even have a random password generated automatically.

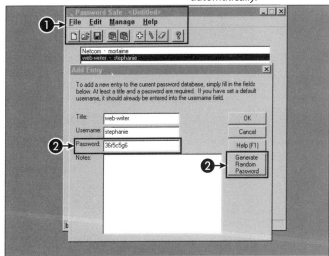

❶ Counterpane Systems' Password Safe is a freeware program that also stores passwords.

❷ You can also generate a random password with Password Safe.

# Personal Workbook

## Q&A

**1** What is *SSL*? What does it stand for?

_____

_____

_____

**2** What are some common SSL servers?

_____

_____

_____

**3** What's the difference between 40-bit and strong encryption?

_____

_____

_____

**4** What is a *certificate authority*?

_____

_____

_____

**5** How can you use user logins to control information on your site?

_____

_____

_____

**6** How do you protect a Web directory with basic authentication?

_____

_____

_____

**7** What's chmod? What can you do with it?

_____

_____

_____

**8** Where should you store your passwords?

_____

_____

_____

ANSWERS: PAGE 448

## EXTRA PRACTICE

1 Create a directory on your Web server called "secure." Change it to grant read-only permissions to Web users.

2 Now, use basic authentication to require users to log in as "user" with the password "Re549ooo." Test the directory in a Web browser.

3 Save the password somewhere safe.

4 Create a list of 12 passwords, one for each month of the year. Change your password every month.

5 If you have SSL on your Web server, design a basic form and place it on the SSL site. Test it by submitting data through the form.

6 Retrieve the encrypted results, or use a password scheme to allow you to access the results in unencrypted form.

## REAL-WORLD APPLICATIONS

✔ You're setting up a business on the Internet and need to take orders online. You already have a merchant account to accept credit cards, but you need to protect your customers' credit cards in transit. You use SSL and certificates to receive orders, and to retrieve them from the Web server.

✔ Your company has an intranet that contains nonclassified internal company information. You use basic authentication to permit all employees to access the internal documents.

✔ You design an online community. You add a user login so people don't have to enter their names and addresses every time they post a message.

## Visual Quiz

What kinds of security features are being used in this transaction? What assurance does the Web site owner have that the person making the order is genuine? What assurance does the customer have that the company is legitimate?

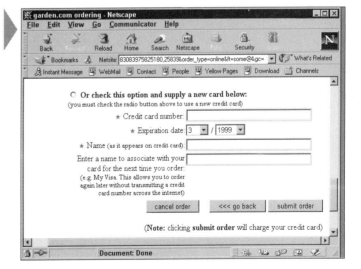

# PART

# VI

# The Web Site as a Whole

In this last part, I show you how to think of your Web site as a unified concept. You learn how to manage all of your Web documents, create and modify a unique "look and feel" for your site, and build traffic and encourage visitors. This part moves beyond designing Web pages into designing entire, integrated sites.

Site management may not seem important to you when you have two or three pages, but it's crucial when you put more than five pages of text and graphics online, or when you develop a site with other people. Chapter 21, "Document Management,"

shows you how to manage your documents for sharing with a Web development team.

Every corporation eventually develops a company "image" with text, font, and graphics identifying the company. Translating a corporate identity to the Web requires a certain amount of finesse, and you learn how to do just that in Chapter 22, "Your Own Look and Feel."

Finally, your Web site is nothing more than a private document without traffic. Several ways to encourage users to visit your site — and come back — are discussed in Chapter 23, If You Build It . . . .

CHAPTER **21**

**MASTER THESE SKILLS**

▶ Controlling Information

▶ Updating the What's New! Page

▶ Using Last Modified Dates

▶ Working in a Team

▶ Marking HTML Changes

▶ Archiving Information

# Document Management

Document management is the process of controlling information through your Web site, updating and maintaining your online content, working with team members on Web sites, and collecting and keeping archives and backups of all your Web files.

When you update a Web site, there are tons of little details that are easy to forget. In fact, all of document management is about the details. Controlling the information is all about determining how users will access your content, using which links and forms to get to the information they need to access. Site maintenance means making sure that every detail of your site is updated correctly: What's New! pages are updated, dates are correct and double-checked, and if any filenames have changed, the links to them have changed accordingly. Teamwork is an exercise in details and cooperation, as anyone who's worked in a team will attest. Archiving and backups are crucial parts to web development; anyone who's lost data to an electrical failure, hardware emergency, or similar computer disaster will understand the importance of keeping a current backup of every page on the system.

As you read this chapter, keep a notebook and your Web site handy. Jot down all the little details about your site that only you would know. Which parts are generated by a script? Will the script need to be updated if the site changes? How will you mark recent changes to a page, and how will you store and test the rough draft copies of your site? Do you work with other Web designers, managers, graphic artists, or programmers? Where do you fit into the team, and what are your responsibilities? Imagine that, tomorrow, you'll be gone from your position, and someone else will have to fill in for you. What will they need to know about running and maintaining your Web site?

Jot down those notes as documentation for your site administration. If your site belongs to a company, those notes will be valuable to others in similar positions, or who may take over if you leave your current position. If it's your own site, you may find yourself lost if you take a hiatus from working on that site to pursue other projects. The notes you make will help you recall how you maintained the site originally, and what your original plans and goals were.

# Controlling Information

Although the main purpose of a Web site is to deliver information and content to the audience, you should always try to control how people access that content as much as possible. In some cases, you may wish to restrict access to some information entirely.

This is the "Information Age," where information and knowledge is bought, sold, traded, given away, and generally used as a kind of worldwide currency. You might have decided to give away all information on your Web site, or you might wish users to trade something (registration information, other information, or money) in return. Your side of the information exchange revolves around publishing your content and deciding if and how people will pay for it.

From the user's perspective, the content had better be worth it if they're going to have to buy or trade for it. And, they have to know that your information is out there.

On the next page, I show an example of how a fictional company might control its content. The company offers three types of content on this site: product information, technical support, and employee information. The product information is offered for free. It's promotional in nature, and the company wants as many people as possible to read about their product, so they can consider using the product. A customer considering a purchase, or looking for general information on a product, can go here.

The technical support site requires a user registration, because the company only offers tech support to its customers. The user registration page requests user data, which is then saved in a database of registered users. It also saves a "cookie" so that the user doesn't have to reregister each time he or she visits this part of the site.

Finally, the employee information pages are protected from unauthorized entry entirely. If you don't have a password, then you can't access that information. Here, the company publishes company-wide memos, human resources documents, the upcoming calendar, and any information they might normally publish on an intranet. The company doesn't put confidential or classified information on this section: that type of data should always be restricted to the most secure networks available.

## TAKE NOTE

### ► CROSS-LINKING CONTENT

In this example, product-specific technical support might only be available from the main home page, or it might be cross-linked from the product page. If it's hyperlinked from the product page, make sure the link goes directly to the product-specific support page, not the main tech support page. If the users are looking for tech support on the product page, they're already lost. Starting them over at the top of another section will only make things worse. Hyperlink to a CGI script that checks for the "registered user" cookie, and goes straight to the product's technical support page, or to the user registration page for technical support.

**CROSS-REFERENCE**
More information on server security and password protection can be found in Chapter 20.

**FIND IT ONLINE**
Read more about content management and navigation at **http://info.med.yale.edu/caim/ manual/sites/site_design.html.**

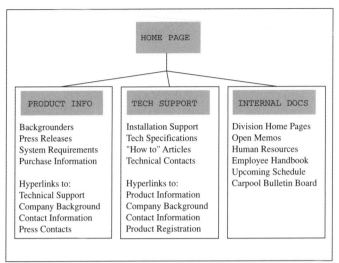

■ *The company's planned information flow, with proposed cross-links.*

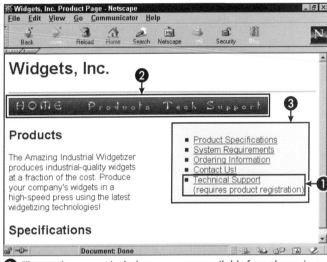

❶ *The product pages include a link to technical support, but note that user registration is required.*

❷ *Notice that the internal company pages are unavailable from the main part of the site.*

❸ *A list of related links provides a quick navigation through the product information pages.*

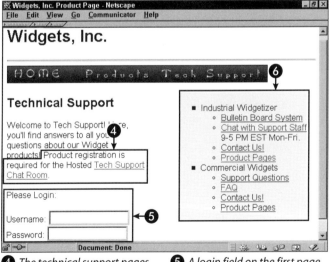

❹ *The technical support pages clearly identify which parts require product registration.*

❺ *A login field on the first page makes it easy for returning visitors to go quickly to the information they need.*

❻ *The links section is subdivided into product sections.*

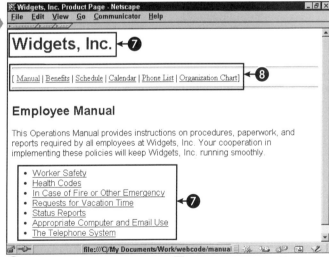

❼ *Internal employee pages need less "flash" and quicker access to important information.*

❽ *A short list of employee documents is available at the top of each page.*

■ *Employees can quickly get to important information, but nothing personal or confidential is exposed online.*

# Updating the What's New! Page

Every good Web site should have a "What's New!" page, a page that is regularly updated with the newest and latest changes to the Web site. Users go to that page when they want to see at a glance if there's any new information or content.

Links to a What's New! page should be on the home page itself, and possibly in the sitewide navigation system (be it a header, footer, frame, or floating remote controller). You should update the What's New! page every time you change something on the page.

Many people put a little graphic that says "New!" on it, to highlight the most recent changes to their sites. That's not a bad idea, but you might want to make that graphic "disappear" after some time has passed. After all, if it's been up there for a month, it's probably not very new anymore, is it?

On the next page, there's a sample JavaScript program demonstrating one way to automate removing a "New!" graphic. You could also use a server-side include, or a server-side script to automatically include or remove an image, or even the text that follows it.

The JavaScript has two parts. First, the JavaScript function called `image_expiration`. That function is the actual script itself. When the Web page loads, a little JavaScript script sends a request to this `image-expiration` function, telling the function the expiration date (`stopdate`) value. The function compares the current date with the expiration date, and only displays the graphic if today's date is before the expiration date. In the bottom-right figure, I also show the JavaScript script you would use in place of the normal `<IMG>` element. Replace the date "November 10, 1998" with whatever expiration date you wish to use.

## TAKE NOTE

### ▶ ANOTHER WHAT'S NEW! SCRIPT EXAMPLE

A more complicated What's New! script might be a server-side program that keeps an index of all Web pages on the server (like a search engine). The What's New! page would search for pages that were last modified within a certain time span, such as two weeks or a month. The search engine would return the document's title, URL (hyperlinked), and any pertinent `<META>` information, such as the keywords or the author's name.

If all Web designers included a `<META>` element with the most recent changes, your What's New! page would be able to include a meaningful list of actual changes to the Web site, not just a listing of every page that's changed or been added to the server.

### ▶ WHAT'S NEW! IN THE NEWS

Sometimes, your What's New! page will also reflect changes to the company, products, or the industry as a whole. While you might not have a Web page on the server explaining those changes, you can still include a short description of the event, and add a hyperlink if one becomes available later.

## CROSS-REFERENCE
Learn how to create a "New!" graphic in Chapter 6.

## SHORTCUT
Use a similar JavaScript program to automatically remove outdated headlines and hyperlinks.

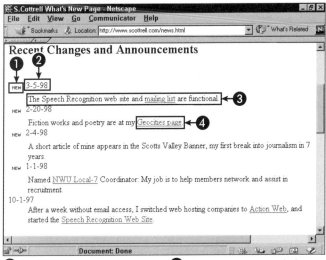

❶ New! graphics provide a quick, colorful cue to the latest information.

❷ Use dates to help readers determine how new your recent changes pages are.

❸ Concise descriptions help users decide if they need to view those changes.

❹ Hyperlinks guide users to the relevant and updated pages.

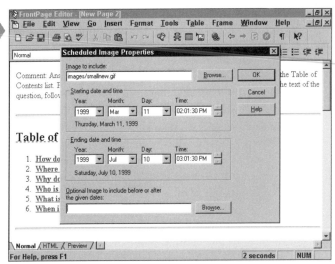

■ FrontPage 98 has Scheduled Image and Scheduled Page Bots to let you easily include an image or file into a document.

## Listing 21-1: Automating a What's New! Image

```
<SCRIPT LANGUAGE="Javascript">
<!--
function image_expiration(stopdate) {   ❶

today = new Date();   ❷
enddate = new Date(stopdate);   ❸
if (today.getTime() < enddate.getTime()) {
  document.write("<IMG SRC=\"new.gif\">");
  }
}
// -->
</SCRIPT>
```

❶ This JavaScript uses the `stopdate` variable (which is set in the HTML file) to stop displaying an image.

❷ Today's date is obtained through the Date() object.

❸ The script compares today's date with the stop date and includes the image if the stop date hasn't passed yet.

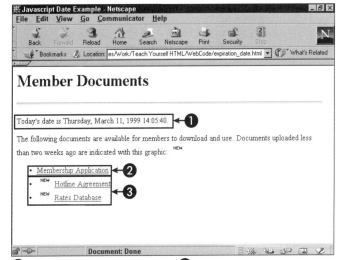

❶ Today's date was generated using a JavaScript, but a server-side include would also have worked.

❷ The first item's expiration date was March 1.

❸ The second and third items expire on March 14.

# Using Last Modified Dates

I n a standard HTTP header, which is sent along with any Web page, there are a few pieces of information you can obtain automatically. The file's size and location, included files, and the Last Modified date. The Last Modified date might not have much to do with how current the document is. It's just the date it was last changed or saved. Since you can change and save a file without actually updating its content in any significant way, the Last Modified date can be a little misleading to Web users who don't understand its limitations. In addition, CGI scripts can change a Web page, also without changing its content, and Web designers sometimes prefer to type in the date by hand, making it a static object just like any piece of text in the Web file.

Personally and professionally, I've found that to be a bad idea. It's not very hard to forget to change the date on a file you've just updated, making your "Current semester schedule" page look like it's from sometime last year. I like to use the Last Modified date to save myself from the embarrassment of having pages that look like they're outdated, even when they're not.

Besides, every item I don't have to change when updating a site is a bonus. There are already too many things to forget.

To insert a Last Modified date using SSI, use `Last Modified: <!#—flastmod virtual="/index.html">` (or use the absolute path to the file you'd like to show). To insert one using JavaScript, you would use `Last Modified (JavaScript): <SCRIPT>document.write(document.lastModified);</SCRIPT>`. Note, however, that both versions depend on the Web server providing a Last Modified date for the Web page.

## TAKE NOTE

### ▶ OTHER HTTP HEADERS YOU CAN USE

You can also include a file's size and location using SSIs, as well as certain other variables, such as the current date and time.

To include the file size with an SSI, type `<!—#fsize virtual="/index.html">`, using the path and filename of whatever document you'd like to show the size for.

Use the `<echo>` tag to include the file's location and the current date and time. `<!—#echo var="DOCUMENT_URI">` gives the local path of the current page. Similarly, use `<!—#echo var="DATE_LOCAL">` to give the local date and time (useful when determining the age of a Web page or using a script to compare them).

### ▶ JAVASCRIPT AND HTTP HEADERS

With JavaScript, you can include even more properties, such as link color variables, referring pages, and title of the document.

To include HTTP headers in JavaScript, read up on JavaScript in Chapter 18. Or, use the same syntax as shown in the above JavaScript example, using `document.URL` for the location, `document.title` for the title, and `document.linkColor` for the RGB value of link colors on the page.

## CROSS-REFERENCE

More information on server-side includes is in Chapter 19.

## FIND IT ONLINE

http://www.apache.org/docs/mod/ mod_include.html has complete documentation for Apache's include variables.

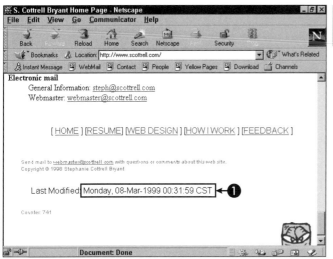

**1** Use the `flastmod` variable to include the Last Modified date in a Web page.

■ Make sure to specify the file's path and name:
`virtual="/index.html"`

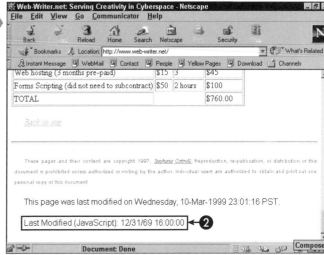

■ You can also use JavaScript to remove the load on the Web server.

**2** Unfortunately, the JavaScript `lastModified` object doesn't work with all Web servers, and returns an incorrect date.

## Listing 21-2: Last Modified and File Sizes

```
<TR>
<TD><A HREF="bookshel.htm">bookshel.htm</A></TD>
<TD><!--#fsize virtual="bookshel.htm" --></TD>
<TD><!--#flastmod virtual="bookshel.htm" -->
</TD>
</TR>
<TR>
<TD><A HREF="calendar.htm">calendar.htm</A></TD>
<TD><!--#fsize virtual="calendar.htm"--></TD>
<TD><!--#flastmod virtual="calendar.htm" -->
</TD>
</TR>
```

(a) (b) (b) (c)

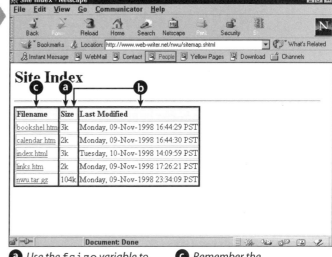

**(a)** Use the `fsize` variable to include the file's size.

**(b)** List file sizes and modification dates to keep up-to-date with your Web site files and changes.

**(c)** Remember the `virtual="filename.html"` when including the size and dates of other files.

# Working in a Team

Because the World Wide Web requires so many different types of specialists, most companies organize a Web team to develop their site. In fact, most individual Web designers also collaborate with other designers to provide the best all-around service to their clients.

As you already know, Web design involves writing, graphic arts, programming, server maintenance and networking, marketing skills, and even publishing knowledge. Although it's possible to produce a site by yourself, the areas about which you are not as knowledgeable will invariably be weaker than those in which you've specialized. So, if you're a graphic artist, the graphics of your site will probably be very good, but the writing or programming might suffer.

A Web team will usually have at least one Web designer whose job is to code the HTML for the site. There might also be a programmer, to provide server-side scripts, a graphic artist to produce company logos and graphics for the site, a database programmer for database-driven Web sites, and a manager who pulls the rest of the team into a functioning group.

If you become part of a Web team, make sure you know what your job is and what you're supposed to do. Do the job you've been hired to do, and know who's supposed to do the rest. Company employees are notorious for asking the wrong person to do a job, usually because they don't know who the right person is. If you're the graphic designer, are you supposed to put little company graphics online, or is that the server administrator's job? Know your job, and be willing to pass the work on to the right person when asked to do something outside your job description.

## TAKE NOTE

### COLLABORATION SOFTWARE

Collaboration software, also called groupware, is used to help members of a department or team work more effectively together. Some groupware is just designed to help prevent scheduling conflicts, identify task lists, and manage contact information.

Group collaboration software can help Web teams work more effectively together. Some collaboration systems provide a document check in/check out feature. Your Web pages and graphics reside on a network computer, which is controlled in part by a workflow software program. When you want to edit a file, you log in and request the file. If you have permission to edit it, and no one else is currently editing it, you can check it out and edit the file as needed. When you're done, you log out, or check in the document so other team members can use it.

---

**CROSS-REFERENCE**

Chapter 22 shows you how to unify the look and feel of your entire Web site.

**FIND IT ONLINE**

http://www.irwa.org/ has information and resources for Webmasters.

# Web Team Tricks

Every Web team manager knows a few tricks to keeping his or her team members happy, productive, and working on their goals. Because every business is different, every Web team is different. But here are a few tricks used by Webmasters everywhere.

Know your goals. Know what the goal is of your Web site, and what your individual goals are in relation to the overarching goal. If your goal is to have the #1 online community within three years and you're a community facilitator, is your goal to increase membership by a certain percent? Retain a certain percentage of members? What should you do to help the team reach the main goal?

Know your audience. Everyone on the team has to know who they're designing the site for. Is it for teens, grandmothers, businessmen, customers, clients, or anyone living in the San Francisco area?

Know your team. What are the jobs and duties of the people on your team, as well as their strengths and weaknesses? Does your programmer overcommit to deadlines? Does your graphic designer like to unwind with Nerf toys? Does your Web designer have a background in tech writing as well as layout? Who are these people, and how will their individual personalities affect how your Web site is designed?

**Table 21-1: SUGGESTED JOBS ON A WEB TEAM**

| Job | Duties |
| --- | --- |
| Web team manager | On large teams, is the main contact for Web-related questions. Manages Web team resources and time, and defines and enforces priorities. |
| Web designer | Designs an overall user interface for the Web site, including layout, colors, and navigation. |
| Graphic designer | Designs and creates graphics for the site. |
| HTML author | Codes HTML and Web pages. Makes changes to existing HTML. Codes forms for CGIs. |
| CGI programmer | Write CGIs, usually in Perl or C, for the web system. |
| Database programmer | Develops and maintains Web database. |
| Server administrator | Provides hardware and software support, maintains the Internet connection. |
| Customer support | Provides direct contact with customer in case of problems with the Web site. |
| Community facilitators | On community sites (chat, BBS, etc.), interacts with users on a daily basis, encouraging users to participate in the community and preventing abuse of the system. |

# Marking HTML Changes

There's no universally agreed upon way to mark changes to a Web document among web designers. You've already learned some useful tools for communicating changes to your Web audience, but there are currently no standard ways to communicate revisions to other members of your Web team, or even to yourself, in HTML.

This section provides a few good suggestions for marking changes in an HTML document. Some of the suggestions use cascading style sheets, but most of my suggestions use two HTML elements you already know: <META> elements and comments.

Use <META> elements to identify yourself. Whenever a team member makes a change to a Web page, he or she should edit a <META> element with the following information: <META name="Last Author" content="Stephanie Cottrell Bryant.">. Teams should use <META> elements to identify the "owner" of the document, someone who has final approval of the document before going live. The top-left code example shows an example of a page using this technique.

One kind of change you might make is to the HTML code; changing the elements to take advantage of newer browser features, or changing the way the site looks through layout or formatting styles. Note all code changes in a comment at the bottom of the document: <!— code changed to remove FONT tags and use style sheets instead. 11/1/98 S.Bryant —>. The date identifies when that change was made, and include your name or initials to identify who made the change. When the document has been approved as a final draft, remove those revision comments before publishing it to your "live" site.

Another type of change is to the content itself. Notes on content changes can be made through a comment in the document itself or onscreen. Use style="text-decoration: line-through;" to cross out text onscreen, indicating that you want to delete the selection, or place comment brackets <!— —> around the selection to remove. Note additions by placing the added text in bold, or by using another style to change the text's color, or to highlight it through a background color. The bottom-left figure shows an example of a site using this kind of revision marks.

## Version Numbers

Programmers use a version numbering system to keep track of changes in software programs, and you can use them for sites that undergo numerous revisions, or that have periodic changes, such as online magazines. Version or issue numbers make it easier to track information by date, and to identify archived information.

Use <META name="version" content="1.0">, or <!— version number 1.0 —> in your first version of the Web site. Every time you make a minor change to the entire site, increase the version by .1 (1.1, for example). When you make a major change to the site, increase the version number by 1.0 (1.0 to 2.0, for example).

---

**CROSS-REFERENCE**

For more information on style sheets, see Chapter 13.

**FIND IT ONLINE**

http://www.webdeveloper.com/categories/html/ html_metatags.html has more information on <META> tags.

## Listing 21-3: Authors and Owners

```
<HTML>
<HEAD>
<META NAME="Author" CONTENT="Stephanie Bryant">  ❶
  <!-- Original author of the document -->
<META NAME="Last_Author" CONTENT="Jen Stamper">  ❷
  <!-- Last person to modify the page -->
<META NAME="Owner" CONTENT="John Bryant">  ❸
  <!-- Person with final approval/ownership -->
```

❶ *The author of the Web page is the person who usually works on it.*

❷ *The* Last_Author *is the last person to modify the page.*

❸ *The document's owner is a manager or the client who has final approval over any changes to the Web site.*

## Listing 21-4: Using Styles for Revisions

```
<STYLE>
.delete {text-decoration: line-through;}
.add {text-decoration: underline;}  ❹
</STYLE>
</HEAD>
<BODY>
<H1>Direction to the Holiday Party</H1>
<HR>
<P>Take Highway 17 North to Scotts Valley, and get off at the Mt. Hermon Road
  exit.</P>  ❺
<SPAN class="delete"><P>Turn right onto Scotts Valley Drive. Turn left at Bean Creek
  Road. Turn left onto Bluebonnet. Turn left onto King's Village Road.</P>
<P>The party is at the roller-rink on the right-hand side of the street.</P></SPAN>
<P><SPAN class="add">Follow Mount Hermon Road to King's Village Road. Turn right. The
  party is at the roller rink on the left.</SPAN>  ❻
```

❹ *Use a style sheet to specify revision marks.*

❺ *A* <SPAN> *element uses the* delete *class to cross out deleted text.*

❻ *Another class underlines all added text.*

■ *A comment at the end of the file describes all the changes made to the file. All comments and revision marks should be removed before going "live."*

# Archiving Information

By its very nature, the Internet is in a constant state of development. It's no longer necessary to put "Under Construction" on a Web site; people assume that the site is always under construction because it's on the Web.

Many Webmasters find themselves a little lost when they actually finish designing and developing the Web site. For myself, I feel a great sense of accomplishment and relief; my clients are generally satisfied by the results, and all that remains is the site maintenance.

Ah, yes. Maintenance. You see, nothing is completely static. Ever. Life changes. Web sites change, too, to reflect the changes in life, the world, and technology. Sites must be updated, altered, and tinkered with in order to keep up-to-date.

But, what a loss to have to change your masterpiece! And what happens if you want to go back and return to the original design or final draft of a Web document? Keeping archives of your work helps prevent data loss (it's a backup of everything you've done), and it provides a chronicle of what did and didn't work on your site's development. If you decide to use revision numbers, those archives will have a handy naming and numbering scheme built-in, and you'll be able to refer to them later.

Would a sidebar work for navigation purposes? Did you try that before? Go to the archive and see what's already been done, and how it was attempted. Wasn't there an article on tropical fish in northern gardens in the Web magazine? Go back through the archives and find it; Web periodicals should have user-searchable archives as well.

An archive is little more than a copy, made on a single date, before a revision is made to the site. You could copy an entire directory, for example, and rename the archive to something like "version3." Or, use compression software to make the archive into a `.zip` or `.gzip` file for storage. Compressed files need a decompression program to be readable, but you can shrink plaintext files like HTML pages by up to 80 or 90 percent.

## UNIX Archive Programs

If you're using a UNIX system, you might be wondering what kind of archive compression program to use. Tar is the most common way in UNIX to archive several files together. Most tar files are then compressed using a compression program like gzip.

To create an archive, telnet to the UNIX server and type `tar -cvf archive.tar directory filename.html filenames.* *.gif`. That will create an archive called `archive.tar`, including all files inside the `directory` directory, `filename.html`, any file starting with filenames. (the * is a wildcard), and all .gif files.

After you create the tar file, you can then compress it with gzip: `gzip archive.tar` would compress the archive to a file called `archive.tar.gz` (gzip automatically adds the .gz extension).

**CROSS-REFERENCE**

Chapter 12 has more information on Web tools you can use to author and enhance your site.

**FIND IT ONLINE**

Complete documentation of gzip is available at http://www.gzip.org/.

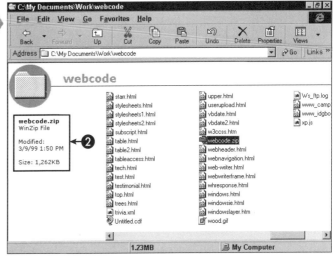

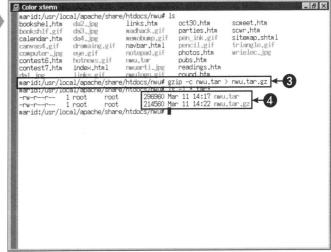

■ Winzip archives are created and used in Windows systems.

❶ The files in the Winzip file have a combined size of 2,148K.

❷ When compressed and archived, the file is just 1.23MB.

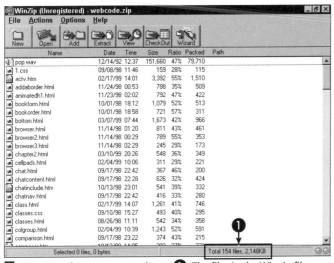

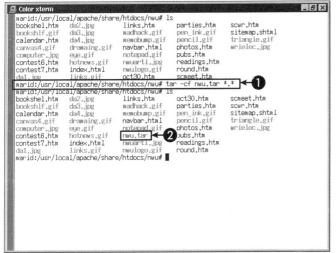

❶ To create an archive in UNIX, first tie all the files together using tar.

❷ The newly created file is the archive.

❸ Next, compress the archive with gzip: gzip nwu.tar.

❹ This compression reduced the original .tar file from 296K to 214K.

# Personal Workbook

## Q&A

**1** Name one way to track visitors to your site.

_____

_____

_____

**2** How do you prevent users from getting bogged down by information?

_____

_____

_____

**3** What's a "What's New!" page, and why is it important?

_____

_____

_____

**4** Name two ways to include the last modified date in a document.

_____

_____

_____

**5** What are some useful HTTP headers you can access?

_____

_____

_____

**6** What's a _Web team_, and who's in it?

_____

_____

_____

**7** Name one way to mark a significant change to a Web page.

_____

_____

_____

**8** How would you store a Web site archive in UNIX?

_____

_____

_____

ANSWERS: PAGE 448

## EXTRA PRACTICE

**1** Create a "What's New!" page for one of your sites. Include a graphic that automatically disappears after two weeks.

**2** Using one of your own sites, evaluate how you might streamline the information presented to your users.

**3** Add a Last Modified date to every page in your Web site, using whatever method works.

**4** Update the What's New! page for the site to reflect those changes.

**5** Create a compressed archive of your Web site when you're done making all your changes. Save the archive to a floppy diskette and store it somewhere safe.

## REAL-WORLD APPLICATIONS

✔ You've just been hired as part of a Web development team. You know what questions to ask of the Web team manager, and who's most likely to be responsible for which jobs.

✔ You've updated your Web site many times, but you can't remember if you updated the What's New! page. Fortunately, you created a site index showing you the last modified dates for all files.

✔ You keep receiving email complaining that the site has too many options. You decide to limit your users' information options as much as possible, to streamline their Web browsing experiences.

✔ Your company decides to "upgrade" to a new server. You archive and copy all the Web files, then save the archive to a Zip disk or tape backup.

## Visual Quiz

What site tools do you see used in this page? Where would you expect a page like this to be linked? What would you expect users would use it for?

_____

_____

_____

_____

_____

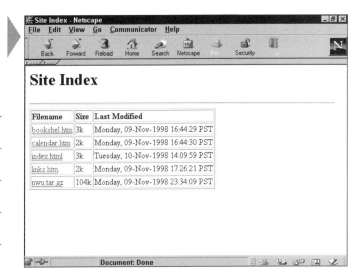

CHAPTER **22**

MASTER
THESE
SKILLS

▶ **Choosing a Look and Feel**
▶ **Creating a Page Banner**
▶ **Creating a Common Navigation Bar**
▶ **Creating Headers and Footers**
▶ **Changing the Look and Feel of Your Site**

# Your Own Look and Feel

By now you know just about everything you need to create a Web site for any purpose. You know a variety of tricks for laying out the content on a page. You know how to link your home page to the other pages on your site. You know how to handle a variety of scripts. You know how to target your intended audience.

But let's think a little more about that last point. One of the ways to reach a particular audience is to tailor your site's "look and feel" to that audience. If you're presenting technical information, you'll want clean lines, a minimum of clutter, and appropriate technical illustrations. If you're engaging in e-commerce, you have to choose imagery and styling to attract and keep the intended audience for your product. Moreover, your Web site will be more comprehensible to your users if you give it a consistent look and feel. At the same time, you can use design elements to make your site distinctive so your visitors will remember it and want to come back.

So, how do you do that? One way to approach the problem is to design a look and feel for your site that can be applied to all the pages. You might start with a banner heading, which you'll learn how to create in this chapter. You should consider your color scheme, and make sure your banner goes with it. When you think about colors, pay attention to elements other than text and background. You don't want to jar your visitors to a business with a bunch of bright pink images on predominantly green pages. A site aimed at teenage girls may stress pinks, purples, and magentas, while one aimed at teenage boys may use almost any colors — the more they clash, the better.

Your page layout is another element of your design that can give your site a distinctive character. You can maintain the layout from page to page with a template or a set of frames.

A vital element of any site is its navigation aids. You can give your site a distinctive look by creating one or more navigation bars, repeated in style (if not in content) from one page to the next. This may be in the form of image maps, text, tables, or frames. You learn to create several kinds of navigation bars in this chapter.

# Choosing a Look and Feel

In earlier chapters you learned to create and use most of the elements you need to create a consistent look and feel, and make your site easy to navigate:

▶ Colors and color schemes
▶ Graphics and icons
▶ Fonts and style sheets
▶ Frames

In designing the look of your site, remember that your users may not have the same equipment as you do. You can easily design a site at a resolution of 1,024    768 that becomes unusable at 640    480. The upper-left figure shows a site that overwhelms with graphic information. A dense background image results in barely legible text. The page is also too wide for a 640    480 browser.

But a design like this one often drives away users before they have the chance to see what's available. Here are some general principles to keep in mind if you want to keep your visitors' attention:

▶ Eighty percent of Web users see long download times as the Web's biggest problem; therefore, be sure to keep your download times short.
▶ A significant proportion of Web users turn off graphics; to reach these visitors, you must provide equivalent text content. If a picture is worth a thousand words, it should ideally be no larger than 4K.
▶ Many users won't use the scroll bars; therefore, make sure that your message is conveyed clearly in the space available in a 640    480 browser window
▶ Too much information can be as much of a turnoff as too little. That includes visual information.

The lesson should be clear: your biggest enemies in attracting and keeping visitors are long download times and sensory overload.

This chapter uses the site shown at the upper right. After the graphics were run through SmartSaver, the CD symbol was found to be a bandwidth hog. The other icons were subsequently reduced to about .5K. Those with the CD were all 1.2 to 1.6K, so the Web author chose a different CD icon with fewer colors. In addition, he saved bandwidth by using only two font styles, except for the banner, and a limited palette. The lower-right figure shows an exceptionally uncluttered and well-designed site. It has no graphics, but by clever use of color and careful grouping, it provides a great deal of information in an easy-to-digest form.

## TAKE NOTE

### ▶ AVOID EXCESSIVE GRAPHICS

To avoid long download times, use small, simple icons, as suggested above, as well as an <HR> tag, which is much more economical than using a GIF image as a separator bar.

### ▶ OPTIMIZE YOUR START PAGE

If you want lots of graphics on your site, at least make sure that your first page downloads quickly. Once you've got your visitors interested, they are more likely to put up with longer downloads.

**CROSS-REFERENCE**
See Chapter 2 for information on choosing and customizing Web colors.

**FIND IT ONLINE**
http://www.pantos.org has many pages of design tips to make your pages easier to use and navigate.

**1** *This site is uncommonly cluttered. Boxed items visually interrupt the overly busy background image.*

**2** *The vertical scroll bar, which might be ignored, reveals two screenfuls of additional information.*

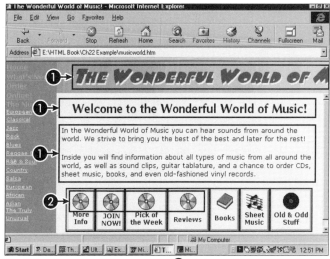

■ *Colors from the CD image are repeated in the icon borders, banner, and left frame, for a consistent appearance.*

**1** *Only two fonts are used, one for headlines, the other for everything else.*

**2** *The icons are a significant drag on download time.*

**3** *Substituting images with fewer colors allowed the icons to be reduced from about 1.4K to 1/2K.*

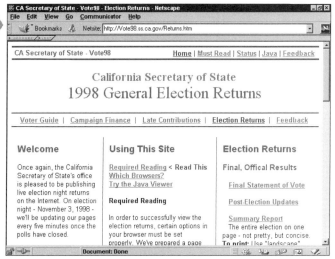

■ *This site uses no graphic elements. Careful layout, using tables, allows the display of a great deal of information without overwhelming the eye. Judicious use of color gives the page a distinctive look without resorting to graphics.*

# Creating a Page Banner

At the simplest, a page banner can be plain text (possibly in a fancy font), on a transparent background. Banners of this type can be quite effective, especially when enhanced with gradient fills, shading, or drop shadows.

The World of Music sample page uses an animated banner, violating every principle I've tried to convey. However, it's in a frame at the top, so it has to load only once. If you do this, be sure to choose a background color for the frame so that it still looks OK at higher resolutions, when there will be a blank space to the right of the banner. The following line specifies the background color, among other things:

```
<BODY topmargin="0" leftmargin="0"
bgcolor="#FFCCFF">
```

To begin, create a background, if you wish. For this example, the background is a banner 600 pixels wide by 60 pixels high, created with Paint Shop Pro. With a navigation bar at the left, this is wide enough to fill a standard 640 480 screen, and not so high as to eat up the available presentation space. While editing the banner, the graphic designer clicked in the light and dark borders of an icon to choose foreground and background colors, and used a linear gradient at 311 degrees so that the gradient ran a bit top to bottom as well as left to right. You can use any graphic file type for the background of an animation. Bitmaps (.BMP files) are said to work best, but it's hard to reduce the colors in them. You might reduce the Color Palette first and then save as a .BMP.

To create the animation, the designer used Ulead's GIF Animator LE. An animation consists of a series of images displayed in sequence. The finer the scrolling on a banner, the more images it requires. By default, GIF Animator sets the quality to Good, which creates 32 separate images of the text. By changing it to Normal, which creates only 20, the designer reduced the file size considerably. If you get the full version of SmartSaver, you can optimize animations as well as GIFs, JPEGs, and PNGs. When used on this banner, the text left ghosts in its path; the designer was stuck with a 151K file.

## TAKE NOTE

### CHOOSING COLORS FOR YOUR ANIMATION

If you've properly reduced your palette, you may find that all the shades available for your scrolling banner are variations of the background. If you want a contrasting banner with a different color drop shadow, you must edit the Global Palette in GIF Animator (choose Edit ⇨ Global Palette). You see a series of squares, each representing one of the colors in the background, but probably several will be the same. Pick a color that's repeated, note the RGB values, and enter the new RGB values you want to use. When you click OK, a dialog box appears. Choose Yes, and click Start Preview.

## CROSS-REFERENCE

For more about animation, see Chapter 6.

## FIND IT ONLINE

To download the free version of Ulead GIF Animator, go to **http://www.webutilities.com/Frwu_ga.htm**.

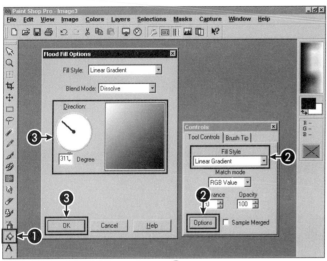

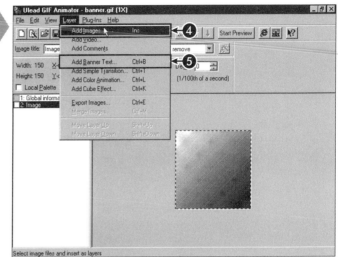

❶ To add a gradient fill background, choose the Paint Can tool in Paint Shop Pro.

❷ Choose a gradient type. Click the Options button.

❸ Choose a direction and blend style, and click OK.

❹ To create a scrolling banner in Ulead GIF Animator, first choose Layer ➪ Add Images. Open the background image you created.

❺ Choose Layer ➪ Add Banner Text.

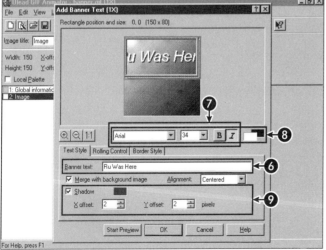

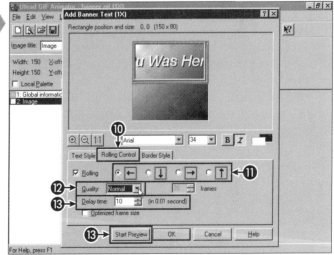

❻ Enter your banner text.

❼ Choose a font, size, and style.

❽ Choose a text foreground color.

❾ For a drop shadow, choose a color and the offset the shadow should have from the text.

❿ Click the Rolling Control tab.

⓫ Choose the direction in which the text should scroll.

⓬ Choose your animation quality.

⓭ Choose the Delay time (the default is 14). Click Start Preview to preview the result.

# Creating a Common Navigation Bar

You can give all your pages a common look and feel — and help your visitors find their way around the site — by creating a common navigation bar linked to the top-level pages. You've already seen an example in Chapter 6, where you saw an image map used as a navigation bar in the left frame of a frames page. However, as you know, graphics download a lot more slowly than text, and if all you're conveying is words, you're using more bandwidth than you need to.

You can reduce the impact of an item such as a navigation bar on download time by placing it in a frame. To do that, you can include your navigation bar in a header frame, place it in a side frame on either side, or create a footer frame for it. Alternatively, you can place one in the body of each page. Many designers favor a navigation bar for the top-level pages in text form at the bottom of a page, and a second navigation bar at the top for top-level pages. These can be graphical, as a series of buttons or an image map, or text-based.

In fact, there's nothing to stop you from using all of these aids to navigation. The World of Music site has a text-based navigation bar in the left frame. The first page has a navigation bar made up of icons. If these icons were reduced considerably in size, they could be used as a common navigation bar in the header. But to save bandwidth, a text navigation bar was created, containing the same items on the foot of all pages except the home page. Specialized pages have an additional text navigation bar at the head. For example, the jazz page has links to subsidiary pages for traditional jazz, mainstream jazz, and contemporary jazz, as well as links to the appropriate books, reviews, and sheet music pages.

You can create a left-side navigation bar in several ways. First, you can place the navigation bar in a separate frame or include it in your main page. If you want to include it on the main page, a common approach is to create a table one column wide, with one cell for each link. Then, you create a table for the page layout, and place the navigation table in the leftmost frame. This means it can be extended as long as you like, and stays with the material as you scroll down the page. It unfortunately takes extra time to load two tables, and they have to be reloaded with each new page.

Putting a navigation bar in a frame means it only has to be loaded once. If it runs longer than a 640  480 browser window, however, you have to permit scrolling, which places an ugly scroll bar in the middle of your page. The World of Music page uses a single paragraph with line breaks to make everything fit.

**CROSS-REFERENCE**

For more information about style tags, see Chapter 13.

**FIND IT ONLINE**

Go to **http://www.spunwebs.com/frmtutor.html** for a complete tutorial on frames.

## Notes about Listing 22-1

Within Listing 22-1, the header contains a style tag, `<A:HOVER {color: red;}>`, which turns the links red when the mouse hovers over them.

To create consistent coloring, the three links in the larger font have a `<style>` tag specifying the color. This overrides the default color used by the page for links and makes them the same color as the topic header "The Music:". This line doesn't need a `<style>` tag, because the `color` attribute can be used for the text.

Note also the tag in the header specifying a font family for the body text. Many visitors will not have the Verdana font installed, so this tag specifies alternative fonts — Arial for PCs and Helvetica for Macs. With this tag, you don't have to specify the font for each line.

### Listing 22-1: World of Music Page Left Frame

```
<HTML>
<HEAD>
<META http-equiv="Content-Type"
content="text/html; charset=iso-8859-1">
<TITLE>Navigation bar</TITLE>
<STYLE>
A:HOVER {color: red;}
BODY {font-family: Verdana, Arial, Helvetica,
Geneva, sans-serif;}
</STYLE>
<BASE target="rtop">
</HEAD>
<BODY topmargin="0" leftmargin="3"
link="#FFFFCC"
  alink="#FF0099" bgcolor="#8080FF">
<P><A href="index.htm" style="color: 00FFFF">
<FONT   size="2"><B>Home</FONT></A></B><BR>
<A href="whatsnew.htm" style="color: 0FFFF">
  <FONT size="2"><B>What's
New</FONT></A></B><BR>
<A href="http://www.musicorder.com/
orderform.htm/"
  style="color: 00FFFF"><FONT size="2">
  <B>Order Online!</FONT></A></B><BR>
<FONT   size=2" color="#00FFFF">
  <B>The Music:</B></A></B><BR>
<A href="classical.htm">
<FONT    size="1">
European Classical</A></FONT><BR>
. . . . . . . . . .
<A href="other.htm"><FONT size="1">
The Truly Unusual</FONT></A></P>
</BODY>
```

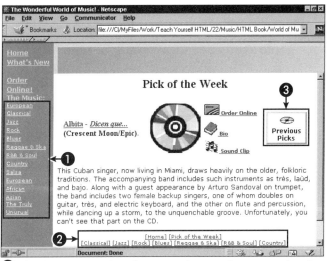

① This site uses a text-based navigation bar in the left frame.

② Another text-based navigation bar appears at the bottom of every page but the home page.

③ A single navigation icon maintains visual continuity.

# Creating Headers and Footers

Another way to control the look and feel of your site is to give your pages headers and footers. Either or both give you a place for navigation bars and other items that should be consistent from page to page.

A header should display your site name, either as text or as a banner, and may include a top-level navigation bar. Some sites use a graphic header that includes image-mapped icons. A search field and its accompanying push-button are not uncommon.

A footer may include such things as a navigation bar (generally in the form of text) an update bot, a copyright notice, or anything else that you want at the foot of every page.

There are basically three ways you can create headers and footers:

▶ A one-column, three-row table
▶ Frames
▶ Simply placing appropriate material at the top and bottom of the pages

There are advantages and disadvantages to each method. A table makes it easy to find the header and footer material when changing the look of your site. On the other hand, tables must be a fixed width. If you make your table 620 pixels wide, your page is sure to fit in any browser. However, if you center some items, they won't be centered at higher resolutions. And if you want different cell backgrounds in some cells, the background won't expand to fill the width of a higher-resolution page.

If you use frames, you need to load the information only once. Unless you keep reloading the frameset as your visitors navigate the site, you're limited to the same information for all your headers or footers, and you "lock out" visitors whose browser can't handle frames.

Finally, you can just set aside portions of your frame as header and footer, and mark them with comments. This technique gives you the most precise control over the contents. Even a graphic banner should be loaded from the cache on the second and subsequent pages, so you needn't worry too much about increasing download time. On the other hand, you must create (or cut and paste) the copy for each page individually; making it harder to redesign the site.

The left side of the following page shows the code for creating a three-cell table. Note that the center cell is designated as having a `height` of "1". This allows the cell to expand to fit its contents.

The right side of the page shows the code for creating a frames page that includes a header, body, and footer. Again, note that the center frame's `height` is "*", which has the same effect as the `height` of "1" in a table.

## TAKE NOTE

### ▶ COMBINING APPROACHES

There's no reason you can't combine these approaches. For example, to create a fixed header, and a footer that appears after the contents, create a page with two frames (one for the header) and set the border off with comments at the end of the content pages.

## CROSS-REFERENCE

For a complete discussion of frames, see Chapter 7. To review tables, see Chapter 4.

## FIND IT ONLINE

http://html.miningco.com/msubtables.htm is a links page leading you to many tutorials on building tables.

### Listing 22-2: Three-Cell Table

```
<TABLE border="0" cellpadding="0"
cellspacing="0" width="620" height="60">
  <TR>
    <TD><!—Header content goes here>
  </TR>
</TABLE>
</DIV><DIV align="left">


<TABLE border="0" cellpadding="0"
cellspacing="0" width="620" height="1">
  <TR>
    <TD><!—Content of main page goes here>
  </TR>
</TABLE>
</DIV><DIV align="left">


<TABLE border="0" cellpadding="3"
cellspacing="0" width="620" height="80">
  <TR>
    <TD><!—Footer content goes here>
  </TR>
</TABLE>
</DIV>
```

▲ *This code sets up a one-column table with three cells for laying out a page.*

■ *This figure shows a page laid out using the frames defined in Listing 22-3.*

❶ *The header and footer always remain on the screen with this arrangement.*

### Listing 22-3: Three Horizontal Frames

```
<FRAMESET framespacing="0" border="false"
frameborder="0" rows="70,*,60">
<FRAME name="header" scrolling="no" noresize
target="subject"src="fheader.htm">
<FRAME name="subject" target="footer"
scrolling="auto" src="fhome.htm">
<FRAME name="footer" scrolling="no" noresize
src="ffooter.htm">
<NOFRAMES>
<BODY><P>This page uses frames, but your
browser doesn't support them.</P></BODY>
</NOFRAMES>
</FRAMESET>
```

▲ *This code creates frames instead of a table for organizing a page.*

# Changing the Look and Feel of Your Site

It never fails. As soon as you've got your site laid out and tweaked to perfection, your boss tells you the company has a new image, and the Web site must be changed accordingly. Count on it. Worse yet, somebody will probably upload the company logo to your site folder, using the same name, and expect it to fit in the height and width tags you've established.

There are steps you can take to reduce the pain of the transition. Following is a checklist of items to be aware of:

- ▶ **Headers:** Will the header change? Will links in it change? Are there new graphics? (Hint: If you've set off the header with comments and `<DIV>` tags, you can make the change once, copy it, and paste it into all the other pages.)
- ▶ **Footers:** Same issues as headers.
- ▶ **Graphics:** Are there new graphics? Are they the same size as the old graphics? Will you have to adjust the `<height>` and `<width>` tags?
- ▶ **Tables:** Will new content alter the proportions of tables? Will a new graphic in a table blow the table out of shape?
- ▶ **Frames:** If your site uses frames, will their sizes need to be adjusted to accommodate new fonts and graphics, or vice versa?
- ▶ **Links:** Has the internal structure of your site changed? Have new pages been added? Make sure your internal navigation aids reflect the change.

Better yet, use an external style sheet, along with `<DIV>` and `<SPAN>` tags for internal formatting. With an external style sheet, you can specify all the details of style for every element on your site once. If some pages have special elements, you can set them off with local `<style>` tags, or use `class` or `id` elements in your style sheet, which you reference at various points on your page as needed. Use the `<DIV>` and `<SPAN>` tags for larger blocks. Then, you can change the global elements by editing the external style sheet, and search your pages for `<style>` tags to find the local items that need changing.

The code on the upper right is the style sheet for the Elements of Magic site shown in the previous section. Part of the procedure to change the look shown on the lower right involved editing the style sheet in Listing 22-4.

## TAKE NOTE

### ▶ BROWSER INCONSISTENCIES

Test any style sheets you use in more than one browser. The page in the illustration contains a SPAN element to turn the "ENTER" link into a button, which has no effect in Internet Explorer. On the other hand, Netscape Navigator didn't render some of the fonts correctly.

### ▶ CHANGING A COLOR SCHEME

To change the colors of your graphics, edit one of the existing images to use the new scheme. Save the resulting palette. Load all the other images to be changed and load and apply the saved palette. You may have to change the color depth several times to complete the job.

**CROSS-REFERENCE**

For a full discussion of style sheets, see Chapter 13.

**FIND IT ONLINE**

Go to **http://www.sitetech.com/** to download a trial version of QuickSite.

## Using Themes

There's another easy way to change the look and feel of your site all at once. Two current WYSIWYG Web-design tools — Microsoft FrontPage 2000 and DeltaPoint QuickSite — include groups of elements such as headers, navigation bars, bullets, buttons, and font styles. You choose a theme and all its elements are applied.

With QuickSite, you are limited to the themes supplied, but you can easily mix and match elements from different themes. FrontPage includes a Theme Designer on the installation CD (you have to install it separately), which lets you create your own themes. You can start with an existing theme, save it under a different name, and then substitute your own backgrounds, graphics, etc. for those that don't fit your design. FrontPage even creates common header and footer zones for you, which you can choose to include in a page on an individual basis.

❶ This element is coded as H1 instead of H2. A color attribute changes the color to green, overriding the element's style.

❷ A table arranges the graphics and text.

❸ <P> tags inherit their text style from the style sheet.

❹ The H5 element defines footer text appearance.

### Listing 22-4: External Style Sheet for Elements of Magic Site

```
P {font: normal demi-bold small "Draft Plate";
font-family: "Draft Plate, Roman, Times New
Roman,  serif"; color: black}

H1 {font: normal bold x-large; font-family:
"Desdemona, Baskerville, serif"; color: black;}
H2 {font: normal bold large; font-family:
"Desdemona, Baskerville, serif"; color: black;}
H3 {font: normal bold medium ; font-family:
"Desdemona, Baskerville, serif"; }
H5 {normal demi-bold smaller "Draft Plate";
font-family: "Draft Plate, Roman, serif";}
A {color: #800080; }
A:HOVER {color: red; }
```

▲ Editing this style sheet gives the Web site in the upper-right corner a different look.

### Listing 22-5: Revised Style Sheet for Elements of Magic Site

```
P {font: normal demi-bold small Lucida
Calligraphy; font-family: Lucida Calligraphy,
script; color: black}
H1 {font: normal bold x-large Agincort; font-
family: Agincort, Lucida Calligraphy, script;
color: green; }
H2 {font: normal bold large Agincort; font-
family: Agincort, Lucida Calligraphy, script;
color: green; }
H3 {font: normal bold medium "Agincort"; font-
family: Agincort, Lucida Calligraphy, script;
color: green; }
H5 {normal demi-bold 8pt Times New Roman;
font-family: Times New Roman, Times, Times
Roman, serif"; color: black; }
A {color: #800080; }
A:HOVER {color: red; }
```

▲ These are the edits that alter the page's look.

# Personal Workbook

## Q&A

**1** Why might you want to minimize the use of graphics on your site?

_____

_____

_____

**2** What are the relative advantages and disadvantages of placing a left-side navigation bar in a frame vs. in a table on the contents pages?

_____

_____

_____

**3** Name three ways to create page headers.

_____

_____

_____

**4** Name three items commonly found in page headers.

_____

_____

_____

**5** Why should you think twice — at least — before putting a scrolling banner on your site?

_____

**6** Name the most important factor affecting the file size of a scrolling banner.

_____

_____

_____

**7** How might an external style sheet help when changing the look and feel of a site?

_____

_____

_____

**8** What six aspects of your site should you review routinely when changing the site's appearance?

_____

_____

_____

ANSWERS: PAGE 449

## EXTRA PRACTICE

**1** Set up a simple page using a style sheet for all font information.

**2** Change the font attributes by editing the style sheet.

**3** Create a banner that scrolls top to bottom against a sunburst background.

**4** Using your company logo for a background, animate your company's slogan scrolling across it.

**5** Create a navigation sidebar using a frame.

**6** Create a navigation sidebar using a table.

## REAL-WORLD APPLICATIONS

✔ Your boss wants you to change your site's color scheme. You examine the Browser Safe Colors chart for appropriate shades, and edit your external style sheet to change the font and background colors.

✔ You also examine your icons, and use the Color Replacer tool to change the dominant colors to match your new scheme.

✔ Your boss wants a new product featured prominently on the home page, with a link to the product's information page on all other pages. You edit the home page, and create a product icon that you place on the right side of the header frame.

✔ The entire structure of your site has changed. You edit the left-side navigation bar accordingly.

## Visual Quiz

Identify the header on this page. Identify the navigation elements. What kinds of navigation elements are there? How is this page geared for its intended audience?

_____

_____

_____

_____

_____

CHAPTER **23**

**MASTER THESE SKILLS**

▶ **Registering with Search Engines**

▶ **Building Traffic with Email and Newsgroups**

▶ **Analyzing Log Files and Reports**

▶ **Incorporating Advertising and Banners**

▶ **Conducting Market Research**

▶ **Leveraging Partnerships**

▶ **Using Online Communities and Content**

# If You Build It...

It's possible to build the most eye-popping, information-packed, accessible Web site ever coded in HTML, publish it to the Net, and still not have a successful Web site. How can that be? Because there's a last, very important step that still needs attention: site promotion.

For your Web site to be truly successful, it needs visitors. Preferably lots of them. The art of luring ever-increasing throngs of people to your Web pages is called building traffic. It's the same thing supermarkets are after when they advertise in the Sunday paper, put up billboards, sponsor community efforts, or send coupons to your home.

You don't have to hire an expert to promote your site (although you could), and you won't have to spend a lot of money. The biggest investment you'll need to make in do-it-yourself site promotion is *time*. And there are even tools to help minimize that.

The most successful traffic-building programs are planned and multidimensional. First, you'll need to think about the types of people you want to bring to your site. They make up your target market. Once you know who they are, you'll need to do a little research to find out where they are. How can you reach them and let them know about your site? What will motivate them to point their browser to your URL?

When it comes to putting your Web site in front of your target market, you have a smorgasbord of options to choose from. Getting listed in Internet directories such as Yahoo! and Infoseek is just the first step. You might also decide to create a targeted email campaign, participate in newsgroups related to your site's content (or even host a new one), distribute your own electronic newsletter, or participate in a banner advertising program. Other opportunities include community building and networking with other Webmasters. The most successful promotional efforts incorporate several of these methods.

There's a generous supply of traffic-building expertise available on the Web. Online marketing resource centers such as Promotion World (**www.promotionworld.com**) and `freeSubmit` `()` make it their business to provide extensive libraries of articles, hints, tips, and expert marketing advice. You've already built your site. Tell people how to find it and why they want to, and the traffic will come.

# Registering with Search Engines

Search engines are often the first place people look to find out who can supply something that is needed, and how to contact them. A large portion of your Web site traffic will come from people who find it using a search engine.

To get your Web pages included in a search engine directory, go to the search engine's Web site and look for a link that says something like "add URL" or "add your site." Click on that link and fill in the form that appears.

Before you begin submitting to search engines, make your site "spider friendly." A few search engines have a human operator visit each submission before including it in their directory, but since they receive huge numbers of submissions each day, many instead use a software program called a "spider." Soon after you submit your pages for inclusion, the spider will visit your site and catalog what it finds there.

What the spider encounters will affect where your pages appear in the directory, or if they appear at all. Your goal is to get your URLs to show up whenever a search engine user enters keywords that relate to your site. You also want them to appear as close to the top of the search results as possible so they won't get lost among thousands of competing matches.

Spiders often use the contents of <META> tags to index a page. Carefully crafted <META> tags will dramatically improve your page's position in search engines. <META> tags go in the <HEAD> section of HTML documents. The two <META> tags you'll be using for search engine purposes are the description and keywords <META> tags. Each <META> tag has two attributes: a keyword identifying the content, and then the content itself.

Use the description <META> tag to provide a summary of your site. For example:

```
<META name ="description" content =
"gocertify.com is a gathering place and
resource center for people interested in
computer professional certification.">
```

Some search engines will use the description tag verbatim in the listing for the page. Others will use it to index your page, and only a few will ignore it.

The keywords <META> tag provides a list of terms that people seeking the types of material on the page might use. For example:

```
<META name ="keywords" content= "certify,
certified, certification, professional
education, computers, training, MCSE, A+, CNE">
```

Search engine spiders also pay close attention to the <TITLE> tag of each page. Take advantage of this by being as specific as possible when naming your pages.

```
<TITLE>Obtaining Computer Professional
Certification</TITLE>
```

is better than

```
<TITLE> Certification <TITLE>
```

## TAKE NOTE

### ▶ <META> TAG SIZE RESTRICTIONS

The different search engines place limits on the length of <META> tags they will consider. Although restrictions vary by search engine, it's a good idea to keep your keywords content to under 1,000 characters and description content to several sentences.

## CROSS-REFERENCE
To review HTML tag syntax, see Chapter 1.

## FIND IT ONLINE
http://searchenginewatch.com/webmasters/index.html tells you how to get your pages prominently listed.

## Customize Every Page

Optimize every page of your site, not just the home page. Think of each page as a minisite, and customize <META> and <TITLE> tags for each. By using page-specific titles and keywords, you're broadening the array of search terms that will lead to your site.

Use the same mindset when submitting your pages to the different search engines. Submit each page separately to each search engine. By getting multiple pages listed, you improve the odds of a search turning up at least one of them. The more paths you make to your site, the easier it will be for visitors to find and follow them.

### Listing 23-2: Adding <META> Elements

```
<HTML>
<HEAD>
<TITLE>
The Speech Recognition Web Site
   speech, speech recognition, voice recognition,
   software, microphones, visually impaired
</TITLE>
<META name="description" content="All about
   speech recognition products, including
   software and hardware.">
</HEAD>
```

❸ Add a <META> description tag for the page. Type **<META name="description" content= "text">**.

### Listing 23-1: Using Title to Build Traffic

```
<HTML>
<HEAD>
<TITLE>
The Speech Recognition Web Site
   speech, speech recognition, voice recognition,
   software, microphones, visually impaired
</TITLE>
</HEAD>
```

❶ Use very specific, descriptive text in your title.

❷ The first few words of your title should still be the main title of the page.

### Listing 23-3: <META> Keywords

```
<HTML>
<HEAD>
<TITLE>
The Speech Recognition Web Site
   speech, speech recognition, voice recognition,
</TITLE>
<META name="description" content="All about
   speech recognition products, including
   software and hardware.">
<META name="keywords" content="speech, speech
   recognition, microphones, visually
impaired">
</HEAD>
```

❹ Add a <META> keywords tag for the page. Type **<META name="keywords" content= "text">**. Use keywords that highlight and identify the content of the page.

413

# Building Traffic with Email and Newsgroups

It's often said that email is the "killer app" of the Internet. That's true in more than one way. Judicious and appropriate application of these tools will boost awareness of your Web site and draw additional traffic to it. Haphazard or indiscriminate use will make people mad at you, and instead of getting visitors to your Web site, you'll get a flood of nasty email messages.

There are many ways — most of them free — to use email to bring traffic at your site. One of the simplest is to turn your everyday online correspondence into an advertising vehicle. This is accomplished by adding a few additional lines at the end of every email message you send out, including newsgroup postings. The extra lines include your Web site URL and one or two sentences geared to generate interest in your site. For example:

```
Anne Martinez (author@gocertify.com)
––––––––––––––––Get Certified And Get Ahead
visit http://gocertify.com
––––––––––––––––––––––
```

The above collection of lines is called a signature. Keep it short and sweet. Signatures should be a footnote to your email, not a screaming billboard. Every once in a while, change your signature to keep it fresh.

You can also use email as a gentle reminder service for people who've visited or expressed interest in your site in the past. One method is to send out occasional, newsy messages about your site. These messages might describe a feature you've added or announce that a key area has been updated.

With a bit more effort, you can compile and distribute a newsletter that covers an industry or technology closely related to your site. The newsletter must provide useful content, not just advertising for your Web pages. Otherwise, nobody will read it and your efforts will be wasted. How-to articles, state of the industry (or technology, or ...) reports, and resource listings make good newsletter fodder. Somewhere within the newsletter, incorporate news about your site, or some other reminder of what's on it and why newsletter recipients should hurry up and point their browsers at your home page.

To send out a regular newsletter or other bulk emailing, you'll first need to amass a list of people to send it to. One of the simplest ways is to include an "add me to your mailing list" link somewhere on your site. The link should lead visitors to a form for submitting their email address, which you then add to your mailing list. If your site includes an autoresponder, configure it to save the email addresses of people who contact it. Your mailing list should also include the address of anyone who sends you site-related email, or otherwise expresses an interest in the information you have to offer.

*Continued*

## TAKE NOTE

### ▶ DON'T BE A SPAMMER

To avoid annoying instead of enticing people, keep your mass-emailings infrequent, and include information on how recipients can remove themselves from your list.

## CROSS-REFERENCE

For information on email and newsgroup features of Microsoft's Internet Explorer, see Chapter 10.

## FIND IT ONLINE

The mailing list management software FAQ can be found at **http://www.greatcircle.com/list-managers/software-faq**.

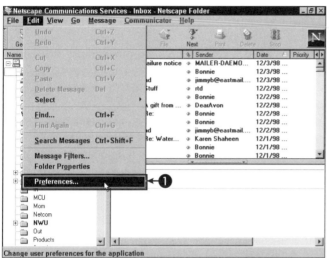

❶ *Email programs can be configured to automatically insert a signature into outgoing messages. To configure Netscape Communicator to do this, select Edit ➪ Preferences from the menu bar.*

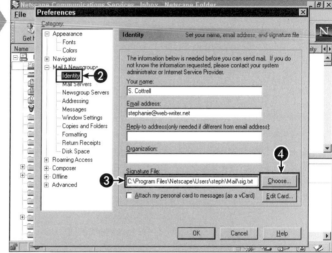

❷ *Select the Mail & Newsgroups ➪ Identity preferences box.*

❸ *Enter the path to a text file with your signature.*

❹ *Or, click the Choose button to browse to your sig file.*

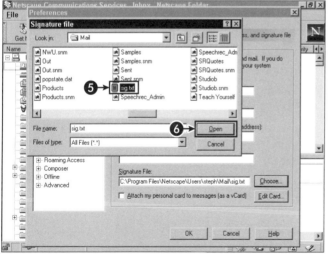

❺ *Use the Explorer to browse to and select your signature text file.*

❻ *Click Open to include that signature file.*

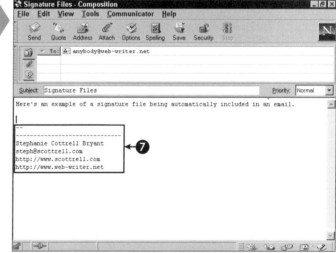

❼ *The contents of the text file will be included in every outgoing message by default.*

■ *To remove the signature for an individual email, just delete the text from the message.*

# Building Traffic with Email and Newsgroups *Continued*

Discussion groups and newsgroups can also be used to entice visitors to your site. Both types of groups facilitate ongoing conversations about a particular topic or subject area. Newsgroup discussions take place via a message board. Postings are stored in a central, online repository. Newsgroup messages can be viewed online, or downloaded for offline reading. Most newsgroups are open to anyone who cares to participate.

Discussion groups are conducted via email. To be part of a discussion group, users have to subscribe. When a message is posted to a discussion group, every subscriber receives a copy via email. Replies are also distributed to everyone on the list. Postings are usually forwarded immediately, although some discussion groups offer a once-a-day digest version.

Because these groups are organized around a particular theme, everyone who participates has some interest in the subject area. Find the groups where potential visitors to your site are likely to hang out, and you'll have a pool of traffic just waiting to be invited.

Posting advertisements for your site to these groups is frowned upon. After all, group members participate because of the information and community; not because they want to be bombarded with advertising. What you can do is put your site in front of group members without forcing it on them.

You do this by becoming an active participant in the group. Look for questions you can answer and problems you can solve. Always close your postings with a signature that mentions your site.

If there aren't any discussion groups devoted to your site's subject area, consider hosting one yourself. Small discussion groups can be managed through your regular mailing software and dial-up modem connection. Set up your email software to check for incoming messages every 20 minutes, and to automatically forward those mailing list messages to members of the group. You can handle address additions and deletions manually.

When the discussion mailing list grows larger, you'll need to move it to a mailing list host, or use mailing list software. Using a mailing list host will dramatically reduce your time investment, because they will handle the administrative end of the discussion group for you. You won't have to deal with adding or removing subscribers, or forwarding hundreds or thousands of messages each day.

Publicize your discussion group by posting subscription information on your Web site. You can also include reference to it in your signature file. The fact that you host the group is good advertising for your site. It also gives you a direct line to people interested in your site's subject matter. As the mailing list grows, your site traffic should grow too.

## TAKE NOTE

### ▶ YOU MAY ALREADY HAVE THE SOFTWARE

Your Web hosting service may already have mailing list management software available for your use. The use of such software is often bundled in with your site hosting package.

## CROSS-REFERENCE

To review how to add hyperlinks to pages, see Chapter 2.

## FIND IT ONLINE

To locate list hosting services, search The List of Lists at http://catalog.com/vivian/interest-group-search.html.

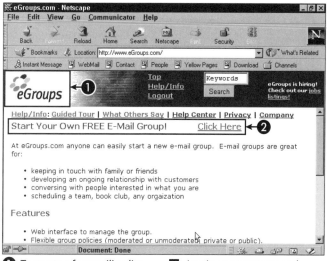

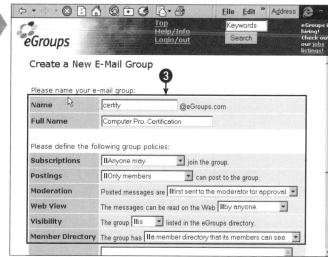

**①** To create a free mailing list related to your Web site, begin by going to the eGroups.com home page.

■ Log in as a new user and complete the new user registration, then return to the home page.

**②** Select Click Here to start a new mailing list.

**③** Fill in the new group form to define the name of your group, who can access it and how, and whether or not you'll have moderator.

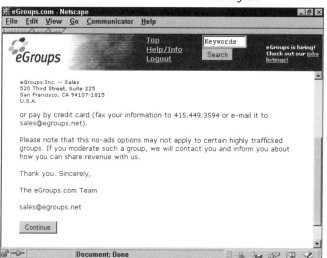

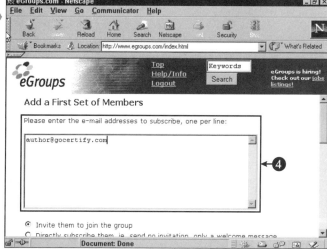

■ A "no ads" option prevents advertisements from appearing in your egroups mailing list. If you wish to create an ad-free list, check this option and click Continue.

**④** Add initial subscribers list

■ Double-check the displayed list description.

■ Click the Finish button. Your mailing/discussion list is now ready to use! Remember to add a "subscribe to the discussion list" link to your Web site's home page.

# Analyzing Log Files and Reports

To judge the success of your promotional efforts, you need to be able to examine traffic to and through your site. Web site analysis programs let you see how many times an individual page is viewed, which page users view first, what site they came from, and daily traffic patterns.

These types of statistics provide important feedback. You can use them to measure the effects of your promotional efforts and assess which are the most effective at achieving your goal of building traffic. To make the best use of site statistics, it's important to understand how they're gathered, as well as what they mean.

Whenever someone accesses your site, their browser is requesting files from your Web server. The request includes information about the requestor and information requested. Most Web servers record these details in a log file.

Log file contents vary depending on what software the Web server is running. Typical detail items include the date and time, name of the file(s) being requested, the type of browser requesting them, the name and domain of the computer making the request, where the user was last, and if errors were encountered while processing the request.

Attempting to directly read and interpret a log file can be a challenge. Fortunately, there are many software products that will translate the apparent gobbledy gook from your log files into meaningful reports. These programs are called log file analyzers. Your Web hosting service may provide a basic analysis program as part of your hosting package. If not, or if the provided software doesn't provide the

information you want, you can purchase a separate analyzer program that accesses the log files on your server. Price ranges vary greatly depending on the features of the software.

Another option is to use a statistics service to provide reports for you. To enable them to do so, you add several lines of HTML to the pages you want tracked. To view your statistics, you sign on to the service's site and enter a password. You may also have the option of having the reports sent to your email address. There are a number of free statistics services that will handle your reporting in exchange for displaying an advertising banner. The scope of the reports you'll receive will be limited, but the price is right, so they're worth a look.

*Continued*

## TAKE NOTE

### ▶ SPIDER TRACKING

Search engine spiders will show up in your log reports, too. Any request for a file named `robots.txt` is a sure sign that a spider or other software robot has been by. You may also spot them based on the host computer name. For example, if the host name **www.lycos.com** appears in your log reports, the Lycos spider has paid your site a visit.

**CROSS-REFERENCE**
For help choosing an editing tool, see Chapter 12.

**FIND IT ONLINE**
For a list of free Web statistics providers, see
**http://home.ici.net/~shreyans/counter.html**.

① SiteTracker is a statistics service. To use it to track your Web traffic, begin by going to the SiteTracker home page.

② Select Sign Me Up from the menu bar.

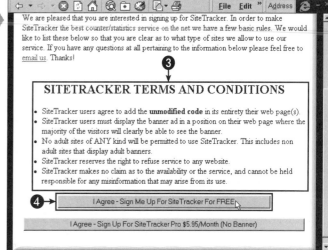

③ Review the terms and conditions.

④ If the terms are acceptable, click on the first I Agree button for free service in exchange for displaying an ad on your site.

⑤ Complete the signup form.
- Record the password you chose in your personal files.
- Click the Signup button at the bottom of the page.

- A page containing your account number and the code for your page will appear. A copy of it will also be sent to your email address.

# Analyzing Log Files and Reports
*Continued*

When reviewing a log analysis report, it's important to interpret the information properly. You've no doubt seen other sites trumpeting the number of hits they receive. But what exactly is a hit? Every time a file is requested from the server, that's a hit. There's no distinction made between graphic files and HTML files. Thus, an all-text page would produce one hit when loaded. Throw four graphics on there and you get five hits, because each graphic is in its own file. So, every view of the page generates five hits.

And it gets worse than that. Let's say a visitor reloads the page — another five hits. A single visitor wandering around in your site can generate dozens to hundreds of hits. As this has become more widely known, hit counts aren't taken as indicative of much of anything.

It's possible to configure log file analysis programs to exclude particular types of hits. It's a good idea to set them to ignore all requests for .gif, .jpg, and .jpeg files, the most commonly used graphics formats on Web pages. By doing that, you can come up with a more meaningful number: page views. The figures in the upper left and upper right of the next page show the difference between excluding or including graphics files.

Since the IP addresses of your visitors will be recorded, it's possible to come up with an estimate of unique visitors to your site. This is one of the more meaningful statistics, although page views can tell you something about how long visitors stay at the site and what they do there. But not all log file analysis programs offer such a report.

Log files and reports generated from them will help you assess the impact of your promotional efforts. You can tell, for example, how many visitors are arriving directly from Yahoo!. If there aren't any, it's time to make sure that you're listed there. Yahoo! is one of the largest sources of traffic for many sites, but they tend to be less than expeditious in adding new listings.

By noting which sites your visitors come from, you can visit the referring sites and scout them out. Perhaps they cover a related subject matter, with forums and or related link lists. If so, those are places you should be frequenting.

To verify your promotional efforts are working, compare your traffic reports for the period before your last promo effort against postcampaign reports. The numbers should be going up. You might even recognize where the additional traffic is coming from. And if you don't see any change, it may be time to switch to alternate promotional methods.

## TAKE NOTE

### WHICH TRACKING SOFTWARE?

Choosing analysis software doesn't require spending hours gathering product information and then comparing features and costs. Ziff-Davis has already done that. All you need to do is read their results at **http://www.zdnet.com/products/content/pcmg/1705/281511.html**.

**CROSS-REFERENCE**
For more on Web hosting services, see Chapter 17.

**FIND IT ONLINE**
Discover the accuracy of Web-traffic statistics at **http://www.zdnet.com/intweek/print/970317/inwk0027.html**.

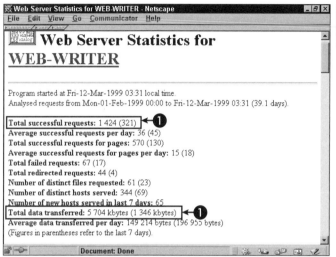

❶ *Learn to properly interpret your site's statistics. Look at the bytes served (5.7MB) and number of pages requested (1421) shown on this report.*

❷ *The Request Report section shows that* .gif *and* .css *files, which are often included in more than one Web page, were the target of many of these requests.*

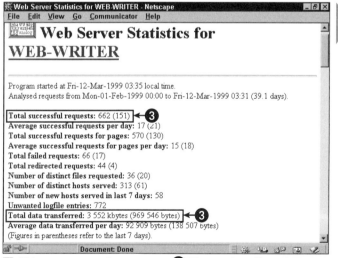

⬛ *This report covers the identical time period, with requests for graphics files excluded from the totals.*

❸ *The number of http requests has fallen to 662. The number of bytes served shows a corresponding drop.*

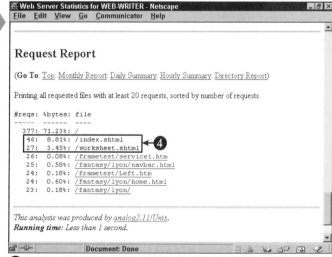

❹ *The Request Report shows that server-parsed HTML files (*.shtml*) were the targets of those requests.*

# Incorporating Advertising and Banners

The rectangular advertisements that appear at the top of virtually every Web site are called banner ads. Clicking on a banner brings the user to the advertiser's Web site. Because banners are prominently placed, and more interesting than a plain hyperlink, they can prove a good way to lure visitors to your site.

At the heart of banner advertising is what's called the "click-through rate." It's the number of times someone actually clicks on the ad and comes to your site divided by the number of times the banner is displayed. Usually these rates are under four percent — often two percent or lower. That means for every 100 times your banner is displayed, only two to four people will decide to visit your site. Another term you'll run across is "impressions." An impression is a display of your banner, whether or not anyone clicks on it.

Banner advertising can be purchased, but it's not the only way to land space for your cyber-billboard on someone else's site. A bevy of banner exchanges have sprung up on the Net. When you sign up for an exchange, you agree to display banners from other exchange members in return for having them display yours.

Rarely is the exchange ratio 1:1. It's more often 2:1 — for every two banners you display, yours will be displayed once. In a banner exchange it's rare to have any control over where you banner will appear. Although most exchanges promise to exclude banners and sites featuring "adult" content, there's no promise that the ad for your certification site won't be shown on someone else's recipe site.

Purchasing advertising space allows you to choose where your banner will appear. You can place it on sites that draw the same type of people who are likely to be interested in your site. Some purchase arrangements are based on actual click-throughs, but many charge per thousand impressions (CPM) of your banner. The click-through rate is likely to be higher with targeted purchase than with exchanges, but then so is the price tag.

Another option is to swap advertising with other sites that are similar to your own. This can be a good way to consistently reach your target market and still avoid purchasing space.

Banner ads can be created with any drawing program that supports the GIF file format. Special banner creation software, like the GIF Construction Set, makes it simple to add attention-getting animation. There are many artists on the Web who specialize in creating advertising banners.

## TAKE NOTE

### ▶ BANNER STANDARDS

Sites and exchanges have specific dimension and file size requirements your banner will have to comply with. The most standard size is 400 pixels wide by 40 pixels high. Using utilities available on the Web, it's possible to compress GIF files to help meet size requirements.

## CROSS-REFERENCE

For more information about images and HTML, see Chapter 2.

## FIND IT ONLINE

Web Site Banner Advertising (**http://www. markwelch.com/bannerad**) contains loads of banner advertising resources.

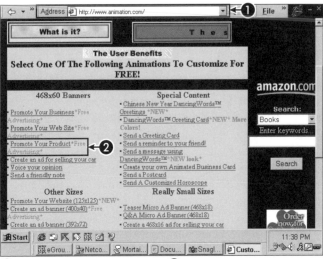

❶ Create an animated banner online in under five minutes by going to the animation. com home page.

❷ Select Promote Your Web Site from the menu.

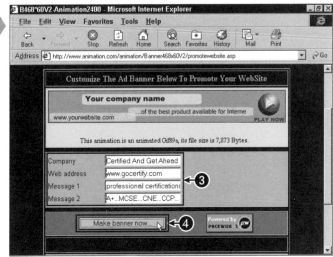

❸ Fill in your company name, home page URL, and message lines.

❹ Click the "Make banner now" button.

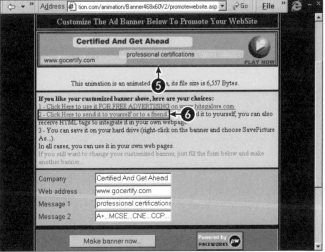

❺ Wait about 30 seconds and your banner will appear.

❻ Click the "send it to a friend" link.

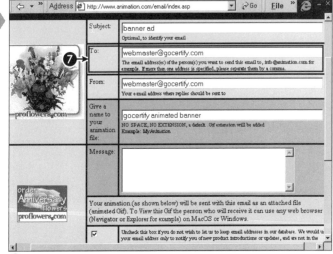

❼ Fill in the form with your own email address in the to field.

■ Click Send. The banner will arrive in your email box ready to use!

# Conducting Market Research

Designing your site by instinct is all well and good, and you might even end up with a successful site. But why risk it? By performing a little up-front research, you can discover what features your visitors are likely to value and have your site design on target from day one. Learning from other people's mistakes is usually less painful than learning from your own.

The goal of your research is to determine what members of your target market like and want. Is arcane but essential information the thing that gets them smiling at the keyboard? Do they thirst for interaction with peers? Or do they prefer nothing but the facts, thank you very much.

Begin with the search engines. Visit Yahoo! and search using key words that members of your target market might use. Use Boolean operators such as OR and AND to include specific words in your search. For example, if your site is for tropical fish enthusiasts, use "tropical fish AND raising." Play around with different keywords and see what comes up.

You're looking for Web sites, forums, and newsgroups. Visit any site that looks promising. Does it appear to be a popular spot for the people you're trying to reach? If so, try to determine why. What features does it offer? Is there a heavily used message board (or conversely, an empty one)? What is the navigation between pages like? Are there subject-specific classified ads? Lots of articles? Things to download?

Don't just focus on what's good about these sites. Look for shortcomings as well. What sets the heavily trafficked sites apart from the uninhabited ones? Does your target market seem to prefer casual, humor-packed sites, or more formal settings? Do graphics seem to draw them, or is text the thing? When you've exhausted what one search engine has to offer, check out at least two others to see what you can find there.

Web sites you find through a search engine will usually provide you with a direct path to the best sites in your genre. Look for link pages, especially those that include descriptions or ratings in addition to hyperlinks.

Your research should also include newsgroups, discussion lists, and forums related to your subject area. Reading the postings on such resources will help you keep your fingers on the pulse of your target market. Bookmark any good finds so you can revisit them regularly.

Keep an eye out for Web sites that might want to swap banners with you, exchange links, or participate in some other mutually beneficial arrangement. You'll mostly be studying your competitors, but if you keep your eyes open, you just might find some partners along the way.

## TAKE NOTE

### ▶ RESEARCH SHORTCUTS

Going through the major search engines one at a time can quickly get tedious. Another option is to use one of the meta-search sites. Meta-search engines will submit your query to numerous search engines, and collate the results for you.

**CROSS-REFERENCE**

For more on catering to your visitors, see Chapter 5.

**FIND IT ONLINE**

An index of meta-search engines can be found at http://guide-p.infoseek.com/Topic/META_search_engines.

## Market-Research Checklist

When you conduct your market research, you should start with a thorough knowledge of your audience. Who do you want to visit your page? What kinds of things do you think they'll be interested in? Here's a list of ways to find related sites to help you decide how to design your Web page, and what kinds of partnerships to create.

There's a difference between commercial and non-commercial sites. Depending on your own site, commercial sites may be competitors. Noncommercial sites rarely compete directly with each other. However, a commercial site is more likely to have more traffic, and there's more potential for powerful partnerships with commercial sites.

▶ List all the keywords associated with your subject matter.

▶ Search for those keywords in a search engine. Visit the first ten sites returned.

▶ Look for visitor counters on the Web pages returned. Estimate how many users visit in a typical month.

▶ Visit any forums or chat rooms on the site. Warning signs: no one's posted in a month, or the chat room is empty.

▶ If several sites have unused community-oriented features (like chat rooms and forums), your audience might not be interested.

▶ Look for heavy repositories of text and information. Some audiences are just interested in how-to information.

▶ "Related Links" pages often have sites that have set up reciprocal links, or that are related to the subject matter. Visit those links for further research.

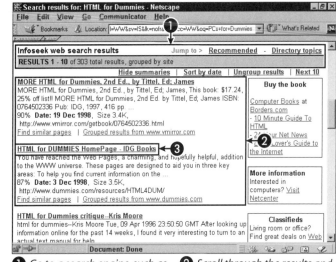

**1** *Go to a search engine, such as* **http://www.go.com**.

■ *Enter keywords members of your target market might use and click the search button.*

**2** *Scroll through the results and read the descriptions.*

**3** *Select a site to visit and click on its hyperlink.*

■ *The HTML for Dummies site is a commercial site targeting beginning Web authors.*

# Leveraging Partnerships

There's competition among Web sites, but there's also a great deal of cooperation. After all, with few exceptions, Webmasters are largely after the same thing: more traffic. A partnership can help both sites get what they want.

The most common type of partnership is link swapping: You provide a link to the other Webmaster's site and he or she adds one to yours. When you find a site that you want to exchange links with, send them an email describing why their visitors would benefit from a link to your site. Explain how your site provides resources that complement the other site's content. Suggest where your link would best fit on the other site; otherwise, it may get buried on a page that never gets visited.

Although some sites may be willing to link to you without qualification, most will expect a mutual arrangement. Acknowledge that you're willing to offer a reciprocal link (or that you have already done so).

Swapping banners or links isn't without drawbacks. Every outside link you add to your site is an invitation for your visitors to leave. You can partially alleviate this problem by coding the links so that the referenced site is opened in a new window. Your own site will still be displayed in its current window. This is accomplished by adding the `target` attribute to your link code. For example:

```
<a href="http://www.gocertify.com" target = "outside">Get Certified And Get Ahead</a>
```

will open a new browser window and load the **www.gocertify.com** page into it. The name "outside" will be associated with the new window. If you add another link that references outside, it will reuse that window.

You can also code "outside" (or any other target name) as the default target for all links on a page. To do this, use the `<BASE>` element. Place it in the `<HEAD>` section of the page, like this:

```
<base href="outside">
```

Then, if you have links on the page that you don't want to open in the same window rather than the one named outside, use the `target` attribute "_top" as in:

```
<a href="http://www.gocertify.com/
bookstore.html" target = "_top">
Visit the book store</a>
```

Another type of partnership involves content sharing. For example, DICE, a computer jobs site, has a job search form that Webmasters can customize and include on their own sites. When visitors enter job specifications and click Submit, a script accesses the DICE database, retrieves jobs that match the query, and displays the results on the query site's customized results page. DICE gets extra traffic to its jobs database, and the query site gets to provide job searching without creating and maintaining the database behind it. This same technique can be used with classified ads and search functions.

---

### TAKE NOTE

▶ **SUPPLY GRAPHICS**

Create several small graphics featuring your site's logo, and offer them to your link partners. They're more eye-catching than plaintext links, and add a little pizzazz to your partner's site, too.

---

**CROSS-REFERENCE**

For more about forms and their uses, see Chapter 8.

**FIND IT ONLINE**

Search the Reciprocal Link Bank (**http://www.duban.com/bio/linkbank/**) for sites to exchange links with.

## Listing 23-4: `<Base>` Elements in Link Exchanges

```
<HEAD>
<TITLE>Links to Speech Recognition
Sites</TITLE>
<BASE target="new_window"> ◄—❶
</HEAD>                  ❷
<BODY>
<P><A HREF="http://www.voicerecognition.com">
  voicerecognition.com</A>
<P><A HREF="http://www.talk-
systems.com">Talking
  Technologies</A>
</BODY>
```

❶ Insert the `<BASE>` element in the `<HEAD>` section.

❷ Make sure the target is a window or frame with an unused name.

❶ This site uses a form to query a database on another Web site.

❷ It also provides a simple link to a second job search site.

## Listing 23-5: `target` Attributes in Link Management

```
<HEAD>
<TITLE>Links to Speech Recognition Sites</TITLE>
<BASE target="new_window">
</HEAD>
<BODY>
<P><A HREF="http://www.voicerecognition.com">
  voicerecognition.com</A>
<P><A HREF="http://www.talk-systems.com">Talking
  Technologies</A>
<P><A HREF="http://www.scottrell.com/Speech/
  articles.html" target="_top">Speech Recognition
  Articles</A></BODY>    └❸
```

❸ Modify links you don't want to open into a new window by adding the `target="_top"` attribute.

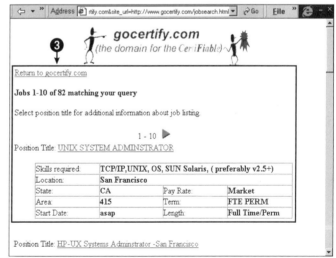

❸ Results of the form job query are displayed on an HTML page on the querying site.

# Using Online Communities and Content

One of the best ways to build traffic at your Web site is to create a virtual community that visitors can join. The key feature of an online community is interaction among visitors. Often, they will be able to provide each other with expert advice, support, and information that you can't. The Webmaster's job is to facilitate the process.

For visitors to interact, they need places to do it. Two common options are chat rooms and message boards. Both can be added to your site with little administrative work. If you can tolerate some advertising, there are businesses that will host your chat and discussion areas at no charge. All you have to do is sign up for the service and paste a little HTML into your Web pages. Some Web design programs, such as Microsoft FrontPage 2000, include templates for creating and managing message boards.

There are two main differences between chat rooms and message boards: response time and archiving. A chat room is a place that site visitors can gather to "talk" with each other in real time. Each chat participant sees a divided screen. Conversations scroll through the top part as they occur. The bottom part includes a text box and a Send button. To join the discussion, the user types in his or her message and hits Send. The message will appear in the top portion of all participants' screens. Anyone who wants to respond can do so immediately. Messages that scroll off the top of the screen disappear; people who aren't present won't get to read the discussion later.

Message boards (sometimes called forums or discussion boards), on the other hand, allow time-delayed conversations. A message is posted, other visitors sign on and read whichever messages interest them, and post a reply if they have one. Past messages remain on the board. Visitors can browse messages and replies in any order, at their leisure.

Remember to provide a way for visitors to interact with you, as well. Provide a prominently located form or link for suggestions, comments, and bug reports. This enables them to tell you what they want so that you can deliver it.

Another key to getting and keeping traffic seems obvious, but is often overlooked: provide useful and fresh content. Visitors who encounter dead links and old news are not likely to return. However, if they encounter fresh content and current information, chances are they'll be back. It's too easy to let site maintenance fall by they wayside, so create a schedule for regular updates, link checks, and enhancements, and adhere to it.

## TAKE NOTE

### CHOOSE YOUR CHAT-ROOM SERVICE CAREFULLY

Although all of the free services will include advertising — that's how they pay for themselves — some incorporate so many blinking, disruptive ads that your users will become annoyed and their browsers may even crash.

**CROSS-REFERENCE**

For information on developing a unique Web site, see Chapter 22.

**FIND IT ONLINE**

Use Site Inspector (**http://www.siteinspector.com/**) to examine and report on your site's search engine readiness.

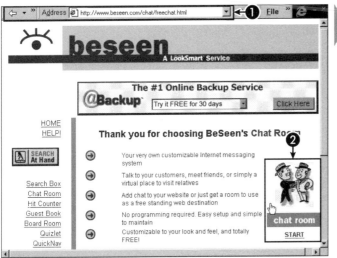

① *To add a free beseen.com chat room to your Web site, begin by going to its Web site.*

② *Click START.*

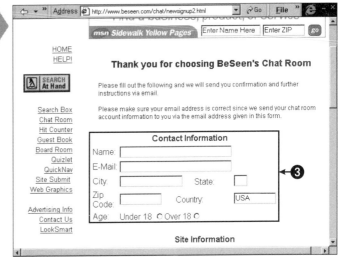

❸ *Fill in the contact information.*

■ *Add your URL, title, description, and content rating.*

■ *Select the categories that best describe your site.*

■ *Read the signup agreement and type **YES** to agree to them. Click the Accept Options button.*

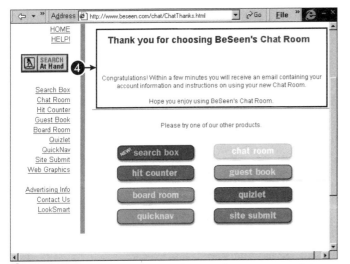

❹ *A confirmation page appears and an email message containing instructions and HTML to add to your Web page will be sent to the email address you entered.*

### Listing 23-6: BeSeen.com Sample Code

```
<!- Begin Beseen.com Button Link ->
<a href="http://pluto.beseen.com/chat/rooms/
    q/10320">
Chat Now </a>
<a href="http://www.beseen.com/b-index.html"
    target="_top">
<img src="http://www.beseen.com/images/
    beseenbutton.gif align=absmiddle height=31
    width=88 alt="Beseen.com"></a>
<!- End Beseen.com Button Link ->
```

▲ *You'll receive an email with code similar to this. Paste it into your Web page wherever you want to include the Chat button.*

# Personal Workbook

## Q&A

**1** Which two <META> tags will help search engines index your site?

_____

_____

_____

**2** Name three ways you can partner with other Webmasters to build traffic.

_____

_____

_____

**3** Why isn't total hit count an accurate measure of Web site traffic?

_____

_____

_____

**4** How is a chat room different from a forum?

_____

_____

_____

**5** What is a _discussion list_ and why might you want to create one?

_____

_____

_____

**6** Name four things you can learn from your site's log files.

_____

_____

_____

**7** What is a _search engine spider_?

_____

_____

_____

**8** How can you tell how successful a competitor's Web site is?

_____

_____

_____

ANSWERS: PAGE 450

## EXTRA PRACTICE

1. Open one of your Web pages and optimize its title.

2. Add a keywords <META> tag to the page.

3. Add a description <META> tag to the page.

4. Modify external links on the page to open in a different browser window.

5. Submit the page to a search engine.

6. Surf the Web and identify three traffic-building partnership opportunities.

## REAL-WORLD APPLICATIONS

✔ You get your site listed with search engines. People looking for the content you offer will be able to find it.

✔ You create a community at your Web site. Communities add value and bring visitors back again and again.

✔ You partner with other Webmasters. Now your site features job searching and classified advertising without you having to administer them yourself.

✔ You analyze your log files. Now you can tell that your partnership with another site isn't producing any traffic and should be reconsidered.

## Visual Quiz

What changes would you make to this Web page to improve its position in search engine results?

_____

_____

_____

_____

_____

_____

```
index.html - Notepad
File  Edit  Search  Help
<HTML>
<HEAD>
  <TITLE>
    ACE
  </TITLE>
</HEAD>
<BODY>

<H1 align="center">Awesome Computer Experts (ACE)</H1>
<P>
<P>We are a consulting firm featuring the top gurus in firewall, IT auditing,

<UL>
  <LI>needs assessment</LI>
  <LI>specification and RFCs</LI>
  <LI>implementation</LI>
  <LI>analysis &amp; design</LI>
  <LI>system security analysis</LI>
  <LI>other consulting</LI>
</UL>
</BODY>
</HTML>
```

# Appendix A:
# Personal Workbook Answers

## Chapter 1

see page 4

**❶ What's the difference between an element and an attribute?**

**A:** An attribute defines the properties for an element.

**❷ Do you always need a closing tag for all elements?**

**A:** No. Some elements are "empty" and do not need to be closed.

**❸ Does any information from the `<HEAD>` element appear on the Web page?**

**A:** No. Only the `<TITLE>` element appears in the Web browser, but not on the page itself.

**❹ How often should you repeat provocative words and phrases, such as "XXX, nudity, videogames" in your `<META>` elements?**

**A:** Never. Unless your site is actually about those topics, or you like receiving hateful e-mail.

**❺ Is it acceptable to include keywords in a `<META>` element that do not appear on the current page, but on other pages within the site?**

**A:** Yes. Don't overdo it, but you can and should include keywords that describe your entire site.

**❻ Which one is an inline element, `<DIV>` or `<SPAN>`?**

**A:** `<SPAN>` is an inline element. `<DIV>` is a block element.

**❼ Do across-site headers and footers add anything valuable to a document's structure?**

**A:** Yes, the user visually reading the site can identify that he or she is still on the same Web site, but the structure is entirely visual, not contextual.

**❽ True or False: You should never use elements that only provide visual markup to the page.**

**A:** False. Use contextual elements when you can and make sure your site is readable to everyone, but don't sacrifice clarity and impact for universality.

### Visual Quiz

**Q:** This Web page is not the home page for the site. What kind of `<META>` elements would you expect to see in the `<HEAD>`, if any? Is this site designed for style or substance? Would you expect to be able to read this site with a text-only browser?

**A:** `<META name="description" content="An article on web design issues for visually-impaired audiences"><META name="keywords" content="web design, web authoring, visually impaired, blind, speech recognition, text-to-speech">` Because it is content-oriented, the site is designed for substance, not style. It should be readable with a text-only Web browser.

# Appendix A: Personal Workbook Answers

## Chapter 2

see page 16

**❶ How do you include a title in the `<HEAD>` section?**

**A:** Enclose it in the `<TITLE>` `</TITLE>` elements.

**❷ What is the link anchor element?**

**A:** `<A>` is the anchor element; `<A href="page.html">` will link to another page.

**❸ How do you include a background graphic?**

**A:** Include `background="image.gif"` in the `<BODY>` element.

**❹ How many heading levels are there?**

**A:** Six. Levels 1–3 are usually larger size font, and 4–6 are usually smaller font (the "fine print").

**❺ In the `<IMG>` element, `height` and `width` are measured in what units?**

**A:** Pixels.

**❻ What does the `<HR>` element do?**

**A:** It adds a horizontal rule line across the page, and creates a new paragraph break.

**❼ Name two accessibility issues discussed in this chapter.**

**A:** Headings and text-to-speech readers; use the `alt` attribute in graphics; colors can be turned off or customized by the user; colorblind users.

**❽ What element do you put at the top of your HTML document?**

**A:** The `<DOCTYPE>` element: `<!DOCTYPE HTML PUBLIC "-//W3C//DTD HTML 4.0//EN" "http://www.w3.org/TR/REC-html40/strict.dtd">`

## Visual Quiz

**Q:** Write out the HTML code required to produce the Web page to the right. Who is the audience for this page? What would you expect to see linked from here?

**A:**

```
<HTML>
<HEAD>
<TITLE>S. Cottrell Bryant Home Page</TITLE>
</HEAD>
<BODY BGCOLOR="#FFFFFF">
<HR>
<H1>Welcome!</H1>
<IMG SRC="images/speechrec.gif" ALT="Click
here for the Speech Recognition Web Site"
ALIGN=Right>
<P>I'm Stephanie Cottrell Bryant, a freelance
technical and business writer specializing in
web-ready words and personable prose. Please
step inside and have a look around my web
site.
   You'll find some information about me and my
work, <A HREF="resume.html">my
resume</A>,(with links to some <A
HREF="resume.html#worksamples"> work
samples</A>, and <A HREF=#contact>my
contact information</A>.</P>
<P>That said, let the tour begin!</P>
<HR>
</BODY>
</HTML>
```

The audience for this page is potential clients of a professional tech writer. There should be links to the resume, work samples, contact information, and possibly links to technical and business writing resources.

# APPENDIX A: PERSONAL WORKBOOK ANSWERS

## Chapter 3

see page 36

**①** How would you put text into a foreign language font that you knew your users would have installed?

**A:** `<FONT face="Cyrillic">Put Text Here.</FONT>`

**②** How do you include a trademark symbol on a Web page?

**A:** Use the `&#153;` character code.

**③** What are the three types available in unordered lists?

**A:** A disc, square, or circle.

**④** Can you nest different types of lists?

**A:** Yes, but be sure to close each list.

**⑤** How do you change the starting value of an ordered list?

**A:** Use the `start` attribute in the `<OL>` element, or the `value` attribute in the first `<LI>` element.

**⑥** Name the two ways to cite sources in HTML 4.0 quotations.

**A:** The `<CITE>` element within the document itself, and the `cite` attribute in the `<Q>` or `<BLOCKQUOTE>` elements.

**⑦** How would you display a fragment of code within a paragraph?

**A:** `<CODE>fragment</CODE>`

**⑧** What's the difference between Emphasis (`<EM>`) and Italic (`<I>`) text?

**A:** Emphasis is a significant element, meaning to add emphasis to the text. Italics are purely visual.

## Visual Quiz

**Q:** What elements are evident on this page? How else could you display this information? Is this the most effective way to show these samples?

**A:** There are three lists on the page: an ordered list, a definition list, and a nested ordered list. You could display the definition list in a table, and the Membership Committee Notes in a hyperlinked table of contents. This is the most efficient way to produce this information, because it requires the least amount of download and display time.

## Chapter 4

see page 54

**①** How do you create a table without a border?

**A:** `<TABLE border=0>`

**②** How many columns are in a table?

**A:** As many as you put into it, but there must be one cell (or enough spanning cells) for each column in each row.

**③** What is *cell spanning*?

**A:** Cell spanning increases the size of the cell by one cell either vertically (`rowspan`) or horizontally (`colspan`).

**④** How do you create a table heading?

**A:** Use the `<TH>` element instead of the `<TD>` for the cell elements. You can also create a row group called `<THEAD>`.

**⑤** Why would you not use the `<COLGROUP>` element?

**A:** Column groups are only fully supported in Internet Explorer 4.0.

# APPENDIX A: PERSONAL WORKBOOK ANSWERS

**6** How do you change the width of a table or its columns?

**A:** Use the `width` attribute: `width` can be defined in pixels or percentage of the browser window.

**7** Why should you use a `summary` attribute, and where?

**A:** The `summary` attribute is like the `alt` attribute in an `<IMG>` element; it provides an alternative for non-graphical browsers. It belongs in the opening `<TABLE>` tag, and its value is a sentence or two to sum up the table's contents.

**8** What's the difference between `align` and `valign`, and what are their respective values?

**A:** `Align` is used for horizontal alignment, and takes the values `left`, `right`, and `center`. `Valign` aligns elements vertically, with the values `top`, `bottom`, `middle` (centered), and `baseline`.

## Visual Quiz

**Q:** What are some design issues with this page? How did the author create it? Identify each table, and any special formatting you see in the table. (Hint: there are nested tables on this page.) When you're done, go to http://www.campdownunder.com/facilities97.html and view the source code.

**A:** The page has a lot of information — too much to be displayed in one long list. The author used tables and cell colors to create a simple display.

# Chapter 5

see page 68

**1** Name two common barriers to accessibility for older users.

**A:** Vision and mobility; older users may not be able to see as well, and may have difficulty using a mouse.

**2** What are the benefits of designing for an intranet?

**A:** The audience is very focused and defined, and you know what hardware and software they're likely to use.

**3** What are the drawbacks of an intranet?

**A:** Information must be quickly accessible. Users will not spend time searching on the intranet for information.

**4** How many Web browsers should you test your Web page on?

**A:** As many as you can get your hands on. At a minimum, you should test it on three browsers.

**5** What's a low-bandwidth alternative to graphics?

**A:** Text with styles or other formatting markup.

**6** Name one problem with animated graphics.

**A:** Distracting, potentially dangerous to epileptics, often confusing.

**7** How can you encourage users to respond to your site?

**A:** Feedback forms, chat rooms, on-line forums, and contests.

**8** What's one of the first steps in designing your Web site?

**A:** Identify the audience and what you want to tell them.

## Visual Quiz

**Q:** Who's the audience for this Web page? What will filling in the form do? What would you change on this site to encourage people to use this service? Would paid advertising work on a site like this?

**A:** The audience for this page consists of new parents and people looking for new baby announcements in the Denver area. Filling in the search form lets you look for a baby announcement, which will include the baby's name, parents' names, birth date, time, and weight. It

# APPENDIX A: PERSONAL WORKBOOK ANSWERS

may also include a picture of the new infant. To encourage people to use the service, you might include a form on the first page for people to fill in with their baby's information. Targeted advertising would work very well on a site like this: the audience is very narrow and well defined.

## Chapter 6

**1** **What are the three graphic file formats that can be used on the Web?**

**A:** GIF, JPEG, and PNG.

**2** **When is a JPEG preferable to a GIF?**

**A:** JPEGs are preferable to GIFs when using complex images, such as photographs.

**3** **What Paint Shop Pro tools might you use to select part of an image?**

**A:** Use the pointer to select part of an image.

**4** **How do you select foreground and background colors in Paint Shop Pro?**

**A:** Use the Color Palette, on the right-hand side of the window.

**5** **What are the three values that define a color?**

**A:** Red, green, and blue values define a color.

**6** **Name three ways you can reduce the download time for an image.**

**A:** Use the appropriate file type (GIF or JPEG), reduce the number of colors used, reduce the image resolution, increase the compression (JPEG only).

**7** **What are the three shapes you can use to define a hot spot in an image map?**

**A:** Rectangles, circles, and polygon shapes are available in image maps.

**8** **What are the advantages and disadvantages of client-side image maps vis-à-vis server-side image maps?**

**A:** Client-side image maps load faster and run without server interaction, but they are browser- and platform-dependent.

### Visual Quiz

**Q:** Identify at least ten of the tools in the Paint Shop Pro Tool Palette.

**A:** Pointer, Zoom, Scale, Move, Shape Select, Freehand Select, Magic Wand, Eyedropper, Paintbrush, Clone Brush, Color Replacer, Retouch, Eraser, Picture Tube, Airbrush, Paintcan (Fill), Text, and Line.

## Chapter 7

**1** **What's the first step in developing your frame?**

**A:** Identify your target audience. Design the frameset. Create a frameset.

**2** **What standard HTML element is not used in a frameset?**

**A:** The <BODY> element.

**3** **How do you create alternate text for a frameset?**

**A:** Place text to show nonframes browsers inside the <NOFRAME> element.

**4** **What attributes are required in a <FRAME> element?**

**A:** The src and name attributes are required in all <FRAME> elements.

**5** **How can you adjust the frame's border and resizing ability?**

**A:** Use the frameborder attribute to make it adjustable or to set its width.

# Appendix A: Personal Workbook Answers

**6** **What HTML element should you use to target hyperlinks in one frame to another frame?**

**A:** `<FRAME target="target_name">`

**7** **What does the `_top` reserved name mean?**

**A:** The `_top` reserved name opens a frame into the entire browser window, replacing all open framesets.

**8** **What happens when a hyperlink target cannot find the named frame?**

**A:** It opens a new window and names it with the unrecognized name.

## Visual Quiz

**Q:** How was this frameset created? What design elements do you see in it? How would you design it differently?

**A:** This frameset uses a two-column frameset. The left-hand navigation bar has two scroll bars but no borders, and the right-hand content frame has a scroll bar as well. This page could be redesigned so that the navigation frame doesn't require scroll bars, for a cleaner look. Navigation links could also be in a horizontal frame on the top or bottom of the site.

## Chapter 8

see page 128

**1** **What kinds of information would you need in a user feedback form?**

**A:** Name, email address, comments and opinions.

**2** **How do you protect your customers' data and let them know you're protecting them?**

**A:** Have a privacy policy that outlines how customer data will be used, and follow it.

**3** **What does the `action` attribute do? What's its value?**

**A:** The `action` attribute determines how the data will be sent to the server; its value is either "GET", "POST "or, "PUT."

**4** **What's the difference between POST and GET?**

**A:** POST sends data to be written to a file on the server, while GET pulls data from the server.

**5** **How do you create a drop-down box?**

**A:** `<SELECT name="itemselect"><OPTION value="item1">Item 1.`

**6** **How do you create a text box? What are the types of text wrapping available?**

**A:** `<TEXTAREA name="textarea1" cols="10" rows="10" wrap="VIRTUAL"></TEXTAREA>`. You can use `"Virtual"`, `"Off"`, and `"Physical"` text wrap.

**7** **Name two ways to gather multiple-choice data.**

**A:** Use a radio button or a checkbox.

**8** **How do you use a graphic instead of a submit button?**

**A:** `<INPUT type="Image" src="image.gif">`

## Visual Quiz

**Q:** How would you have designed this form differently? What form elements are obvious? How did the designer create each visible field?

**A:** This form uses the `<PRE>` element to make the form elements line up. That's unnecessary for the form, which could use a layout table to achieve the same effect. The text input fields are the most obvious elements in the form here. They were created using `<INPUT TYPE=Text NAME="fieldname" SIZE="100">`. The radio buttons use `<INPUT TYPE=Radio NAME="MailingList" VALUE="no" CHECKED>`. The checkbox uses `<INPUT TYPE=Checkbox NAME="Contact" VALUE="Contact">`.

# APPENDIX A: PERSONAL WORKBOOK ANSWERS

## Chapter 9

see page 144

**1** What are three uses for the `<META>` element?

**A:** The `<META>` element can automatically refresh the page, provide information to search engines, and play background sound files.

**2** When and why do you need special character entities?

**A:** Special characters are used for foreign language sites, symbols, and mathematical notation.

**3** Name three ways to incorporate sound files into your Web page.

**A:** Use the `<EMBED>` element, a `<META>` element to play a background sound, or a plug-in.

**4** Name two popular plug-in programs.

**A:** RealAudio, Shockwave, QuickTime, and Acrobat Reader.

**5** Name three ways to incorporate mathematical notation into your Web page.

**A:** Use a mathematics plug-in, `<CODE>` elements, graphics, and Math ML.

**6** Name at least one possible disadvantage to incorporating multimedia into your site, and how to overcome it.

**A:** Multimedia files are sometimes hard to create, but you can hire someone to do it for you, or buy multimedia clips ready-made.

**7** What is internationalization, and what is localization? How do they differ?

**A:** Internationalization is making your site accessible to other languages and cultures. Localization means making your site accessible to a specific locale (using language, culture, dialect, and idioms).

**8** How do you automatically redirect a user from one Web page to another?

**A:** `<META HTTP-EQUIV=REFRESH CONTENT="A;` `URL="http://www.mydomain.com ">`

### Visual Quiz

**Q:** Try creating a `<META>` element with keywords for the site shown in the figure using standard `<META>` tags. Then, check the site on the Web and view the actual keywords used.

**A:**

```
<META NAME="Description" CONTENT="A speech
  recognition site for writers and people
  purchasing speech recognition products.">
<META NAME="Keywords" CONTENT="Speech
  Recognition, Speech Recognition, Voice
  Recognition, Dragon NaturallySpeaking, IBM
  SimplySpeaking, IBM ViaVoice, Speech
  Recognition purchase">
```

## Chapter 10

see page 166

**1** How do you install additional Internet Explorer components?

**A:** Go to Microsoft's Web site and use the AutoInstall program.

**2** What's the History button and what does it do?

**A:** The History button opens a list of sites you've been to in the last several days.

**3** What's the quickest way to enter the URL for Yahoo!'s site?

**A:** Type **yahoo** in the Location bar.

# Appendix A: Personal Workbook Answers

**④** **What search options are built into Internet Explorer and Outlook Express?**

**A:** Web page searches are included in Internet Explorer and people searches are in Outlook Express.

**⑤** **What is an *active channel*?**

**A:** An active channel is a Web page that uses "server push" to automatically update the page as needed.

**⑥** **How do you change the background wallpaper in Active Desktop?**

**A:** Go to the Display Control Panel and change the background with the Background tab.

**⑦** **Where do you add, delete, or hide your Active Desktop items?**

**A:** In the Display Control Panel, under the Web tab.

**⑧** **How or why would you change from HTML to plaintext for composing email?**

**A:** Use plaintext when sending messages to mailing lists, people you don't know, and people who don't use an HTML-compliant email reader.

## Visual Quiz

**Q:** Write out the code for this wallpaper. What Active Desktop items do you see here? What should happen when the search query is entered?

**A:**

```
<!DOCTYPE HTML PUBLIC "-//W3C//DTD HTML
4.0//EN"
  "http://www.w3.org/TR/REC-
html40/strict.dtd">
<HTML>
<HEAD>
<STYLE>
A:LINK.whitebg        {background: #FFFFFF;
  color: #000099;}
</STYLE>
```

```
  <TITLE>Garden Wallpaper</TITLE>
</HEAD>
<BODY BGCOLOR="#003300" TEXT="#FFFF00"
  LINK="#FFFFFF">
<IMG SRC="images/pinkamy.jpg" WIDTH=116
HEIGHT=592
  HSPACE=0 VSPACE=0 BORDER=0 ALT="Pink
Amaryllis"
  ALIGN="Left" style="top: 0%; left: 0%;">
<DIV style="float: right; width: 175;">
<IMG SRC="images/rose.jpg" WIDTH=160
HEIGHT=158
  BORDER=0 ALT="">
</DIV>
<P style="border: 1pt; background: #FFFFFF;
color:
  #000000;">
<!- Begin Yahoo Search Form ->
<form method="GET"
  action="http://search.yahoo.com/bin/search">
  <img src=
"http://www.yahoo.com/images/recip/1yahoo.gif"
  width=104 height=21 align=top alt="[ Yahoo!
]">
  <input type="text" name="p" value=""
size=18>
  <input type="submit" name="name">
  <font size=1>
  <a class=whitebg href=
  "http://www.yahoo.com/search.html">
  options</a>
  </font>
</form>
<!- End Yahoo Search Form ->
</P>
<P style="padding-top:4cm; padding-left:4cm;">
<IMG SRC="images/emily.jpg" WIDTH=338
HEIGHT=196
```

```
    BORDER=0 ALT="Emily Dickenson's Garden">
</P>
</BODY>
</HTML>
```

The Active Desktop items consist of the included Web page in the middle of the screen, and a usable Web page for the background. When you enter a search query, the results should open up in the background, as if you had used Yahoo!'s Web site to search for the item.

## Chapter 11

see page 188

**❶ What installation options are available in Netscape Communicator?**

**A:** Custom and Typical.

**❷ How do you view the source code in Communicator?**

**A:** Select View ➪ Source from the menu bar.

**❸ Name three ways to open a page in Netscape Navigator.**

**A:** File ➪ Open, typing the URL into the location bar, and clicking a hyperlink or bookmark.

**❹ How do you change the home page URL?**

**A:** Edit ➪ Preferences, choose Navigator, and enter the new home page.

**❺ How do you set up your preferences to not send HTML messages by default? By user?**

**A:** Select Edit ➪ Preferences and use the Formatting tab to change the default. Change the settings by user in the Address Book.

**❻ How do you file a new bookmark into a folder?**

**A:** Select Bookmarks ➪ File Bookmark ➪ FolderName.

**❼ How do you delete a bookmark?**

**A:** Select Bookmarks ➪ Edit Bookmarks. Choose the bookmark and press the Delete key.

**❽ How do you make a hyperlink in Composer?**

**A:** Select the text or image to link and click the Link button on the toolbar.

### Visual Quiz

**Q:** What elements do you see in this message in Composer? Is there a way to send the same information without using HTML? Do you think the sender knows if the recipient can receive HTML mail? What are some ways you would use HTML in mail most effectively? When would you not use it?

**A:** This Composer message uses a table, a graphic, table background and text colors, and font styles. The same information could be sent in a standard email, using an attachment to send the graphic. Since the sender is emailing her mother, she probably knows what mail client the recipient is using. You could use HTML to send hyperlinks, graphics, lists, and tables more effectively. You should not use HTML in email when you don't know what mail program the recipient is using, or to send email to a large group of people, such as a mailing list.

# Appendix A: Personal Workbook Answers

## Chapter 12

see page 206

**1** **What are some important features in a WYSIWYG editor?**

**A:** The ability to directly edit and manipulate generated code, a reliable preview, and advanced layout tools.

**2** **What are the drawbacks to using a WYSIWYG editor?**

**A:** Most WYSIWYG editors don't promote cross-browser compatibility, and few allow you to directly edit the HTML code.

**3** **How important is a preview mode in tag-based editors?**

**A:** Preview modes are useful in tag-based editors, although you can also preview the Web page in your browser.

**4** **What other types of programs would you expect to find in a Web editing package?**

**A:** Image mappers and creators, FTP programs, site management tools, and link or HTML validation tools.

**5** **How do commercial graphics programs differ from shareware programs?**

**A:** Commercial graphics programs are usually more expensive and have advanced layers, filtering, and similar design tools.

**6** **Name one advantage of a shareware program over a commercial graphics program.**

**A:** You can try out shareware programs before you buy them. They're also less expensive. Some of the shareware graphics programs are as advanced as commercial programs.

**7** **Why is the** DOCTYPE **so important to HTML Validation tools?**

**A:** The DOCTYPE declaration tells the validator which version of HTML you're using.

**8** **When creating server-side scripts, what information will you probably need to provide?**

**A:** You'll need to know your Web server's domain, full server path, and the location of the programming language, such as Perl.

### Visual Quiz

**Q** **What kind of HTML editor is shown here? How would you create a new Web page using it? How would you include HTML elements and images? What do you like and dislike about this kind of Web editing program?**

**A:** This is a text-based HTML editor. You would create a new page with the File ➪ New menu, or by clicking the New Page icon on the toolbar. To include HTML elements and images, you must type them in directly.

## Chapter 13

see page 226

**1** **How do you create a local style sheet?**

**A:** Enclose the entire style sheet inside a <STYLE> element.

**2** **Replace the following using inline styles:** <FONT COLOR="#8B008B" SIZE=4 FACE="Arial">.

**A:** style="color: #8B008B; font-size: 4; font-family: Arial;"

**3** **What part of the box is defined by** padding?

**A:** The padding is the space between the border and the element's contents (images, text, and so on).

# Appendix A: Personal Workbook Answers

**④ What kinds of border styles can you use?**

**A:** none, dotted, dashed, solid, double, groove, ridge, inset, and outset

**⑤ How do you use a floating element?**

**A:** style="float: right;"

**⑥ How many times can you use an ID in a given document?**

**A:** You can only use an ID once in any given document.

**⑦ How do you include an external style sheet?**

**A:** <LINK rel="STYLESHEET" type="text/css" href="styles.css">

**⑧ What values does the** speak **property accept?**

**A:** normal, none, spell-out

## Visual Quiz

**Q:** What font and color properties do you see used in this page? What positioning properties? Could you produce the same effect with other layout and color elements? How?

**A:**
```
BODY { font-family: Arial; color: #0000FF;
  background: #66CCFF; }
P { text-align: left; text-indent: 10pt; }
DIV { border-color: #330066; border-width:
5pt;
  border-style: groove; margin: 5pt; width:
  200pt; position: relative; left: 100pt; }
```
The font and colors are set in the <BODY> style declaration, and the positioning is defined in both the <P> and <DIV> styles. You could achieve the same effect with <FONT> elements and tables.

# Chapter 14

see page 246

**❶ What are the key components of a well-formed XML document?**

**A:** There must be a root element and all other elements must nest properly within the structure, all text elements are enclosed in balanced tags, all attribute values are enclosed in quotes, all empty tags must either close with /> or a closing tag, and the document cannot use markup characters in the text stream.

**❷ What is an** *element declaration*?

**A:** An element declaration is a statement that identifies one item in an XML document. The declaration identifies the item by name and data type. It can also be used to create the hierarchy of elements in the XML document.

**❸ How does a DTD work?**

**A:** A DTD contains the structure information for the content.

**❹ How do you get XML onto the Web?**

**A:** Convert the XML document into HTML using a processor, or have all users view the XML with an XML-compliant browser, like Internet Explorer 5.

**❺ What's a** *channel*?

**A:** A channel is a subscription path between your readers and your Web site. Using a channel, you can automatically inform users when the Web site has been updated.

**❻ What is an** <EMPTY> **element?**

**A:** An <EMPTY> element does not contain character data. Its attributes determine its content value.

# Appendix A: Personal Workbook Answers

**7** Identify the documents used to render an XML document.

**A:** XML content document, which may contain the DTD; DTD, which may be a separate document, and XSL style sheet.

**8** What is the difference between a parsed and unparsed element?

**A:** A parsed element is understood by the XML processor or browser. It is generally character data. An unparsed element is one that is not understood by the processor. This is used for binary data, such as images, sound, and video.

## Visual Quiz

Q: Create a DTD for the document shown on the right.

**A:**
```
<Root_Element>
<Child_Element/>
<TRAVELOGUE/>
<COUNTRY>
<NAME>United States</NAME>
  </COUNTRY>
<STATE>
<NAME>Nevada</NAME>
  </STATE>
<CITY>
<NAME>Las Vegas</NAME>
  </CITY>
<DATE>
<ARRIVAL>October 23, 1998</ARRIVAL>
<DEPARTURE>October 25, 1998</DEPARTURE>
  </DATE>
<COMMENTS>The wedding was
beautiful.</COMMENTS>
</Root_Element>
```

# Chapter 15

see page 276

**1** How do you use `<META>` elements to create a new cookie?

**A:** 
```
<META HTTP-EQUIV="Set-Cookie"
content="cookievalue=HomePage;
expires=Saturday, 30-Nov-98 23:00:00
GMT; path=/cookies; domain=.domain.com">
```

**2** What security restrictions are there for cookies?

**A:** Cookies cannot write to or access files on your hard drive, except the cookie file.

**3** Name two limitations of JavaScript, deliberate or otherwise.

**A:** JavaScript has the same limitations as cookies (cannot write or access your hard drive) and is dependent on the browser to work.

**4** What method do you use to display the current date in JavaScript?

**A:** Use the `Date()` method to get the current date.

**5** What is a *script function*? How do you call one in the document body?

**A:** A function is a small script program; you call one with an event handler: `onClick=functionName()`.

**6** How do you access cookies with JavaScript?

**A:** Use the `document.cookie` object.

**7** Name two differences between JavaScript and VBScript.

**A:** VBScript is not case-sensitive, is optimized for scripting ActiveX, and has a slightly different punctuation syntax.

**8** **What attribute is required in an `<APPLET>` tag?**

**A:** The code attribute, which specifies the applet's source class, is required in all `<APPLET>` elements.

## Visual Quiz

**Q:** What scripting elements do you see in this example? Which scripting language is this script probably written in? How would you rewrite this script to make it more user friendly?

**A:** This script uses a random number generator, and a pop-up dialog box. The language is VBScript, and you could rewrite this script to have the lottery number in the Web page itself change when you click the button.

## Chapter 16

see page 294

**1** **What's the biggest different between Microsoft and Netscape's DHTML?**

**A:** Microsoft's implementation of the DOM includes the `document.all` object.

**2** **What's a *spec sheet,* and why would you create one for DHTML?**

**A:** A spec sheet provides a blueprint for programs, and may be useful for DHTML authors in planning their dynamic Web pages.

**3** **What are the `name` and `id` elements used for in Dynamic HTML?**

**A:** `name` and `id` attributes help identify objects in DHTML.

**4** **How do you dynamically change an element's style properties?**

**A:** Include
`document.all.element_id.style.propertyName = property_value` in your script.

**5** **What array would you use to switch between style sheets?**

**A:** Use `document.styleSheets[#]` to select a style sheet.

**6** **Name two arrays in Dynamic HTML.**

**A:** `applets[]`,`images[]`,`forms[]`, `styleSheets[]`,`anchors[]`,`embeds[]`,`frames[]`, `links[]`,`scripts[]`,`classes[]`,and `ids[]`.

**7** **How do you change the position of an object in DHTML?**

**A:** `document.all.objectID.style.left = 100px.` `document.all.objectID.style.top = 100px`

**8** **What parameter do you use for sorting columns in data-bound DHTML?**

**A:** To sort data records, add `<PARAM NAME="SortColumn" VALUE="ColumnName">`.

## Visual Quiz

**Q:** What DHTML elements are evident in this figure? What would you expect to happen if you put a different name in the text field? How many functions do you think this application has?

**A:** This DHTML script uses data binding to dynamically display the results of a database query. Unchecking the box removes the style sheet formatting on the name column. When you change the "Filter by Last Name" field, the page changes to reflect your filter data. This application has three functions: `highlight`, `goForward`, and `goBack`.

# Appendix A: Personal Workbook Answers

## Chapter 17

see page 308

**❶** How does Netscape implement the DOM?

**A:** Netscape's implementation does not include the `document.all` and other objects.

**❷** What arrays are available in Netscape's DOM?

**A:** `anchors[]`, `applets[]`, `classes[]`, `embeds[]`, `forms[]`, `ids[]`, `images[]`, `layers[]`, `links[]`, `plugins[]`, `tags[]`.

**❸** How would you create a layer?

**A:** Place the elements you want in the layer into a `<LAYER>` element.

**❹** What element should you use for sites that don't display layers correctly?

**A:** Use the `<NOLAYER>` element.

**❺** How do you change the style of elements inside a layer?

**A:** `document.layers[].styleProperty= propertyValue`

**❻** How do you move a layer to the right?

**A:** `document.layerID.moveBy(-100, 0)`

**❼** How do you change which layer is on top of other layers?

**A:** `document.layerID.moveAbove(otherLayerID)`

**❽** How do you include a dynamic font in a Web page?

**A:** Create a font definition file, then use `@fontdef url(http://home.netscape.com/fonts/font-file.pfr);` in your `<STYLE>` element.

## Visual Quiz

**Q:** What DHTML elements do you see present in this figure? How would you expect this page to behave? What other ways can you think of to present this information?

**A:** There are two layers in this figure. When you click on one, it brings the layer forward, covering the other layer. You could also present the information in these layers in a standard Web page.

## Chapter 18

see page 324

**❶** What three things should you determine first about a Web hosting company?

**A:** Storage space, transfer rate, and transfer speed.

**❷** How much storage space will you probably need for a basic Web site?

**A:** Less than 5MB.

**❸** What's a popular Web server setup that uses only free software?

**A:** Linux operating system with Apache Web server.

**❹** Name three important features in a collocation service?

**A:** Twenty-four-hour monitoring, adequate security systems, an immaculate environment, and a clean power supply are important factors in collocating your server.

**❺** What's the major drawback of graphical FTP programs?

**A:** It's very easy to "drag and destroy" pages, directories, even entire Web sites.

**6** How do you open an FTP connection to an FTP or Web server?

**A:** Type **open ftp.domain.com** at the FTP prompt.

**7** How would you upload all the HTML files in a directory to your Web server?

**A:** Go to the directory on the Web server and type **mput *.html.**

**8** What's the difference between ASCII and binary in FTP modes?

**A:** Use ASCII for plaintext files, and binary for everything else.

## Visual Quiz

**Q:** Which of these files is a binary file? Which ones are ASCII files? How do you download a file from this page? How would you go to the previous directory?

**A:** The file `chapt17figs.zip` is a binary file. All the other ones are ASCII files. You would download a file from this page by clicking it, or by right-clicking and choosing "Save link as …." To go up a directory, click the "Up to a higher level directory" link.

# Chapter 19

see page 346

**1** What does *CGI* stand for?

**A:** CGI stands for Common Gateway Interface.

**2** What programming languages are used in CGI?

**A:** You can use any programming language, but Perl and C are by far the most popular.

**3** Why would an API or application environment be preferable to CGI?

**A:** CGI scripts slow down the Web server; an API runs seamlessly with the server, so the overhead is minimal.

**4** Name one CGI environment variable — when or how would you use it?

**A:** `ENV{DOCUMENT_ROOT}`; use it when you want to include the document path in a script.

**5** What's the first step in writing a CGI script?

**A:** Create a spec sheet and plan out what the script will do.

**6** Where do your script's input variables come from?

**A:** Input variables usually come from a form.

**7** Name two things to look for when modifying or adapting a script.

**A:** Make sure the environment variables are correct, and that the location of the programming language is accurate.

**8** What is a *version number*?

**A:** A version number is the number of times a program has been rewritten or undergone a major revision.

## Visual Quiz

**Q:** Write a specification sheet for this form (the field names are shown inside the fields). What would you want to do with the data? Would you protect the data from unauthorized access?

**A:**

```
Name: Guestbook Form CGI Script
Date: Today   Author: You
Purpose: To take user data from a web form and
append it to the top of a guestbook file. The
value of the email field should also be made
into a hyperlink of the form
   <A HREF="mailto:email">email</A>
```

# Appendix A: Personal Workbook Answers

Fields: name, email, and comments
Files: guestform.html - submits the data to
the CGI
guestbook.cgi - performs the scripting
guestbook.html - the output file that the CGI
script will append to.
The guestform.html file should be publicly available,
but the guestbook.html page could either be protected or not, depending on if you want the whole
world to also read your guest book.

## Chapter 20

**see page 362**

**1** **What is *SSL*? What does it stand for?**

**A:** Secure Sockets Layer is the standard way to encrypt
and transfer data over the Internet.

**2** **What are some common SSL servers?**

**A:** Apache Stronghold, Netscape Commerce Server, and
Microsoft Internet Information Server.

**3** **What's the difference between 40-bit and strong
encryption?**

**A:** Forty-bit encryption can be exported, and is easily broken in a matter of days. Strong encryption takes longer
to decode.

**4** **What is a *certificate authority*?**

**A:** A certificate authority checks the identity of certificate
companies and issues an electronic certificate that
"vouches" for them.

**5** **How can you use user logins to control information
on your site?**

**A:** Require user login to prevent or monitor access to specific documents, or to track user behavior.

**6** **How do you protect a Web directory with basic
authentication?**

**A:** On UNIX, change the .htaccess file in the Web
directory.

**7** **What's *chmod*? What can you do with it?**

**A:** chmod is the UNIX program that allows you to change
permissions for individual files and directories, allowing
read, write, or execute permissions.

**8** **Where should you store your passwords?**

**A:** Store your passwords in a secure location, be it an
encrypted file on your hard drive, or a slip of paper or
notebook in a locked drawer in your office.

### Visual Quiz

**Q:** **What kinds of security features are being used in this
transaction? What assurance does the Web site owner
have that the person making the order is genuine?
What assurance does the customer have that the
company is legitimate?**

**A:** An SSL Web server is encrypting the transaction. The
Web site owner uses cookies and password-protected
pages to ensure that the person making the order is
genuine. The customer can check the server's certificate
to be sure it's genuine as well.

## Chapter 21

**see page 380**

**1** **Name one way to track visitors to your site.**

**A:** Track users with cookies, login forms, and counters.

**2** **How do you prevent users from getting bogged
down by information?**

**A:** Prevent information overload by providing consistent,
intuitive navigation and clearly identified cross-links to
help lost users find their way.

**❸ What's a "What's New!" page, and why is it important?**

**A:** A "What's New!" page shows recent changes and updates to the Web site; it's important for showing users what pages to visit next.

**❹ Name two ways to include the last modified date in a document.**

**A:** Use a server-side include, or use JavaScript.

**❺ What are some useful HTTP headers you can access?**

**A:** `LAST_MODIFIED`, `DOCUMENT_URI`, and `DATE_LOCAL`.

**❻ What's a *Web team*, and who's in it?**

**A:** A Web team is the group of Web professionals who design a Web site; there may be programmers, administrators, Web designers, and graphic artists on a Web team.

**❼ Name one way to mark a significant change to a Web page.**

**A:** You can change the version number, add a `<META>` element or comment, and add it to the What's New! page.

**❽ How would you store a Web site archive in UNIX?**

**A:** Use `tar` and `gzip` to compress and store an archive in UNIX.

## Visual Quiz

**Q:** What site tools do you see used in this page? Where would you expect a page like this to be linked? What would you expect users would use it for?

**A:** The FileSize and LastModified server-side includes are in this page. You could use a page like this for a What's New! page or for a Web site quick-navigation page. Users would use a page like this to quickly find new information and to navigation the site.

# Chapter 22

see page 396

**❶ Why might you want to minimize the use of graphics on your site?**

**A:** To keep download times short.

**❷ What are the relative advantages and disadvantages of placing a left-side navigation bar in a frame vs. in a table on the contents pages?**

**A:** A left-side navigation bar in a frame needs to be loaded only once, and thus can be an image map without too much impact on download time; however, it must fit in a limited space or have a scroll bar. When placed in a table on the contents page, it can be any length and scrolls with the contents, but it must be included in every page and downloaded with each.

**❸ Name three ways to create page headers.**

**A:** With a frame, with a table, with comments.

**❹ Name three items commonly found in page headers.**

**A:** A banner, a navigation bar, a search field, and somebody else's banner ad.

**❺ Why should you think twice — at least — before putting a scrolling banner on your site?**

**A:** Scrolling banners generally require rather large files, which can impact download time severely. They can also become an annoying distraction.

**❻ Name the most important factor affecting the file size of a scrolling banner.**

**A:** The number of frames.

**❼ How might an external style sheet help when changing the look and feel of a site?**

**A:** You can change many design elements just by editing a single file.

# APPENDIX A: PERSONAL WORKBOOK ANSWERS

**⑧** **What six aspects of your site should you review routinely when changing the site's appearance?**

**A:** Headers, footers, graphics, tables, frames, and links.

## Visual Quiz

**Q:** Identify the header on this page. Identify the navigation elements. What kinds of navigation elements are there? How is this page geared for its intended audience?

**A:** The header is "Magical World Builder's Guide," and the navigation elements consist of the navigation sidebar on the right. This page, as a long article, is very text-oriented.

## Chapter 23

see page 410

**❶** **Which two `<META>` tags will help search engines index your site?**

**A:** `<META name ="description" content = "Place your description here.">` and `<META name ="keywords" content= "keyword, key-word2, keyword3">`

**❷** **Name three ways you can partner with other Webmasters to build traffic.**

**A:** Exchange links and banners, sharing content, and contributing to community sites together.

**❸** **Why isn't total hit count an accurate measure of Web site traffic**

**A:** Hit counts measure all hits to the page, including reloading, images, included files, and so forth.

**❹** **How is a chat room different from a forum?**

**A:** A chat room is conducted in real time. People may leave a forum and return later to post messages.

**❺** **What is a *discussion list*, and why might you want to create one?**

**A:** A discussion list is an email list; people tend to interact with email more often than they do with on-Web lists and forums.

**❻** **Name four things you can learn from your site's log files**

**A:** You can learn the IP address of people requesting Web pages, browser type, time of day, and which files were requested.

**❼** **What is a *search engine spider*?**

**A:** A search engine spider is a program that follows hyperlinks across the Internet, cataloging and indexing sites on the way.

**❽** **How can you tell how successful a competitor's Web site is?**

**A:** Look for your competitors by searching for your site's category in search engines, link pages, and newsgroups.

## Visual Quiz

**Q:** What changes would you make to this Web page to improve its position in search engine results?

**A:** Add `<META>` elements to include descriptive keywords and description, a more descriptive `<TITLE>` element, and a few subheadings to help create more structure in the page.

# Appendix B:
# HTML 4 Reference

The bulk of this appendix helps you identify attributes of specific HTML elements. Elements are listed by name, and include the attributes permitted and the description of the element. Table B-1 is not a substitute for reading the rest of this book, but it will help you find a tag fast.

The rest of this appendix lists where you should look on the Web for more HTML information.

| Table B-1: HTML ATTRIBUTE REFERENCE | | |
| --- | --- | --- |
| **Element** | **Attributes Allowed** | **Description** |
| `<A>` | `charset, coords,dir,href,hreflang,id,lang,name,onblur, onclick,ondblclick,onfocus,onkeydown,onkeypress,onkeyup, onmousedown,onmousemove,onmouseout,onmouseover,onmouseup, rel,rev,shape,style,tabindex,target,title,type` | Creates an anchor for hyperlinks. |
| `<ABBR>` | `class,dir,id,lang,onclick,ondblclick,onkeydown,onkeypress, onkeyup,onmousedown,onmousemove,onmouseout,onmouseover, onmouseup,style,title` | Indicates an abbreviation. |
| `<ADDRESS>` | `class,dir,id,lang,onclick,ondblclick,onkeydown,onkeypress, onkeyup,onmousedown,onmousemove,onmouseout,onmouseover, onmouseup,style,title` | Indicates an email address block element. |
| `<APPLET>` | `align,alt,archive,class,code,codebase,height,hspace,id,name, object,style,title,vspace,width` | Inserts a Java applet. |
| `<AREA>` | `accesskey,alt,class,coords,dir,href,id,lang,nohref,onblur, onclick,ondblclick,onfocus,onkeydown,onkeypress,onkeyup, onmousedown,onmousemove,onmouseout,onmouseover,onmouseup, shape,style,tabindex,target,title` | Specifies an area on a client-side image map. |

# Appendix B: HTML 4 Reference

## Table B-1: HTML ATTRIBUTE REFERENCE

| Element | Attributes Allowed | Description |
|---|---|---|
| <B> | class, dir, id, lang, onclick, ondblclick, onkeydown, onkeypress, onkeyup, onmousedown, onmousemove, onmouseout, onmouseover, onmouseup, style, title | Bold text. |
| <BASE> | href, target | Document base URL and target. |
| <BASEFONT> | color, face, id, size | Document base font styles. |
| <BDO> | class, dir, id, lang, style, title | Bidirectional override. |
| <BIG> | class, dir, id, lang, onclick, ondblclick, onkeydown, onkeypress, onkeyup, onmousedown, onmousemove, onmouseout, onmouseover, onmouseup, style, title | Use large text. |
| <BLOCKQUOTE> | cite, class, dir, id, lang, onclick, ondblclick, onkeydown, onkeypress, onkeyup, onmousedown, onmousemove, onmouseout, onmouseover, onmouseup, style, title | Indicates a long quotation. |
| <BODY> | alink, background, bgcolor, class, dir, id, lang, link, onclick, ondblclick, onkeydown, onkeypress, onkeyup, onload, onmousedown, onmousemove, onmouseout, onmouseover, onmouseup, onunload, style, text, title, vlink | Start the document body. |
| <BR> | clear, class, id, style, title | Insert a single line break. |
| <BUTTON> | accesskey, class, dir, disabled, id, lang, name, onblur, onclick, ondblclick, onfocus, onkeydown, onkeypress, onkeyup, onmousedown, onmousemove, onmouseout, onmouseover, onmouseup, style, title, tabindex, type, value | Create a push button. |
| <CAPTION> | align, class, dir, id, lang, onclick, ondblclick, onkeydown, onkeypress, onkeyup, onmousedown, onmousemove, onmouseout, onmouseover, onmouseup, style, title | Caption text for a table. |
| <CENTER> | class, dir, id, lang, onclick, ondblclick, onkeydown, onkeypress, onkeyup, onmousedown, onmousemove, onmouseout, onmouseover, onmouseup, style, title | Center this block-level element. |
| <CITE> | class, dir, id, lang, onclick, ondblclick, onkeydown, onkeypress, onkeyup, onmousedown, onmousemove, onmouseout, onmouseover, onmouseup, style, title | Provide a citation. |

## Table B-1: HTML ATTRIBUTE REFERENCE

| Element | Attributes Allowed | Description |
|---|---|---|
| `<CODE>` | `class, dir, id, lang, onclick, ondblclick, onkeydown, onkeypress, onkeyup, onmousedown, onmousemove, onmouseout, onmouseover, onmouseup, style, title` | Inline code fragment. |
| `<COL>` | `align, char, charoff, class, dir, id, lang, onclick, ondblclick, onkeydown, onkeypress, onkeyup, onmousedown, onmousemove, onmouseout, onmouseover, onmouseup, span, style, title, valign, width` | Specifies a table column. |
| `<COLGROUP>` | `align, char, charoff, class, dir, id, lang, onclick, ondblclick, onkeydown, onkeypress, onkeyup, onmousedown, onmousemove, onmouseout, onmouseover, onmouseup, span, style, title, valign, width` | Specifies a table column group. |
| `<DD>` | `class, dir, id, lang, onclick, ondblclick, onkeydown, onkeypress, onkeyup, onmousedown, onmousemove, onmouseout, onmouseover, onmouseup, style, title` | Definition list description. |
| `<DEL>` | `cite, class, dir, id, lang, onclick, ondblclick, onkeydown, onkeypress, onkeyup, onmousedown, onmousemove, onmouseout, onmouseover, onmouseup, style, title` | Deleted text (for revision marking). |
| `<DFN>` | `class, dir, id, lang, onclick, ondblclick, onkeydown, onkeypress, onkeyup, onmousedown, onmousemove, onmouseout, onmouseover, onmouseup, style, title` | First time the term is defined. |
| `<DIR>` | `class, compact, dir, id, lang, onclick, ondblclick, onkeydown, onkeypress, onkeyup, onmousedown, onmousemove, onmouseout, onmouseover, onmouseup, style, title` | Directory listing. |
| `<DIV>` | `align, class, dir, id, lang, onclick, ondblclick, onkeydown, onkeypress, onkeyup, onmousedown, onmousemove, onmouseout, onmouseover, onmouseup, style, title` | Block-level container. |
| `<DL>` | `class, compact, dir, id, lang, onclick, ondblclick, onkeydown, onkeypress, onkeyup, onmousedown, onmousemove, onmouseout, onmouseover, onmouseup, style, title` | Definition list. |
| `<DT>` | `class, dir, id, lang, onclick, ondblclick, onkeydown, onkeypress, onkeyup, onmousedown, onmousemove, onmouseout, onmouseover, onmouseup, style, title` | Definition list term. |

# Appendix B: HTML 4 Reference

## Table B-1: HTML ATTRIBUTE REFERENCE

| Element | Attributes Allowed | Description |
|---|---|---|
| <EM> | class, dir, id, lang, onclick, ondblclick, onkeydown, onkeypress, onkeyup, onmousedown, onmousemove, onmouseout, onmouseover, onmouseup, style, title | Emphasis. |
| <FIELDSET> | class, dir, id, lang, onclick, ondblclick, onkeydown, onkeypress, onkeyup, onmousedown, onmousemove, onmouseout, onmouseover, onmouseup, style, title | Group of fields in a form. |
| <FONT> | class, color, dir, face, id, lang, size, style, title | Change font styles. |
| <FORM> | accept-charset, action, class, dir, enctype, id, lang, method, onclick, ondblclick, onkeydown, onkeypress, onkeyup, onmouse down, onmousemove, onmouseout, onmouseover, onmouseup, onreset, onsubmit, style, target, title, | Create interactive form. |
| <FRAME> | class, frameborder, id, longdesc, marginheight, marginwidth, name, noresize, scrolling, src, style, title | Create a frame (usually within a frameset). |
| <FRAMESET> | cols, class, id, onload, onunload, rows, style, title | Create a set of frames. |
| <H1-H6> | align, class, dir, id, lang, onclick, ondblclick, onkeydown, onkeypress, onkeyup, onmousedown, onmousemove, onmouseout, onmouseover, onmouseup, style, title | Headings, levels 1 through 6. |
| <HEAD> | dir, lang, profile | Document head information. |
| <HR> | align, class, id, noshade, onclick, ondblclick, onkeydown, onkeypress, onkeyup, onmousedown, onmousemove, onmouseout, onmouseover, onmouseup, size, style, title, width | Horizontal rule. |
| <HTML> | dir, lang, version | Root element. |
| <I> | , class, dir, id, lang, onclick, ondblclick, onkeydown, onkeypress, onkeyup, onmousedown, onmousemove, onmouseout, onmouseover, onmouseup, style, title | Italics. |
| <IFRAME> | align, class, frameborder, height, id, longdesc, marginheight, marginwidth, name, scrolling, src, style, title, width | Create an inline frame. |
| <IMG> | align, alt, border, class, dir, height, hspace, id, ismap, lang, longdesc, onclick, ondblclick, onkeydown, onkeypress, onkeyup, onmousedown, onmousemove, onmouseout, onmouseover, onmouseup, src, style, title, usemap, vspace, width | Insert a graphic. |

## Table B-1: HTML ATTRIBUTE REFERENCE

| Element | Attributes Allowed | Description |
|---|---|---|
| `<INPUT>` | accept, accesskey, align, alt, checked, class, dir, disabled, id, lang, maxlength, name, onblur, onchange, onclick, ondblclick, onfocus, onkeydown, onkeypress, onkeyup, onmousedown, onmousemove, onmouseout, onmouseover, onmouseup, onselect, readonly, size, src, style, title, tabindex, type, usemap, value | Form field. |
| `<INS>` | cite, class, dir, id, lang, onclick, ondblclick, onkeydown, onkeypress, onkeyup, onmousedown, onmousemove, onmouseout, onmouseover, onmouseup, style, title | Inserted text (for revisions). |
| `<ISINDEX>` | class, dir, id, lang, prompt, style, title | Same as INPUT type=text. |
| `<KBD>` | class, dir, id, lang, onclick, ondblclick, onkeydown, onkeypress, onkeyup, onmousedown, onmousemove, onmouseout, onmouseover, onmouseup, style, title | Keyboard or monospace text formatting. |
| `<LABEL>` | accesskey, class, dir, for, id, lang, onblur, onclick, ondblclick, onfocus, onkeydown, onkeypress, onkeyup, onmousedown, onmousemove, onmouseout, onmouseover, onmouseup, style, title | Label for form fields. |
| `<LEGEND>` | accesskey, align, class, dir, id, lang, onclick, ondblclick, onkeydown, onkeypress, onkeyup, onmousedown, onmousemove, onmouseout, onmouseover, onmouseup, style, title | Adds a caption to a fieldset. |
| `<LI>` | class, dir, id, lang, onclick, ondblclick, onkeydown, onkeypress, onkeyup, onmousedown, onmousemove, onmouseout, onmouseover, onmouseup, style, title, type, value | List item. |
| `<LINK>` | charset, class, dir, href, hreflang, id, lang, media, onclick, ondblclick, onkeydown, onkeypress, onkeyup, onmousedown, onmousemove, onmouseout, onmouseover, onmouseup, rel, rev, style, target, title | Creates an independent link (style sheets, scripts, and so on). |
| `<MAP>` | class, dir, id, lang, name, onclick, ondblclick, onkeydown, onkeypress, onkeyup, onmousedown, onmousemove, onmouseout, onmouseover, onmouseup, style, title | Start defining a client-side image map. |
| `<MENU>` | class, compact, dir, id, lang, onclick, ondblclick, onkeydown, onkeypress, onkeyup, onmousedown, onmousemove, onmouseout, onmouseover, onmouseup, style, title | Creates a single-column menu list. |

# APPENDIX B: HTML 4 REFERENCE

## Table B-1: HTML ATTRIBUTE REFERENCE

| Element | Attributes Allowed | Description |
|---|---|---|
| `<META>` | `content, dir, http-equiv, lang, name, scheme` | Provides information about the document. |
| `<NOFRAMES>` | `class, dir, id, lang, onclick, ondblclick, onkeydown, onkeypress, onkeyup, onmousedown, onmousemove, onmouseout, onmouseover, onmouseup, style, title` | Alternate text to display if frames are unavailable. |
| `<NOSCRIPT>` | `class, dir, id, lang, onclick, ondblclick, onkeydown, onkeypress, onkeyup, onmousedown, onmousemove, onmouseout, onmouseover, onmouseup, style, title` | Alternate content for browsers without scripting capabilities. |
| `<OBJECT>` | `align, archive, border, class, classid, codebase, codetype, dir, height, hspace, id, lang, name, onclick, ondblclick, onkeydown, onkeypress, onkeyup, onmousedown, onmousemove, onmouseout, onmouseover, onmouseup, standby, style, title, tabindex, type, usemap, vspace, width` | Embeds an object of any media type. |
| `<OL>` | `compact, class, dir, id, lang, onclick, ondblclick, onkeydown, onkeypress, onkeyup, onmousedown, onmousemove, onmouseout, onmouseover, onmouseup, start, style, title, type` | Create an ordered list. |
| `<OPTGROUP>` | `class, dir, disabled, id, label, lang, onclick, ondblclick, onkeydown, onkeypress, onkeyup, onmousedown, onmousemove, onmouseout, onmouseover, onmouseup, style, title` | Groups `<OPTION>` fields together. |
| `<OPTION>` | `class, dir, disabled, id, label, lang, onclick, ondblclick, onkeydown, onkeypress, onkeyup, onmousedown, onmousemove, onmouseout, onmouseover, onmouseup, selected, style, title, value` | Choices in `<SELECT>` fields. |
| `<P>` | `align, class, dir, id, lang, onclick, ondblclick, onkeydown, onkeypress, onkeyup, onmousedown, onmousemove, onmouseout, onmouseover, onmouseup, style, title` | Block-level paragraph. |
| `<PARAM>` | `id, name, type, value, valuetype` | Parameters for applets, objects, and so on. |
| `<PRE>` | `class, dir, id, lang, onclick, ondblclick, onkeydown, onkeypress, onkeyup, onmousedown, onmousemove, onmouseout, onmouseover, onmouseup, style, title, width` | Preformatted text style. |

## Table B-1: HTML ATTRIBUTE REFERENCE

| Element | Attributes Allowed | Description |
|---|---|---|
| `<Q>` | `class, dir, id, lang, onclick, ondblclick, onkeydown, onkeypress, onkeyup, onmousedown, onmousemove, onmouseout, onmouseover, onmouseup, style, title` | Inline quotation. |
| `<S>` | `class, dir, id, lang, onclick, ondblclick, onkeydown, onkeypress, onkeyup, onmousedown, onmousemove, onmouseout, onmouseover, onmouseup, style, title` | Strikethrough text formatting. |
| `<SAMP>` | `class, dir, id, lang, onclick, ondblclick, onkeydown, onkeypress, onkeyup, onmousedown, onmousemove, onmouseout, onmouseover, onmouseup, style, title` | Sample program or script. |
| `<SCRIPT>` | `charset, language, src, type` | Script statements and programs. |
| `<SELECT>` | `class, dir, disabled, id, lang, multiple, name, onblur, onchange, onclick, ondblclick, onfocus, onkeydown, onkeypress, onkeyup, onmousedown, onmousemove, onmouseout, onmouseover, onmouseup, size, style, title, tabindex` | Multiple-choice selection field. |
| `<SMALL>` | `class, dir, id, lang, onclick, ondblclick, onkeydown, onkeypress, onkeyup, onmousedown, onmousemove, onmouseout, onmouseover, onmouseup, style, title` | Use small text. |
| `<SPAN>` | `class, dir, id, lang, onclick, ondblclick, onkeydown, onkeypress, onkeyup, onmousedown, onmousemove, onmouseout, onmouseover, onmouseup, style, title` | Inline container. |
| `<STRIKE>` | `class, dir, id, lang, onclick, ondblclick, onkeydown, onkeypress, onkeyup, onmousedown, onmousemove, onmouseout, onmouseover, onmouseup, style, title` | Strikethrough text formatting. |
| `<STRONG>` | `class, dir, id, lang, onclick, ondblclick, onkeydown, onkeypress, onkeyup, onmousedown, onmousemove, onmouseout, onmouseover, onmouseup, style, title` | Emphasize text strongly. |
| `<STYLE>` | `class, dir, lang, media, type` | Specifies style sheet information. |
| `<SUB>` | `class, dir, id, lang, onclick, ondblclick, onkeydown, onkeypress, onkeyup, onmousedown, onmousemove, onmouseout, onmouseover, onmouseup, style, title` | Subscript. |

**Table B-1: HTML ATTRIBUTE REFERENCE**

| Element | Attributes Allowed | Description |
|---|---|---|
| `<SUP>` | `,class,dir,id,lang,onclick,ondblclick,onkeydown,` `onkeypress,onkeyup,onmousedown,onmousemove,onmouseout,` `onmouseover,onmouseup,style,title` | Superscript. |
| `<TABLE>` | `align,bgcolor,border,cellpadding,cellspacing,class,dir,` `frame,id,lang,onclick,ondblclick,onkeydown,onkeypress,` `onkeyup,onmousedown,onmousemove,onmouseout,onmouseover,` `onmouseup,rules,style,title,summary,width` | Create a table. |
| `<TBODY>` | `align,char,charoff,class,dir,id,lang,onclick,ondblclick,` `onkeydown,onkeypress,onkeyup,onmousedown,onmousemove,` `onmouseout,onmouseover,onmouseup,style,title,valign` | Indicates the table body. |
| `<TD>` | `abbr,align,axis,bgcolor,char,charoff,class,colspan,dir,` `headers,height,id,lang,nowrap,onclick,ondblclick,on` `keydown,onkeypress,onkeyup,onmousedown,onmousemove,` `onmouseout,onmouseover,onmouseup,rowspan,style,title,` `valign,width` | Indicates a table cell. |
| `<TEXTAREA>` | `accesskey,class,cols,dir,disabled,id,lang,name,onblur,` `onchange,onclick,ondblclick,onfocus,onkeydown,onkeypress,` `onkeyup,onmousedown,onmousemove,onmouseout,onmouseover,` `onmouseup,onselect,readonly,rows,style,title,tabindex` | Creates a multiline text field. |
| `<TFOOT>` | `align,char,charoff,class,dir,id,lang,onclick,ondblclick,` `onkeydown,onkeypress,onkeyup,onmousedown,onmousemove,` `onmouseout,onmouseover,onmouseup,style,title,valign` | Indicates the table's footer. |
| `<TH>` | `align,axis,bgcolor,char,charoff,class,colspan,dir,headers,` `height,id,lang,nowrap,onclick,ondblclick,onkeydown,onkey` `press,onkeyup,onmousedown,onmousemove,onmouseout,onmo` `useover,onmouseup,rowspan,style,title,valign,width` | A table header cell. |
| `<THEAD>` | `align,char,charoff,class,dir,id,lang,onclick,ondblclick,` `onkeydown,onkeypress,onkeyup,onmousedown,onmousemove,` `onmouseout,onmouseover,onmouseup,style,title,valign` | Indicates the table head. |
| `<TITLE>` | `dir,lang` | Specifies the document title. |

**Table B-1: HTML ATTRIBUTE REFERENCE**

| Element | Attributes Allowed | Description |
|---|---|---|
| `<TR>` | `abbr,align,bgcolor,char,charoff,class,dir,id,lang,` `onclick,ondblclick,onkeydown,onkeypress,onkeyup,onmouse` `down,onmousemove,onmouseout,onmouseover,onmouseup,style,` `title,valign` | Start a table row. |
| `<TT>` | `class,dir,id,lang,onclick,ondblclick,onkeydown,onkeypress,` `onkeyup,onmousedown,onmousemove,onmouseout,onmouseover,` `onmouseup,style,title` | Use teletype or monospace text formatting (similar to `<KBD>`). |
| `<U>` | `class,dir,id,lang,onclick,ondblclick,onkeydown,` `onkeypress,onkeyup,onmousedown,onmousemove,onmouseout,` `onmouseover,onmouseup,style,title` | Underline formatting. |
| `<UL>` | `class,compact,dir,id,lang,onclick,ondblclick,onkeydown,` `onkeypress,onkeyup,onmousedown,onmousemove,onmouseout,` `onmouseover,onmouseup,style,title,type` | Start an unordered list. |
| `<VAR>` | `class,dir,id,lang,onclick,ondblclick,onkeydown,onkeypress,` `onkeyup,onmousedown,onmousemove,onmouseout,onmouseover,` `onmouseup,style,title` | An inline program argument or variable. |

## More Resources

More resources are available on the Web, and I highly recommend going there for further reference, as the online resources will be updated more often than this book.

For the complete list of HTML elements, see **http://www.w3.org/TR/REC-html40/index/elements.html**.

For the HTML attributes, see **http://www.w3.org/TR/REC-html40/index/attributes.html**.

Cascading style sheets properties are available at **http://www.w3.org/TR/REC-CSS2/propidx.html**.

The Document Object Model specification is available at **http://www.w3.org/TR/REC-DOM-Level-1/**.

Be sure to check out the Microsoft Developer's Network at **http://msdn.microsoft.com**.

Netscape's DevEdge Online is at **http://developer.netscape.com/**.

# Appendix C:
# About the CD-ROM

The CD-ROM included with this book contains several programs to help you learn HTML. In addition to these, there are literally thousands of programs on the Internet for you to download and use, on every computer platform available.

Some of these programs are also discussed in Chapter 12, and I encourage you to check out this chapter for some ideas and suggestions on choosing the right program for the job.

Shareware programs are fully functional, free trial versions of copyrighted programs. If you like particular programs, register with their authors for a nominal fee and receive licenses, enhanced versions, and technical support. Freeware programs are free, copyrighted games, applications, and utilities. You can copy them to as many PCs as you like—free—but they have no technical support.

### Adobe Acrobat Reader

A reader for the cross-platform PDF document format; PDF files are often distributed on the Web when layout and appearance are crucial.

### Allaire HomeSite

A popular tag-based HTML editing program that includes a preview mode for quick browsing of your Web page.

### Coffee-Cup Style HTML Editor, Style Sheet Maker, and other tools

A collection of useful tools for creating Web pages, style sheets, Java applets, and image maps.

### CSE HTML Validator

An HTML validation tool, useful for checking to make sure your Web pages won't "break" other browsers.

### Dreamweaver

Macromedia's Dreamweaver is an HTML authoring program that helps you use dynamic layers in your Web documents.

### Ipswitch WSFTP LE

A graphical FTP upload and download program.

# Appendix C: About the CD-ROM

## Jasc Software Paint Shop Pro

A fully featured image-editing program, complete with animated GIF support.

## Live Image

A very useful image mapping utility; formerly MapThis!

## Microsoft Internet Explorer 5

One of the two most popular Web browsers.

## Munica FormPAL

A form and script generator.

## Netscape Communicator

The *other* most popular Web browser distributed.

## Nico Mak Computing's WinZip

A very popular compression utility for Windows.

## TetraNet Software's Linkbot

A free link checker to verify that all links on your site still work.

## WebGenie's CGI Star Pro

A CGI script generator; works for UNIX and Windows NT servers.

## WebManage Technologies NetIntellect Lite

A log analysis tool to generate reports from your raw server log files.

# Glossary

## A

**access**  When a client retrieves a file from a Web server.

**accessibility**  Universal usability of a Web site by people of any ability, using any type of input or output device (speech recognition, Braille or screen readers, nonstandard pointing devices, TTY).

**Active**  A proprietary Microsoft technology that enables the Web browser to embed and control applications and files into a Web page.

**address book**  A file or series of files that store names, email addresses, and contact information for use with an email client program.

**alignment**  Content placement in relation to the page's margins: left, right, or centered.

**animation**  A multiple-frame graphic, Shockwave file, or Java animation applet that appears to be moving on the screen.

**API**  Application Programming Interface: In Web servers, a programming environment for writing embedded programs for server-side scripts and other server tasks.

**applet**  A Java miniprogram that runs a small application entirely embedded into a Web page.

**application**  A standalone program with a useful purpose. A JavaScript program, Java applet, or even a series of Web pages can serve as a full-featured application.

**architecture**  The combination of microchip type and hardware that identifies a particular series of computers (x86, SPARC, Macintosh, and so on).

**archive**  A file or series of files that store other files for future reference or as a backup in case of emergency.

**ASCII**  Plain text data that is not encoded or compressed in any way.

**attribute**  Modifiers to an HTML element. An attribute determines how the element will be displayed.

**attribute declaration**  In XML, an attribute declaration defines how attributes may be used, and in which elements.

**aural style sheet**  A cascading style sheet that contains properties specific to aural Web browsers.

## B

**background**  When used as an attribute for the <BODY> element, the background image to use. When used as a style sheet property, the background color of the element being defined.

**bandwidth**  The rate of data transfer over a connection.

**basic authentication**  A username and password are required to access the file or directory, but the transaction (including password) is not necessarily encrypted.

**binary**  Encoded or compressed data, such as images, archives, programs, or any file that is not ASCII.

# GLOSSARY

**block element** An HTML element that is assumed to have a break after its closing tag.

**bookmark** In Netscape, a frequently visited page whose location you choose to save on disk.

**border** A line or edge around an element, such as a table or image.

**browser-specific** Elements and features that only work on one or two browsers and are not an Internet standard.

**buttonize** To turn a computer graphic so that it looks like a clickable button.

## C

**cache** The space on your hard drive where the Web browser stores temporary files.

**carpal-tunnel syndrome** A common affliction among people who use computers a lot. Carpal-tunnel syndrome (and related repetitive-stress injuries, or RSIs) usually affects the hands and is caused by poor typing posture and overuse.

**case-sensitive** Capitalization makes a difference.

**cell** An individual "box" in a table.

**certificate** A file that identifies one entity on the Web to another. Most often used by secure Web servers to identify themselves to customer and Web users.

**CGI** Common Gateway Interface: a programming interface to enable an anonymous Web user to run a program on a Web server (such as a Perl script).

**channels** A Web site that can be dynamically updated using Internet Explorer's client-pull technology.

**charset** A charset, or character set, is a list of symbols and characters that can be used in a document. For example, the Japanese alphabet uses a separate character set from the Western-Latin alphabet.

**chat** A real-time interactive medium in which users can communicate with each other instantly.

**child element** Any element that is included inside another HTML element.

**class** A style sheet selector that enables you to apply a style definition to any element by using the optional `class` attribute.

**client** The user's part of a network connection; the client computer or program only handles a few connections at a time, and all those connections are initiated by itself.

**clip art** Free or inexpensive graphics that can be plugged into any document; always check the copyright and royalty statements for the right to use any clip art you find.

**collocation** The practice of keeping your server's hardware at another company's facility in order to take advantage of better Internet connectivity, security, environmental controls, and maintenance and monitoring options.

**code** The underlying instructions to the computer; HTML source code is uncompiled and easily read by anyone.

**column** Vertical display of data in a table.

**comment** A text string that is not displayed in the Web browser.

**community** A Web site, or series of Web sites, in which Internet users can interact with each other, as well as with the sites' owners.

**compression** Using an algorithm to reduce a file's size by removing unnecessary data.

**content** The text, images, and multimedia files that go into a Web page.

**content rating** The practice of describing any potentially offensive content in a `<META>` element or comment to provide parental control over their kids' Web browsing experience.

**contextual element** An element that provides information about the meaning of the item being marked up, not merely visual information on how it should be displayed.

**cookies** A file or collection of files that store little bits of information to help Web designers make their sites more interactive, or to provide a personalized user experience.

**counter** A script or server-side-include that counts and displays the number of hits the referring page has received.

**cross-browser compatibility** Making a Web site compatible in most, if not all, Web browsers (usually by using Web standards).

**data** Information, generally transmitted or stored electronically with computers.

**database** A file or series of files that store individual pieces of data, such as names in an address book database or products in a catalog database.

**definition list** An HTML list with two types of list items: the term and the definition.

**designer** A Web professional who organizes, authors, or implements a Web site.

**dialog box** A separate window that pops up to ask a question or provide an alert or warning to a user; dialog boxes usually require a response before they will close.

**document** `<BODY>` The part of a document that contains the viewable content of a Web page.

**document colors** The background, text, and hyperlink colors used in a document, as defined in the document's `<BODY>` element or in a style sheet.

**document** `<HEAD>` The part of a document that contains information about a Web page, but no viewable content.

**Document Type Declaration (DOCTYPE)** The DTD is a document that defines how HTML elements should be displayed, as well as which attributes go with which elements.

**documentation** The records of what was done, or how to do something. Usually applies to programs, and includes information on what parts of the program do, meanings of variable names, and any bugs encountered.

**DOM** The Document Object Model, a way to name every object in a document for scripting purposes.

**domain name** A unique identifier on the Internet to enable people to connect to an individual computer system.

**download** To transfer data from a remote computer onto the one you're working on (the local computer).

**drag-and-drop** The experience of clicking on an item, holding down the mouse key while moving the mouse, and dropping the item in another location on the screen.

**dynamic font** A Netscape-specific technology that enables Web designers to include a specific font with their Web pages, to be used when displaying the page.

**Dynamic HTML** Making HTML interactive and changeable with scripting languages and the DOM.

**element** An HTML tag that marks up a document's content.

# GLOSSARY

**element declaration**  In XML, declaring an element's name and usage in the DTD.

**email**  Electronic mail: a technology that allows for the rapid and simple exchange of messages over the Internet, using Standard Mail Transfer Protocol (SMTP).

**embedded object**  Any file, usually multimedia, that uses the <EMBED> element to place the file into a Web document, complete with a tools for the associated multimedia player to run.

**encryption**  The process of scrambling data so that it cannot be read without applying special algorithms to decode it.

**endnote**  A note or comment included at the end of a document.

**entity declaration**  In XML, declaring an item that will be replaced by an external source file or by commonly used data, such as an email address or copyright notice.

## F

**FAQ**  Frequently Asked Questions: a help file in the form of a question-and-answer session.

**favorites**  A collection of files used by Microsoft Internet Explorer to save the locations of frequently visited pages.

**file permissions**  The rights to read, write, or run files, as given to individuals, groups, and anonymous users.

**filter**  In graphics programs, a filter is a special effect that can be applied to the graphic or to a selected area of the graphic.

**firewall**  A combination of hardware and software placed between two networks (such as an internal network and the Internet) to limit transactions to authorized traffic only.

**font**  The typeface used by text.

**footnote**  A note or comment included at the end of a page.

**form**  In HTML, an element that enables users to input data, which is then processed either through a client-side script, or through a CGI program.

**form field**  An individual element for collecting user data.

**form method**  The process by which the form will be sent to a Web server — "GET" or "PUT."

**frame**  An individual pane in a frameset, which enables you to view one Web page at a time.

**frameset**  A series of panes that appear in a Web browser window simultaneously, and that can show multiple Web pages at the same time.

**FTP**  File Transfer Protocol: a standard, stable method for uploading and downloading files over a network.

**function**  In programming and scripting, a part of the program that contains a series of instructions, and that can later be called or used in the program to perform that series of instructions multiple times.

## G

**GIF**  A graphical file format that is best suited for line art.

**GUI**  Graphical User Interface: the graphical part of a program, usually using windows and dialog boxes (vs. a text-based, command-line interface, which is generally more difficult to learn and to use).

## H

**headings**  In HTML, headings are a visual and structural way to organize and lay out a document.

**hidden fields** Form fields that are not viewable by the user, but that are transmitted with the field data nonetheless.

**hits** Accesses to a Web page. Hits are generally defined as unique accesses of the Web page, not including the graphics within it.

**host** The name of the computer or program on a domain, such as the "www" in *www.domain.com*, or "local2" in *local2.domain.com*.

**HTML** Hypertext Markup Language, the collection of markup elements that tells Web browsers how to display data and information from a Web page.

**HTTP** Hypertext Transfer Protocol is a computer "language" used by computers when transferring Web documents (http://).

**HTTP header** Information automatically sent along with a Web document when transferred by HTTP. It can include the filename, size, date, and any additional headers as specified in the <META> elements.

**hyperlink** A word, phrase, or image that uses HTML markup to provide a clickable spot. When a user clicks a hyperlink, the Web browser opens whatever page specified in the HTML markup.

**I**

**icon** A small image to help navigate or provide a visual signifier about the text.

**ID** A style sheet selector that must be unique within an individual web page, and that can use any styles.

**image map** A single graphic with multiple hyperlinks.

**inline element** An element that does not presume a line or paragraph break when it's closed.

**indexing** The process of using a Web crawler or "spider" program to scan Web sites for common keywords, and to store those in a centrally located search engine.

**input** To accept data from a Web site, usually via a form field.

**interactivity** Accepting user input and responding to it dynamically.

**internal bookmark** In HTML, a hyperlink destination within a Web page.

**internationalization** Making your site accessible to other languages and cultures.

**Internet** An international, publicly available network of computers connected using standard networking protocols to communicate and transfer information.

**Internet Explorer** Microsoft's Web browser, now embedded into new Windows operating systems.

**intranet** An internal, private network of computers, often behind a firewall.

**IP address** A unique number used by computers to identify each other on the internet; dial-up customers often have dynamic IP addresses to conserve the number of IPs available.

**ISP** Internet Service Provider: the company or organization that provides Internet access to an individual or company.

**Java** A full-featured, cross-platform programming language developed by Sun Microsystems.

**JavaScript** A client-side scripting language developed by Netscape.

# GLOSSARY

**JPEG** A graphical file format that is best suited for photographs.

**Jscript** Microsoft's implementation of JavaScript: Jscript and JavaScript are not 100 percent compatible with each other.

## L

**layer** A Netscape-specific Dynamic HTML element that enables Web authors to create and control part of a Web page with scripts.

**layout** The visual placement of text paragraphs, images, and other elements in a document.

**link** See *hyperlink*.

**link verification** Using a Web crawler or "spider" to check all the links on your Web page and make sure they're all valid.

**localization** Making your site accessible to a specific culture, language, and locale.

**log** A file that records each access of a Web server, the files accessed, and additional information such as time, date, and IP address of the client.

**look and feel** A combination of document colors, graphics, and navigation tools that provides a consistent public image.

## M

**mailing list** An interactive discussion group by email.

**mailto:** The protocol to use instead of `http://` to create an email link.

**margin** The space around an element's exterior.

**media descriptor** In style sheets, the type of browser that will be rendering the Web page.

**META tags** HTML elements that provide additional information, such as HTTP headers, file refresh or expiration times, author names, keywords, and any content you may wish to provide.

**method** See *form method*.

**monitoring** Keeping a constant watch on a Web site's response times, availability, and traffic.

**monospace font** A font that provides the same amount of space for each letter, regardless of the letter's actual width: `this is a monospace font`.

**Mozilla** The precursor to Netscape Navigator, and now an open-source Web browser movement.

**multimedia** Any combination of text, graphics, audio, video, and virtual reality.

## N

**name** In HTML, an optional attribute that theoretically enables every element to be scripted.

**navigation** The tools, visual or otherwise, that a Web site provides for users to get from one part of the site to another.

**nesting** Placing an element inside another HTML element. Nesting usually refers to the same type of element, such as lists and tables. Some elements cannot be nested.

**Netscape Communicator** The Web browser packages developed and distributed by Netscape Corporation.

**network** A group of computers connected together through some type of networking protocol, such as TCP/IP (for the Internet).

**newsgroup** A threaded discussion group that uses the NNTP protocol to send and retrieve messages worldwide.

**nonstandard Web browser** A Web browser that doesn't conform to HTML 4, or that renders Web pages in some widely variant way from the most common browsers, Netscape Navigator and Microsoft Internet Explorer.

**objects** An element listed in the Document Object Model, and that is manipulated or used by a client-side script.

**online** Connected to the Internet.

**open source** Any program, technology, or library whose source code is freely available in an uncompiled form, usually for the purpose of development by individual programmers.

**operating system** Software that provides all the basic services, such as access to hardware devices, memory, and the processor, to software programs.

**ordered list** A numbered list.

**output** The data or results that are returned when a user requests information from a Web server. Usually refers to query results.

**padding** The space between the border of an element, if any, and the element's content itself (such as the text, graphics, or embedded file).

**palette** The range of colors available in any graphics program.

**parent element** An element that contains or controls (in scripting) another element.

**password** A private word, phrase, or text string used to verify that you are who you say you are on the computer.

**perl** A simple, common, uncompiled programming language used for CGIs.

**pixel** The smallest addressable unit on a screen.

**platform** The combination of architecture (hardware) and operating system (software) that makes a unique computing environment (Windows NT on Intel vs. Windows NT on DECAlpha, for example).

**plug-ins** Third-party applications that are installed into another application as an integrated program, such as the Shockwave plug-in for Netscape Communicator.

**pop-up box** A dialog box that opens above other application windows and queries the user.

**positioning** Onscreen placement of HTML objects in relation to the upper left-hand corner of the screen (absolute positioning), or in relation to other objects (relative positioning).

**preferences** In a Web browser, the menu you use to set font colors, starting pages, mail and news identities, security features, and similar options.

**proprietary** Closed-development technology or programs; proprietary technologies must be licensed by any company wishing to implement them in a program, and are not overseen by any standards committees.

**proxy server** A server that makes connections on your behalf, then returns the results to you. Often used in firewalls and to provide caching services to large networks.

# GLOSSARY

## R

**reserved name** A word, in programming, that cannot be used for variable or function names because it already has a special purpose in the programming language.

**RGB Values** The Red, Green, and Blue values that make up a color in HTML.

**row** Data displayed horizontally in a table.

**RSI** Repetitive Stress Injury: any injury caused by using the afflicted body part too many times in the same way. Often experienced in the hands by people using a keyboard too much.

## S

**sans serif font** Fonts like Arial and Helvetica that do *not* have serifs, the little lines at the ends of the stems and arms of letters (the "foot" on a letter "l," for example).

**screen resolution** The number of pixels wide and tall that a monitor can display.

**script** A small program that can do a limited set of instructions.

**scripting** The process of applying a script to an HTML element in a client-side script such as JavaScript.

**scrolling** The process of using arrow keys or scroll bars to view content that is offscreen due to limited screen size, but which is part of the current document.

**search engine** A Web site or program that catalogs and indexes Web sites and then enables users to search for individual sites by keyword, description, or similar criteria.

**secure server** A Web server that uses SSL or a similar encryption technology to protect all data transferred between it and client machines.

**security zones** In Microsoft Internet Explorer, a security zone is an area, such as the local network, intranet, or the Internet, for which you have set special security permissions.

**serif font** Fonts like Times New Roman and Times that *do* have little lines at the ends of the stems and arms of letters (the "foot" on a letter "l," for example).

**server** In a network transaction, the server handles multiple connections, originating from many different computers, to move information from one place to another.

**SGML** Standard Generalized Markup Language: a method of describing markup languages to provide structural, syntactical, and visual information for document content (does not necessarily apply to Web or even electronic documents).

**signature file** A text file or line that is automatically attached to the bottom of your outgoing email messages.

**source** See *code.*

**spam** The practice of sending out unsolicited email, usually of a commercial nature, to people who didn't ask for it and usually don't want it, or of sending such inappropriate messages to public forums, such as newsgroups, guestbooks, and mailing lists.

**spec sheet** A preliminary document outlining how a program or application should behave, and what variables or data it will use.

**specification** A description of how to implement a technology. The HTML specification describes how to implement HTML in Web browsers so that Web authors can use it effectively.

**SSI** Server-Side Includes: A server-based method of including data, files, and information into Web pages before they're displayed in the Web browser.

**SSL** Secure Sockets Layer: A security standard for TCP/IP communications, most commonly used with HTTP.

**stationery** In Internet Explorer, a premade email message template that uses both graphics and HTML.

**style property** An individual characteristic of an HTML element that is changed or otherwise defined using a style sheet or the `style` attribute.

**style selectors** An HTML attribute (ID or class) that applies style properties to the element containing the attribute, without changing the element.

**style sheet** A file or section in a Web document that describes how to visually render individual HTML elements in a Web browser.

**submit button** A form field that sends the form's data to a script.

**subscript** Text that is set just below the normal line of text.

**superscript** Text that "floats" above the normal line of text.

**syntax** A specific way to write source code in order to be understandable by a computer.

# T

**table** A grid to display data efficiently in rows and columns. Also used for layout purposes on the Web.

**tag** The string of characters, usually beginning with < and ending with >, that opens or closes an HTML element.

**Tag-based editor** An editor that shows the HTML tags onscreen as you edit your page, and that has shortcuts to help you find and remember all the HTML elements.

**TCP/IP** Transmission Control Protocol/Internet Protocol: When used together, they form the primary way that data is transferred over the Internet. IP specifies the format of data packets being sent, and TCP defines how to reassemble them once they've arrived, and how to recover dropped packets.

**template** A predesigned document that enables you to "fill in the blanks" to easily design an attractive and useful document.

**text-based editor** An HTML editor that requires you to type in all HTML elements by hand.

**text-only browser** A Web browser that only displays text — no graphics, multimedia, or often even tables.

**thumbnail image** A smaller version of an image to facilitate faster downloading of image catalogs and to provide a preview.

**toolbar** A series of buttons and icons in a program that provide shortcuts and tools for you to use in the program.

**top-level domain** Top-level domains are the last part of a domain name, such as .com, .net. .gov, .edu, etc.

**traffic** The amount of bandwidth being used by the network at any given time. A lot of traffic to your server means a lot of hits, but also slower connection times.

**TWAIN-compliant** A standards-compliant scanner, camera, or similar input device.

# GLOSSARY

# U

**unordered list**  A bulleted list.

**upload**  Transferring data or files from your local computer to a remote machine.

**URI**  Uniform Resource Identifiers: formerly known as a URL, this is the location of a document or file on the Internet.

**URL**  Uniform Resource Locators: the identifying address of an Internet document or file (usually a Web page).

**urlencoding**  A method of encoding special characters, such as slashes, in a URL so a server or other program (such as an operating system) can understand them.

**Usenet**  A collection of newsgroups organized and controlled by the organization known as Usenet.

**user**  An individual who accesses a Web site or uses a program.

**username**  An individual's online account name that identifies them to others. Email addresses often use the form `username@hostname.domain.com`.

**uuencode**  Originally known as UNIX-to-UNIX Copy, a way to encode binary files as text for the purpose of transmitting them with text-only programs, such as email.

# V

**validation**  Running a program to double-check to be sure all HTML used in a Web page conforms to the W3C's HTML 4 standards.

**value**  In an HTML element, attributes often have values to modify the way the element looks or behaves.

**variables**  In programming and scripting, a named place where pieces of data can be stored and retrieved for use in programs.

**VBScript**  A proprietary Microsoft scripting language that is similar in syntax to Visual Basic.

# W

**W3C**  World Wide Web Consortium: the standards committee for recommending Web standards such as HTML, CSS, and XML.

**Web browser**  The computer program used by an Internet user to view Web pages.

**Web hosting**  The practice of using another company's Web server to make your Web pages available on the Internet.

**Web page**  An individual page written in HTML.

**Web site**  A collection of related Web pages connected by hyperlinks and generally maintained by a single individual or team.

**Web team**  A group of people working on a Web site together.

**WebTV**  An evolving technology that enables people to surf the Internet using a television instead of a computer.

**whiteboard**  A program that provides a simple drawing surface, usually usable by more than one person at a time.

**whitespace**  The unused space around text and images in desktop and Internet publishing.

**wizard**  A small program, often included in other programs, that automates a complex task or guides you through an otherwise unfamiliar concept.

**word wrap**  When the words in a document automatically wrap to the next line when the text reaches to the edge of the available viewing area, whether it's an input box or window.

**World Wide Web**  All of the Web sites and pages on the Internet.

**WYSIWYG**  What You See Is What You Get: a type of editor in which you edit the document as you preview how it will look in a Web browser.

**XML**  eXtensible Markup Language: a superset of HTML that enables you to apply different document type definitions to a Web page.

**XSL**  Style sheets as applied in XML.

# Index

# Index

# Index

# Index

# Index

# INDEX

# IDG BOOKS WORLDWIDE, INC.
# END-USER LICENSE AGREEMENT

READ THIS. You should carefully read these terms and conditions before opening the software packet(s) included with this book ("Book"). This is a license agreement ("Agreement") between you and IDG Books Worldwide, Inc. ("IDGB"). By opening the accompanying software packet(s), you acknowledge that you have read and accept the following terms and conditions. If you do not agree and do not want to be bound by such terms and conditions, promptly return the Book and the unopened software packet(s) to the place you obtained them for a full refund.

1. **License Grant.** IDGB grants to you (either an individual or entity) a nonexclusive license to use one copy of the enclosed software program(s) (collectively, the "Software") solely for your own personal or business purposes on a single computer (whether a standard computer or a workstation component of a multiuser network). The Software is in use on a computer when it is loaded into temporary memory (RAM) or installed into permanent memory (hard disk, CD-ROM, or other storage device). IDGB reserves all rights not expressly granted herein.

2. **Ownership.** IDGB is the owner of all right, title, and interest, including copyright, in and to the compilation of the Software recorded on the disk(s) or CD-ROM ("Software Media"). Copyright to the individual programs recorded on the Software Media is owned by the author or other authorized copyright owner of each program. Ownership of the Software and all proprietary rights relating thereto remain with IDGB and its licensers.

3. **Restrictions On Use and Transfer.**

   (a) You may only (i) make one copy of the Software for backup or archival purposes, or (ii) transfer the Software to a single hard disk, provided that you keep the original for backup or archival purposes. You may not (i) rent or lease the Software, (ii) copy or reproduce the Software through a LAN or other network system or through any computer subscriber system or bulletin-board system, or (iii) modify, adapt, or create derivative works based on the Software.

   (b) You may not reverse engineer, decompile, or disassemble the Software. You may transfer the Software and user documentation on a permanent basis, provided that the transferee agrees to accept the terms and conditions of this Agreement and you retain no copies. If the Software is an update or has been updated, any transfer must include the most recent update and all prior versions.

4. Restrictions On Use of Individual Programs. You must follow the individual requirements and restrictions detailed for each individual program in Appendix B of this Book. These limitations are also contained in the individual license agreements recorded on the Software Media. These limitations may include a requirement that after using the program for a specified period of time, the user must pay a registration fee or discontinue use. By opening the Software packet(s), you will be agreeing to abide by the licenses and restrictions for these individual programs that are detailed in Appendix B and on the Software Media. None of the material on this Software Media or listed in this Book may ever be redistributed, in original or modified form, for commercial purposes.

# End-User License Agreement

**5. Limited Warranty.**

**(a)** IDGB warrants that the Software and Software Media are free from defects in materials and workmanship under normal use for a period of sixty (60) days from the date of purchase of this Book. If IDGB receives notification within the warranty period of defects in materials or workmanship, IDGB will replace the defective Software Media.

**(b) IDGB AND THE AUTHOR OF THE BOOK DISCLAIM ALL OTHER WARRANTIES, EXPRESS OR IMPLIED, INCLUDING WITHOUT LIMITATION IMPLIED WARRANTIES OF MERCHANTABILITY AND FITNESS FOR A PARTICULAR PURPOSE, WITH RESPECT TO THE SOFTWARE, THE PROGRAMS, THE SOURCE CODE CONTAINED THEREIN, AND/OR THE TECHNIQUES DESCRIBED IN THIS BOOK. IDGB DOES NOT WARRANT THAT THE FUNCTIONS CONTAINED IN THE SOFTWARE WILL MEET YOUR REQUIREMENTS OR THAT THE OPERATION OF THE SOFTWARE WILL BE ERROR-FREE.**

**(c)** This limited warranty gives you specific legal rights, and you may have other rights that vary from jurisdiction to jurisdiction.

**6. Remedies.**

**(a)** IDGB's entire liability and your exclusive remedy for defects in materials and workmanship shall be limited to replacement of the Software Media, which may be returned to IDGB with a copy of your receipt at the following address: Software Media Fulfillment Department, Attn.: Teach Yourself HTML 4, IDG Books Worldwide, Inc., 7260 Shadeland Station, Ste. 100, Indianapolis, IN 46256, or call 1-800-762-2974. Please allow three to four weeks for delivery. This Limited Warranty is void if failure of the Software Media has resulted from accident, abuse, or misapplication. Any replacement Software Media will be warranted for the remainder of the original warranty period or thirty (30) days, whichever is longer.

**(b)** In no event shall IDGB or the author be liable for any damages whatsoever (including without limitation damages for loss of business profits, business interruption, loss of business information, or any other pecuniary loss) arising from the use of or inability to use the Book or the Software, even if IDGB has been advised of the possibility of such damages.

**(c)** Because some jurisdictions do not allow the exclusion or limitation of liability for consequential or incidental damages, the above limitation or exclusion may not apply to you.

**7. U.S. Government Restricted Rights.** Use, duplication, or disclosure of the Software by the U.S. Government is subject to restrictions stated in paragraph (c)(1)(ii) of the Rights in Technical Data and Computer Software clause of DFARS 252.227-7013, and in subparagraphs (a) through (d) of the Commercial Computer — Restricted Rights clause at FAR 52.227-19, and in similar clauses in the NASA FAR supplement, when applicable.

**8. General.** This Agreement constitutes the entire understanding of the parties and revokes and supersedes all prior agreements, oral or written, between them and may not be modified or amended except in a writing signed by both parties hereto that specifically refers to this Agreement. This Agreement shall take precedence over any other documents that may be in conflict herewith. If any one or more provisions contained in this Agreement are held by any court or tribunal to be invalid, illegal, or otherwise unenforceable, each and every other provision shall remain in full force and effect.

# CD-ROM Installation
# Instructions

This book's CD-ROM is cross-platform: you can mount it on a PC (using Windows 95, Windows 98, or Windows NT 4.0), Macintosh, or UNIX. To view the contents of the CD-ROM, insert it in your computer's CD-ROM drive and then do the following:

1. Open Windows Explorer (or the equivalent) on your platform of choice.
2. Double-click the icon for your CD-ROM drive.
3. To select a folder containing a particular application, click it.
4. If needed, click subfolder icons until you find the subfolder in which the installation program is located. The installation program is usually named `install.exe` or `setup.exe`. Some programs are archived; use an archive program to uncompress and install them. WinZip, a common compression utility, is also included on this CD-ROM.
5. If the subfolder contains a readme file, click the file and read it before starting the installation.
6. To install the program, double-click the icon representing the installation program.
7. After installing the program, close all the windows associated with the installation.